AF782571

# UNITED STATES–EUROPEAN COMMUNITY TRADE RESOURCES

# UNITED STATES–EUROPEAN COMMUNITY TRADE RESOURCES

**John S. Gordon**
**Timothy Harper**

**John Wiley & Sons, Inc.**

**New York • Chichester • Brisbane • Toronto • Singapore**

This text is printed on acid-free paper.

Copyright © 1993 by John Wiley & Sons, Inc.

All rights reserved. Published simultaneously in Canada.

Reproduction or translation of any part of this work beyond that permitted by Section 107 or 108 of the 1976 United States Copyright Act without the permission of the copyright owner is unlawful. Requests for permission or further information should be addressed to the Permissions Department, John Wiley & Sons, Inc.

This publication is designed to provide accurate and authoritative information in regard to the subject matter covered. It is sold with the understanding that the publisher is not engaged in rendering legal, accounting, or other professional services. If legal advice or other expert assistance is required, the services of a competent professional person should be sought. *From a Declaration of Principles jointly adopted by a Committee of the American Bar Association and a Committee of Publishers.*

***Library of Congress Cataloging in Publication Data:***

Gordon, John S., 1944–
United States–European Community trade resources / John S. Gordon, Timothy Harper
p. cm.
Includes index.
ISBN 0-471-55667-X
1. Business information services—United States—Directories. 2. Foreign trade promotion—United States—Information services—Directories. 3. United States—Commerce—Information services—Handbooks, manuals, etc. 4. Business information services—European Economic Community countries—Directories. 5. Foreign trade promotion—European Economic Community countries—Information services—Directories. 6. European Economic Community countries—Commerce—Information services—Handbooks, manuals, etc.
I. Harper, Timothy, 1950– . II. Title.
HF54.52.U5G67 1993
016.65—dc20 93-17471

Printed in the United States of America

10 9 8 7 6 5 4 3 2 1

# ACKNOWLEDGMENTS

Thanks and acknowledgments would fill another book. The authors wish to express their thanks to the many state and federal officials in the United States and to the many local and national government authorities in the EC member states who shared the information and resources that made this work possible. Especially helpful were the staff of the U.S. Department of Commerce's US&FCS District Office in Seattle and the staff of the Office of European Community Affairs in Washington, DC; Jeanne Cobb and Bill King of the Washington State Department of Trade and Economic Development; the directors of numerous trade organizations; the librarians at the law firm of Bogle and Gates in Seattle, and the Seattle First Bank library; and the U.S. Council on International Business.

We would also like to acknowledge assistance from the American Chambers of Commerce in Europe, from state and federal government trade officials in Europe, and particularly from the trade and information offices of the European Commission and the 12 European Community member states. Private individuals and companies too numerous to mention were also extremely helpful.

For the U.S. section of this resource guide, John S. Gordon would like to acknowledge the support of his family: Martha Gordon, Dr. Susan L. Warme, and Jayne K. Bell; the encouragement of his editors, and the confidence of his associates.

Tim Harper would like to recognize the invaluable contributions of his London-based associate Thor Valdmanis, a Canadian-Latvian journalist whose exhaustive research in Britain and elsewhere was instrumental in guaranteeing the comprehensive quality of the listings for the European Community and its member nations.

# CONTENTS

# INTRODUCTION

This book is directed to the corporations and individuals that import from, export to, invest in, and otherwise interact with one or more of the European Community (EC) countries. It is a guide to resources in the United States and the EC that gives interested parties the ability to accomplish their objectives. All of the agencies, institutions, service organizations, and private companies identified in this trade resource are specialists available to help Americans do business in the EC.

Part One focuses on resources in the United States. It is presented in thirteen chapters. Chapters 1 and 2 identify public sector resources:

- Agencies and departments of the federal government charged to help American firms achieve corporate profitability in foreign markets
- State organizations that exist to promote increased employment in their states by working to increase exports and international trade activity
- U.S. offices of EC member states and regions that are in the United States to attract new investment.

Chapters 3–7 identify research and trade facilitation resources:

- Publications dealing directly with the EC—its markets, dynamics, laws, regulations, and business opportunities
- Libraries of information specific to the EC and to international trade
- Trade organizations that can support and assist a corporation's market entry, expansion, or investment goals
- Nonprofit or bilateral organizations that provide information, facilitation, access to government policymakers, and the formal and informal personal networks that are critical to long-term success in any market.

Private sector resources are listed in Chapters 8 and 11:

- U.S.-based legal resources that specialize in Europe—how to find them and optimize their value
- Trade consulting firms with acknowledged abilities

- Accounting, finance, and insurance organizations active in the EC and international markets generally
- International marketing organizations that get business done.

There is significant overlap among the trade consultants, accountants, and marketing organizations. There are thousands of firms that offer these services to the public, so the user is directed to additional resources to broaden the resource base beyond the listed firms.

Chapters 12 and 13 identify some of the operational resources needed to capitalize on opportunities in the EC. These resources include translation, language, and travel information services, and the logistics/transportation service firms that move the products in a timely and professional manner.

Many of the U.S. agencies, companies, and service providers have branches or affiliates in the EC. Where possible, these are listed by country so the reader may take advantage of those relationships. Contact is best made through the U.S. headquarters organization.

Part Two provides information on comparable organizations in Europe, on a country-by-country basis. The trade resources for each EC member state are prefaced with an introduction to that country's business practices and a brief statistical profile.

The country listings consist of European-based firms, or branches of U.S. firms that are independently managed in the EC. An American exporter, importer, or investor (generally a direct investor rather than a portfolio investor) may want to get advice from a United States trade consultant while at the same time make contact with a European trade consultant specializing in the opposite activity from within the EC. This resource guide is designed to give the American executive quick and targeted access to relevant trade resources in the United States and the EC. The executive can shop for information, advice, contacts, services, finance, and consulting services on both sides of the Atlantic.

Listings in this resource guide are largely alphabetical, with no preferential order intended, and no recommendations are implied. The fact that a company is not listed does not imply inferior services; it is impossible in the rapidly changing environment of U.S.-EC trade to list every potentially valuable resource. Individual chapters provide direction on finding additional resources.

Some organizations belong within fairly narrow specialties, while others have broad and overlapping services. Some banks and accountants may also provide trade consulting services; site location services may be offered by consultants, accountants, law firms, and marketing organizations, in addition to the site selection services listed in Chapter 5. Some trade and marketing consultants may offer logistics services, thereby broadening the lists of logistics vendors in Chapter 13.

This resource guide provides the initial contact points—names, numbers, and so on—to begin building the network of people in the United States and in the EC that is essential to the success of every international business venture.

# PART ONE

# United States Resources

# 1

# FEDERAL GOVERNMENT ORGANIZATIONS

The U.S. government can be a major resource of information, guidance, and assistance, for any company that is doing business in or planning to do business with the European Community (EC). A host of agencies have input and influence in the field of international trade. The activities of the principal organizations are identified here. Agencies that have a peripheral impact on trade with the EC have also been listed, with contact information. The principal organizations are:

- U.S. Department of Commerce (DOC)
- U.S. Department of Agriculture (DOA)
- U.S. Department of State (DOS)
- U.S. Trade Representative (USTR)
- U.S. Department of Transportation
- U.S. Department of the Treasury (Customs Service)
- U.S. International Development Cooperation Agency
- U.S. Department of Education
- U.S. Department of Energy
- Export-Import Bank of the United States (EximBank)
- U.S. International Trade Commission

The U.S. Department of Commerce (DOC) is the lead agency and the principal corporate export/international trade resource at the federal level. Within Commerce, the International Trade Administration (ITA) deals with international trade, while the Small Business Administration (SBA) has an Office of International Trade whose activities overlap those of the ITA. Other agencies have an impact and their actions can have long-term negative effects on corporate activity within the EC. For example, the political mission of the Department of State is not always compatible with the export development objectives of other departments.

## DEPARTMENT OF COMMERCE

### Office of European Community Affairs

The OECA is the central contact point in ITA for information on the EC and its impact on U.S. business. OECA's Single Internal Market Information Service (SIMIS) provides a number of services, including:

- A basic information packet on EC 1992
- *Europe Now,* a quarterly newsletter
- Specialized guides to EC legislation
- Information on EC duties, taxes, and customs requirements
- Informational seminars
- Individualized business counseling.

SIMIS maintains a comprehensive database of EC directives, regulations, and other information published by the EC, the U.S. government, and the private sector. Contact:

Single Internal Market Information Service (SIMIS), Office of European Community Affairs, U.S. Department of Commerce
Rm. 3036, 14th & Constitution Ave., NW, Washington, DC 20230
202-482-5276; Fax: 202-482-2155

The OECA produces a variety of documents relating to EC regulations, directives, and proposals, including:

*List of EC 1992 Directives and Proposals.* This is updated regularly and provides a running report on legislative initiatives shaping the EC.

*Business Guide to EC Internal Market Legislation.* These briefs analyze EC 1992 issues and directives and their effects on U.S. business. Available titles include:

*Chemicals and European Community Directives*

*EC Labor Policy*

*EC Liberalizes Transportation Rules and Upgrades the Infrastructure*

*EC Telecommunications*

*EC Testing and Certification Procedures*

*Environmental Policy*

*Regulations on Food and Beverages*

*Intellectual Property Protection*

*Medical Devices*

### Office of Western Europe

The Office of Western Europe (OWE), like the Office of European Community Affairs, is part of the International Economic Policy group.

These are the *country desks*. Country desk officers provide information on new marketing or exporting opportunities specific to their assigned country. Desk officers provide information on national regulations, trade data, market characteristics, growth rates, and other matters. Any question relating to the country in question is fair game to put to the country desk officer. For the EC, the contact is:

U.S. Department of Commerce, Office of Western Europe, Washington, DC 20230

(*Note:* Personnel assignments change, therefore personnel are not listed)

| *Country* | *Telephone (202)* | *Country* | *Telephone (202)* |
|---|---|---|---|
| Belgium | 482-5041 | Ireland | 482-2177 |
| Denmark | 482-3254 | Italy | 482-2177 |
| European Community | 482-5276 | Luxembourg | 482-5401 |
| France | 482-6008 | Netherlands | 482-5401 |
| Germany | 482-2434 | Portugal | 482-3945 |
| Greece | 482-3945 | Spain | 482-3945 |
| | | United Kingdom | 482-3478 |

In addition to the country desk personnel, the ITA has a Trade Development group, with personnel assigned to four specific industry sectors:

| *Industry Group/Office* | *Telephone (202)* |
|---|---|
| Technology and Aerospace Industries | 482-1872 |
| Aerospace | 482-4222 |
| Computers, business equipment | 482-2990 |
| Microelectronics, med. equip., inst. | 482-2010 |
| Telecommunications | 482-4466 |
| Basic Industries | 482-0575 |
| Automotive affairs | 482-0554 |
| Materials, minerals, chemicals | 482-0575 |
| Energy, environment, infrastructure | 482-5226 |
| Service Industries and Finance | 482-5261 |
| Export trading companies | 482-5131 |
| Finance, countertrade | 482-5131 |
| Service industries | 482-3575 |
| Textiles, Apparel, Consumer Goods | 482-3737 |
| Textiles, apparel | 482-2043 |
| Consumer goods | 482-0337 |

Specific industry group personnel have been assigned to assist businesses regarding their industry group and its interaction with the European Community. Contact:

| *Industry Office* | *Telephone (202)* |
|---|---|
| Textiles and Apparel | 482-3587 |
| Service Industries | 482-3575 |
| Basic Industries | 482-0606 |
| Telecommunications | 482-4466 |
| Automotive Affairs | 482-4036 |
| Consumer Goods | 482-5783 |
| Financial Services | 482-0349 |
| Capital Goods/Int'l. Construction | 482-2474 |
| Aerospace | 482-4222 |

## U.S. and Foreign Commercial Service Offices in the United States

The US&FCS is the public contact point within the International Trade Administration. District and branch offices in the United States are the primary access points to obtain and use a broad range of export marketing and information resources from the Department of Commerce. The district offices of the US&FCS are staffed with trade specialists whose function is to assist U.S. corporations in their efforts to increase export and international investment activity. There are US&FCS officers assigned to each foreign service post maintained by the U.S. government, so the U.S.-based personnel can deal with their contemporaries in each country of the EC (and elsewhere around the world).

Services and information available from the U.S. Department of Commerce through the district offices of the US&FCS include:

- *Export Counseling*. Trade Specialists, assigned to an industry sector in addition to their usual counseling duties, help companies gain access to the tremendous amount of information available on the National Trade Data Bank. They counsel on strategies and guide companies in the development of export marketing plans. They also conduct seminars and training programs for the business community.
- *Market Information*. In addition to communicating sales leads developed by the foreign posts of the US&FCS, the district office can assist companies in using and evaluating the market data generated by the various offices and departments of the government.
- *Commercial News USA* is a biweekly magazine on export trade and export markets.
- The *Agent-Distributor Service* is a customized search for interested and qualified foreign representatives.
- The *Gold Key Service* is offered by a number of US&FCS posts abroad. It includes identification and introduction to potential trade partners, translation services, orientation meetings, market

research, limited office facilities on site, and guidance in developing strategies for a specific market.

- The *National Trade Data Bank (NTDB)* is a CD-ROM-based database of market and economic information, updated monthly. Every business that seeks to profit from international business activity should subscribe to this database. The cost is nominal, the information is timely and immediately applicable. Chapter 2 lists the libraries that subscribe to the NTDB and hold the information available to the public. The Appendix on page 28 contains a summary of the documents available on the NTDB, by agency or organization. A more complete description is provided in Appendix A at the end of Part I. (See p. 278.)
- *Market Access and Assistance.* In addition to the Agent/Distributor Service, the US&FCS supports or sponsors Overseas Trade Missions, Overseas Trade Fairs, Overseas Video and Catalog Shows, and Matchmaker Events where U.S. firms are matched with qualified potential market partners for exports, joint ventures, or licensing arrangements.

Contact the closest district office to arrange a meeting with the District Director, a trade specialist, or members of the District Export Council.

US&FCS District Offices are listed by state. The correct mailing address for each office begins:

U.S. Department of Commerce
International Trade Administration
U.S. and Foreign Commercial Service

| *State* | *Office Location* |
|---|---|
| Alabama | Rm. 302, Berry Bldg., 2015 Second Ave. North, Birmingham 35203, 205-731-1331 |
| Alaska | Suite 319, World Trade Center, 4201 Tudor Center Dr., Anchorage 99508, 907-271-6237 |
| Arizona | 2901 N. Central Ave., Suite 970, Phoenix 85012, 602-640-2513 |
| Arkansas | 425 West Capitol Ave., Suite 700, Little Rock 72201, 501-324-5794 |
| California | 11000 Wilshire Blvd., Rm. 9200, Los Angeles 90024, 310-575-7105 |
| | 3300 Irvine Blvd., Suite 305, Newport Beach 92660-3198, 714-660-1688 |
| | 6363 Greenwich Dr., Suite 230, San Diego 92122, 619-557-5395 |
| | 250 Montgomery St., 14th Fl., San Francisco 94104, 415-705-2301 |

| *State* | *Office Location* |
|---|---|
| | 5201 Great American Parkway, Suite 333, Santa Clara 95054-1127, 408-291-7625 |
| Colorado | 1625 Broadway, Suite 680, Denver 80202, 303-844-3246 |
| Connecticut | Rm. 610 B, Federal Bldg., 450 Main St., Hartford 06103, 203-240-3530 |
| Delaware | *See* Philadelphia, PA |
| District of Columbia | *See* Gaithersburg, MD |
| Florida | Suite 224, Federal Bldg., 51 SW First Ave., Miami 33130, 305-536-5268 |
| | 128 N. Osceola Ave., Clearwater 34615, 813-461-0011 |
| | 200 E. Robinson St., Suite 695, Orlando 32801, 407-648-6235 |
| | 107 W. Gaines St., Rm. 366G, Tallahassee 32399-2000, 904-488-6469 |
| Georgia | Plaza Square North, Suite 310, 4360 Chamblee-Dunwoody Rd., Atlanta 30341, 404-452-9101 |
| | 120 Barnard St., Rm. A-107, Savannah 31401, 912-652-4204 |
| Hawaii | P.O. Box 50026, Rm. 4106, 300 Ala Moana Blvd., Honolulu 96850, 808-541-1782 |
| Idaho | 700 W. State St., 2nd Fl., Boise 83720, 208-334-3857 |
| Illinois | 55 East Monroe St., Rm. 1406, Chicago 60603, 312-353-4450 |
| | Illinois Institute of Technology, 201 E. Loop Rd., Wheaton 60187, 312-353-4332 |
| | 515 North Court St., P.O. Box 1747, Rockford 61110-0247, 815-987-4347 |
| Indiana | 11405 N. Pennsylvania St., Suite 106, Carmel (Indianapolis) 46032-6905, 317-582-2300 |
| Iowa | Rm. 817, Federal Bldg., 210 Walnut St., Des Moines 50309, 515-284-4222 |
| Kansas | 151 N. Volutsia, Wichita 67214-4695, 316-269-6160 |

| *State* | *Office Location* |
|---|---|
| Kentucky | Rm. 636B, Gene Snyder Courthouse and Customshouse Bldg., 610 West Broadway, Louisville 40202, 502-582-5066 |
| Louisiana | 432 World Trade Center, # 2 Canal Street, New Orleans 70130, 504-589-6546 |
| Maine | 77 Seawall St., Augusta 04330, 207-622-8249 |
| Maryland | 413 U.S. Customhouse, 40 South Gay St., Baltimore 21202, 301-962-2560 |
| | c/o National Institute of Standards & Technology, Bldg. 11, Gaithersburg 20899, 301-975-3904 |
| Massachusetts | World Trade Center, Suite 307, Commonwealth Pier Area, Boston 02210, 617-565-8563 |
| Michigan | 1140 McNamara Bldg., 477 Michigan Ave., Detroit 48226, 313-226-3650 |
| | 300 Monroe NW, Grand Rapids 49503, 616-456-2411 |
| Minnesota | 108 Federal Bldg., 110 South 4th Street, Minneapolis 55401, 612-348-1638 |
| Mississippi | 201 West Capital St., Suite 310, Jackson 39201-2005, 601-965-4388 |
| Missouri | 8182 Maryland Ave., Suite 303, St. Louis 63105, 314-425-3302 |
| | Rm. 635, 601 East 12th St., Kansas City 64106, 816-426-3141 |
| Montana | *See* Portland, OR |
| Nebraska | 11133 "O" Street, Omaha, 515-284-4222 |
| Nevada | 1755 East Plumb Lane, # 152, Reno 89502, 702-784-5203 |
| New Hampshire | 601 Spauling Turnpike, Suite 29, Portsmouth 03302, 603-334-6074 |
| New Jersey | Suite 100, 3131 Princeton Pike Bldg., Trenton 08648, 609-989-2100 |
| New Mexico | 851 University Blvd., SE # 203, Albuquerque 87106, 505-246-6205 |
| New York | 1312 Federal Bldg., 111 West Huron St., Buffalo 14202, 716-846-4191 |
| | Rm. 3718, 26 Federal Plaza, New York 10278, 212-264-0634 |

| *State* | *Office Location* |
|---|---|
| | 111 East Ave., Suite 220, Rochester 14604, 716-263-6480 |
| North Carolina | Suite 400, 400 West Market St., Greensboro 27401, 919-333-5345 |
| North Dakota | *See* Omaha, NE |
| Ohio | 9504 Federal Bldg., 550 Main St., Cincinnati 45202, 513-684-2944 |
| | Rm. 600, 668 Euclid Ave., Cleveland 44114, 216-522-4750 |
| Oklahoma | 6601 Broadway Extension, Oklahoma City 73116, 405-231-5302 |
| | 440 S. Houston St., Tulsa 74127, 918-581-7650 |
| Oregon | Suite 242, One World Trade Center, 121 SW Salmon, Portland 97204, 503-326-3001 |
| Pennsylvania | 660 American Avenue, Suite 201, King of Prussia (Philadelphia) 19406, 215-962-4980 |
| | 2002 Federal Bldg., 1000 Liberty Ave., Pittsburgh 15222, 412-644-2850 |
| Puerto Rico | Rm. G-55, Federal Bldg., Chardon Ave., San Juan (Hato Rey) 00918, 809-766-5555 |
| Rhode Island | 7 Jackson Walkway, Providence 02903, 401-528-5104 |
| South Carolina | Suite 172, Strom Thurmond Federal Bldg., 1835 Assembly St., Columbia 29201, 803-765-5345 |
| | J.C. Long Bldg., 9 Liberty St., Charleston 29424, 803-727-4361 |
| South Dakota | *See* Omaha, NE |
| Tennessee | Suite 114, Parkway Towers, 404 James Robertson Parkway, Nashville 37219-1505, 615-736-5161 |
| | 301 E. Church St., Knoxville 37915, 615-549-9268 |
| | 22 North Front St., Suite 200, Memphis 38103, 901-455-4137 |
| Texas | World Trade Center, 2050 N. Stemmons Freeway, S. 170, Dallas 75242-0787, 214-767-0542 |
| | # 1 Allen Center, 500 Dallas, Suite 1160, Houston 77002, 713-229-2578 |
| | 410 E. 5th St., Suite 320A, Austin 78701, 512-482-5939 |

| *State* | *Office Location* |
| --- | --- |
| Utah | Suite 105, 324 South State St., Salt Lake City 84111, 801-524-5116 |
| Vermont | *See* Boston, MA |
| Virginia | 8010 Federal Bldg., 400 North 8th St., Richmond 23240, 804-771-2246 |
| Washington | 3131 Elliott Ave., Suite 290, Seattle 98121, 206-553-5615 |
| | 320 N. Johnson St., Suite 350, Kennewick 99336, 509-735-2751 |
| West Virginia | Suite 807, 405 Capitol St., Charleston 25301, 304-347-5123 |
| Wisconsin | Rm. 596, 517 East Wisconsin Ave., Milwaukee 53202, 414-297-3473 |
| Wyoming | *See* Denver, CO |

## Bureau of Export Administration

Every U.S. export requires a license. Regulations, administration, and enforcement of these license requirements is done by the Bureau of Export Administration (BXA). The bureau publishes and enforces the export control laws of the United States to prevent the transfer of goods or information that is inconsistent with our national interests. Exporters should purchase a copy of the *Export Administration Regulations.* These regulations direct exporters on how to comply with the law and complete the licensing process. The regulations are updated throughout the year. The BXA also produces *The OEL Insider,* a quarterly newsletter on export licensing issues. Exporters should note that the government presumes you have knowledge of the laws and that any failure to comply is deliberate. Additions, amendments, or deletions to the Export Administration Regulations are published in the Federal Register and are effective on the date of publication. Contact:

Bureau of Export Administration, U.S. Department of Commerce, P.O. Box 273, Washington, DC 20044, 202-582-4911

*Office of Export Licensing, Regional Offices*

Western Regional Office, 3300 Irvine Ave., Suite 345, Newport Beach, CA 92660, 714-660-0144

Western Region, Northern California Branch, 5201 Great American Parkway, Suite 226, Santa Clara, CA 95054, 408-748-7450

Eastern Regional Office, 547 Amherst St., Nashua, NH 03063, 603-598-4300

*Office of Export Enforcement*

Enforcement Hotline 800-424-2980
Intelligence Division 202-582-8208

Boston Field Office, 10 Causeway St., Rm. 350, Boston, MA 02222, 617-565-6030

Chicago Field Office, 2400 Devon St., Suite 300, Des Plaines, IL 60018, 312-353-6640

Dallas Field Office, 525 Griffin St., Rm. 622, Dallas, TX 75202, 214-767-9294

Los Angeles Field Office, 2601 Main St., Suite 310, Irvine, CA 92072, 714-251-9001

Miami Field Office, 200 S. Andrews Ave., Suite 500, Fort Lauderdale, FL 33301, 305-356-7540

New York Field Office, 26 Federal Plaza, Rm. 3704, New York, NY 10278, 212-264-1365

San Jose Field Office, 96 N. Third St., Suite 250, San Jose, CA 95112, 408-291-4204

Washington Field Office, P.O. Box 1838, Springfield, VA 22151, 703-487-4950

## ■ National Institute of Standards and Technology

One of the principal concerns of U.S. business with the advent of the Single Market in Europe is the creation of new or revised standards to which U.S. firms must conform. There is a belief that these European standards have been created to keep U.S. products out. That is incorrect. The EC has created a series of product and performance standards that must be met by all companies operating in the EC. This includes the French, English, German, Spanish, Dutch, Japanese, American, or companies from any other country.

The National Institute of Standards and Technology (NIST) has prepared an extensive summary of the EC initiatives on standards, and other related materials. These can be obtained by contacting:

GATT Inquiry Point/Technical Office, Office of Standards Code and Information, National Institute of Standards and Technology, Administration Bldg., Rm. A 629, Gaithersburg, MD 20899, 301-965-4040

National Center for Standards Certification
Same address and telephone
GATT Hotline: 301-975-4041

The Office of Standards Code and Information has also established an EC hotline, to report on draft European standards developed for electrotechnical standardization and the European Telecommunications Standards Institute. The hotline also reports on standards-related EC directives identified from the *Official Journal of the EC.* Telephone 301-921-4164.

The Single Internal Market Information Service (SIMIS) published an overview paper *EC Product Standards under the Internal Market Program, April 1, 1992* that provides a comprehensive overview of the process. Interested parties should telephone SIMIS and request a copy.

The standards bodies of the EC have enabled NIST to identify U.S.-based organizations that can certify compliance with one or more of the EC standards applicable to a product, process, or manufacturing activity (e.g., ISO 9000). NIST does not warrant the quality or validity of any of the programs offered. Review and compare the offered services and the scope of the registrar's accreditation, before selecting a registration program. North American Quality System Registration Organizations include:

ABS Quality Evaluations, Inc., 263 North Belt East, Houston, TX 77060, 713-873-9400

American Association for Laboratory Accreditation, 656 Quince Orchard Rd., # 304, Gaithersburg, MD 20878-1409, 301-670-1377

American Association for Quality System Registration, 656 Quince Orchard Rd., # 340, Gaithersburg, MD 20878-1409, 301-990-1775

American European Services, 1054 31st St., NW, Suite 120, Washington, DC 20007

American Gas Association Laboratories Quality, 8501 East Pleasant Valley Rd., Cleveland, OH 44131, 216-525-4990

AT&T Quality Registrars, 1090 E. Duane Ave., Sunnyvale, CA 94086, 408-522-5377

650 Liberty Ave., Union, NJ 07083, 908-851-3058

1259 S. Cedar Crest Blvd., Allentown, PA 18103, 215-770-3285

BQS, Inc., 110 Summit Ave., Montvale, NJ 07645, 800-624-5892

British Standards Institution Quality Assurance, Office 20, 8000 Towers Crescent Dr., Suite 1350, Vienna, VA 22181, 703-760-7828

Bureau Veritas Quality International (NA), Inc., 509 North Main St., Jamestown, NY 14701, 800-937-9311

Det Norske Veritas Industrial Services, Inc., 16340 Park 10 Place, Suite 100, Houston, TX 77084, 713-579-9003

Entela, Inc., 3033 Madison Ave., Grand Rapids, MI 49548-1289, 616-247-0515

ETL Testing Laboratories/Intertek Services Corp., Industrial Park, Cortland, NY 13045, 502-150-9000

Intertek, 9900 Main St., Suite 500, Fairfax, VA 22301-3969, 703-476-9000

ISO Registrars, Inc., 3000 Town Center, Suite 2960, Southfield, MI 48075, 313-356-4510

Perry Johnson Registrars, Inc., 3000 Town Center, Suite 2960, Southfield, MI 48075, 800-800-0450

KEMA USA, 4379 County Line Rd., Chalfont, PA 18914, 215-822-4281

Lloyd's Register Quality Assurance, Ltd., 33–41 Newark St., Hoboken, NJ 07030, 201-963-1111

MET Electrical Testing Co., 916 W. Patapsco Ave., Baltimore, MD 21230, 410-354-2200

National Quality Assurance, 1146 Massachusetts Ave., Boxborough, MA 01719, 508-635-9256

National Sanitation Foundation, 3475 Plymouth Rd., P.O. Box 130140, Ann Arbor, MI 48113-0140

National Standards Authority of Ireland, 5 Medallion Centre, Greeley St., Merrimack, NH 03054, 603-424-7070

Quality Control Systems and Services, P.O. Box 4417, San Clemente, CA 92672, 800-423-8060

Quality Systems Registrars, Inc., 1555 Naperville/Wheaton Rd., Suite 206, Naperville, IL 60563, 708-778-0120

Scott Technical Services, 34 Channing St., Suite 400, Newton, MA 02158, 617-527-7032

SGS Yarsley Quality Accredited Firms, 1415 Park Ave., Hoboken, NJ 07030, 201-792-2400

Southwest Research Institute, 6220 Culbra Rd., San Antonio, TX 78288, 512-522-3145

Testwell Craig Laboratories, Inc., 47 Judson St., Ossining, NY 10562

Tri-Tech Services, Inc., 4700 Clairton Blvd., Pittsburgh, PA 15236, 412-884-2290

TUV America, Inc., 5 Cherry Hill Dr., Danvers, MA 01923, 508-777-7999

TUV Rheinland of North America, Inc., 12 Commerce Rd., Newtown, CT 06470, 203-426-0888

Twin City Testing Corp., 662 Cromwell Ave., St. Paul, MN 55114, 612-641-9318

Underwriters Laboratories, Inc., 1285 Walt Whitman Rd., Melville, NY 11747-3081

Vincotte USA, Inc., 10497 Town and Country Way, Suite 900, Houston, TX 77024, 713-465-2850

## U.S. Small Business Administration

The Small Business Administration (SBA), another bureau within the U.S. Department of Commerce, also provides information and resources to exporters. These resources include the Export Information System mentioned in the National Trade Data Bank, the Service Corps of Retired Executives (SCORE), reference libraries, business planning tools, and counseling services. SBA operates under a mandate to provide services to small business in America: the definition of a small business for SBA program purposes differs by industry SIC code. Some small businesses eligible for SBA support employ more than 1000 people or have revenues in excess of US $ 100 million or total assets of over US $ 1 billion.

SCORE is staffed by volunteer retired executives. Those with international business experience provide counseling and assistance in the development of international business plans, strategies, and operations.

The data program services of SBA can be accessed through the SBA's regional business centers. There are over 275 SBA documents and other publications on its "Small Business Consultant" disc, and other CD-ROM-based information is also available.

Each regional office has a Regional International Trade Officer. To utilize the resources of the SBA international programs, contact:

Central Office and Office of International Trade, 409 3rd St., NW, 6th Fl., Washington, DC 20416, 202-205-6720

General Information: 800-827-5722

Region I, 155 Federal St., 9th Fl., Boston, MA 02110

Region II, 111 West Huron St., Rm. 1311, Buffalo, NY 14202

Region III, 475 Allendale Rd., Suite 201, King of Prussia, PA 19406

Region IV, 1375 Peachtree St., NE, 5th Fl., Atlanta, GA 30367-8102

Region V, 300 S. Riverside Plaza, Suite 1975, Chicago, IL 60606-6617

Region VI, 8625 King George Dr., Bldg. C, Dallas, TX 75235-3391

Region VII, 911 Walnut St., 13th Fl., Kansas City, MO 64106

Region VIII, 999 18th St., Suite 701, Denver, CO 80202

Region IX, 71 Stevenson St., 20th Fl., San Francisco, CA 94105-2939

Region X, 2615 4th Ave., Suite 440, Seattle, WA 98121-1233

District International Trade Officers are located in district offices in every state. The Blue pages (government) of the telephone book list the addresses and telephone numbers of the SBA District Offices. Cities with district offices include:

| | |
|---|---|
| Alabama | Birmingham |
| Alaska | Anchorage |
| Arizona | Phoenix |
| Arkansas | Little Rock |
| California | Fresno<br>Glendale<br>Sacramento<br>Santa Ana<br>San Diego<br>San Francisco |
| Colorado | Denver |
| Connecticut | Hartford |
| Delaware | Wilmington |
| District of Columbia | |
| Florida | Coral Gables<br>Jacksonville |
| Georgia | Atlanta |
| Hawaii | Honolulu |
| Idaho | Boise |
| Illinois | Chicago<br>Springfield |
| Indiana | Indianapolis |
| Iowa | Cedar Rapids<br>Des Moines |
| Kansas | Wichita |
| Kentucky | Louisville |
| Louisiana | New Orleans |
| Maine | Augusta |
| Maryland | Baltimore |
| Massachusetts | Boston<br>Springfield |
| Michigan | Detroit |
| Minnesota | Minneapolis |
| Mississippi | Gulfport<br>Jackson |
| Missouri | St. Louis<br>Springfield |
| Montana | Helena |
| Nebraska | Omaha |
| Nevada | Las Vegas |
| New Hampshire | Concord |
| New Jersey | Camden<br>Newark |
| New Mexico | Albuquerque |
| New York | Albany<br>Buffalo<br>Elmira<br>Melville<br>New York<br>Rochester<br>Syracuse |
| North Carolina | Charlotte |
| North Dakota | Fargo |
| Ohio | Cleveland<br>Columbus |
| Oklahoma | Oklahoma City |
| Oregon | Portland |
| Pennsylvania | King of Prussia<br>Harrisburg<br>Pittsburgh<br>Wilkes-Barre |
| Rhode Island | Providence |
| South Carolina | Columbia |
| South Dakota | Sioux Falls |
| Tennessee | Nashville |
| Texas | Corpus Christi<br>Dallas<br>El Paso |

| | | | |
|---|---|---|---|
| Texas (*cont.*) | Harlingen<br>Houston<br>Lubbock<br>San Antonio | Washington | Seattle<br>Spokane |
| Utah | Salt Lake City | West Virginia | Charleston |
| Vermont | Montpelier | Wisconsin | Madison<br>Milwaukee |
| Virginia | Richmond | Wyoming | Casper |

## National Oceanic and Atmospheric Administration

This organization, commonly known as NOAH, manages the National Marine Fisheries Service (NMFS). The NMFS and NOAH are charged to support the interests of U.S. fisheries and fishery exporters. The NMFS also provides fee based inspection services for fishery products for export.

*National or Regional Office*

National Marine Fisheries Service, 1335 East-West Highway, Silver Spring, MD 20910, 301-427-2379

Alaska Region, NMFS, P.O. Box 21668, Juneau, AK 99802, 907-586-7221

Southeast Region, NMFS, 300 South Ferry St., Rm. 2016, Terminal Island, CA 90731, 213-514-6677

Northeast Region, NMFS, One Blackburn Dr., Gloucester, MA 01930, 508-281-9300

Southwest Region, NMFS, 9450 Koger Blvd., St. Petersburg, FL 33702, 813-893-3141

Northwest Region, NMFS, 7600 Sand Point Way, Seattle, WA 98115, 206-527-6150

The NMFS inspection service is situated in four offices. They are:

National Marine Fisheries Service, 1335 East-West Highway, Silver Spring, MD 20910, 301-427-2379

Alaska Region, NMFS, P.O. Box 21668, Juneau, AK 99802, 907-586-7221

Southeast Region, NMFS, 300 South Ferry St., Rm. 2016, Terminal Island, CA 90731, 213-514-6677

Northeast Region, NMFS, One Blackburn Dr., Gloucester, MA 01930, 508-281-9300

Southwest Region, NMFS, 9450 Koger Blvd., St. Petersburg, FL 33702, 813-893-3141

Southeast Inspection Office, 9450 Koger Blvd., St. Petersburg, FL 33702, 813-893-3155

## DEPARTMENT OF AGRICULTURE

Agriculture is a major export industry, and the EC is a major market. Subsidy and support programs proliferate, and the United States and EC continue to trade with each other. The Department of Agriculture actively promotes exports through the Foreign Agricultural Service (FAS), with an export promotion and support budget that approximates that of total U.S. agricultural exports. Contact:

Foreign Agricultural Service
International Trade Policy Division
Western Europe Group
202-720-1322; (Fax) 202-690-2079

Foreign Agricultural Service
Information Division
U.S. Department of Agriculture
202-720-7014; (Fax) 202-690-2079

The USDA has a number of international trade-oriented publications. Many are noted on page 278. To order publications or program information, write to the Information Division at Room 4644 South Bldg. at the above address.

A complete description of the Department of Agriculture export support and promotion programs is contained in their publication no. 1497 *Food & Agriculture EXPORT DIRECTORY 1993.*

### ■ Commodity and Marketing Programs

The FAS provides marketing support to industry groups, trade associations, State departments of agriculture, and regional associations. Specialists provide research and analysis to individuals and other entities interested in specific markets and products. Commodity and marketing program contacts are:

| *Commodity/Program* | *Telephone (202)* |
|---|---|
| Dairy, Livestock, Poultry | 720-8031 |
| Forest Products | 720-0638 |
| Grain and Feed | 720-6219 |
| High Value Products/ Services | 720-6343 |
| Horticultural/Tropical Products | 720-6590 |
| Marketing Operations | 720-4327 |
| Oilseeds and Products | 720-7037 |

| *Commodity/Program* | *Telephone (202)* |
|---|---|
| Tobacco, Cotton, and Seeds | 720-9494 |

## Export Credit Programs

USDA provides concessional financing and extended financing to support the export of U.S. commodities. These are the PL 480 program (Food for Peace) and CCC (Commodity Credit Corporation) program. Contact:

| *Program* | *Telephone (202)* |
|---|---|
| PL 480 Operations | 720-3664 |
| CCC Operations | 720-6211 |

## Services to Exporters

The FAS offers Trade Leads generated from its offices around the world, Foreign Buyer Lists from a database of over 13,000 foreign firms in over 70 countries, and publications such as *AgExporter.* FAS offices in the EC include:

| *Country* | *Address* |
|---|---|
| Belgium | Agricultural Minister-Counselor, U.S. Mission to the EC, USEC, APO New York, NY, 09667-1030 |
| Denmark | Agricultural Counselor, American Embassy, Copenhagen, APO New York, NY 09170 |
| France | Agricultural Counselor, American Embassy, Paris, APO New York, NY 09777 |
| Germany | Agricultural Attache, U.S. Embassy Office, Berlin, APO New York, NY 09742 |
| | Agricultural Counselor, American Embassy, Bonn, Box 385, APO New York, NY 09080 |
| | Agricultural Trade Officer, American Consulate General, Hamburg, APO New York, NY 09215-0002 |
| Greece | Agricultural Counselor, American Embassy, Athens, APO New York, NY 09255-0006 |
| Ireland | Agricultural Minister-Counselor, Dublin, U.S. Department of Agriculture, FAS, Washington, DC 20250-6000 |
| Italy | Agricultural Officer, American Consulate General, Milan, Box M, APO New York, NY 09794 |
| | Agricultural Counselor, American Embassy, Rome, APO New York, NY 09794-0007 |

| *Country* | *Address* |
|---|---|
| | Agricultural Attache for Food and, Agricultural Affairs, U.S. Mission to the U.N., American Embassy, Rome, APO New York, NY 09794-0007 |
| Netherlands | Agricultural Attache, American Embassy, The Hague, APO New York, NY 09159-7011 |
| Portugal | Agricultural Attache, American Embassy, Lisbon, APO New York, NY 09678-0002 |
| Spain | Agricultural Counselor, American Embassy, Madrid, APO New York, NY 09285-8500 |
| United Kingdom | Agricultural Minister-Counselor, American Embassy, London, Box 48, FPO New York, NY 09509 |

### ■ Inspection Services

The USDA Animal and Plant Health Inspection Service inspects and certifies plant and animal products for export. This office also provides U.S. exporters with import requirements of foreign nations. Contact:

Animal and Plant Health Inspection Service or Veterinary Services (VS)

Plant Protection and Quarantine (PPQ), Federal Bldg., 6505 Belcrest Rd., Hyattsville, MD 20782, 301-436-8537

## DEPARTMENT OF STATE

The State Department is interested in the political implications of the European Community for many reasons: prestige, power, influence, and the political future of the region. The Foreign Service Act directs Ambassadors to promote U.S. exports in their respective host countries. Contact:

U.S. Department of State, Commercial, Legislative and Public Affairs, 21st & C St., NW, Washington, DC 20520, 202-647-1942

Bureau of European Community Affairs, Office of EC/OECD Affairs, 202-647-2395; (Fax) 202-647-9959

Office of Economic and Business Affairs, Office of Developed Country Trade, 202-647-6956, 202-647-1420; (Fax) 202-647-6540

## UNITED STATES TRADE REPRESENTATIVE

The U.S. Trade Representative (USTR) is the President's chief adviser on international trade policy, develops and coordinates implementation of international trade policy, and is the chief negotiator for international trade agreements. The USTR also provides policy guidance on: expansion of U.S. exports; the General Agreement on Tariffs and Trade (GATT); trade policy with regard to unfair trade practices; bilateral trade and commodity issues; and policy research on trade, commodities, and direct investment. The USTR has offices in Washington, DC and Geneva, Switzerland:

Office of the U.S. Trade Representative, 600 17th St., NW, Washington, DC 20506, 202-395-3230; (Fax) 202-395-3911

Europe and the Mediterranean, 202-395-3320; (Fax) 202-395-3911

Director, Technical Trade Barriers, 202-395-3063; (Fax) 202-395-3911

U.S. Trade Representative, Geneva, 1-3 Avenue de La Paix, 1202 Geneva, Switzerland, 41 22 749 5241

## DEPARTMENT OF TRANSPORTATION

The Maritime Administration administers federal laws and programs to develop and maintain the U.S. merchant marine. The Office of Market Development conducts programs to increase the use of U.S. flag vessels. MARAD publishes information on its programs and on U.S. flag shipping services. Contact:

U.S. Department of Transportation, Maritime Administration, 400 7th St., SW, Washington, DC 20590

Office of Market Development, 202-366-5517

Office of Policy and International Affairs, 202-366-4544

## DEPARTMENT OF THE TREASURY

The Treasury is actively interested in the European Community for at least three reasons:

1. Impacts of EC economic union on the U.S. monetary policy
2. Treatment of U.S. financial institutions in the EC
3. Treatment of EC financial institutions in the U.S.

The EC member states are the dominant foreign investors and holders of hard assets (land, stock, and other portfolio assets, in addition to actively managed corporate equities) in the United States, with Japan a close second due to the size of their short-term portfolios. The nature of this sizeable investment by EC citizens (corporate and otherwise) warrants close attention by the Treasury. They can also provide practical information to U.S. firms regarding the EC. Contact:

Office of Industrial Relations, and Global Analysis
202-566-3856; (Fax) 202-786-8446

Office of International Banking, and Portfolio Investment
202-566-5628; (Fax) 202-633-0887

Office of International Investment
202-343-9150; (Fax) 202-786-8453

Office of International Trade
202-566-8108; (Fax) 202-633-7831

U.S. Customs is a branch of the Treasury Department. Customs implements the import control activities of the U.S. government through its district and regional offices. Customs provides information on Drawback (see p. 277). Customs also receives copies of the Shipper's Export Declaration, a document that must be submitted with nearly every export shipment. The SED is a license reporting and information capture document used by the Bureau of Export Administration to enforce U.S. export regulations, and by the Bureau of the Census to compile information on export transactions.

U.S. Customs offices are listed in the Government section of the telephone book, under "Customs Service."

## INTERNATIONAL DEVELOPMENT COOPERATION AGENCY

The U.S. International Development Cooperation Agency (IDCA) mission is to ensure that development goals are part of executive branch decisions on trade, finance, monetary affairs, technology, and other economic issues affecting less developed nations. The Agency for International Development (AID), the Overseas Private Investment Corporation (OPIC), and the Trade and Development Program (USTDP) are part of the IDCA. For more information on the IDCA, contact:

U.S. International Development Cooperation Agency, 321 21st St., NW, Washington, DC 20523, 202-647-8578

### Agency for International Development

AID provides economic assistance programs to help developing countries improve their economic and productive resources. It promotes economic and political stability in friendly countries. AID is not active in the EC, but its development assistance can benefit U.S. or EC-based companies. Contact:

Agency for International Development, 320 21st St., NW, Washington, DC 20523, 202-647-8578

### Overseas Private Investment Corporation

OPIC supports U.S. private investment in over 100 developing countries. Its programs provide for loan or lease guarantees, investment guarantees, and a limited amount of direct equity participation by the agency. OPIC was the subject of some debate in the 1992 election campaign because OPIC investments create offshore industries that compete directly with U.S.-based producers. The definition of the OPIC mission does not address this anomaly. OPIC loan, investment and lease guarantees, and investments can benefit U.S. corporations and their related entities. For additional information on OPIC programs, see: Gordon, John S. *Alternative Finance: Techniques and Strategies.* (Dayton, OH: Global Training Center, Inc., 1992). Contact:

Overseas Private Investment Corporation, 1615 M St., NW, Washington, DC 20527, 202-457-7092, 800-424-6742

### U.S. Trade and Development Program

The USTDP funds feasibility studies performed by U.S. firms for development projects in developing countries. Program logic is: if planning and feasibility study work is done by U.S. firms, the follow-on work will accrue to one or more U.S. firms. Regrettably, the nonreimbursable funding is not contingent on this consideration and the program does not require any specific participation by U.S. contractors or vendors in the development project itself. Contact:

U.S. Trade and Development Program, State Annex 16, Rm. 309, Washington, DC 20523, 703-875-4357

## DEPARTMENT OF EDUCATION

The Department of Education Business and International Trade Education Program awards grants to post-secondary institutions to support education and training programs in international trade. Contact:

Program Officer
Business and International Education Program
U.S. Department of Education, Rm. 3053, ROB-3, 7th & D St., SW, Washington, DC 20202, 202-708-8764

## DEPARTMENT OF ENERGY

The Department of Energy (DOE) has a number of programs to promote U.S. exports of energy goods, services, and technology. These programs and contact telephone numbers are:

*Committee on Renewable Energy Commerce and Trade*
Provides comprehensive advice on markets, financing and information on export guidelines. Staff Director: 202-586-5517.

*Coal and Technology Export Program*
Promotes the export of clean coal products and services. Program Manager in the Office of Fossil Energy: 202-586-7297.

*FE/AID Database and International Energy Development Opportunities*
DOE has two programs available through the Agency for International Development. The FE/AID Database provides energy related trade leads (contact 202-586-9680), and the FE/AID International Energy Development Opportunities Program provides financial support to U.S. companies for pre-feasibility studies regarding international energy trade and development opportunities. Contact: 202-586-7297.

*The Bureau of International Affairs and Energy Emergency Eastern Europe Development Program*
This program focuses on energy development in Eastern Europe. Contact: 202-586-1189.

*The Export Assistance Initiative*
This is a program within DOEs Bureau of International Affairs. Its purpose is to:

(1) identify overseas opportunities for U.S. companies,
(2) assist these firms in taking advantage of these opportunities,
(3) identify trade barriers and work with other government agencies to remove them,
(4) advocate changes to U.S. laws that restrict trade, and
(5) identify financing alternatives for U.S. companies.

Contact the Bureau of International Affairs: 202-586-0153.

## EXPORT-IMPORT BANK OF THE UNITED STATES

The Eximbank is a government agency that helps finance the sale of U.S. goods and services. Eximbank has three principal types of programs:

- *Working Capital Guarantee Program.* Eximbank guarantees up to 100 percent of the principal and interest on commercial loans to small and medium-sized U.S. companies that need financing to produce U.S. goods for export. The program can be for a single export sale or for a revolving line of credit requirement. While there is no stated minimum, U.S. banks are the access point and their practical minimum is in excess of US$ 50,000.
- *Loans.* Eximbank provides loans directly to foreign buyers of U.S. capital equipment and services, or through an intermediary lender (U.S. or foreign). Intermediary loans enable commercial

lenders or exporters to provide fixed rate financing to foreign buyers. Eximbank also guarantees commercial loans to foreign buyers of U.S. goods and services. Eximbank loans and guarantees cover 85 percent of the contract price and the foreign buyer is required to make a 15 percent down payment. There are fees for the programs.

- *Insurance.* Eximbank provides commercial and political risk insurance policies on single or repetitive export sales or leases to foreign buyers. Policies can be tailored to the needs of exporters and financial institutions. Insurance usually covers 100 percent of the political risks and 90 to 95 percent of the political risks, plus a portion of the interest. These policies can be used to secure financing by commercial lenders.

Eximbank has a regional loan and guarantee office in Los Angeles and five insurance service offices across the United States. Contact Export Import Bank of the United States at:

*Loan and Guarantee Programs*

811 Vermont Ave., NW, Washington, DC 20571-0999,
202-566-4490; (Fax) 202-566-7524

West Coast Office, 11000 Wilshire Blvd., Suite 9103, Los Angeles, CA 90024, 310-575-7425; (Fax) 310-575-7428

*Export Credit Insurance Programs*

New York Regional Office, 212-513-4292; (Fax) 212-513-4704

Chicago Regional Office, 312-641-1915; (Fax) 312-641-2292

Houston Regional Office, 713-589-8182; (Fax) 713-589-8184

Miami Regional Office, 305-372-8540; (Fax) 305-372-5114

Los Angeles Regional Office, 310-322-1152; (Fax) 310-322-2041

Eximbank has an advisory and information service on 800-424-5201. Additional information on Eximbank programs is presented on page 215.

## INTERNATIONAL TRADE COMMISSION

The ITC was established as the U.S. Tariff Commission in 1916. By the 1970s, it had evolved into a quasi-judicial agency charged with administering trade remedy laws, subject to court review. The ITC:

- Determines whether domestic industries are injured or subject to injury by increased levels of imports
- Takes action to counteract unfair import trade practices
- Determines if domestic industries are injured by imports sold at less than fair value (dumped or subsidized)

- Provides the government and the public with technical information and advice on trade and tariff matters
- Conducts studies and compiles data on trade and tariff issues.

The Trade Remedy Assistance Office provides assistance to businesses seeking relief under U.S. trade remedy laws. The trade remedies addressed by this office include: anti-dumping, countervailing duties, patent infringements, trademarks infringement, copyright infringement, denial of U.S. rights under trade agreements, and other discriminatory acts by foreign countries. Contact:

U.S. International Trade Commission, 500 E. St., SW,
Washington, DC 20436, 202-205-2000

Trade Remedy Assistance Office, 800-343-9822

## OTHER AGENCIES

Each of the following agencies may create or enforce laws or regulations that impact the international activities of U.S. companies. If your company has had contact with any of these agencies, it would be useful to determine their interest in your international business ventures.

*Department of Justice*
Antitrust Division, Foreign Commerce Section
202-514-2464; (Fax) 202-514-4508

*Department of Labor*
Bureau of International Labor Affairs, Office of International
Economic Affairs, 202-523-6096; (Fax) 202-523-4071

*Environmental Protection Agency*
Office of International Activities, 202-260-4886; (Fax) 202-260-8512

*Food and Drug Administration*
Office of Health Affairs, 301-443-6143; (Fax) 301-443-1309

*U.S. Information Agency*
Office of European Affairs, 202-619-4563; (Fax) 202-619-6821

*Securities and Exchange Commission*
Office of Economic Analysis, 202-272-7359; (Fax) 202-272-7132

## APPENDIX

Summary of NTBD Documents

1. Board of Governors of the Federal Reserve System
   - Foreign Exchange Spot Rates
   - Foreign 3-Month Interest Rates
   - Stock Price Indices for the G-10 Countries (most of the EC)

U.S. 3-Month CD Interest Rates
Weighted Average Exchange Value of the Dollar

2. Central Intelligence Agency
   *Handbook on Economic Statistics*
   *World Factbook*
3. Export-Import Bank of the United States
   Quarterly Report
4. Overseas Private Investment Corporation
   OPIC Program Summaries
5. Office of the United States Trade Representative
   *National Trade Estimate Report on Foreign Trade Barriers*
   Trade Projections Report to the Congress
6. U.S. Department of Agriculture
   Foreign Production, Supply & Distribution of Ag Commodities
7. U.S. Department of Commerce, Bureau of Economic Analysis
   Fixed Reproducible Tangible Wealth Estimates
   Foreign Direct Investment in the United States: BOP Basis
   International Services
   National Income & Product Accounts, Quarterly and Annual Series
   Operations of U.S. Affiliates of Foreign Companies
   Operations of U.S. Parent Companies & Their Foreign Affiliates
   U.S. Assets Abroad & Foreign Assets in the United States
   U.S. Business Acquired & Established by Foreign Direct Investors
   U.S. Direct Investment Abroad: Position, Capital, Income
   U.S. Expenditures for Pollution Abatement & Control (PAC)
   U.S. International Transactions (Balance of Payments)
   U.S. Merchandise Trade (Balance of Payments Basis)
8. U.S. Department of Commerce, Bureau of the Census
   Exports from Manufacturing Establishments
   Merchandise Trade-Imports by Commodity
   Merchandise Trade-Exports by Commodity
   Merchandise Trade-Imports by Country
   Merchandise Trade-Exports by Country
   Total Mid-Year Populations & Projections through 2050
   Trade & Employment
9. U.S. Department of Commerce, Bureau of Export Administration
   BXA Today
   Bureau of Export Administration Annual Report
   Export Licensing Information
10. U.S. Department of Commerce, International Trade Administration
    Business America
    *A Basic Guide to Exporting*
    Domestic & International Coal Issues and Markets

Eastern Europe Looks for Partners
EC 1992: A Commerce Department Analysis of EC Directives
Europe Now: A Report
Export Programs: A Business Directory of U.S. Government Resources
Foreign Direct Investment in the U.S.—Annual Transactions
Foreign Traders Index
Investment Guides
Market Research Reports: Country Marketing Plans; Industry Sector Analyses; Foreign Economic Trends
North American Free Trade Agreement (NAFTA) Information
Trade Promotion Coordinating Committee Calendar of Events
U.S. Foreign Trade Update—Monthly Analysis
U.S. Industrial Outlook
U.S. Manufacturers Trade Performance—Quarterly Report

11. U.S. Department of Commerce, National Institute of Standards and Technology
    GATT Standard Code Activities of NIST
    Organizations Conducting Standards Related Activities
    National Standards & Metric Information Program
12. Department of Labor, Bureau of Labor Statistics
    International Labor Statistics
    International Price Indexes
13. Department of Energy, Energy Information Administration
    International Energy Annual
14. Department of State, Bureau of Public Affairs
    Background Notes
    Key Officers of Foreign Service Posts
    Resource Guide to Doing Business in Central & Eastern Europe
15. U.S. Department of Commerce, Small Business Administration
    SBA Export Information System (XIS)
16. U.S. International Trade Commission
    Trade between U.S. & Non-Market Economy Countries
17. U.S. Department of Commerce, Office of Business Analysis
    NTDB Browse Manual
    Sources of Trade Information and Contacts
18. University of Massachusetts, MISER
    States of Origin of U.S. Exports

To subscribe to the NTDB contact:

U.S. Department of Commerce, Office of Economic Analysis,
HCHB Rm. 4885, Washington, DC 20230, 202-482-1986

The Department of Commerce operates a Trade Information Center directory of export information. It directs inquirers to the export services that should meet their needs. Telephone 800-872-8723.

# 2

# STATE AND REGIONAL ORGANIZATIONS

## STATE ORGANIZATIONS

Each state has an economic development office, though it may be named finance, investment, insurance, industry and trade, or market development. These economic development or market development offices were formed to support the growth of sales and employment, therefore the tax base, of state-based companies. Some states have very sophisticated international marketing and service support organizations; others have only nominal support for international business activities. Trade development offices can be of value to mid-sized, emerging, and small firms; they offer limited benefits to major national and multinational corporations.

State trade offices concentrate on the leading in-state industry sectors. Agricultural promotion for international markets is handled by the state's department of agriculture or the local extension office of the U.S. Department of Agriculture.

A number of states maintain offices in one or more EC countries. Because exports have over the past decade been one of the engines of economic growth in the United States, (the other was the tremendous growth in deficit spending at the Federal level), governors and state legislators are very interested in programs to support international trade, particularly exports. It will be useful to cultivate a positive working relationship with those legislators that oversee or control the state's economic development and commerce programs and expenditures.

### ■ State Trade Promotion Offices

State trade promotion offices are listed by state. If a state has an office in one or more EC countries, the country is listed after the state office. Following this state listing, there is a list of state offices by EC member state.

| *State* | *Office Location* |
|---|---|
| Alabama | Alabama Development Office, International Marketing Division, 401 Adams Ave., Montgomery 36130, 205-242-0400<br>Germany |
| Alaska | Alaska Office of International Trade, 3601 C St., Suite 798, Anchorage 99503, 907-561-5585 |
| Arizona | Arizona Department of Commerce, International Trade and Investment Division, 3800 North Central, Suite 1500, Phoenix 85012 |
| Arkansas | Arkansas Industrial Development Commission, One State Capitol Mall, Rm. 4C 300, Little Rock 72201, 501-682-1121<br>Belgium |
| California | California State World Trade Commission, 1121 L St., Suite 310, Sacramento 95814, 916-324-5511<br>Germany, United Kingdom |
| Colorado | Colorado International Trade Office, 1625 Broadway, Suite 680, Denver 80202, 303-892-3850<br>Belgium |
| Connecticut | Connecticut Department of Economic Development, International Division, 865 Brook St., Rocky Hill 06067, 203-258-4243<br>Germany |
| Delaware | Business Development, Division of Economic Development, 99 Kings Highway, Box 1401, Dover 19903, 302-739-4271 |
| District of Columbia | D.C. Office of International Business, 1250 I St., NW, Suite 1003, Washington 20005, 202-727-1576 |
| Florida | Division of International Trade and Development, Florida Department of Commerce, 366 Collins Bldg., 107 West Gaines St., Tallahassee 32399-2000, 904-488-9050<br>Belgium, Germany, United Kingdom |
| Georgia | Department of Industry, Trade and Tourism, P.O. Box 1776, Atlanta 30301, 404-656-3571<br>Belgium |
| Hawaii | Trade and Industry Development, Department of Planning and Economic Development, P.O. Box 2359, Honolulu 96804, 808-548-7719 |
| Idaho | Division of International Business, Idaho Department of Commerce, 700 West State St., Boise 83720, 208-334-2470 |

| *State* | *Office Location* |
|---|---|
| Illinois | International Business Division, Illinois Department of Commerce and Community Affairs, 100 West Randolph, Suite C-400, Chicago 60601, 312-814-7164<br>Belgium |
| Indiana | International Trade Division, Indiana Department of Commerce, One North Capitol, Suite 700, Indianapolis 46204-2288, 317-232-3527<br>Netherlands |
| Iowa | Division of International Trade, Iowa Department of Economic Development, 200 East Grand Ave., Des Moines 50309, 515-242-4729<br>Germany |
| Kansas | Trade Development Division, Kansas Department of Commerce, 700 Harrison St., 13th Fl., Topeka 66603-3957, 913-296-4027<br>Belgium |
| Kentucky | Office of International Trade, Kentucky Commerce Cabinet, Capitol Plaza Tower, 24th Fl., Frankfort 40601, 502-564-2170<br>Belgium |
| Louisiana | Louisiana Department of Economic Development, P.O. Box 94185, Baton Rouge 70804-9185, 504-342-4320<br>Netherlands |
| Maine | International Commerce, Department of Economic & Community Development, State House Station 59, Augusta 04333, 207-289-5700 |
| Maryland | International Trade, Maryland International Division, 401 East Pratt St., Suite 752, Baltimore 21202, 410-333-8180<br>Belgium |
| Massachusetts | Office of International Trade, 100 Cambridge St., Rm. 902, Boston 02202, 617-367-1830<br>Germany, United Kingdom |
| Michigan | International Office, Michigan Department of Commerce, P.O. Box 30225, Lansing 48909, 517-373-6390<br>Belgium |
| Minnesota | Office of International Marketing, Minnesota Trade Office, 1000 MN World Trade Center, 30 East 7th St., St. Paul 55101-4902, 612-297-4227<br>France, United Kingdom |

| *State* | *Office Location* |
|---|---|
| Mississippi | International Trade and Investment, Department of Economic Development, P.O. Box 849, Jackson 39205, 601-359-6672<br>Germany |
| Missouri | Business Development, Department of Economic Development, P.O. Box 118, Jefferson City 65102, 314-751-4999<br>Germany |
| Montana | International Trade Office, Montana Department of Commerce, 1424 9th Ave., Helena 59620, 406-444-3923 |
| Nebraska | Department of Economic Development, 301 Centennial Mall South, P.O. Box 94666, Lincoln 68509, 402-471-3111 |
| Nevada | International Program, Nevada Commission on Economic Development, 5151 South Carson, Carson City 89710, 702-687-4325 |
| New Hampshire | Department of Resources and Economic Development, 105 Loudon Rd., Bldg. 2, Concord 03301, 603-271-2591 |
| New Jersey | Division of International Trade, Department of Commerce and Economic Development, P.O. Box 47024, Newark 07102, 201-648-3518<br>United Kingdom |
| New Mexico | Office of International Trade, Economic Development and Tourism Department, 1100 St. Francis Dr., Santa Fe 87503, 505-827-0272 |
| New York | International Division, Department of Economic Development, 1515 Broadway, 51st Fl., New York 10036, 212-827-6210<br>Germany, Italy, United Kingdom |
| North Carolina | International Division, North Carolina Department of Economic & Community Development, 430 North Salisbury St., Raleigh 27611, 919-733-7193<br>Germany |
| North Dakota | North Dakota World Trade, 1833 East Bismarck Expressway, Bismarck 58504, 701-221-5300 |
| Ohio | International Trade Division, Department of Development, 77 South High St., 29th Fl., P.O. Box 1001, Columbus 43266-0101, 614-466-2317<br>Belgium, Germany |

| *State* | *Office Location* |
| --- | --- |
| Oklahoma | International Trade and Investment, Oklahoma Department of Commerce, P.O. Box 26980, Oklahoma City 73126-0980, 405-841-217<br>Germany |
| Oregon | International Trade Division, Oregon Economic Development Department, One World Trade Center, 121 Southwest Salmon, Suite 300, Portland 97204, 503-229-5625 |
| Pennsylvania | Office of International Development, Pennsylvania Department of Commerce, 463 Forum Bldg., Harrisburg 17112, 717-783-1356<br>Belgium, France, Germany |
| Rhode Island | International Trade Division, Department of Economic Development, 7 Jackson Walkway, Providence 02903, 401-277-2601<br>Belgium |
| South Carolina | South Carolina State Development Board, International Business Division, P.O. Box 927, Columbia 29202, 803-737-0400<br>Germany |
| South Dakota | Export, Trade and Marketing Division, Governor's Office of Economic Development, 711 Wells Ave., Capitol Lake Plaza, Pierre 57501, 605-773-5735 |
| Tennessee | International and National Marketing Division, Department of Economic and Community Development, 320 6th Ave. North, 7th Fl., Nashville 37243-0405, 615-741-5870 |
| Texas | International Trade Relations, Texas Department of Commerce, P.O. Box 12728, Austin 78711, 512-320-9672<br>Germany |
| Utah | International Business Development, Economic and Industrial Development Division, 324 South State St., Suite 200, Salt Lake City 84111, 801-538-8737<br>Belgium |
| Vermont | Department of Economic Development, Pavilion Office Bldg., Montpelier 05602, 802-828-3221 |
| Virginia | Trade Development Group, Virginia Department of Economic Development, P.O. Box 798, Richmond 23206-0798, 804-371-8107<br>Belgium |

| *State* | *Office Location* |
|---|---|
| Washington | Washington State Department of Trade and Economic Development, 2001 Sixth Ave., 26th Fl., Seattle 98121, 206-464-7143<br>France |
| West Virginia | Governor's Office of Community and Industrial Development, State Capitol, Rm. M-146, Charleston 25306, 305-558-2234 |
| Wisconsin | Bureau of International Development, Department of Development, P.O. Box 7970, Madison 53707, 608-266-9487<br>Germany |
| Wyoming | International Trade Office, Wyoming Division of Economic and Community Development, 4th Fl. North, Barrett Bldg., Cheyenne 82002, 307-777-6412 |

*State Trade and Investment Offices in the European Community, by Country**

| | |
|---|---|
| Belgium | Arkansas<br>Colorado<br>Florida<br>Georgia<br>Illinois<br>Kansas<br>Kentucky<br>Maryland<br>Michigan<br>Ohio<br>Pennsylvania<br>Rhode Island<br>Utah<br>Virginia |
| France | Minnesota<br>Pennsylvania<br>Washington |
| Germany | Alabama<br>California<br>Connecticut<br>Florida<br>Iowa<br>Massachusetts |
| Germany (*cont.*) | Mississippi<br>Missouri<br>New York<br>North Carolina<br>Ohio<br>Oklahoma<br>Pennsylvania<br>South Carolina<br>Texas<br>Wisconsin |
| Italy | New York |
| Netherlands | Indiana<br>Louisiana |
| United Kingdom | California<br>Florida<br>Massachusetts<br>Minnesota<br>New Jersey<br>New York |

* Some state offices in the EC are serviced by a service agency or are maintained on a part-time basis. Contact the U.S.-based trade development office to determine the services offered by their EC office.

Denmark, Greece, Ireland, Luxembourg, Portugal, and Spain have no U.S. state trade development offices.

## U.S. REGIONAL ORGANIZATIONS

### ■ Small Business Development Centers

Small Business Development Centers (SBDCs) are no-charge business consulting service centers funded jointly by the Small Business Administration (SBA) and state and local governments. There are over 750 SBDCs across the United States. All centers provide access to international trade services, and some centers concentrate specifically on international trade assistance.

This assistance can include general export information, training seminars and workshops, market research assistance, export counseling, development of export market plans, development of trade leads, assistance with overseas trade shows, international trade finance, packaging language translation services, and more.

To contact the SBDC in your area, telephone the local office of the Small Business Administration (SBA) and ask for information. Nineteen states have SBDCs that concentrate on international trade; they provide international trade counseling and support services to small and emerging business.

| *State* | *SBDC Contact Information* |
|---|---|
| Alabama | Alabama International Trade Center, University of Alabama at Birmingham, 400 North Martha Parham, Tuscaloosa 35487-0396, 205-348-7621 |
| California | Export Small Business Development Center, 110 E. Ninth St., Suite A761, Los Angeles 90079, 213-892-1111, 800-371-1110 |
| | Export Small Business Development Center Satellite, 300 Esplanade Dr., Suite 1020, Oxnard 93030, 805-981-4633 |
| Florida | Florida Atlantic University, P.O. Box 3091, Boca Raton 33431, 407-338-2273 |
| | Small Business Development Center, University of Central Florida, P.O. Box 2500, Bldg. Ceba II, Orlando 32816, 407-823-5554 |
| | University of West Florida, College of Business, Bldg. 8, Pensacola 33251, 904-474-2908 |

| *State* | *SBDC Contact Information* |
|---|---|
| Georgia | International Trade Development Center, University of Georgia, Chicopee Complex, 1180 East Broad St., Athens 30602, 404-542-5760 |
| | Small Business Development Center, Clayton State College, P.O. Box 285, Morrow 30260, 404-961-3440 |
| | Small Business Development Center, Kennesaw College, P.O. Box 444, Marietta 30061, 404-423-6450 |
| Illinois | Illinois World Trade Center College, 321 North Clark St., Suite 550, Chicago 60610-4714, 312-467-0550 |
| | International Trade Center, Bradley University, Lovelace Hall, Peoria 61625, 309-677-3075 |
| Louisiana | Louisiana International Trade Center, University of New Orleans, 368 Business Administration, New Orleans 70148 |
| Maine | Small Business Development Center, University of Southern Maine, 96 Falmouth St., Portland 04103, 207-780-4420 |
| Massachusetts | Small Business Development Center, University of Massachusetts, Amherst 01003, 413-545-5580 |
| Michigan | Center for International Business Development, Michigan State University, 6 Kellogg Center, East Lansing 48824-1035, 517-353-4336 |
| Mississippi | Small Business Development Center, International Trade Center, Millsaps College, Jackson 39210, 601-354-5201 |
| New York | Small Business Development Center, State University College at Buffalo, 1300 Elmwood Ave., Buffalo 14222, 716-878-4030 |
| | Small Business Development Center, Rockland Community College, 145 College Rd., Suffern 10901, 914-356-0381 |
| Ohio | Small Business Development Center, Lake County Economic Development Center, Lakeland Community College, Mentor 44080, 419-243-8191 |
| Oklahoma | Small Business Development Center, Rose State College, 6420 Southeast 15th, Midwest City 73110, 405-733-7348 |
| Oregon | Small Business Development Center, Portland Community College, One World Trade Center, 121 SW Salmon St., Suite 210, Portland 97204, 503-274-7482 |

| *State* | *SBDC Contact Information* |
| --- | --- |
| Pennsylvania | Small Business Development Center, Lehigh University International Trade Center, 301 Broadway, Bethlehem 18015, 215-758-3930 |
| | Small Business Development Center, Gannon University, Carlisle Bldg., 3rd Fl., Erie 16541, 814-871-7714 |
| | Small Business Development Center, Pennsylvania State University of Harrisburg, Crags Bldg., Route 30, Middletown 17057, 717-948-6069 |
| | Wharton School of Business, University of Pennsylvania, Vance Hall, 4th Fl., Philadelphia 19104, 215-898-4861 |
| | Small Business Development Center, Duquesne University, Rockwell Hall, Rm. 10 Concourse, 600 Forbes Ave., Pittsburgh 15282, 412-434-6233 |
| Rhode Island | Small Business Development Center, Bryant College, 450 Douglas Pike, Smithfield 02917-1284, 401-232-6407 |
| Tennessee | Small Business Development Center, International Trade Center, Memphis State University, Memphis 38152, 901-678-2500 |
| Texas | North Texas Small Business Development Center, International Trade Resource Center, 2050 Stemmons Freeway, Suite 150, Dallas 75258, 214-653-1777 |
| | Small Business Development Center, University of Houston, 601 Jefferson St., Suite 2330, Houston 77002, 713-752-8404 |
| | South Texas Border Small Business Development Center, University of Texas at San Antonio, San Antonio 78285-0660, 512-224-0791 |
| Washington | International Trade Institute, North Seattle Community College, 9600 College Way North, Seattle 98103, 206-527-3732 |

## District Export Councils

District Export Councils (DECs) are comprised of a select corps of trade experts dedicated to providing leadership and guidance to the international business community, and providing counsel to the U.S. Department of Commerce on emerging export development issues. President Nixon directed the establishment of DECs in 1973. Their activities are supported by the District Offices of the U.S. and Foreign Commercial Service (see p. 9). Each state has an active DEC, however, Nebraska, North Dakota, and South Dakota are combined with Iowa.

Each District Export Council has about 30 volunteer members from the business community (1500+ nationwide), appointed to four-year terms by the U.S. Secretary of Commerce. Selection is based on the individual's ability to contribute energetic leadership, a leadership position in the local business community, thorough knowledge of day-to-day international operations, a keen interest in export development, and the willingness to devote time to council activities (state government and SBA members are appointed on an ex officio basis).

The mission of each DEC is to encourage and support:

- Exports that strengthen individual companies and stimulate U.S. economic growth.
- Export expansion activities by working with the US&FCS district offices.
- Opportunities to promote greater export activity at the local level by developing trade assistance networks.

Through:

- Counseling of local and regional businesses.
- Identification of export financing sources for business.
- Programs to create a greater export awareness in their local business communities.
- Identification of issues that impact export trade and implementation for constructive suggestions for improvement.
- Supporting programs and services of US&FCS district offices.
- Building local export assistance partnerships with other organizations.
- International education at the community level.

The focus of each DEC is to assist and support the expansion of export and international activity within the region served. DEC members are available to counsel corporate managers and executives on the issues and opportunities involved in exporting and international trade.

The members of each DEC have a demonstrated interest in assisting, counseling, and supporting the growth and expansion of international trade and investment by other corporations operating within their region. Interested companies can contact DEC through the district office of the US&FCS.

## ■ EC Regional Organizations Located in the United States

Many states have offices in the EC in order to develop trade and investment. A number of EC members or local governments have established offices in the United States. These offices have been formed to promote trade with or through a region or governmental entity. The following organizations, listed by their home country, provide resources to the U.S.-based firm planning to enter or expand in the EC. The objective of each organization is to increase trade and investment between corporations in the United States and the state or region listed, unless noted.

| *EC Location* | *Organization, U.S. Location, and Objective* |
|---|---|
| Belgium | Consul General of Belgium, 6100 Wilshire Blvd., Suite 1200, Los Angeles, CA 90048, 213-857-1244 |
| Flanders | Flanders Investment Office, 70 Walnut St., Wellesley, MA 02181, 617-239-8225 |
| | Increase foreign investment in Flanders (primarily Dutch speaking Belgium), service industries, European business centers. |
| Denmark | Royal Danish Embassy, 3200 Whitehaven St., NW, Washington, DC 20008-3683, 202-234-4300 (see Chapter 2 for consulates) |
| | Danish Trade Office, 229 Peachtree St., NE, Suite 1008, Atlanta, GA 30303, 404-588-1588 |
| | Danish Trade Office, 19120 Detroit Rd., Cleveland, OH 44116, 216-331-0550 |
| | Danish Trade Office, 1777 South Harrison St., Suite 500, Denver, CO 80210, 303-692-9090 |
| | Danish Trade Office, 15710 JFK Blvd., Suite 260, Houston, TX 77032, 713-442-9004 |
| | Danish Trade Office, 1402 Third Ave., Suite 220, Seattle, WA 98101, 206-624-9638 |
| France | Invest in Europe (DTAR), 1801 Avenue of the Stars, Suite 410, Los Angeles, CA 90067 |
| | Invest in France Agency, 610 Fifth Ave., Suite 301, New York, NY 10020, 212-757-9340 |
| | Midi-Pyrenees Industrial Development Agency, DML & Associates, 420 Lexington Ave., Rm. 406, New York, NY 10170, 212-867-7328 |
| | To attract high-technology manufacturing operations into the Toulouse region of France. |
| Germany | Berlin Economic Development Corporation, 185 Devonshire St., Boston, MA 02110, 617-556-8890 |
| | German Information Center, 950 Third Ave., New York, NY 10022, 212-888-9840 |

| *EC Location* | *Organization, U.S. Location, and Objective* |
|---|---|
| | The Ports of Bremem/Bremerhaven, Carl F. Ewig, Inc., Ewighaus, 910 Oak Tree Rd., South Plainfield, NJ 07080, 908-756-3944<br>also<br>Peter F. Blaich, 655 Redwood Highway, Suite 306, Mill Valley, CA 94941, 415-381-1106<br>To attract shipping traffic through the ports, for onward shipment throughout the EC, for storage, distribution, communication, truck and rail transport. The ports are served by over 15 scheduled ocean liner services (conference and non-conference). |
| Greece | Greek Trade Office, 150 E. 58th St., Suite 1701, New York, NY 10022 |
| Ireland | Industrial Development Authority, 50 W. San Fernando St., Suite 830, San Jose, CA 95113, 408-294-9903 |
| Italy | Italian Trade Commissioner, 1801 Avenue of the Stars, Suite 700, Los Angeles, CA 90067, 213-879-0950 |
| Luxembourg | Luxembourg Board of Economic Development, 801 Second Ave., New York, NY 10017, 212-391-3476 |
| Netherlands | Netherlands Foreign Investment Agency, One Rockerfeller Plaza, New York, NY 10020, 212-246-1434<br>601 California St., San Francisco, CA 94108, 415-981-1468<br>11755 Wilshire Blvd., Los Angeles, CA 90025, 213-477-8288<br>To attract foreign investment into and trade through the Netherlands. This agency promotes the work force, the distribution systems, and access to the EC, and the port facilities. |
| Portugal | Portuguese Trade Commission, 590 Fifth Ave., New York, NY 10036, 212-354-4610 |
| Spain | Spanish Commercial Office, 350 S. Figueroa St., Suite 946, Los Angeles, CA 90071, 213-628-1406 |
| United Kingdom | British Trade and Investment Office, 845 Third Ave., 11th Fl., New York, NY 10022, 212-745-0495 |

| *EC Location* | *Organization, U.S. Location, and Objective* |
| --- | --- |
| | Devon & Cornwall Development, 300 Unicorn Park Dr., Woburn, MA 01801, 617-932-9697<br>To attract industrial development, manufacturing, communications services, R&D. This organization places particular emphasis on the healthcare and electronics industries. |
| | Kent Enterprise Office, 320 Walnut St., Suite 204, Philadelphia, PA 19106, 800-486-0040<br>To attract investment in manufacturing industries such as publishing, food processing, transportation parts and components, pharmaceutical and personal care products. Emphasis is on access to the EC and the UK market. Traditionally known as the "garden of England" and home to the UK terminus of the channel tunnel. |
| | Merseyside Development Corporation, 7700 Leesburg Pike, Suite 307, Falls Church, VA 22043, 800-872-1632<br>To attract leisure, commercial and industrial development by providing low cost labor, first class training, and access to the major markets in the UK. |
| Wales | Wales Development International, 104 Carnegie Center, Suite 216, Princeton, NJ 08540, 609-452-2323<br>3390 Peachtree Rd., NE, Suite 1000 Atlanta, GA 30326, 404-364-6588<br>4590 MacArthur Blvd., Suite 550, Newport Beach, CA 92660, 714-252-8298<br>8410 West Brynmawr Ave., 4th Fl., Chicago, IL 60631, 312-380-1515<br>To attract diversified manufacturing investment into this region, by providing investment assistance in many forms. Wales has been successful in attracting a significant percentage of the new investment going into the EC market. Particular emphasis is placed on communications and information technology. |

# 3

# PUBLICATIONS

The European Single Market has been written about from all perspectives, at all levels, and all disciplines. What information sources work? How can corporate management—executive, finance, credit, risk management, marketing and sales, transportation and logistics, manufacturing, and administration—acquire background and analysis on its important issues. Many of the publications that corporate managers will find useful and informative in their investigation of the EC and in their management of activities with that marketplace are discussed next.

Publications are sorted by *public sector* publishers or publications, and *private sector* publications. Within the public sector, the two principal publishers are the U.S. government, and the Commission of the European Communities.

## PUBLIC SECTOR PUBLICATIONS

### ■ U.S. Government Publications

*AgExporter*

U.S. Department of Agriculture Foreign Agricultural Service, Washington, DC 20250, 202-720-8732

This is a monthly magazine.

*AID Procurement Information Bulletin*

USAID Office of Small and Disadvantaged Business Utilization/ Minority Resource Center, Washington, DC 20523-1414, 703-875-1551

This bulletin advertises notices of intended procurement of AID financed commodities.

*Business America*

Superintendent of Documents, U.S. Government Printing Office, Washington, DC 20402

This bi-weekly publication of the U.S. Department of Commerce is focused to help U.S. companies export. Articles deal with markets, U.S. trade initiatives, industry sector analyses, country summaries, and more. Features include a review of the current trade position of the United States, export success stories, a calendar of meetings and events, a summary of upcoming trade exhibitions.

*Europe NOW*

Single Internal Market Information Service, U.S. Department of Commerce, Rm. 3036, 14th Street and Constitution Ave., NW, Washington, D.C. 20230

Issued six times per year, this is a newsletter of the Office of European Community Affairs within the International Economic Policy division of the International Trade Administration. The newsletter is focused on the European Community. Articles identify prospective market opportunities, legal requirements, business conditions, EC and U.S. legislative and regulatory updates, the status of agreements within the EC, and information on seminars and conferences relating to the EC.

*Annual Trade Estimate Report on Foreign Trade Barriers*

Superintendent of Documents, Washington, DC 20402-9328

This annual report documents foreign trade barriers to U.S. exports, by country and by type of barrier. Trade barriers included in this report can be government laws, regulations, policies, or practices that either protect domestic products from foreign competition or artificially stimulate exports of particular products.

*The Effects of Greater Economic Integration within the European Community on the United States*

United States International Trade Commission, Washington, DC 20436

This series of reports, nos. 2204, 2268, 2318, 2368, 2501 (4/92) is a comprehensive overview, by the staff of the U.S. International Trade Commission, of the major features of the EC program that impact U.S. trade. These include: Standards, Testing, and Certification; Public Procurement and Internal Energy Markets; the Financial Sector; Customs Controls; Transportation; Competition Policy and Company Law; Taxation; National Quantitative Restrictions; and Intellectual Property.

*EC 1992: A Commerce Department Analysis of European Community Directives*

U.S. Department of Commerce

International Trade Administration.

This series updates the status of EC directives, and provides analysis on their implications for U.S. firms.

*European Single Market: Issues of Concern to U.S. Exporters*
U.S. General Accounting Office, P.O. Box 6015,
Gaithersburg, MD 20877, 202-275-6241
This is one of a series of reports submitted to the Chairman, Subcommittee on International Trade, Committee on Finance, U.S. Senate. The other reports are: *U.S. Government Efforts to Assist Small and Medium Sized Exporters; U.S. Financial Services' Competitiveness Under the Single Market Program;* and *European Initiatives: Implications for U.S. Defense Trade and Cooperation.*

The Single Internal Market Information Service (SIMIS) of the Office of Europe within the International Trade Administration (U.S. Department of Commerce) actively produces information on the European Community and the Single Market (p. 6).

### *EC Government Publications*

*Eurocom*
Director of Press and Public Affairs, Commission of the European Communities, 3 Dag Hammarskjold Plaza, 305 East 47th St., New York, NY 10017
This is a monthly bulletin of European Community economic and financial news.

*Euromemo*
European Community Information Service, 2100 M St., NW, Washington, DC 20037
This is a monthly one-page memo announcing publications, press releases, brochures, and other information.

*Europe*
Delegation of the Commission of the European Communities, 2100 M St. NW, Ste. 700, Washington, DC 20037
This "magazine of the European Community" is published 10 times per year. It is a general newsmagazine about the EC: business, fashion, lifestyles, and other topics of general interest to business.

*Official Publications of the European Communities*
Unipub, 4611-F Assembly Dr., Lanham, MD 20706-4391
Unipub is a central resource for official publications of a number of government organizations, including: The European Community, the British Government Publisher, UNESCO, the United Nations, the General Agreement on Tariffs and Trade, the World Bank, the International Monetary Fund, the Organization for Economic Cooperation and Development, the Food and Agricultural Organization of the UN, and the International Labor Organization. This comprehensive directory of publications include the following:

*Common Standards for Enterprises.* Explains the European Standards Systems

*Panorama of EC Industry.* Details on over 180 industry sectors within the EC

*Subscriptions: Business and Industry*

*Industrial Trends: Monthly Statistics* provides information on industrial activity within the EC.

*Iron and Steel: Monthly Statistics* provides short term economic statistics on this industry.

*Results of the Business Survey Carried out Among Managements in the Community: Monthly* gives results from business surveys carried out in the EC.

*Finance*

*International Capital Markets: Developments and Prospects.* An annual survey.

*The ECU Report.* looks at the benefits and costs of a single currency.

*The Single Financial Market: Second Edition.* Reports on the creation and integration of the financial markets, and the liberalization of capital movements.

*Subscriptions: Finance*

*Money and Finances: Quarterly* provides structural indicators, and quarterly and monthly time series data.

*ECU-EMS Information: Monthly* indicates private and official use of the ECU, the evolution of the ECU exchange rate, price indices, and tables of interests and issues of securities denominated in the ECU capital markets.

*Economics*

*OECD Economic Surveys.* Each book provides a detailed economic analysis of each country, and include short-term forecasts and analysis of medium-term problems.

*One Market, One Money.* Examines the overall financial and economic impacts of the monetary union of Europe.

*Subscriptions: Economics*

*European Community Quarterly.* Contains annual economic reports, communications on significant economic developments, and borrowing and lending activities within the Community.

*Trade and Tariffs*

*Trade Policy Review Series.* Reviews individual GATT member countries. Each report contains a trade policy analysis prepared by the GATT secretariat.

*TARIC: Integrated Tariff of the European Communities. Volumes 1–4.* Shows the various rules applying to specific products when imported into or exported from the EC.

*Customs Tariff and Trade Schedule: Official Journal.* This Journal documents the rules and provisions of EC tariffs, and the schedule of customs duties by product categories.

*Analytical Tables of External Trade—Exports and Imports.* Statistical compilations on the performance of EC export and import trade by member state.

*Exchange Arrangements and Exchange Restrictions: Annual Report.* Published by the IMF, this report provides a detailed description of exchange controls and restrictions of all IMF member countries.

*Subscriptions: Trade and Tariffs*

*External Trade: Monthly Statistics.* Monthly trade statistics for the EC and each member state, by country and commodity.

*Communications*

*Audiovisual Production in the Single Market.* This report provides an analysis of the industry and its future.

*Telecommunications in Europe: Free Choice for the User in Europe's 1992 Market.* This report gives an in-depth review of the characteristics of the European market for telecommunications technology, programs, and applications.

*Law and Legislation*

*The Community Legal Order.* Covers the main features of the Community's legal system, descriptions of Community law, the EC treaties, national and international law.

*Rules Governing Medicinal Products in the European Community.* These six volumes present the rules for this product segment: rules for human use, for marketing organizations, guidelines on quality, safety and efficacy, good manufacturing practice, veterinary medicines.

*A New Community Standards Policy: Current Standards Policy.* Provides all current proposals and actions on EC standards policy.

*Subscriptions: Law and Legislation*

*Official Journal of the European Communities.* Published daily, this provides current information on: directives, ECU developments, budgets, agreements, council decisions, more.

*Public Contracts and Tenders Supplements to the Official Journal.* Lists all notices of public works contracts, public supply contracts, and invitations to tender. More than 150 contracts are published in each issue.

*Socioeconomics*

*A Social Portrait of Europe.* Provides comprehensive data on populations, households, education, employment, working conditions, standards of living, health, environment, and more.

*A Guide to Working in Europe Without Frontiers.* This is a guide for the professions including consultants, architects, transporters, insurance agents, lawyers, and others.

*Subscriptions: Energy*

*Energy in Europe.* Three issues per year present the short-term energy outlook for the EC, statistical data and analysis, policy developments, research programs, conferences, and publications.

*Subscriptions: Agribusiness*

*Agricultural Prices Quarterly, Rapid Reports: Agriculture and Agriculture Yearbook.* Trends in monthly EC producer prices/indices, agricultural inputs and productions. Contains nominal and deflated prices, recent developments, diagrams and indexed tables. Provides country comparative information.

*Transportation*

*Transport Information 1991.* This paper covers the basic assumptions regarding transport requirements for the EC and West/East transport. It details the international transport issues and infrastructure requirements for the EC countries.

*Subscriptions: Transportation*

*Europa Transport: Market Developments.* Quarterly reviews, and annual reports, on the EC goods transport market, transport nodes, general market appraisals.

*Reference*

*The Europa World Yearbook.* This is a comprehensive guide to each country of the world. Directories are included to facilitate contacts with various service and support sectors of each economy.

*Basic Statistics of the European Communities.* Provides general statistical data on the European Communities for the most recent year. Includes illustrations and tables.

*CD-ROM Products*

*SCAD+CD.* Contains over 100,000 abstracts on a wide range of Community information sources.

*Publications: Office for Official Publications of the European Communities*
L-2985, Luxembourg

This catalog is published quarterly, and comprises the monographs and collections published by the Institutions of the EC during the prior period, as well as current periodicals. Publications are listed in these headings: Institutional questions, customs union and commercial policy, agriculture, silviculture and fisheries, employment and labour, social questions, laws and procedures, transport, competition and undertakings, finance, economic questions-consumer, external relations, energy, regional policy, environment, scientific and technical research, information, education and culture, and statistics.

*Target 1992*
Commission of the European Communitie
Directorate-General Audiovisual, Information, Communication and Culture, and Directorate-General Enterprise Policy, Distributive Trades, Tourism and Cooperatives, Rue de la Loi 200—B-1049, Brussels, Belgium

This monthly newsletter on the single internal market reports on happenings within the EC. It has sections titled: Decisions, Initiatives, Seen from Abroad, and SMEs (Small and Medium-sized Enterprises). Each issue also contains statistical information on one or more aspects of EC trade or business activity.

*United Nations Publication Catalog*
United Nations, 2 United Nations Plaza, Rm. DC2, Dept. 421, New York, NY 10017, 800-253-9646

This is the annual catalog of publications of the United Nations. It includes all titles currently available from the United Nations. Publications are cataloged by Reference, Political science, Social science, Law, Environment, Economics, Educational aids, Periodicals, and Mimeographed documents.

## PRIVATE SECTOR PUBLICATIONS

*ABC Europ Production-Europex*
ABC Publishing Group, P.O. Box 4034, D-6100, Darmstadt, Germany

Western Hemisphere Publishing Corporation, P.O. Box 710, Newcastle, CA 95658, 916-823-3532

This two-volume reference directory is a guide to manufacturers in 32 countries in Europe. By alphabet and product classification, it contains names, addresses, and telecommunications data.

*American Export Register*
Thomas Publishing Company, International Division, Five Penn Plaza, New York, NY 10001, 212-629-1177

This publication lists over 43,000 U.S. companies under 4200 categories with over 200,000 separate listings. Company information is alphabetical and by product or service. Listing in the register is free.

*Business Credit*
National Association of Credit Management, 8815 Centre Park Dr., Ste. 200, Columbia, MD 21045-2117

Published 10 times per year, this magazine is targeted to member credit executives. The NACM has 60 affiliated associations across the United States, and an international subsidiary association Finance, Credit and International Business (FCIB). There are over 750 FCIB member firms in the U.S. and abroad. Members of NACM, or FCIB, are credit and financial executives primarily representing manufacturers, wholesalers, financial institutions, and service organizations. There are over 38,000 members.

*Corporate Finance*
Euromoney Publications plc, 145 Hudson St., 7th Fl., New York, NY, 10013
This monthly magazine deals with international corporate finance.

*Corporate Handbook to the European Community*
United States Council for International Business, 1212 Avenue of the Americas, New York, NY 10036, 212-575-0327
This handbook, written in May 1990, provides a background on the EC, the structure of its institutions, legal instruments, how law is created, and other information.

*Directory of U.S Importers* and *Directory of U.S. Exporters*
The Journal of Commerce, 445 Marshall St., Phillipsburg, New Jersey 08865, 800-222-3056
These annual business directories contain business profiles on over 35,000 U.S. companies actively engaged in import (16,000) or export (19,000), with products listed by HTS or Schedule B number.

*EC-US Business Report*
C&M International Ltd., 1001 Pennsylvania Ave., NW, Washington, DC 20004-2505
This monthly report, more substantial than a newsletter, contains a commentary on a timely legal issue, a special in-depth report, a report on legislation pending before the EC and the U.S. legislatures, and reports of topical interest within each of the EC and the U.S. These cover such subjects as dumping, competition, communications, employment, energy, foreign investment, government contracts, and trade issues.

*Euromoney*
Euromoney Inc., 145 Hudson St., 7th Fl., New York, NY. 10013
This is a monthly magazine that deals with international banking and finance. Articles and editorials may be of interest to corporate finance officers.

*European Community Country Profiles*
International Division Publications, U.S. Chamber of Commerce, 1615 H Street NW, Washington, DC 20062
Each profile contains background data on the political, economic, trade and investment environment of each country and a list of country specific contacts. The data is updated on a regular basis.

*European Focus*
KPMG European Business Centre, 54 Avenue Louise, 1050 Brussels, Belgium

This is a bi-monthly review of European political, legislative and economic developments. Sections deal with company law, financial services, world trade, industry, the Single Market, funding, and other rotating subjects.

*EuroSphere*
KPMG Peat Marwick, 767 Fifth Ave., New York, NY 10153
This bi-monthly newsletter provides summary information on business within the EC, including a Country Profile, an issue update, and industry reports.

*Exporter's Encyclopedia*
Dun's Marketing Services, 3 Sylvan Way, Parsippany, NJ 07054-3896, 800-526-0651
This is an annual handbook covering more than 220 world markets. Information includes the basics of export transactions, and specific export sales information to each market covered.

*Export Reference Manual*
Bureau of National Affairs, Inc., 1231 25th St. NW, Washington, DC 20037, 301-258-1033
This three-volume loose leaf reference manual is updated weekly. Similar in concept to the *Exporter's Encyclopedia,* the *Export Reference Manual* provides comprehensive information on business conditions, export and trade practices in each market covered.

*Export Today*
Trade Communications, Inc., 733 15th St., NW, Ste. 1100, Washington, DC 20005
This magazine is published 9 times per year. Editorial and articles deal with export practices, trade finance, export business services, country information.

*Financial Times*
F.T. Publications Inc., 14 East 60th St., New York, NY 10022, 800-628-8088
This international business news daily publishes a North American edition in two sections. Section I provides news on international events, Europe, the Americas and World Trade, the UK, Business and Law, Technology, and the Arts. Section II covers International Companies and Finance, International Capital Markets, UK Companies, Commodities and Agriculture, and the Stock Markets.

*Financial World*
Financial World Partners, 1328 Broadway, New York, NY 10001, 212-594-5030
This is a bi-weekly financial news magazine that deals with international business issues.

*Foreign Trade*
Defense & Diplomacy, Inc., 6849 Old Dominion Dr., Ste. 200, McLean, VA 22101
This bi-monthly magazine contains practical trade related articles and commentary from international trade professionals. Editorial and articles deal with financing, shipping, transportation, country profiles, and current trade legislation.

*Global Trade*
North American Publishing Co., 401 N. Broad St., Philadelphia, PA 19108
This is a monthly magazine targeted to high volume shippers and exporters. Articles and editorials deal with transportation, shipping, the logistics of trade, international finance, customs practices, and the freight forwarding industry.

*Guide to Distributorship Agreements*
Publication 441, ICC Publishing Corporation, 156 Fifth Ave., New York, NY 10010, 212-206-1150

*Incoterms 1990*
Publication 460, ICC Publishing Corporation, 156 Fifth Ave., New York, NY 10010, 212-206-1150
Incoterms are the internationally accepted terms of sale/terms of trade used in international trade. These 13 terms of sale range from ExWorks to Delivered Duty Paid, and include the shipping terms common to international trade: FOB, CIF, and CFR (cost and freight). The Incoterms establish the responsibilities of each party regarding the handling of shipments.

*International Banking, A Legal Guide*
International Financial Law Review, Euromoney Publications plc., Nestor House, Playhouse Yard, London, EC4V 5EX
This 1991 publication summarizes banking laws and regulations in 37 different countries or regions worldwide. There are sections on each EC country, and a section on the EC as an entity.

*International Economic Insights*
Institute for International Economics, 11 DuPont Circle, NW, Washington, DC 20036-1207, 202-328-9000
A by-monthly publication with regular features on finance, Europe, and international data. Articles cover international economic issues from a variety of perspectives. The Institute for International Economics is the only major research center in the United States devoted wholly to international economic concerns.

*International Trade Finance Report*
The Morgan Williams Group, Inc., P.O. Box 22, Rutherford, NJ 07070, 201-030-2137
This is a monthly newsletter for international finance, credit, and risk management professionals.

*International Trade Reporter*
Bureau of National Affairs, Inc., 1231 25th St., NW, Washington, DC 20037, 202-452-4200
This is a set of international trade information reports: *Current Reports* is a weekly newsletter that provides notification of trade policy developments in the United States and abroad; *Import Reference Manual* is a guide to customs and import trade law; *Export Reference Manual* is noted above; *Decisions* provides digests and full texts of judicial and administrative decisions in major fields of import law.

*Newsletter, United States Council for International Business*
U.S. Council for International Business, 1212 Avenue of the Americas, New York, NY 10036, 212-354-4480
This is a newsletter for members of the U.S. Council for International Business.

*1992 Directory of EEC Information Sources, 4th ed.*
Euroconfidential, S.A. BP29, B-1330 Rixensart, Belgium

*1992: The European Community's Internal Market Program*
MAPI, 1200 Eighteenth St., NW, Washington, DC 20036
This study contains suggestions to help business adjust to and prepare for the opportunities available within the new internal market.

*1993 Guide to EC Grants and Loans*
Euroconfidential S.A. (see above)

*Profitable Exporting: A Complete Guide to Marketing Your Products Abroad, 2nd ed., 1993*
John Wiley & Sons, Inc., 605 Third Ave., New York 10158-0012
This book by John S. Gordon is a comprehensive introduction to the strategy and practices of exporting and managing a corporate export function. The book also reviews the impact and implications of the EC Single Market program.

*Schmitthoff's Export Trade, 9th ed.*
Stevens & Sons, c/o Sweet & Maxwell Ltd, South Quay Plaza, 183 Marsh Wall, London, England
The book by Clive M. Schmitthoff is written for lawyers and businesspeople from a British perspective. It has eight parts: International Sale of Goods, Marketing Organization, Financing Exports, Insurance of Exports, Transportation of Exports, International Commercial Dispute Settlement, Construction and long term contracts, and Customs law. The book is comprehensive.

*Sizing Up U.S. Export Disincentives*
Institute for International Economics, 11 DuPont Circle, NW, Washington, DC 20036-1207, 202-328-9000
This book by J. David Richardson seeks to identify the export disincentives inherent in U.S. export controls, foreign policy sanctions, environmental and other regulations, inadequate public spending on export financing, export promotion and economic infrastructure, and more.

*The Economist*
111 W. 57th St., New York, NY 10019
This is a British-based weekly business magazine that covers global business, political, and economic events. Frequent surveys are inserted, dealing with countries or business segments or other sectoral situations, e.g., International Banking, a Survey of Europe's Internal Market.

*The Europe of 1992: An American Business Perspective*
National Association of Manufacturers, 1331 Pennsylvania Ave., NW, Ste. 1500, North Tower, Washington, DC 20004-1703
This is the fourth report of the National Association of Manufacturers on the EC's plan to create a single internal market. It examines EC-92 from the perspective of its implications for manufacturers: technical standards, procurement policies, and monetary union.

*The Exporter*
Trade Data Reports, Inc., 34 West 37th St., New York, NY 10018
This is a monthly magazine targeted to the growing or frequent exporter. The articles and editorial content deal with marketing, distribution, trade finance, export regulations, and timely strategic issues.

*The Export Yellow Pages*
District Office, U.S. Department of Commerce
Published by a public/private partnership including the Office of Export Trading Company Affairs, U.S. Department of Commerce International Trade Administration. This directory lists U.S. manufacturers, by product type, export trading and management companies, export service providers, and technical assistance firms.

*The International Directory of Importers-Europe*
Interdata, 1480 Grove St., Healdsburg, CA 95448, 707-433-3900
A two-volume directory of over 32,000 importers in 19 European nations. Information is presented alphabetically under commodity headings.

*The Journal of European Business*
Faulkner & Gray, Inc., Eleven Penn Plaza, New York, NY 10001, 212-967-7000
This periodical is published 6 times a year. It is targeted to managing executives of larger corporations.

*Trade & Culture*

Trade & Culture Inc., 7127 Hartford Rd., Baltimore, MD 21234, 410-426-2906

This bi-monthly magazine attempts to blend cultural insights with business fundamentals. It covers its self-defined 22 world trade zones in feature columns.

*Trade Finance*

Euromoney Publications plc, Oakfield House, Perrymount Rd., Haywards Heath, Sussex RH16 3DH, Great Britain

This monthly magazine deals with large scale international trade finance. Editorials and articles address: export credits, country information, deals and transactions, countertrade and offset, forfaiting, creditwatch situations, and market information.

*Washington International Business Report*

International Business-Government Counselors, Inc., 818 Connecticut Ave. NW, 12th Fl., Washington, DC 20006, 202-872-8181

This monthly newsletter is an analytical review and outlook on major government developments affecting international trade and investment.

*World Trade*

Taipan Press, Inc., 500 Newport Center Dr., Ste. 450, Newport Beach, CA 92660

This monthly magazine is comparable in format to the better known general business magazines such as *BusinessWeek* and *Forbes*. Editorials are focused and demanding, articles deal with marketing, finance, export and investment strategies, franchising, and transportation. Standing departments address trade statistics, travel tips, trade fairs, and so on.

# 4

# EC DEPOSITORY AND OTHER LIBRARY RESOURCES

There are three main library resources for information on the European Community, in addition to the resources identified earlier. These library resources are the EC Depository libraries, the U.S. Government Depository libraries, and those libraries across the United States that subscribe to the National Trade Data Bank. An additional resource is the U.S. Government Bookstore chain.

EC Depository libraries hold EC official documents and publications, U.S. Government Depository libraries hold official U.S. government documents and publications. The National Trade Data Bank (NTDB) is a CD-ROM database containing over 120,000 U.S. government documents and publications dealing with international trade data and information.

## EUROPEAN COMMUNITY DEPOSITORY LIBRARIES

The EC has established a network of libraries in the United States to allow access to all official EC publications. Each of these depository institutions automatically receives one copy of each EC institution's periodical and nonperiodical publications. Of particular note is the *Official Journal of the European Communities,* the equivalent of our Federal Register. The C section includes proposed legislation and important notices; the L section contains the final texts of legislation. Depositories also receive the legislative proposals and communications of the Commission in their original, COM document form.

The following is a list of publications, databases, legislative documents, research tools, national directives and implementing measures, and other types of information available in each EC Depository library. Depository libraries are listed after this list.

## Publications and Databases

- Procedures for Making Laws
  - The Commission
  - The Council of Ministers
  - The European Parliament
  - The Economic and Social Committee
  - The Court of Justice
- Legislative Documents and Research Tools
  - Official Journal
  - Directory of Community Legislation in Force
  - The Commission
  - The European Parliament
  - The Economic and Social Committee
  - The Council of Ministers
  - Documents Catalog
  - Compilations
- Annual Reports and Informational Documents
  - General Report on the Activities of the Community
  - Bulletin of the European Communities
  - Report on Competition Policy
  - The Agricultural Situation in the Community
  - Report on Social Development
  - Social Europe Review and Supplements
  - Energy in Europe
  - Innovation and Technology Transfer
  - XIII Magazine and XIII News Review
  - Court of Auditors Annual Report
  - European Economy and Supplements
  - Annual Report and Bulletin of the Economic and Social Committee
  - Review of the Council's Work
  - European Perspectives Series
  - European Political Cooperation Documentation Bulletin
- Biographic and Other Guides
  - SCAD Bulletin
  - Publications of the European Communities
  - Eurostat Catalogue: Publications and Electronic Services
  - Dictionary of Acronyms for EC Action Plans and Programmes
- Statistical and Economic Publications
  - General Statistics
  - Economy and Finance
  - Population and Social Conditions
  - Energy and Industry
  - Agriculture, Forestry, and Fisheries
  - Foreign Trade

Commission-Draft Proposals—Internal Working Documents
Commission-Information Memos
Commission-Proposal for Council Directive—COM Document
Commission-Proposal—Official Journal
Opinions-Economic and Social Committee
Opinions-Official Journal—Economic and Social Committee
European Parliament Committee Reports
European Parliament—First Reading-Minutes-Official Journal
European Parliament—Verbatim Text-Official Journal
Commission-Proposals and Amended Proposals
Council of Ministers—Press Release
Council of Ministers—Common Position
European Parliament—Second Reading: Documents, Readings, Official Journal, Debates
Commission-Amended Proposal—COM Document and Re-Examined Proposal
Council of Ministers—Press Release
Final Text—Official Journal

## ■ Print Research Tools

*Directory of Community Legislation in Force*
*Index to the Official Journal*
*General Report on the Activities of the EC*
*Bulletin of the EC and Supplement*
*Review of the Council's Work*
*Annual Report and Bulletin, the Economic and Social Committee*
*Fact Sheets on the European Parliament*
*Recent Publications of the European Communities*
*Publications of the Court of Justice.*

## ■ EC Depository Libraries in the United States (Not All States Have EC Depository Libraries.)

| | |
|---|---|
| Arizona | The University of Arizona, University Library, International Documents, Tucson 85721 |
| Arkansas | University of Arkansas, USAR Library, Documents Dept., 33rd and University, Little Rock 72204 |

| | |
|---|---|
| California | Stanford University, The Hoover Institute, Central Western Europe Collection, Stanford 94305 |
| | University of California-Berkeley, Documents Dept., General Library, Berkeley 94720 |
| | University of California-Los Angeles, Von Kleinschmidt Library, International Documents, Los Angeles 90089 |
| | University of California-Los Angeles, Public Affairs Service, University Research Library, International Documents, Los Angeles 90024 |
| | University of California-San Diego, Central Library, Documents Dept., La Jolla 92093 |
| Colorado | University of Colorado-Boulder, Library, Government Publications, P. O. Box 184, Boulder 80309 |
| Connecticut | Yale University, Government Documents Center, Seeley G. Mudd Library, 38 Mansfield, New Haven 06520 |
| District of Columbia | The American University, Center for Research & Documentation on the EC, 305 Bender Library, Massachusetts & Nebraska Ave., NW, Washington 20016 |
| | The Library of Congress, Exchange and Gift Division, IGO-EUCOM, 10 First St., SE, Washington |
| Florida | University of Florida, Libraries, Documents Dept., Libraries West, Gainsville 32611 |
| Georgia | Emory University, School of Law, Law Libraries, Atlanta 30322 |
| Hawaii | University of Hawaii, Library-Government Documents, 2550 The Mall, Honolulu 96822 |
| Illinois | Northwestern University, Government Publications Dept., The University Library, Evanston 60201 |
| | University of Chicago, Joseph Regenstein Library, Documents Dept., 1100 East 57th St., Chicago 60637 |
| | Library of International Relations, Illinois Institute of Technology, 77 S. Wacker Dr., Chicago 60606 |
| | University of Illinois, Law Library, 504 East Pennsylvania Ave., Champaign 61820 |
| Indiana | Indiana University, Library, Documents Dept., Bloomington 47405 |
| | University of Notre Dame, Memorial Library, Document Center, Notre Dame 46556 |

| | |
|---|---|
| Iowa | University of Iowa Libraries, Government Publications Dept., Iowa City 52242 |
| Louisiana | University of New Orleans, Earl K. Young Library, New Orleans 70143 |
| Kansas | The University of Kansas, Government Documents Collection, Spencer Research Library, Lawrence |
| Kentucky | University of Kentucky, Government Publications Dept., Margaret I. King Library, Lexington 40506 |
| Maine | University of Maine, Law Library, 24 Deering Ave., Portland 04102 |
| Massachusetts | Harvard University, Law School Library, Collection Development, Langdell Hall-Law 431, Cambridge 02138 |
| Michigan | University of Michigan, The Law Library, Serials Dept., Ann Arbor 43109-1210 |
| | Michigan State University, Library, Documents Dept., East Lansing 48824-1048 |
| Minnesota | University of Minnesota, Government Publications, 409 Wilson Library, Minneapolis 55455 |
| Missouri | Washington University, John M. Olin Library, Lindell and Skinner Blvds., St. Louis 63130 |
| Nebraska | University of Nebraska at Lincoln, University Libraries, Acquisitions Dept., Lincoln 68588-0410 |
| New Jersey | Princeton University, Documents Division, Library, Princeton 08544 |
| New Mexico | The University of New Mexico, Zimmerman Library, Social Science Collection, Albuquerque 87131 |
| New York | Council on Foreign Relations, Inc., 58 East 68th St., New York 10021 |
| | New York Public Library, Grand Central Station, Research Library, ECN & Pub Aff., New York 10017 |
| | New York University, School of Law Library, 40 Washington Square South, New York 10012 |
| | State University of New York, University Library, Government Publications, 1400 Washington Ave., Albany 12222 |
| | State University of New York Library, Government Documents Dept., Lockwood Library Bldg., Buffalo 14260 |
| North Carolina | Duke University Library, Public Documents Dept., Durham 27706 |

| | |
|---|---|
| Ohio | Ohio State University Library, Documents Division, 1858 Neil Ave. Mall, Columbus 43210 |
| Oklahoma | University of Oklahoma, Government Documents Collection, Bizzell Memorial Library-Rm. 440, 401 West Brooks, Norman 73019 |
| Oregon | The University of Oregon, Library, Documents Section, Eugene 97403 |
| Pennsylvania | Pennsylvania State University, The University Library, Documents Section, University Park 16802 |
| | University of Pennsylvania, Van Pelt Library, Serials Dept., Philadelphia 19104 |
| | University of Pittsburgh, Hillman Library, G-72, Gift and Exchange, Pittsburgh 15260 |
| South Carolina | University of South Carolina, Thomas Cooper Library, Documents/Microfilm Dept., Columbia 29208 |
| Texas | University of Texas, School of Law Library, Foreign Law Librarian, 727 East 26th St., Austin 78705 |
| Utah | University of Utah, Marriott Library, International Documents Section, Documents Division, Salt Lake City 84112 |
| Virginia | The University of Virginia, The Alderman Library, Government Documents, Charlottesville 22903 |
| Washington | University of Washington, Libraries, Government Publications Division, FM-25, Seattle 98195 |
| Wisconsin | University of Wisconsin, The Memorial Library, Documents Dept., 728 State St., Madison 53706 |

## U.S. LIBRARIES WITH THE NATIONAL TRADE DATA BANK

The National Trade Data Bank, a CD-ROM database, contains over 120,000 documents of export-related information and has a Foreign Traders Index of over 40,000 contacts. This information is available at each library listed here. Interested corporations and individuals can subscribe to the National Trade Data Bank for a nominal fee. The information is updated monthly for subscribers.

| | |
|---|---|
| Alabama | Auburn University, Draughon Library, Microforms & Documents Dept., Mell St., Auburn 36849-5606, 205-844-1703 |

| | |
|---|---|
| | Birmingham Public Library, Government Documents Dept., 2100 Park Place, Birmingham 35203, 205-226-3680 |
| | Samford University, Harwell G. Davis Library, Government Documents Dept., 800 Lakeshore Dr., Birmingham 35229, 205-870-2847 |
| | University of Alabama in Huntsville Library, Government Documents, P.O. Box 2600, Huntsville 35816, 205-895-6526 |
| | Jacksonville State University, Houston Cole Library, Pelham Rd., Jacksonville 36265, 205-782-5238 |
| | Air University Library/SAS, Maxwell Air Force Base, Rm. 122, Bldg. 1405, Maxwell Air Base 36112-55, 205-953-2888 |
| | University of South Alabama Library, Government Documents Dept., Mobile 36688, 205-460-7024 |
| | Spring Hill College, Thomas Byrne Memorial Library, Documents Dept., 4000 Dauphin St., Mobile 36608, 205-460-2381 |
| | Alabama Public Library Service, 6030 Monticello Dr., Montgomery 36130, 205-277-7330 |
| | Auburn University at Montgomery Library, Documents Dept., CD 1-3, 7300 University Dr., Montgomery 36117-3596, 205-244-3650 |
| | University of Alabama, Amelia Gayle Gorgas Library, Government Documents Dept., Box 870266 Selectives in CD 4-7, Tuscaloosa 35487-0266, 205-348-6046 |
| | University of Alabama, School of Law Library, 101 Paul Bryant Dr., Tuscaloosa 35487, 205-348-1107 |
| Alaska | Anchorage Municipal Libraries, Z.J. Loussac Public Library, Acquisitions, 3600 Denali St., Anchorage 99503-6093, 907-261-2970 |
| | University of Alaska at Anchorage Library, 3211 Providence Dr., Anchorage 99508, 907-786-1874 |
| | University of Alaska, Elmer E. Rasmuson Library, Documents Collection, 310 Tanana Dr., UAF, Fairbanks 99775-1007, 907-474-7624 |
| | Alaska State Library, Government Publication Service, P.O. Box 11057, Juneau 99811-0571, 907-465-2927 |

| | |
|---|---|
| | University of Alaska Southeast, William A. Egan Library, Serial Dept., 11120 Glacier Highway, Juneau 99801, 907-789-4568 |
| Arizona | Northern Arizona University, Cline Library, Government Documents, Box 6022, Flagstaff 86011-6022, 602-523-6808 |
| | Glendale Public Library, 5959 West Brown St., Glendale 85302, 602-435-4901 |
| | Mesa Public Library, Documents, 64 East First St., Mesa 85201, 602-644-3086 |
| | Phoenix Public Library, 12 East McDowell Rd., Phoenix 85004, 602-534-0596 |
| | Grand Canyon University, Fleming Library, P.O. Box 11097, 3300 West Camelback Rd. 85017, Phoenix 85061, 602-249-3300(329) |
| | Department of Library Archives, and Public, Records—Federal Documents, Third Fl., State Capitol—Research Div., 1700 West Washington, Phoenix 85007, 602-542-4417 |
| | Yavapai College Library, 1100 East Sheldon St., Prescott 86301, 602-776-2274 |
| | Arizona State University, College of Law Library, Government Documents Dept., Tempe 85287-7806, 602-965-4860 |
| | Arizona State University, Hayden Library, Government Documents Service, Tempe 85287-1006, 602-965-3387 |
| | University of Arizona, Main Library, Government Documents Dept., Main Library, Tucson 85721, 602-621-6433 |
| Arkansas | Ouachita Baptist University, Riley-Hickingbotham Library, OBU Box 3742, 410 Ouachita St., Arkadelphia 71923, 501-246-4531(122) |
| | Hendrix College, Olin C. Bailey Library, 1601 Harkrider St., Conway 72032, 501-450-1288 |
| | University of Arkansas, Mullins Library, Government Documents Dept., Fayetteville 72701, 501-575-4524 |
| | Arkansas State Library, Documents Service Section, One Capitol Mall, Little Rock 72201, 501-682-2326 |

Central Arkansas Library System, Main Library, (Little Rock Public Library), 700 Louisiana St., Little Rock 72201, 501-370-5952

University of Arkansas at Little Rock, Ottenheimer Library, Documents Dept., 2801 South University Ave., Little Rock 72204, 501-569-8811

University of Arkansas at Little Rock, Pulaski County Law Library, 400 West Markham Ave., Little Rock 72201, 501-324-9444(243)

Harding University, Brackett Library, Government Documents Dept., Station A, 900 East Center Ave.—Box 928, Searcy 72143-5591, 501-279-4251

Arkansas State University, Dean B. Ellis Library, Government Documents, P.O. Box 2040, State University 72467, 501-972-3077(6)

California

Anaheim Public Library, 500 West Broadway, Anaheim 92805, 714-999-1880

Humboldt State University, Library—HSU, Documents Dept., Arcata 95521, 707-826-3419

California State University, Bakersfield Library, Government Publications Section, 9001 Stockdale Highway, Bakersfield 93311-1099, 805-664-3256

University of California, General Library, Government Documents Dept., Berkeley 94720, 415-643-9346

Carson Regional Library, County of Los Angeles, Government Publications Unit, 151 East Carson St., Carson 90745, 310-830-0901

California State University, Dominguez Hills Univ. Library, Educational Resources Center, 800 East Victoria St., Carson 90747, 213-516-3758

California State University, Chico Library, Government Publications, Chico 95929, 916-898-6802

Claremont Colleges, Honnold/Mouth Library, Government Publications Dept., 800 Dartmouth St., Claremont 91711, 714-621-8000(3861)

Culver City Library, L.A. County Public Library, 4975 Overland Ave., Culver City 90230, 213-559-1676

University of California, Shields Library, Government Documents Dept., Davis 95616, 916-752-1624

Fresno County Free Library, 2420 Mariposa St., Fresno 93721, 209-488-2976

California State University at Fresno, Henry Madden Library, Government Documents Dept., 5200 N. Barton Ave., Fresno 93740-0034, 209-278-2335

California State University at Fullerton, University Library, P.O. Box 4150, Attn: Documents Section, Fullerton 92634, 714-449-7035

Garden Grove Regional Branch, Orange County Public Library, 11200 Stanford Ave., Garden Grove 92640, 714-530-0711

Gardena Library, Los Angeles County Public Library, 1731 West Gardena Blvd., Gardena 90247, 213-323-6363

California State University at Hayward, Library—Documents Unit, 25800 Carlos Bee Blvd., Hayward 94542-3052, 415-881-3815

Huntington Park Public Library, San Antonio Region, 6518 Miles Ave., Huntington Park 90255, 213-583-1461

University of California, Irvine, Main Library, Government Publications and Microforms Dept., P.O. Box 19557, Irvine 92713, 714-856-7290

University of California at San Diego, Central University Library, C-0175P, Government Documents, 9500 Gilman Dr., La Jolla 92093, 619-534-1249

Angelo M. Iacoboni Public Library, Government Publications Collection, 4990 Clark Ave., Lakewood 90731, 213-866-1777

Long Beach Public Library, 101 Pacific Ave., Long Beach 90822-1097, 213-590-6944

California State University, Long Beach Library, Government Documents, 1250 Bellflower Blvd., Long Beach 90840-1901, 213-985-7816

University of Southern California, Doheny Memorial Library, Government Documents Dept., University Park MC-0182, Los Angeles 90089-0182, 213-740-5192

Occidental College, Mary Norton Clapp Library, Documents Division, 1600 Campus Rd., Los Angeles 90041, 213-259-2810

Los Angeles Public Library, SERIALS DIVISION, 361 South Anderson St., Los Angeles 90033, 213-612-3335

California State University, Los Angeles, University Library, Government Publications Section, 5151 State University Dr., Los Angeles 90032, 213-343-3960

University of California, University Research Library, Public Affairs Service, 405 Hilgard Ave., Los Angeles 90024-1575, 213-825-3135

Loyola Law School, William M. Rains Library, 1440 West Ninth St., Los Angeles 90015-1295, 213-736-1191

Pepperdine University, Payson Library, 24255 Pacific Coast Highway, Malibu 90263, 213-456-4279

Montebello Regional Library, 1550 West Beverly Blvd., Montebello 90640, 213-722-6551

Norwalk Regional Library, Los Angeles County Public Library, 12350 Imperial Highway, Norwalk 90650, 213-868-0775

Oakland Public Library, Documents Dept., 125 Fourteenth St., Oakland 94612, 415-273-3138

Pasadena Public Library, 285 East Walnut St., Pasadena 91101, 818-405-4048

California Institute of Technology, Millikan Memorial Library 1-32, 1201 California Blvd., Pasadena 91125, 818-356-6419

Contra Costa County Library, Documents Section, 1750 Oak Park Blvd., Pleasant Hill 94523-4497, 415-646-6434

University of California—Riverside, Library Government Publication Dept., 900 University Ave., Riverside 92521, 714-787-3714

Sacramento Public Library, Central Library—Federal Docs., 828 I St., Sacramento 95814, 916-449-5660

California State Library, Government Publications Sect., 914 Capitol Mall, Sacramento 94237-0001, 916-653-0085

University of the Pacific, McGeorge School of Law Library, 3282 Fifth Ave., Sacramento 95817, 916-739-7010

California State University, Sacramento Library, Government Documents Dept., 2000 Jed Smith Dr., Sacramento 95819, 916-278-5672

National University Law Library, 8380 Miramar Rd., San Diego 92126-4431, 619-492-5185

San Diego Public Library, 820 E St., San Diego 92101, 619-236-5552

San Diego State University Library, Government Publications Div., San Diego 92182-0511, 619-594-6990

University of San Diego, Alcala Park, School of Law Library, Alcala Park, San Diego 92110, 619-260-6813

San Francisco Public Library, Business/Science/Documents Dept., Civic Center, San Francisco 94102, 415-557-4470

San Francisco State University, J. Paul Leonard Library, Government Documents Dept., 1630 Holloway Ave., San Francisco 94132, 415-338-1557

University of San Francisco, Richard A. Gleeson Library, Documents Section, San Francisco 94117-1080, 415-666-2040

San Jose State University, Clark Library, Government Publications Dept., One Washington Square, San Jose 95192-0028, 408-924-2814

California Polytechnic State University, Robert F. Kennedy Library, Documents and Maps Dept., San Luis Obispo 93407, 805-756-1364

Marin County Free Library, Rms. 409–410, Documents Dept., Civic Center Administration Bldg., San Rafael 94903, 415-499-7551

University of California—Santa Barbara Library, Government Publications Dept., Santa Barbara 93106, 805-893-4109

University of Santa Clara, Orradre Library, Documents Dept., Santa Clara 95053, 408-554-5436

University of California—Santa Cruz, McHenry Library, Government Publications, Santa Cruz 95064, 408-459-3318

Sonoma County Library, 3rd & E St., Santa Rosa 95404, 707-545-0831

Stanford University Libraries, Jonsson Library of Government Documents, Att: Green Library, Stanford 94305, 415-725-1030

Public Library of Stockton, and San Joaquin County, 605 North El Dorado St., Stockton 95202, 209-944-8230

Torrance Public Library, 3301 Torrance Blvd., Torrance 90503, 213-618-3421

Solano County Library System, John F. Kennedy Library, 505 Santa Clara St., Vallejo 94590, 707-553-5354

West Covina Regional Library, 1601 West Covina Parkway, West Covina 91790, 818-962-3541

Whittier College, Wardman Library, Government Documents, 13406 East Philadelphia, Whittier 90608, 213-907-4246

Colorado

Aurora Public Library, 14949 East Alameda Dr., Aurora 80012, 303-340-2251

University of Colorado at Boulder, Norlin Library, Government Publications, Campus Box 184, Boulder 80309-0184, 303-492-8834

University of Colorado, School of Law Library, Campus Box 402/ Fleming Law Bldg., Kittredge Loop South, Boulder 80309, 303-492-2704

Colorado College, Tutt Library, 1021 North Cascade Ave., Colorado Springs 80903-32, 719-389-6660

University of Colorado at Colorado Springs Library, 1420 Austin Bluffs Parkway, Colorado Springs 80933-71, 719-593-3175

Auraria Library, Government Documents, Lawrence at Eleven St., Denver 80204, 303-556-3532

Denver Public Library, Government Publications Dept., BS/GPD, 1357 Broadway, Denver 80203, 303-640-8874

University of Denver, Penrose Library, Government Documents Dept., P.O. Box 100600, Denver 80250, 303-871-3426

Colorado State University Libraries, Documents Depts., Fort Collins 80523, 303-491-1881

Colorado School of Mines, Arthur Lakes Library, U.S. Documents, Fourteenth and Illinois, Golden 80401, 303-273-3697

Mesa State College, Tomlinson Library, 1200 College Place, Grand Junction 81502, 303-248-1864

University of Northern Colorado, James A. Michener Library, Government Publications Service, Greeley 80639, 303-351-2987

Western State College, Leslie J. Savage Library, Gunnison 81231, 303-943-7012

Jefferson County Public Library, Lakewood Branch, 10200 West 20th Ave., Lakewood 80215, 303-232-7833

University of Southern Colorado Library, 2200 North Bonforte Blvd., Pueblo 81001, 303-549-2333

Connecticut

Bridgeport Public Library, Reference Dept., Government Documents, 925 Broad St., Bridgeport 06604, 203-576-7422

Western Connecticut State University, Ruth A. Haas Library, Government Documents Dept., 181 White St., Danbury 06810, 203-797-4118

Connecticut State Library, 231 Capitol Ave., Hartford 06106, 203-566-4889

Hartford Public Library, 500 Main St., Hartford 06103, 203-293-6058

Trinity College Library, 300 Summit St., Hartford 06106, 203-297-2270

Wesleyan University, Olin Library, Middletown 06457, 203-347-9411(2140)

Central Connecticut State University, Elihu Burritt Library, 1615 Stanley St., New Britain 06050, 203-827-7528

Yale University—Seeley G. Mudd Library, Government Documents Center, 38 Mansfield St., New Haven 05620, 203-432-3212

Southern Connecticut State University, Hilton C. Buley Library, Government Documents Collection, 501 Crescent St., New Haven 06515, 203-397-4370

Connecticut College, C.E. Shain Library, Reference Dept., 270 Mohegan Ave., New London 06320, 203-439-2655

| | |
|---|---|
| | Ferguson Library, One Public Library, Stamford 06904, 203-964-1000(225) |
| | University of Connecticut, Homer Babbidge Library U-5RP, Research and Information Service Dept., 369 Fairfield Rd., Storrs 06268, 203-486-0626 |
| | Silas Bronson Public Library, 267 Grand St., Waterbury 06702, 203-574-8225 |
| | Teikyo Post University, Traurig Library & Learning, Resources Center, 800 Country Club Rd., Waterbury 06723-2540, 203-596-4564 |
| | University of New Haven, Marvin K. Peterson Library, Documents Dept., 300 Orange Ave., West Haven 06516, 203-932-7189(7189) |
| Delaware | Delaware Technical and Community College, Southern Campus Library, Route 18, Georgetown 19947, 302-856-9033 |
| | University of Delaware Library, Government Documents/Maps, Newark 19717-5267, 302-831-2238 |
| District of Columbia | Library of Congress, Congressional Research Service, Library Services Division, 101 Independence Ave., Washington 20540, 202-707-7456 |
| | District of Columbia Public Library, Document Dept., 901 G St., NW, Washington 20001, 202-727-1117 |
| | Georgetown University Law Center, Edward Bennett Williams Library, 111 G St., NW, Washington 20002, 202-662-9155 |
| | Georgetown University Library, Government Documents Dept., 37th and O Sts., NW, Washington 20013, 202-687-1870 |
| | Department of State Library, IS/OIS/LR Rm. 2442-C, 2201 C St., NW, Washington 20520-2442, 202-647-2053 |
| | Department of the Treasury Library, Main Treasury Bldg., Rm. 5030, 1500 Pennsylvania Ave., NW, Washington 20220, 202-566-2777 |
| | George Washington University, Melvin Gelman Library, Government Documents Dept., 2130 H St., NW, Washington 20052, 202-994-6846 |

George Washington University, National Law Center, Jacob Burns Law Library, 716 20th St., NW, Washington 20052, 202-994-8545

U.S. General Accounting Office, Office of Library Service, Room 6430 also Rm. 7016, 441 G St., NW, Washington 20548, 202-275-4304

Department of the Army, Pentagon Library ANRAL, Pentagon, Rm. 1A518, Washington 20310, 202-697-3411

Library of Congress, Serial and Government Publications Division, Madison Bldg., Rm. 133, 1st & Independence Ave., SE, Washington 20540, 202-707-2958

Board of Governors of The Federal Reserve System—Research Library, 20th St. and Constitution Ave., NW, Washington 20551, 202-452-3334

U.S. Senate Library, The Capitol Bldg., Rm. S-332, Washington 20510, 202-224-2445

American University, Washington College Law Library, 4400 Massachusetts Ave., NW, Washington 20016, 202-885-2679

Florida

Florida Atlantic University, S.E. Wimberly Library, Documents Division, Boca Raton 33431, 407-367-3788

Manatee County Public Library, Information Service Dept., 1301 Barcarrota Blvd., West, Bradenton 34205, 813-748-5555

Seminole County Public Library System, Documents Depository, 215 North Oxford Rd., Casselberry 32707, 407-339-4000(146)

Clearwater Public Library System, 100 North Osceola Ave., Clearwater 34615, 813-462-6916

University of Miami, Otto G. Richter Library, Government Publications, 1300 Memorial Dr., Coral Gables 33124, 305-284-3155

Stetson University, DuPont-Ball Library, Campus Box 8418, 421 North Woodland Blvd., Deland 32720, 904-822-7185

Nova University, Shepard Broad Law Center, Law Library, 3305 College Ave., Fort Lauderdale 33314, 305-760-5767

Indian River Community, College Library, 3209 Virginia Ave., Fort Pierce 34981-9003, 407-468-4757(4318)

Broward County Main Library, Government Documents, 100 South Andrews Ave., Ft. Lauderdale 33301, 305-357-7444

University of Florida Libraries, Documents Dept., Library West, Gainesville 32611, 904-392-0367

University of Florida, College of Law Library, Legal Information Center, Southwest Second Ave. at 25th St., Gainesville 32611, 904-392-0417

Jacksonville Public Library, 122 North Ocean St., Jacksonville 32202, 904-630-1962

Jacksonville University, Carl S. Swisher Library, 2800 University Blvd., North, Jacksonville 32211, 904-744-3950(4262)

University of North Florida, Thomas G. Carpenter Library, 4567 St. Johns Bluff Rd. South, Jacksonville 32216, 904-646-2617

Florida Institute of Technology, Evans Library, 150 West University Blvd., Melbourne 32901-6996, 407-768-8000(7531)

St. Thomas University Library, Documents Dept., 16400 Northwest 32nd Ave., Miami 33054, 305-628-6670

Miami-Dade Public Library, Documents Division, 101 West Flagler St., Miami 33130, 305-375-5028

Florida International University Library, Tamiami Campus, Documents Section, 8th St., South West 107th Ave., Miami 33199, 305-348-3137

Florida International University, North Miami Campus, Library Documents Section, North Miami 33181, 305-940-5722

University of Central Florida Library, Documents Dept., 4000 Central Florida Blvd., Orlando 32816-0666, 407-823-2563

Bay County Public Library, Caller Box 2625, 25 West Government St., Panama City 32402-2625, 904-769-4131

University of West Florida, John C. Pace Library, 11000 University Parkway, Pensacola 32514, 904-474-2410

Selby Public Library, 1001 Blvd. of the Arts, Sarasota 34236, 813-951-5501

State Library of Florida, R.A. Gray Bldg., Documents Section, 500 South Bronough, Tallahassee 32399-0250, 904-487-2651(135)

Florida State University, Strozier Library, Documents/Maps/Micromaterials F.S.U., Tallahassee 32306-2047, 904-644-6061

Tampa Hillsborough, County Public Library, Documents Section, 900 North Ashley Dr., Tampa 33602, 813-223-8871

University of South Florida, Library LIB 122, Documents Unit, 4202 E. Fowler Ave., Tampa 33620-5400, 813-974-2726

University of Tampa, Merle Kelce Library, 401 West Kennedy Blvd., Tampa 33606, 813-253-6231

Rollins College, Olin Library, Government Documents, 1000 Holt Ave., Winter Park 32789-4499, 407-646-2683

Georgia

Georgia Southwestern College, James Earl Carter Library, Americus 31709, 912-928-1341

University of Georgia Libraries, Government Documents Dept., Jackson St., Athens 30602, 404-542-0664

Atlanta-Fulton Public Library, Government Documents, Ivan Allen Dept., 1 Margaret Mitchell Square, Atlanta 30303, 404-730-1908

Georgia Institute of Technology, Price Gilbert Memorial Library, 225 North Ave., NW, Atlanta 30332, 404-894-4519

Emory University, Robert W. Woodruff Library, Documents Center, Atlanta 30322, 404-727-0130

Atlanta University Center, Robert W. Woodruff Library, 111 James P. Brawley Dr., SW, Atlanta 30314, 404-522-8980(110)

Georgia State University, William Russell Pullen Library, Documents Unit, 100 Decatur St., SE, Atlanta 30303, 404-651-2185

Augusta College, Reese Library, 2500 Walton Way (10), Augusta 30910, 404-737-1748

Columbus College, Simon Schwob Memorial Library, Algonquin Dr., Columbia 31993-2399, 404-568-2042(9)

| | |
|---|---|
| | Mercer University, Stetson Memorial Library, 1130 Edgemont Ave., Macon 31207, 912-752-2934 |
| | Georgia Southern College, Zoah S. Henderson Library, Government Documents Dept., Statesboro 30460, 912-681-5117 |
| | Valdosta State College Library, 1500 N. Patterson, Valdosta 31698, 912-333-5867 |
| Hawaii | University of Hawaii at Hilo, Edwin H. Mookini Library, Government Documents Dept., 523 West Lanikaula St., Hilo 96720-4091, 808-933-3525 |
| | Hawaii State Library, Federal Documents Section, 478 South King St., Honolulu 96813, 808-586-3476 |
| | University of Hawaii, Hamilton Library, Government Documents Collection, 2550 The Mall, Honolulu 96822, 808-956-8230 |
| | Brigham Young University, Hawaii Campus, Joseph F. Smith Library, 55-220 Kulanui St., Laie 96762, 808-293-3880 |
| | Wailuku Public Library, 251 High St., Wailuku 96793, 808-244-3946 |
| Idaho | Idaho State Library, 325 West State St., Boise 83702, 208-334-2150 |
| | Boise State University Library, Government Documents, 1910 University Dr., Boise 83725, 208-385-1264 |
| | University of Idaho Library, Documents Section, Moscow 83843, 208-885-6344 |
| | Idaho State University, Eli Oboler Library, Documents Division, 850 S 9th, Pocatello 83209-8089, 208-236-3045 |
| | Ricks College, David O. McKay Learning Resources Center, Documents Dept., Rexburg 83460-0405, 208-356-2353 |
| Illinois | Southern Illinois University at Carbondale, Morris Library, Documents Center, Carbondale 62901, 618-453-2708 |
| | University of Illinois, Law Library, 504 East Pennsylvania Ave., Champaign 61820, 217-244-3044 |
| | Eastern Illinois University, Booth, Library-Documents, Charleston 61920, 217-581-6092 |

University of Illinois at Chicago Library, Documents Dept., 801 South Morgan St., Chicago 60607, 312-996-2738

University of Chicago Library, Documents Section, 1100 East 57th St., Chicago 60637, 312-702-8767

Loyola University of Chicago, E.M. Cudahy Memorial Library, 6525 North Sheridan Rd., Chicago 60626, 312-508-2627

Chicago Public Library, Government Publications Dept., Harold Washington Square, 400 State St., Chicago 60611, 312-269-3021

DePaul University, Law Library, 25 East Jackson Blvd., Chicago 60604, 312-341-8121(2377)

Illinois Institute of Technology, Paul Galvin Library IIT Center, Government Documents, 35 West 33rd St., Chicago 60616, 708-682-6050

Chicago State University, Paul and Emily Douglas Library, Government Publications/Rm. 204/Library Bldg., Ninety Fifth St. at King Dr., Chicago 60628, 312-995-2284

Northeastern Illinois University, Ronald Williams Library, Documents Dept., 5500 North St. Louis Ave., Chicago 60625, 312-583-4050(4474)

Northern Illinois University, Founders Memorial Library, Government Publications Dept., DeKalb 60115-2868, 815-753-9841

Oakton Community College Library, 1600 East Golf Rd., Des Plaines 60016, 312-635-1644

Southern Illinois University at Edwardsville, Love Joy Memorial Library, Edwardsville 62026, 618-692-2632

Principa College, Marshall Brooks Library, Documents Dept., Elsah 62028, 618-374-5074

Northwestern University Library, Government Publications Dept., Evanston 60201-2300, 708-491-3130

Freeport Public Library, 314 West Stephenson St., Freeport 61032, 815-233-3000

Galesburg Public Library, 40 East Simmons St., Galesburg 61401, 309-343-6118

Illinois Benedictine College, Theodore F. Lownik Library, 5700 College Rd., Lisle 60532-0900, 312-960-1500(852)

Western Illinois University, Government Publications & Legal Reference Library, Macomb 61455, 309-298-2723

Monmouth College, Hewes Library, 700 East Broadway, Monmouth 61462, 309-457-2195

Mount Prospect Public Library, Documents Dept., Government Information Center, 10 South Emerson St., Mount Prospect 60056, 708-253-5675

Illinois State University, Milner Library, Documents Dept., School and College Sts., Normal 61761, 309-438-7441

Oak Park Public Library, 834 Lake St., Oak Park 60301, 312-383-8200(1221)

Illinois Valley Community College, Jacobs Library, Documents Dept. R.R. # 1, 2578 East 350th Rd., Oglesby 61348-1099, 815-224-2720(397)

Bradley University, Cullom-Davis Library, 1511 West Bradley Ave., Peoria 61625, 309-677-2840

Rosary College, Rebecca Crown Library, 7900 West Division St., River Forest 60305, 312-366-2490(331)

Rockford Public Library, 215 North Wyman St., Rockford 61101, 815-965-6731(158)

Lewis University Library, Route # 53, Romeoville 60441, 815-838-0500(307)

Illinois State Library, Federal Documents Dept., 300 South Second St., Springfield 62701-1796, 217-782-4887

Poplar Creek Public Library, 1405 South Park Ave., Streamwood 60107, 312-837-6800

Governors State University, University Library, Documents Dept., University Park 60466, 312-534-5000(2232)

University of Illinois at Urbana-Champaign, Documents Library, Rm. 200 D Library, 1408 West Gregory Dr., Urbana 61801, 217-244-2058

Wheaton College, Buswell Memorial Library, Government Documents, Wheaton 60187, 312-260-3990

Woodstock Public Library, 414 West Judd St., Woodstock 60098, 815-338-0542

Indiana

Anderson University, Charles E. Wilson Library, Periodicals & Government Documents, Anderson 46012-3462, 317-641-4275

Anderson Public Library, Government Publications, 111 East 12th St., Anderson 46016-1499, 317-641-2456

Indiana University Library, Documents Dept., 10th and Jordan Sts., Bloomington 47405, 812-855-6924

Indiana University, Law Library, School of Law, Bloomington 47405, 812-855-9666

University of Southern Indiana, Library Service, Documents Dept., 8600 University Blvd., Evansville 47712, 812-464-1834

Allen County Public Library, 900 Webster St., Fort Wayne 46801, 219-424-7241(2240)

Indiana University-Purdue University at Fort Wayne, Helmke Library, 2101 East Coliseum Blvd., Fort Wayne 46805-1499, 219-481-6511

Gary Public Library, Information Center, 220 West Fifth Ave., Gary 46402, 219-886-2484(36)

Indiana University, Northwest Library, Documents Dept., 3400 Broadway, Gary 46408, 219-980-6946

De Pauw University, Roy O. West Library, Greencastle 46135, 317-658-4419

Hanover College, Duggan Library, Box 287, Hanover 47243, 812-866-7164

Huntington College, RichLyn Library, Government Documents Service, 2303 College Ave., Huntington 46750, 219-356-6000(1062)

Indianapolis-Marion County Public Library, Newspaper Periodical Division, 40 East Saint Clair St., Indianapolis 46206, 317-269-1724

Indiana State Library, Serials/Documents Section, 140 North Senate Ave., Indianapolis 46204, 317-232-3686

Indiana University-Purdue University at Indianapolis, University Library X, 815 West Michigan St., Indianapolis 46202, 317-274-8337

Muncie Public Library, 301 East Jackson St., Muncie 47305, 317-747-8200

| | |
|---|---|
| | Ball State University, Alexander M. Bracken Library, Government Publications Service, 2000 University Ave., Muncie 47306, 317-285-1110 |
| | Indiana University, Southeast Library, 4201 Grantline Rd., New Albany 47150, 812-941-2489 |
| | University of Notre Dame, Theodore M. Hesburgh Library, Documents Center, Notre Dame 46556-5629, 219-239-5268 |
| | Indiana University at South Bend, Franklin D. Schurz Library, 1700 Mishawaka Ave., South Bend 46634, 219-237-4442 |
| | Indiana State University, Cunninghan Memorial Library, Documents Unit, Terre Haute 47809, 812-237-2629 |
| | Valparaiso University, Moellering Memorial Library, Valparaiso 46383, 219-464-5771 |
| | Purdue University Libraries, HSSE Library, Documents Dept., 1535 Stewart Center, West Lafayette 47907, 317-494-2837 |
| Iowa | Iowa State University, William Robert and Ellen Sorge, Parks Library, Government Publications Section, Ames 50011-2140, 515-294-6304 |
| | University of Northern Iowa, Donald O. Rod Library, Documents and Maps, Cedar Falls 50613, 319-273-6327 |
| | Drake University, Cowles Library, Government Publications Dept., 2507 University Ave., Des Moines 50311, 515-271-2975 |
| | Loras College, Wahlert Memorial Library, 1450 Alta Vista, Dubuque 52001, 319-588-7125 |
| | Grinnell College, Burling Library, Documents Dept., P.O. Box 805, Grinnell 50112, 515-269-3353 |
| | University of Iowa Libraries, Government Publications Dept., Washington & Madison Sts., Iowa City 52242, 319-335-5925 |
| | North Iowa Area Community College Library, Government Documents, 500 College Dr., Mason City 50401, 515-421-4326 |
| Kansas | Benedictine College, North Campus Library, Documents, Second and Division Sts., Atchison 66002, 913-367-5340(513) |

Bakers University, Collins Library, Documents Dept., P.O. Box 65, Baldwin City 66006-0065, 913-594-6451(389)

Dodge City Community College, Learning Resources Center, 2501 North 14th Ave., Dodge City 67801-2399, 316-227-9285

Emporia State University, William Allen White Library, Government Documents Dept., 1200 Commercial, Emporia 66801, 316-343-1200(5049)

Fort Hays State University, Forsyth Library, Documents Dept., 600 Park St., Hays 67601, 913-628-4340

University of Kansas, Government Documents and Maps, Library, 6001 Malott Hall, Lawrence 66045, 913-864-4660

Kansas State University, Farrell Library, Documents Unit, Manhattan 66506, 913-532-7449

Pittsburg State University, Leonard H. Axe Library, Government Documents, Pittsburg 66762, 316-235-4889

Kansas Wesleyan University, Memorial Library, Documents Dept., 100 East Claflin, Salina 67401-6196, 913-827-5541(234)

Johnson County Library, Documents Dept., 8700 West Shawnee Mission Parkway, Shawnee Mission 66201, 913-831-1550(325)

Kansas State Library, 3rd Fl. Statehouse, Capitol Bldg., Topeka 66612, 913-296-3296

Wichita State University, Ablah Library, Documents Dept., Box 68, Wichita 67208 316-689-3155

Kentucky

Ashland Community College Library, University of Kentucky, 1400 College Dr., Ashland 41101, 606-329-2999(543)

Union College, Abigail E. Weeks Memorial Library, 310 College St., Barbourville 40906, 606-546-4151(242)

Western Kentucky University, Helm-Cravens Library, Government Services Unit, Bowling Green 42101, 502-745-6108

Lindsey Wilson College, Katie Murrell Library, 210 Lindsey Wilson St., Columbia 42728, 502-384-2126

Centre College, Grace Doherty Library, Danville 40422, 606-236-5211(447)

Kentucky State University, Paul G. Blazer Library, East Main St., Frankfort 40601, 502-227-6852

Kentucky Department of Libraries and Archives, State Library Service Division, Federal Documents Section, 300 Coffee Tree Rd., Frankfort 40602-0537, 502-875-7000(219)

Northern Kentucky University, W. Frank Steely Library, Highland Heights 41076, 606-572-5455

University of Kentucky Libraries, Government Publications/Maps Dept., Lexington 40506-0039, 606-257-8400

Louisville Free Public Library, 301 West York St., Louisville 40203-2257, 502-561-8617

University of Louisville, Ekstrom Library, Belknap Campus, Government Publications Dept., Louisville 40292, 502-588-8754

Morehead State University, Camden-Carroll Library, Morehead 40351, 606-783-2160

Kentucky-Wesleyan College, Library Learning Center, 3000 Frederica St., Owensboro 42301, 502-926-3111(135)

Eastern Kentucky University, John Grant Crabbe Library, Richmond 40475, 606-622-1791

Cumberland College, Norma Perkins Hagan Memorial Library, 821 Walnut St., Williamsburg 40769, 606-549-2200(4329)

Louisiana

Southern University, John B. Cade Library, Southern Branch Post Office, Baton Rouge 70813, 504-771-2853

Louisiana State University, Middleton Library, Government Documents Dept./Business Administration, Baton Rouge 70803-3312, 504-388-2570

Southeastern Louisiana University, Sims Memorial Library, P.O. Drawer 896, SLU, Sycamore Ave., Hammond 70402, 504-549-3966

| | |
|---|---|
| | University of Southwestern Louisiana, Dupre Library Documents Div., USL Box 40199, 302 East Saint Mary Blvd., Lafayette 70503, 318-231-6030 |
| | McNeese State University, Lether Frazer Memorial Library, Documents Dept., P.O. Box 91445, Beauregard St., Lake Charles 70609, 318-475-5740 |
| | Northwestern State University of Louisiana, Watson Memorial Library, Natchitoches 71497, 318-357-4466 |
| | New Orleans Public Library, Business and Science Division, 219 Loyola Ave., New Orleans 70140, 504-596-2583 |
| | Our Lady of Holy Cross, College Library, 4123 Woodland Dr., New Orleans 70131-7399, 504-394-7744(102) |
| | University of New Orleans, Earl K. Long Library, Government Documents Division, Lake Front, New Orleans 70148, 504-286-7276 |
| | Loyola University, Government Documents Library, 6363 St. Charles Ave., New Orleans 70118, 504-865-3258 |
| | Tulane University, Howard-Tilton Memorial Library, Documents Dept., 7001 Freret St., New Orleans 70118, 504-865-5683 |
| | Southern University at New Orleans, Leonard S. Washington Library, 6400 Press Dr., New Orleans 70126, 504-282-5227 |
| | Louisiana Technical University, Prescott Memorial Library, Government Documents Dept., Ruston 71272, 318-257-4962 |
| | Shreve Memorial Library, 424 Texas St., Shreveport 71101, 318-226-5888 |
| | Nicholls State University, Ellender Memorial Library, P.O. Box 2028, Leighton Dr., Thibodaux 70310, 504-448-4670 |
| Maine | Bowdoin College Library, Documents Dept., Brunswick 04011, 207-725-3298 |
| | Maine Maritime Academy, Nutting Memorial Library, Box C-1, Castine 04420, 207-326-4311(265) |
| | Bates College, George and Helen Ladd Library, Documents Dept., Lewiston 04240, 207-786-6268 |

University of Maine, Raymond H. Fogler Library, Tri-State Regional, Documents Depository, and Microforms Dept., Orono 04469, 207-581-1681

Portland Public Library, 5 Monument Square, Portland 04101-4072, 207-871-1700(736)

University of Maine, School of Law, Garbrect Law Library, 246 Deering Ave., Portland 04102, 207-780-4827

Louis B. Goodall Memorial Library, 238 Main St., Sanford 04073, 207-324-4714

Maryland

U.S. Naval Academy, Nimitz Library 10A, Documents Dept., Annapolis 21402-5029, 410-267-3268

Enoch Pratt Free Library, Documents Division, 400 Cathedral St., Baltimore 21201, 410-396-5426

University of Baltimore, Langsdale Library, 1420 Maryland Ave., Baltimore 21201, 410-625-3318

Johns Hopkins University, Milton S. Eisenhower Library, Government/Publication/Maps Law Dept., Shafer Hall, 34th and Charles St., Baltimore 21218, 410-338-8360

Morgan State University, Soper Library, Hillen Rd. and Cold Spring Lane, Baltimore 21239, 410-319-3451

U.S. Department of Agriculture, National Agricultural Library, Serial Section, Rm. 002, 10301 Baltimore Blvd., Beltsville 20705, 301-344-4021

University of Maryland, Baltimore County, Albin O. Kuhn Library & Gallery, Government Documents, Catonsville 21228-5398, 410-455-2358

Washington College, Clifton M. Miller Library, Washington Ave., Chestertown 21620, 410-778-2800(241)

University of Maryland at College Park, Hornbake Library, Government Documents/Maps Units, College Park 20742, 301-405-9168

Patuxent River Central Library, U.S. Naval Air Station NAS/NATC, Bldg. 407, Patuxent River 20670, 301-863-1931

Montgomery County Public Library, Rockville Branch, 99 Maryland Ave., Rockville 20850, 301-217-3800

| | |
|---|---|
| | Salisbury State University, Blackwell Library, 1101 Camden Ave., Salisbury 21801, 410-543-6131 |
| | Towson State University, Albert S. Cook Library, Towson 21204, 410-830-3267 |
| Massachusetts | University of Massachusetts, University Library, Government Documents Collections, Amherst 01003, 413-545-2765 |
| | State Library of Massachusetts, Documents Dept., Rm. 442, State House, Boston 02133, 617-727-6279 |
| | Northeastern University, Dodge Library, 360 Huntington Ave., Boston 02115, 617-437-4968 |
| | Boston Public Library, Government Documents Dept., 666 Boylston St., Boston 02117, 617-536-5400(227) |
| | Suffolk University, Law Library, 41 Temple St., Boston 02114, 617-573-8608 |
| | Boston University School of Law, Pappas Law Library, 765 Commonwealth Ave., Boston 02215, 617-353-4790 |
| | Harvard Law School Library, Langdell Hall, Depository, 1545 Massachusetts Ave., Cambridge 02138, 617-495-4516 |
| | Massachusetts Institute of Technology, Libraries, Documents Section, Rm. 14E-210, Cambridge 02139, 617-253-7057 |
| | Harvard College Library, Government Documents & Microforms Division, Cambridge 02138, 617-495-2479 |
| | Boston College, Thomas P. O'Neill Jr. Library, Government Documents Dept., 140 Commonwealth Ave., Chestnut Hill 02167, 617-552-3354 |
| | University of Lowell, O'Leary Library, South Campus, Wilder St., Lowell 01854, 508-934-4589 |
| | Tufts University, Wessell Library, Arts and Sciences Library, Government Publications and Maps, Medford 02155, 617-628-5000(2057) |
| | Boston College, Law School Library, 885 Center St., Newton Center 02159, 617-552-4407 |
| | Southeastern Massachusetts University Library, Documents Section, P.O. Box 6, Old Westport Rd., North Dartmouth 02747, 508-999-8740 |

| | |
|---|---|
| | Stonehill College, Cushing-Martin Library, Washington St., North Easton 02357, 508-230-1203 |
| | Springfield City Library, Documents Section, 220 State St., Springfield 01103, 413-739-3871(422) |
| | Brandeis University Library, Documents Collection, 415 South St., Waltham 02254, 617-736-4673 |
| | Wellesley College, Margaret Clapp Library, Documents Collection, Wellesley 02181, 617-235-0320(2100) |
| | Gordon College, Jenks Learning Resource Center, Winn Library, 255 Grapevine Rd., Wenham 01984-1895, 508-927-2306(4345) |
| | Williams College Library, Sawyer Library, John G. Ames Documents Collection, Williamstown 01267, 413-597-2515 |
| | University of Massachusetts Medical Center, Lamar Soutter Library, 55 Lake Ave. North, Worcester 01655, 508-856-2473 |
| Michigan | Albion College, Stockwell-Mudd Library, Documents, 602 East Cass St., Albion 49224, 517-629-0384 |
| | University of Michigan, Harlan Hatcher Graduate Library, Documents Center, Ann Arbor 48109, 313-764-0410 |
| | Benton Harbor Public Library, 213 East Wall St., Benton Harbor 49022, 616-926-6139(12) |
| | Detroit Public Library, 5201 Woodward Ave., Detroit 48202-4093, 313-833-9165 |
| | Wayne State University, Purdy/Kresge Library, Documents Section, 5265 Cass Ave., Detroit 48202, 313-577-1603 |
| | Michigan State University, Documents Library, East Lansing 48824-1048, 517-353-8601 |
| | Oakland Community College, Martin Luther King Learning, Resource Center Orchard Ridge Campus, 27055 Orchard Lake Rd., Farmington Hill 48018, 313-471-7736 |
| | Flint Public Library, 1026 East Kearsley St., Flint 48502, 313-232-7111(258) |
| | University of Michigan at Flint, Library, Documents Unit, Flint 48502-2186, 313-762-3418 |

Michigan Technological University, J. Robert Van Pelt Library, Documents Dept., 1400 Townsend Dr., Houghton 49931-1295, 906-487-2506

Western Michigan University, Dwight B. Waldo Library, Government Documents Dept., Kalamazoo 49008, 616-387-5208

Library of Michigan, Government Documents Unit, 717 West Allegan St., Lansing 48909, 517-373-8927

Livonia Public Library, Civic Center Branch—Adult Svc., 32777 Five Mile Rd., Livonia 48154, 313-421-7338(619)

Schoolcraft College Library, 18600 Haggerty Rd., Livonia 48152-2696, 313-462-4400(5323)

Northern Michigan University, Lydia M. Olson Library, Government Documents Dept., Marguette 49855, 906-227-2112

Hackley Public Library, 316 West Webster Ave., Muskegon 49440-1281, 616-722-7276

St. Clair County Library, 210 McMorran Blvd., Port Huron 48060, 313-987-7323(22)

Royal Oak Public Library, 222 East Eleven Mile Rd., Royal Oak 48068, 313-541-1470

Hoyt Public Library, 505 Janes St., Saginaw 48605, 517-755-0904

Lake Superior State College, Kenneth Shouldice Library, Sault Ste., Marie 49783, 906-635-2651

Northwestern Michigan College, Mark Osterlin Library, 1701 East Front St., Traverse City 49684, 616-922-1065

Delta College, Learning Resources Center, Federal Depository, Mackinaw and Delta Rds., University Center 48710, 517-686-9560

Minnesota

St. John's University, Alcuin Library, Collegeville 56321, 612-363-3101

Washington County Library, Parkgrove Branch, 7900 Hemingway Ave., Cottage Grove 55016, 612-459-2040

Duluth Public Library, 520 West Superior St., Duluth 55802, 218-723-3805

University of Minnesota, Duluth Library, Rm. 370, 10 University Dr., Duluth 55812, 218-726-6157

Dakota County Library, 1340 Wescott Rd., Eagan 55123, 612-452-9600

Southdale-Hennepin Area Library, Government Documents, 7001 York Ave. South, Edina 55435, 612-830-4977

Mankato State University, Memorial Library, MSU Box 19, P.O. Box 8400, Maywood & Ellis, Mankato 56001, 507-389-5154

Southwest State University Library, Marshall 56258, 507-537-6233

University of Minnesota, 409 Wilson Library, Government Publications, 309 Nineteenth Ave. South, Minneapolis 55455, 612-626-7520

Minneapolis Public Library, Government Documents Dept., 300 Nicollet Mall, Minneapolis 55401, 612-372-6536

University of Minnesota, Law School Library, Documents Depts., 229 Nineteenth Ave. South, Minneapolis 55455, 612-625-5596

Moorhead State University, Livingston Lord Library, Documents Dept., Moorhead 56560, 218-236-2349

University of Minnesota at Morris, Rodney A. Briggs Library, Documents Dept., Morris 56267, 612-589-6176

St. Olaf College, Rolvaag Memorial Library, 1510 St. Olaf Ave., Northfield 55057, 507-663-3226

Carleton College, The Library, Government Documents, One North College St., Northfield 55057, 507-663-4266

St. Cloud State University, Learning Resources Center, Library Documents Section, 720 4th Ave. South, St. Cloud 56301, 612-255-2086

St. Paul Public Library, Government Publications, 90 West 4th St., St. Paul 55102, 612-292-6178

Minnesota State Law Library, 25 Constitution Ave., St. Paul 55155, 612-297-7661

University of Minnesota, St. Paul Campus Library, 1984 Buford Ave., St. Paul 55108, 612-624-4799

Gustavus Adolphus College, Folke Bernadotte Memorial Lib., Government Documents, St. Peter 56082, 507-933-7556

| | |
|---|---|
| | Winona State University, Maxwell Library, Sanborn and Johnson Sts., Winona 55987, 507-457-5148 |
| Mississippi | Delta State University, W.B. Roberts Library, Government Documents, Cleveland 38733, 601-846-4440 |
| | University of Southern Mississippi, Joseph A. Cook Memorial Library, Southern Station Box 5053, Hattiesburg 39401-5053, 601-266-4252 |
| | Mississippi Library Commission, Documents Section, 1221 Ellis Ave., Jackson 39209, 601-359-1036(153) |
| | Millsaps College, Millsaps-Wilson Library, 1701 North State St., Jackson 39210, 601-974-1072 |
| | Mississippi State University, Mitchell Memorial Library, Documents Department—Drawer 5408, Hardy Rd., Mississippi State 39762, 601-325-7660 |
| | University of Mississippi, J.D. Williams Library, Government Documents Dept., 106 Old Gym Bldg., University 38677, 601-232-7465 |
| Missouri | Southeast Missouri State University, Kent Library, Government Documents Dept., One University Plaza, Cape Girardeau 63701-4799, 314-651-2751 |
| | University of Missouri at Columbia, Ellis Library, Government Documents, Columbia 65201, 314-882-0748 |
| | Westminster College, Reeves Library, 501 Westminster Ave., Fulton 65251, 314-642-3361(244) |
| | Missouri State Library, 2002 Missouri Blvd., Jefferson City 65102, 314-751-4552 |
| | Lincoln University, Inman E. Page Library, 820 Chestnut St., Jefferson City 65101, 314-681-5509 |
| | Missouri Southern State College Library, Government Documents, Newman and Duquesne Rds., Joplin 64801, 417-625-9342 |
| | University of Missouri at Kansas City, General Library, Government Documents Dept., 5100 Rockhill Rd., Kansas City 64110, 816-276-1536 |
| | Kansas City Missouri Public Library, Documents Division, 311 East Twelfth St., Kansas City 64106, 816-221-2685(44) |

Northeast Missouri State University, Pickler Memorial Library, Kirksville 63501, 816-785-4534

Northwest Missouri State University, B.D. Owens Library, Maryville 64468, 816-562-1629

University of Missouri-Rolla, Curtis Laws Wilson Library, Documents Section, Rolla 65401, 314-341-4007

St. Charles City Community Library District, Kisker Rd. Branch, 1000 Kisker Rd., St. Charles 63304, 314-447-7323

Lindewood College, Margaret Leggart Bulter Library, St. Charles 63301, 314-949-4820

St. Louis Public Library, Documents Dept., 1301 Olive St., St. Louis 63103, 314-539-0377

Washington University, John M. Olin Library, Government Publications Unit, One Brookings Dr.—Campus Box 1061, St. Louis 63130-4899, 314-935-5475

Washington University of St. Louis, Law Library, Mudd Bldg., 1 Brookings Dr., St. Louis 63130, 314-889-6484

St. Louis University, Law Library, 3700 Lindell Blvd., St. Louis 63108-3478, 314-658-2756

St. Louis University, Pius XII Memorial Library, 3650 Lindell Blvd., St. Louis 63108, 314-658-3105

University of Missouri at St. Louis, Thomas Jefferson Library, 8001 Natural Bridge Rd., St. Louis 63121, 314-553-5061

Southwest Missouri State University, Duane G. Meyer Library, 901 South National, Springfield 65804-0095, 417-836-4532

Central Missouri State University, Ward Edwards Library, Government Documents, South and College St., Warrensburg 64093, 816-429-4149

Montana

Eastern Montana College Library, Documents Dept., 1500 North 30 St., Billings 59101-0298, 406-657-1656

Montana State University, Renne Library, Documents Dept., Bozeman 59717, 406-994-6658

Montana College of Mineral Science and Technology Library, Documents Division, Park St., Butte 59701, 406-496-4286

| | |
|---|---|
| | Northern Montana College, Vande Bogart Library, Havre 59501, 406-265-3706(3037) |
| | Montana State Library, 1515 6th Ave. East, Helena 59620, 406-444-5431 |
| | Carroll College, Corette Library, Capital Hill, Helena 59625, 406-442-1295 |
| | University of Montana, Maureen & Mike Mansfield Lib., Documents Division, Missoula 59812, 406-243-6700 |
| Nebraska | University of Nebraska at Kearney, Calvin T. Ryan Library, Government Documents Dept., Kearney 68849-0700, 308-234-8542 |
| | University of Nebraska at Lincoln, College of Law Library, East Campus, Lincoln 68583-0902, 402-472-8302 |
| | University of Nebraska at Lincoln, D.L. Love Memorial Library, Documents Dept., Lincoln 68588-0110, 402-472-2562 |
| | Nebraska Library Commission, Federal Documents Dept., 1420 P St., Lincoln 68508, 402-471-2045 |
| | Creighton University, Reinert/Alumni Library, California at 24th St., Omaha 68178, 402-280-2219 |
| | University of Nebraska at Omaha, University Library, Documents Dept., 60th and Dodge St., Omaha 68182-0237, 402-554-3258 |
| | Omaha Public Library, W. Dale Clark Library Business, Science, Technology Dept., 215 South 15th St., Omaha 68102, 402-444-4817 |
| Nevada | Nevada State Library, Capitol Complex, 401 North Carson St., Carson City 89710, 702-687-5160 |
| | University of Nevada at Las Vegas, James Dickinson Library, Government Documents, 4505 Maryland Parkway, Las Vegas 89154, 702-739-3409 |
| | Las Vegas-Clark County, Library District, 833 North Las Vegas Blvd., Las Vegas 89101, 702-382-3493 |
| | Washoe County Library, Government Documents Dept., 301 South Center St., Reno 89501, 702-785-4507 |
| | University of Nevada Libraries, Government Publications Dept., Reno 89557-0044, 702-784-6579 |
| New Hampshire | Franklin Pierce Law, Center Library, 2 White St., Concord 03301, 603-228-1541(130) |

New Hampshire State Library, 20 Park St., Concord 03301, 603-271-2239

University of New Hampshire Library, Documents, Durham 03824, 603-862-1777

Dartmouth College Library, Hanover 03755, 603-646-3616

Manchester City Library, 405 Pine St., Manchester 03104-6199, 603-624-6550

St. Anselm College, Geisel Library, 87th St. Anselm Dr., Manchester 03102, 603-641-7306

New Hampshire College, H.A.B. Shapiro Memorial Library, 2500 North River Rd., Manchester 03104, 603-668-2211(2166)

Nashua Public Library, 2 Court St., Nashua 03060, 603-594-3412

New Jersey

Rutgers University Paul Robeson Library, 300 North 4th St., Camden 08102, 609-757-6037

East Brunswick Public Library, 2 Jean Walling Civic Center, East Brunswick 08816, 201-390-6765

Glassboro State College, Savitz Library, Government Publications, Route # 322, Glassboro 08028, 609-863-6317

Johnson Free Public Library, 275 Moore St., Hackensack 07601, 201-343-4169(215)

Irvington Public Library, Civic Square, Irvington 07111, 201-372-6400

Jersey City Public Library, Documents Dept., 472 Jersey Ave., Jersey City 07302, 201-547-4517

Rider College, Franklin F. Moore Library, 2083 Lawrenceville Rd., Lawrenceville 08648-3099, 609-895-5241

Drew University Library, 36 Madison Ave., Madison 07940, 201-408-3480

Ramapo College Library, 505 Ramapo Valley Rd., Mahwah 07430, 201-529-7500(7907)

Burlington County Library, West Woodlane Rd., Mount Holly 08060, 609-267-9660 37

Rutgers University, Alexander Library, Government Documents Dept., 169 College Ave., New Brunswick 08903, 201-932-7007

Rutgers, the State University, John Cotton Dana Library, 185 University Ave., Newark 07102, 201-648-5910

Newark Public Library, U.S. Documents Division, 5 Washington St., Newark 07101, 201-733-7812

Stockton State College Library, Jimmie Leeds Rd. and College Dr., Pomonam 08240-9988, 609-652-4532

Princeton University, Firestone Library, Documents Division, Princeton 08544, 609-258-3178

Fairleigh Dickinson University, Messler Library, U.S. Government Documents, 207 Montross Ave., Rutherford 07070, 201-460-5069

New Jersey State Library, U.S. Documents, CN-520, 185 West State St., Trenton 08625-0520, 609-292-6220

Montclair State College, Harry A. Sprague Library, Government Documents Dept., Upper Montclair 07043, 201-893-7145

Wayne Public Library, 475 Valley Rd., Wayne 07470, 201-694-4272(31)

Woodbridge Public Library, George Frederick Plaza, Woodbridge 07095, 201-634-4450(216)

New Mexico

University of New Mexico, General Library, Government Publications & Maps Dept., Albuquerque 87131, 505-277-7180

University of New Mexico, School of Law Library, 1117 Standford Dr., NE, Albuquerque 87131, 505-277-0677

New Mexico State University Library, Documents Division Dept. 3475, Box 30006, Las Cruces 88003-0006, 505-646-3737

New Mexico Highlands University, Donnelly Library, Las Vegas 87701, 505-454-3333

New Mexico State Library, 325 Don Gaspar Ave., Santa Fe 87503, 505-827-3825

Western New Mexico University, J. Cloyd Miller Library, Silver City 88062, 505-538-6406

New Mexico Institute of Mining & Technology, Martin Speare Memorial Library, Government Documents Dept., Campus Station, Socorro 87801, 505-835-5740

| | |
|---|---|
| New York | New York State Library, Cultural Education Center, Documents/Gift & Exchange Section, Empire State Plaza, Albany 12230, 518-474-3940 |
| | Albany Law School, Schaffer Law Library, 80 New Scotland Ave., Albany 12208, 518-445-2385 |
| | State University of New York at Albany, University Library, Government Publications Dept., 1400 Washington Ave., Albany 12222, 518-442-3549 |
| | State University of New York at Binghamton, Glenn G. Bartle Library, Government Documents Dept., Vestal Parkway, East, Binghamton 13901, 607-777-4907 |
| | State University of New York, at Brockport, Drake Memorial Library, Brockport 14420, 716-395-2197 |
| | Brooklyn Public Library, Business Library, 280 Cadman Plaza, West, Brooklyn 11201, 718-522-4064 |
| | Brooklyn College Library, Government Documents Division, Bedford Ave. and Ave. H, Brooklyn 11210, 718-780-5332 |
| | Brooklyn Public Library, Social Science-Division, Grand Army Plaza, Brooklyn 11238, 718-780-7746 |
| | State University of New York at Buffalo, Charles B. Sears Law Library, Documents Dept., O'Brian Hall, Amherst Campus, Buffalo 14260, 716-636-2084 |
| | Buffalo and Erie County Library, Documents Division, Lafayette Square, Buffalo 14203, 716-858-7149 |
| | State University of New York at Buffalo, Lockwood Memorial Library, Government Documents Dept., Amherst Campus, Buffalo 14260, 716-636-2817 |
| | St. Lawrence University, Owen D. Young Library, Canton 13617, 315-379-5473 |
| | State University of New York, College at Cortland, Memorial Library Documents Section, P.O. Box 2000, Cortland 13045, 607-753-4042 |
| | East Islip Public Library, 381 East Main St., East Islip 11730, 516-286-1600(325) |
| | Elmira College, Gannett Tripp Learning Center, Elmira 14901, 607-734-3911(287) |
| | Queens College, Benjamin S. Rosenthal Library, Documents Dept., 65-30 Kissena Blvd., Flushing 11367, 718-997-3700 |

CUNY Law School at, Queens College, CUNY Law Library, 65-21 Main St., Flushing 11367, 718-575-4263

Adelphi University, Swirbul Library, Federal Documents Dept., South Ave., Garden City 11530, 516-877-3587

State University of New York at Geneseo, Milne Library, Documents Dept., Geneseo 14454, 716-245-5593

Long Island University, B. Davis Schwarts Memorial Lib., C.W. Post Center, Greenvale 11548, 516-299-2142(2842)

Colgate University, Everett Needham Case Library, Documents, Maps Microforms Dept., Hamilton 13346, 315-824-7508

Hofstra University Library, Axinn Library, Documents Dept., Hempstead 11550, 516-463-5972

Hofstra University, School of Law Library, Hempstead 11550-1009, 516-463-5905

Cornell University Library, 110 - B. Olin Library, Serials Dept., Ithaca 14853-5301, 607-255-5118

Cornell University, Albert R. Mann Library, Cornell University Acquisitions Division, Ithaca 14853-4301, 607-255-7953

Cornell Law Library, Myron Taylor Hall, Ithaca 14853-4901, 607-255-5862

St. John's University Library, Grand Central and Utopia Parkway, Jamaica 11439, 718-990-6071

Queens Borough Public Library, Documents Dept., 89-11 Merrick Blvd., Jamaica 11432, 718-990-0769

U.S. Merchant Marine Academy, Schuyler Otis Bland Library, Steamboat Rd., Kings Point 11024, 516-773-5505

Thrall Library, 22 Orchard St., Middletown 10940, 914-342-5877

State University College at New Paltz, Sojourner Truth Library, Government Documents Dept., New Paltz 12561, 914-257-3662

New York University, Law Library, 40 Washington Square South, New York 10012, 212-998-6323

New York Public Library, Astor Branch, 476 Fifth Ave., New York City 10018, 212-930-0586

Columbia University Libraries, Documents Service Center, Rm. 327, 420 West 118th St., New York City 10027, 212-854-1523

New York University, Elmer Holmes Bobst Library, Social Science/Documents Center, 70 Washington Square South, New York City 10012, 212-998-2602

New York Public Library, Lenox Branch, 476 Fifth Ave., New York City 10018, 212-930-0586

Columbia University, School of Law Library, 435 West 116th St., New York City 10027, 212-854-8413

Dowling College Library, Government Documents, Idle Hour Blvd., Oakdale 11769, 516-244-3283

State University of New York at Oswego, Penfield Library, Documents Center, Oswego 13126, 315-341-3566

State University College at Plattsburgh, Benjamin F. Feinberg Library, Government Documents Collection, Plattsburgh 12901, 518-564-5192

State University of New York, College of Potsdam, Frederick W. Crumb Memorial Library, Pierrepont Ave., Potsdam 13676, 315-267-2479

Clarkson University, Harriet Call Burnap Memorial Library, Schuler Educational Resources Center, Potsdam 13676, 315-268-2292

Rochester Public Library, Serials/Documents Dept., 115 South Ave., Rochester 14604, 716-428-7343

University of Rochester, Rush Rhees Library, Government Documents Micotext Center, Wilson Blvd., Rochester 14627, 716-275-4484

Union College, Schaffer Library, Schenectady 12308, 518-370-6635

St. Thomas Aquinas College, Lougheed Library, Route 340, Sparkill 10976, 914-359-9500(291)

State University of New York at Stony Brook, Frank Melville Jr. Memorial Lib., Reference/Government Documents, Stony Brook 11794, 516-632-7161

Syracuse University, Byrd Library, Maps and Government Information Dept., 222 Waverly Ave., Syracuse 13244-2010, 315-443-4176

Onondaga County Public Library, The Galleries of Syracuse, Government Documents Information Service, 447 South Salina St., Syracuse 13202-2494, 315-448-4636(323)

Troy Public Library, Government Documents, 100 Second St., Troy 12180, 518-274-7071(9)

Nassau Library System, Documents Collection, 900 Jerusalem Ave., Uniondale 11553, 516-292-8920(260)

U.S. Military Academy Library, Government Documents Collection, Bldg. 757, West Point 10996-1799, 914-938-2230

Pace University, Law Library, 78 North Broadway, White Plains 10603, 914-422-4273

North Carolina

University of North Carolina at Asheville, D. Hiden Ramsey Library, Government Documents, One University Heights, Ashville 28804-3299, 704-251-6639

Appalachian State University, Carol Grotnes Belk Library, Government Documents, Boone 28608, 704-262-2820

University of North Carolina at Chapel Hill, Davis Library CB #3912, BA/SS Dept.-Documents, Chapel Hill 27599, 919-962-1151

Public Library of Charlotte and Mecklenburg County, 310 North Tryon St., Charlotte 28202, 704-336-6221

Queens College, Everett Library, Documents Dept., 1900 Selwyn Ave., Charlotte 28274-0001, 704-337-2278

University of North Carolina at Charlotte, J. Murrey Atkins Library, Documents Dept., Charlotte 28223, 704-547-2243

Western Carolina University, Hunter Library, Documents Unit, Cullowhee 28723, 704-227-7252(27)

Davidson College Library, P.O. Box 1837, Davidson 28036, 704-892-2154

North Carolina Central University, James E. Shepard Library, Government Documents Center, 1801 Fayetteville St., Durham 27707, 919-560-6097

Duke University, William R. Perkins Library, Public Documents and Maps Dept., Durham 27706, 919-684-2380

North Carolina Agricultural and Technical State University, F.D. Bluford Library, 1601 East Market St., Greensboro 27411, 919-334-7617

University of North Carolina at Greensboro, Walter Clinton Jackson Library, Documents /Microforms Division, Greensboro 27412-5201, 919-334-5251

East Carolina University, J.Y. Joyner Library, Documents Dept., East Fifth St., Greenville 27858-4353, 919-757-6533

Pembroke State University, Mary Livermore Library, Documents Dept., Pembroke 28372, 919-521-4214(655)

North Carolina State University, D.H. Hill Library-Box 7111, Documents Dept., Raleigh 27695-7111, 919-737-3280

Department of Cultural Resources, Division of State Library, Documents Branch, 109 East Jones St., Raleigh 27611, 919-733-3270

Catawba College, Corriher-Linn-Black Library, Documents Dept., 2300 West Innes St., Salisbury 28144, 704-637-4448(3147)

University of North Carolina at Wilmington, William M. Randall Library, 601 South College Rd., Wilmington 28403-3297, 919-395-3277

Barton College, Hackney Library, Lee St., Wilson 27893, 919-237-3161(389)

Forsyth County Public Library, Main, Government Documents/Periodical Dept., 660 West Fifth St., Winston-Salem 27101, 919-727-2220

Wake Forest University, School of Law Library, 216 Carswell Hall, Winston-Salem 27109, 919-759-5052

Wake Forest University, Z Smith Reynolds Library, Box 7777, Reynolds Station, Winston-Salem 27109, 919-761-5828

North Dakota

North Dakota State University Library, Documents Office, P.O. Box 5599, Fargo 58105, 701-237-8863

University of North Dakota, Chester Fritz Library, University Station, Grand Forks 58202, 701-777-4630

Valley City State University, Allen Memorial Library, 101 College St., SW, Valley City 58072-4098, 701-845-7275

Ohio

Akron-Summit County Public Library, 55 South Main St., Akron 44326, 216-762-7621(460)

University of Akron, Bierce Library, Government Documents, 315 East Buchtel Ave., Akron 44325-1708, 216-972-6052

Mount Union College Library, Documents Dept., 1972 Clark Ave., Alliance 44601, 216-823-3842

Ashland University Library, Documents Dept., 401 College Ave., Ashland 44805-3796, 419-289-5410

Ohio University, Alden Library, Government Documents Dept., Athens 45701, 614-593-2718

Bluffton College, Musselman Library, 280 West College Ave., Bluffton 45817, 419-358-3272

Bowling Green State University, Jerome Library, Documents Dept., Bowling Green 43403, 419-372-7826

Malone College, Everett L. Cattel Library, 515 25th St., NW, Canton 44709, 216-471-8324

University of Cincinnati, University Libraries, Langsam Library-Documents Unit, Cincinnati 45221-0033, 513-556-1873

Public Library of Cincinnati, and Hamilton County, Central Library, 800 Vine St., Library Square, Cincinnati 45202-2071, 513-369-6968

Cleveland Public Library, Documents Collection, 325 Superior Ave., Cleveland 44114-1271, 216-623-2870

Case Western Reserve University, Freiberger Library, 11161 East Blvd., Cleveland 44106, 216-368-6512

Cleveland State University Library, 1860 East 22nd St., Cleveland 44115, 216-687-2365

State Library of Ohio, Documents Dept., 65 South Front St., Columbus 43266-0334, 614-644-1971

Public Library of Columbus and Franklin County, General Reference Division, 96 South Grant Ave., Columbus 43215, 614-645-2710

Ohio State University Libraries, Documents Division, 1858 Neill Ave. Mall, Columbus 43210, 614-292-6175

Dayton and Montgomery County Public Library, Documents Dept., 215 East Third St., Dayton 45402, 513-227-9522

Wright State University Library, Government Documents Dept., Col. Glenn Highway, Dayton 45435, 513-873-2533

University of Dayton, Roesch Library, 300 College Park Dr., Dayton 45469-0001, 513-229-4263

Ohio Wesleyan University, L.A. Beeghly Library, 43 University Ave., Delaware 43015, 614-368-3250

Kenyon College Libraries, Olin Library & Chalmers Mem. Library, Documents Dept., Gambier 43022-9623, 614-427-5658

Denison University Libraries, William H. Doane Library, Documents Dept., Granville 43023, 614-587-6512

Hiram College, Teachout-Price Memorial Library, Hiram 44234, 216-569-5358

Kent State University Libraries, Government Documents Dept., Kent 44242, 216-672-2388

Marietta College, Dawes Memorial Library, Marietta 45750-3030, 614-374-4757(5536)

Miami University at Middletown, Gardner-Harvey Library, 4200 East University Blvd., Middletown 45042, 513-424-4444(293)

Oberlin College, Document Library, Oberlin 44074, 216-775-8285

Miami University, King Library, Documents Dept., Oxford 45056, 513-529-3342

Shawnee State University Library, 940 Second St., Portsmouth 45662, 614-355-2515

Toledo-Lucas County Public Library, Social Science Dept., 325 Michigan St., Toledo 43624, 419-259-5245

University of Toledo Library, Documents Dept., 2801 West Bancroft St., Toledo 43606, 419-537-4485

John Caroll University, Grasselli Library, 20700 North Park Blvd., University Heights 44118, 216-397-4711

Otterbein College, Courtright Memorial Library, Documents, 138 West Main St., Westerville 43081, 614-898-1115

College of Wooster, Andrews Library, Government Publications Dept., Wooster 44691, 216-263-2279

Worthington Public Library, 805 Hartford St., Worthington 43085, 614-885-3138

Youngstown State University, William F. Maag Library, Government Documents Dept., 410 Wick Ave., Youngstown 44555, 216-742-1717

Public Library of Youngstown, and Mahoning County, Reference Dept., 305 Wick Ave., Youngstown 44503, 216-744-8636(45)

Oklahoma

East Central Oklahoma, State University, Linscheid Library, Ada 74820-6899, 405-332-8000(369)

Northwestern Oklahoma State University, J.W. Martin Library, Alva 73717, 405-327-1700(219)

Southern Nazarene University, R.T. Williams Learning, Resources Center, 4115 North College, Bethany 73008, 405-491-6350(6546)

Southeastern Oklahoma State University, Henery G. Bennett, Memorial Library STA A, North 6th St., Durant 74701, 405-924-0121(565)

Central State University Library, Government Documents Dept., Edmond 73034-0192, 405-341-2980(2904)

University of Oklahoma Libraries, Bizzell Memorial Library, Government Documents, 401 West Brooks St., Norman 73019, 405-325-3141

Oklahoma City University, Dulaney Browne Library, 2501 North Blackwelder, Oklahoma City 73106, 405-521-5073(5065)

Oklahoma Department of Libraries, U.S. Government Documents, 200 NE 18th St., Oklahoma City 73105-3298, 405-521-2502(252)

Oklahoma State University, Edmon Low Library, Documents Dept., Stillwater 74078, 405-744-9770

Northeastern Oklahoma State University, John Vaughan Library, Learning Resources Center, Government Publications Dept., Tahlequah 74464-7098, 918-456-5511(3245)

| | |
|---|---|
| | Tulsa City-County Library System, 400 Civic Center, Tulsa 74103, 918-596-7946 |
| | University of Tulsa, McFarlin Library, Government Documents, 600 South College Ave., Tulsa 74104-3189, 918-631-3597 |
| | Southwestern Oklahoma State University, Al Harris Library, Documents Dept., Weatherford 73096-3002, 405-774-3031 |
| Oregon | Southern Oregon State, College Library, Documents, 1250 Siskiyou Blvd., Ashland 97520, 503-552-6850 |
| | Oregon State University Library, Documents Division, Corvallis 97331, 503-754-2761 |
| | University of Oregon Library, Documents and Public Affairs Service, Eugene 97403-1299, 503-686-3070 |
| | Pacific University, Harvey W. Scott Memorial Library, 2043 College Way, Forest Grove 97116, 503-357-6151(2437) |
| | Eastern Oregon State College, Walter M. Pierce Library, 1410 L Ave., La Grande 97850, 503-962-3523 |
| | Western Oregon State College, College Library, 345 Monmouth Ave., Monmouth 97361-1396, 503-838-8893 |
| | Portland State University, Branford P. Millar Library, 934 SW Harrison, Portland 97207, 503-725-4126 |
| | Library Association of Portland, Science and Business Dept., 801 SW 10th Ave., Portland 97205, 503-248-5123 |
| | Williamette University, Main Library, 900 State St., Salem 97301, 503-370-6312 |
| | Oregon State Library, State Library Bldg., Salem 97310-0640, 503-378-4368 |
| Pennsylvania | Muhlenberg College, Trexler Library, 2400 Chew St., Allentown 18104-5586, 215-821-3560 |
| | Bethel Park Public Library, 5100 West Library Ave., Bethel Park 15102, 412-835-2207(264) |
| | Lehigh University Libraries, Linderman Library No. 30, Government Documents/Lib.& Computer Ctr., Packer Ave., Bldg. #8A, Bethlehem 18015, 215-758-3053 |

California University of Pennsylvania, Louis L. Manderino Library, Government Documents Section, California 15419, 412-938-4049

Dickinson College, Boyd Lee Spahr, Government Documents, West High St., Carlisle 17013, 717-245-1397

Robert Morris College Library, Acquisitions Dept., Narrows Run Rd., Coraopolis 15108, 412-262-8255

East Stroudsburg University, Kemp Library, Government Documents Section, Smith and Normal Sts., East Stroudsburg 18301, 717-424-3150

Erie County Library System, 3 South Perry Square, Erie 16501, 814-451-6927

Thiel College, Langenheim Memorial Library, Documents Dept., Greenville 16125, 412-589-2127

State Library of Pennsylvania, Government Publications Sect., Box 1601 Rm. 46, Walnut Ave. and Commonwealth Ave., Harrisburg 17105, 717-787-2327

Haverford College, Magill Library, Haverford 19041, 215-896-1166

Franklin and Marshall College, Shadek-Fackenthal Library, P.O. Box 3003, Lancaster 17604-3003, 717-291-3844

Bucknell University, Ellen Clarke Bertrand Library, Lewisburg 17837, 717-524-3230

Allegheny College, Lawrence Lee Pelletier Library, North Main St., Meadville 16335, 814-332-3769

Millersville University, Helen A. Ganser Library, Millersville 17551, 717-872-3617

Bucks County Community College Library, Swamp Rd., Newtown 18940, 215-968-8010

St. Joseph's University, Drexel Library, 5600 City Ave., Philadelphia 19131, 215-660-1904

Free Library of Philadelphia, Government Documents Dept., Logan Square, 1901 Vine St., Philadelphia 19103, 215-686-5329

Temple University, Paley Library, Documents Unit, 13th & Berks Mall, Philadelphia 19122, 215-787-3187

University of Pennsylvania, Serials Dept., 3420 Walnut St., Philadelphia 19104-6278, 215-898-7563

Drexel University Library, W.W. Hagerty Library, Government Documents Sections, 32nd & Chestnut Sts., Philadelphia 19104, 215-895-2782

La Roache College, John J. Wright Library, 9000 Babcock Blvd., Pittsburgh 15237, 412-367-9300(170)

Carnegie Library of Pittsburgh, Allegheny Regional Branch, Allegheny Square, Pittsburgh 15212, 412-321-0389

Carnegie Library of Pittsburgh, Government Documents Dept., 4400 Forbes Ave., Pittsburgh 15213, 412-622-3175

University of Pittsburgh, Hillman Library, Government Publications, G-8, Pittsburgh 15260, 412-648-7717

Reading Public Library, 100 South Fifth St., Reading 19602, 215-374-4548

Scranton Public Library, Albright Memorial Bldg., North Washington and Vine Sts., Scranton 18503, 717-348-3009

Shippensburg University, Ezra Lehman Memorial Library, Documents Dept., Shippensburg 17257, 717-532-1634

Slippery Rock University, Bailey Library, Documents Dept., 35 East Central Loop, Slippery Rock 16057-1389, 412-738-2638

Swarthmore College, McCabe Library, Documents Collection, 500 College Ave., Swarthmore 19081, 215-328-8503

Pennsylvania State University Libraries, Pattee Library, C-207, University Park 16802, 814-863-1345

Villanova University, Law School Library, Garey Hall, Villanova 19085, 215-645-7027

Warren Library Association, Warren Public Library, 205 Market St., Warren 16365, 814-723-4650(16)

West Chester University, Francis Harvey Green Library, Documents Dept., High St. & Rosedale Ave., West Chester 19383, 215-436-3206

King's College, D. Leonard Corgan Library, 14 West Jackson St., Wilkes-Barre 18711, 717-826-5840

Lycoming College Library, Documents Dept., Academy St., Williamsport 17701, 717-321-4082

| | |
|---|---|
| Rhode Island | Barrington Public Library, 281 County Rd., Barrington 02806, 401-247-1923 |
| | University of Rhode Island Library, Government Publications Office, Kingston 02881, 401-792-4610 |
| | Brown University, John D. Rockefeller Jr. Library, Documents Dept., Prospect St., Providence 02912, 401-863-2522 |
| South Carolina | University of South Carolina at Aiken, Gregg-Graniteville Library, 171 University, Parkway, Aiken 29801, 803-648-3320 |
| | The Citadel Military College, Daniel Library, Serials & Documents Dept., Charleston 29409, 803-792-5128 |
| | Baptist College of Charleston, L. Mendel Rivers Library, 9200 University Blvd., Charleston 29418, 803-863-7946 |
| | College of Charleston, Robert Scott Small Library, Collection Development Documents, Charleston 29424, 803-792-8020 |
| | Clemson University, Robert Muldrow Cooper Library, Public Documents Units, Clemson 29634-3001, 803-656-5174 |
| | University of South Carolina, Coleman Karesh Law Library, 1515 Green St., Columbia 29208, 803-777-5898 |
| | South Carolina State Library, Documents Dept., 1500 Senate St., Columbia 29201, 803-734-8666 |
| | University of South Carolina, Thomas Cooper Library, Documents/Microforms Dept., Green and Sumter Sts., Columbia 29208, 803-777-4841 |
| | University of South Carolina, Coastal Carolina College, Kimbel Library/Reference Dept., P.O. Box 1954, Conway 29526, 803-349-2410(2404) |
| | Greenville County Library, 300 College St., Greenville 29601, 803-242-5000(241) |
| | Furman University, James B. Duke Library, Government Documents Dept., Greenville 29613, 803-294-2190 |
| | Lander College, Jackson Library, Greenwood 29649, 803-229-8366 |

| | |
|---|---|
| | Winthrop College, Dacus Library, Documents Dept., Oakland Ave., Rock Hill 29733, 803-323-2131(25) |
| | Spartanburg County Public Library, 333 South Pine St., Spartanburg 29304, 803-596-3505 |
| South Dakota | Northern State College, Beulah Williams Library, Documents Dept., 14 and Washington State, Aberdeen 57401-7198, 605-622-7774 |
| | South Dakota State University, Hilton M. Briggs Library, Box 2115, Brookings 57007-1098, 605-688-5576 |
| | South Dakota State Library, Federal Documents Dept., State Library Bldg., 800 Governors Dr., Pierre 57501-2294, 605-773-3131 |
| | Rapid City Public Library, 610 Quincy St., Rapid City 57701, 605-394-4171 |
| | South Dakota School of Mines and Technology, Deveraux Library, Government Documents, 501 East Saint Joseph St., Rapid City 57701, 605-394-1255 |
| | Sioux Falls Public Library, 201 North Main Ave., Sioux Falls 57102, 605-339-7082 |
| | Augustana College, Mikkelsen Library and Learning, Resources Center, 29th & Summit, Sioux Falls 57197, 605-336-4921 |
| | Black Hills State University, E. Y. Berry Library Learning, Center/Documents Dept., 1200 University Ave., Spearfish 57783, 605-642-6358 |
| | University of South Dakota, I.D. Weeks Library, Documents, Vermillion 57069, 605-677-6091 |
| Tennessee | King College, E.W. King Library, East State St., Bristol 37620, 615-652-4795 |
| | Chattanooga-Hamilton County, Bicentennial Library, Government Documents Dept., 1001 Broad St., Chattanooga 37402, 615-757-5351 |
| | Tennessee Technological University, Jere Whitson Memorial Library, Box 5066, Cookeville 38505, 615-372-3841 |
| | Lambuth College, Luther L. Gobbel Library, 705 Lambuth Blvd., Jackson 38301, 901-425-3290 |

East Tennessee State University, Sherrod Library, Documents/Law/Maps/Dept., P.O. Box 22450A, Johnson City 37614-0002, 615-929-5334

University of Tennessee at Knoxville, John C. Hodges Library, 1015 Volunteer Blvd., Knoxville 37996-1000, 615-974-0011

Knox County Public, Library System Lawson McGhee-Library, 500 West Church Ave., Knoxville 37902, 615-544-5711

University of Tennessee at Martin, Paul Meek Library, Martin 38238-5047, 901-587-7065

Memphis State University Libraries, Government Documents, Memphis 38152, 901-678-2206

Memphis-Shelby County, Public Library and Information Center, 1850 Peabody Ave., Memphis 38111, 901-725-8893

Vanderbilt University, Alyne Queener Massey, Law Library, Documents Dept., Nashville 37203, 615-322-2568

Tennessee State University, Brown-Daniel Library, Government Documents Center, 3500 John A. Merritt Blvd., Nashville 37209-1561, 615-320-3678

Vanderbilt University Library, Central Documents, Unit 419, 419 21 Ave., Nashville 37240-0007, 615-322-2838

Fisk University Library, Government Documents, 17th Ave. North & Meharry Blvd., Nashville 37203-0351, 615-329-8641

Public Library of Nashville, and Davidson County, Eight Ave. North at Union, Nashville 37203, 615-862-5843

Texas

Abilene Christian University, Margaret & Herman Brown Lib., Box 8177/Documents, 1600 Campus Court, Abilene 79699-8177, 915-674-2477

Arlington Public Library, 101 East Abram St., Arlington 76010, 817-459-6905

University of Texas at Arlington Library, Government Publications/Maps, 701 South Cooper St., Arlington 76019, 817-273-3000(4968)

University of Texas at Austin, Edie and Lew Wasserman, Public Affairs Library, Sid Richardson Hall 3.243, Austin 78712-1282, 512-471-4486

University of Texas at Austin, General Libraries/Documents, PCL 2.402, Austin 78713, 512-471-5944

University of Texas at Austin, Tarlton Law Library, Documents Collection, 727 East 26th St., Austin 78705, 512-471-7251(7250)

Texas State Library, United States Documents, 1201 Brazos, Austin 78711, 512-463-5455

Lamar University, Mary & John Gray Library, Government Document Dept., Box 10021—Lamar University Station, 4400 Martin Luther King Parkway, Beaumont 77710, 409-880-8129

Howard Payne University, Walker Memorial Library, Brownwood 76801, 915-643-7813

West Texas State University, Cornette Library/Documents, P.O. Box 748 W.T. Station, Second Ave. & 26th St., Canyon 79016, 806-656-2204

Texas Agricultural and Mechanical University, The Sterling Evans Library, Documents Division, College Station 77843, 409-845-2551

East Texas State University, James Giliam Gee Library, Government Documents, East Texas Station, Commerce 75428, 214-886-5726

Corpus Christi State University Library, 6300 Ocean Dr., Corpus Christi 78412, 512-994-2341

Southern Methodist University, Fondren Library, Documents Dept., Dallas 75275, 214-692-2331

Dallas Public Library, Government Publications Division, 1515 Young St., Dallas 75201, 214-670-1452

Dallas Baptist University, Vance Memorial Library, Learning Center, 3000 Mount Creek Parkway, Dallas 75211-9299, 214-333-5211

North Texas State University Libraries, P.O. Box 5188, Highland St., Denton 76203, 817-565-2870

University of Texas - Pan American Library, Government Documents Division, 1201 West University Dr., Edinburg 78539-2999, 512-381-3304

El Paso Public Library, Documents/Genealogy Section, 501 North Oregon St., El Paso 79901, 915-543-5475

University of Texas at El Paso Library, Documents and Maps Dept., El Paso 79968-0582, 915-747-5685

Fort Worth Public Library, 300 Taylor St., Fort Worth 76102, 817-870-7721

Texas Christian University, Mary Couts Burnett Library, Box 32904, Fort Worth 76129, 817-921-7669

Nicholson Memorial Library System, 625 Austin St., Garland 75040-6365, 214-205-2502

University of Houston, Clear Lake, Alfred R. Neumann, 2700 Bay Area Blvd., Houston 77058, 713-283-3910

Rice University, Fondren Library, Government Publications & Special Resources, 6100 South Main St., Houston 77251-1892, 713-523-2417

Houston Public Library, Government Documents Section, 500 McKinney Ave., Houston 77002, 713-247-1622

University of Houston, M.D. Anderson Library, Documents Division, 4800 Calhoun Rd., Houston 77004, 713-749-1163

University of Houston, School of Law Library, Documents Dept., 4800 Calhoun Blvd., Houston 77204-6390, 713-749-3191(3106)

North Harris County College, South Campus, Learning Resources Center, 2700 W.W. Thorne Dr., Houston 77073, 713-443-5491

Sam Houston State University, Newton Gresham Library, Collection Development Dept., Huntsville 77341, 409-294-1629

Irving Public Library System, 801 West Irving Blvd., Irving 75060, 214-721-2606

Texas Arts and Industries University, James C. Jernigan Library, Government Documents, Kingsville 78363, 512-595-2918

Laredo Jr. College, Harold R. Yeary Library, Government Documents Section, West End Washington St., Laredo 78040-4395, 512-721-5280

Texas Tech University Libraries, Documents Dept., Lubbock 79409-0002, 806-742-2236

Stephen F. Austin State University, Steen Library, Documents Dept., Box 13055 SFA Station, Nacogdoches 75962, 409-568-1574

University of Texas at Dallas, McDermott Library, Government Documents, P.O. Box 830643, Campbell & Floyd, Richardson 75083-0643, 214-690-2627

St. Mary's University, Academic Library, One Camino Santa Maria, San Antonio 78284, 512-436-3441

Trinity University, Elizabeth Coates Maddux Lib., Documents Dept., 715 Stadium Dr., San Antonio 78284, 512-736-7430

San Antonio College Library, 1001 Howard St., San Antonio 78284, 512-733-2598

University of Texas at San Antonio Library, Government Documents Dept., 6900 N Loop 1604 W, San Antonio 78285-0671, 512-691-4583

Southwest Texas State University Library, Documents Dept., J.C. Kellam Bldg., San Marcos 78666-4604, 512-245-3686

Texas Lutheran College, Blumberg Memorial Library, 1000 West Court St., Seguin 78155, 512-372-8100

Austin College, Gladys Abell Library Center, 900 North Grand, Sherman 75090, 214-813-2536

University of Houston-Victoria/Victoria Coll. Library, 2602 North Ben Jordan, Victoria 77901, 512-576-3151(283)

Baylor University, Moody Memorial Library, Government Documents Dept., B. U. Box 7148, Waco 76798-7148, 817-755-2157(6735)

Midwestern State University, Moffett Library, 3400 Taft St., Wichita Falls 76308-2099, 817-692-6611(4177)

Utah

Utah State University, Merrill Library and Learning, Resources Center, UMC-30, Documents Dept., Logan 84322-3000, 801-750-2683

Weber State College, Stewart Library, Documents Dept., # 2901, 3750 Harrison Blvd., Ogden 84408-2901, 801-626-7187

Brigham Young University, Harold B. Lee Library, Documents and Maps Dept., 1356 HBLL, Provo 84602, 801-378-4090

University of Utah, Marriott Library, Documents Division, Salt Lake City 84112, 801-581-8394

| | |
|---|---|
| Vermont | University of Vermont, Bailey/Howe Library, Documents/Maps Dept., Burlington 05405, 802-656-2503 |
| | Castleton State College, Calvin Coolidge Library, Castleton 05735, 802-468-5611(361) |
| | Lyndon State College, Samuel Reed Hall Library, Lyndonville 05851, 802-626-9371(151) |
| | Middlebury College, Egbert Starr Library, Middlebury 05753, 802-388-3711(5493) |
| Virginia | George Mason University, School of Law Library, 3401 North Fairfax Dr., Arlington 22201, 703-841-7131 |
| | U.S. Patent and Trademark Office, Scientific Technology Library, Crystal Mall #1 1E11, 2021 Jefferson Davis Highway, Arlington 22202, 703-308-4472 |
| | Virginia Polytechnic Institute and State Univ., Carol M. Newman Library, Documents/Special Formats Dept., Blacksburg 24061-0434, 703-231-5257 |
| | University of Virginia, Alderman Library, Government Documents, Charlottesville 22903-249, 804-924-3133 |
| | University of Virginia, Arthur J. Morris Law Library, Documents Dept., Charlottesville 22901, 804-924-3504 |
| | Emory and Henry College, Kelly Library, Emory 24327, 703-944-4121(3209) |
| | George Mason University, Fenwick Library, Government Documents, 4400 University Dr., Fairfax 22030, 703-323-2877 |
| | Mary Washington College, The Library, Fredericksburg 22401-5358, 703-899-4586 |
| | Hampton University, Collis P. Huntington Memorial Library, East Queens St., Hampton 23668, 804-727-5561 |
| | James Madison University, Carrier Library, Harrisonburg 22807, 703-568-6929 |
| | Virginia Military Institute, J.T.L. Preston Library, Lexington 24450, 703-464-7296 |
| | Norfolk Public Library System, 301 East City Hall Ave., Norfolk 23510, 804-441-2579 |

| | |
|---|---|
| | U.S. Armed Forces Staff College Library, Documents Dept., 7800 Hampton Blvd., Norfolk 23511-6097, 804-444-5155 |
| | Old Dominion University Library, Government Publications Dept., Hampton Blvd., Norfolk 23529-0256, 804-683-4168 |
| | Virginia State University, Johnston Memorial Library, Documents Dept., Petersburg 23803, 804-524-5582 |
| | University of Richmond, Boatwright Memorial Library, Government Publications, Richmond 23173, 804-289-8851 |
| | Virginia Commonwealth University, James Branch Cabell Library, Documents Service Box 2033, 901 Park Ave., Richmond 23284-2033, 804-367-1104 |
| | Virginia State Law Library, Supreme Court Bldg., 100 North Ninth St., Richmond 23219, 804-786-2075 |
| | College of William and Mary, Earl Gregg Swem Library, Documents Dept., Williamsburg 23185, 804-221-3065 |
| Washington | King County Library System, Bellevue Public Library, 11501 Main St., Bellevue 98004, 206-455-6632 |
| | Western Washington University, Mable Zoe Wilson Library, Documents Division, 516 High St., Bellingham 98225, 206-676-3075 |
| | Eastern Washington University, John F. Kennedy Library, Documents Dept., Mail Stop No. 84, Cheney 99004, 509-359-7894 |
| | Highline Community College Library, 25-1D, 2400 South 240th St., Des Moines 98198-9800, 206-878-3710(288) |
| | Central Washington University Library, Documents Dept., Walnut 14th Ave., Ellensburg 98926, 509-963-1542 |
| | Everett Public Library, 2702 Hoyt Ave., Everett 98201-3556, 206-259-8010 |
| | Washington State Library, Government Publications, 16th & Water, Olympia 98504-2478, 206-753-4027 |
| | North Olympic Library System, Port Angeles Branch, Documents Division, 207 South Lincoln, Port Angeles 98362, 206-457-4464 |

Washington State University, Holland Library TSD/Documents, Documents Processing Section, Pullman 99164-5610, 509-335-2580

Seattle Public Library, Documents Unit, 1000 4th Ave., Seattle 98104, 206-386-4177

University of Washington, Suzzallo Library, Government Publications Division MS FM-25, Seattle 98195, 206-543-4664

Spokane Public Library, Documents Dept., West 906 Main Ave., Spokane 99201-0976, 509-838-3361(736)

Gonzaga University, School of Law Library, East 600 Sharp, Spokane 99220, 509-328-4220(3754)

University of Puget Sound, Collins Memorial Library, Documents Dept., 1500 North Warner St., Tacoma 98416, 206-756-3229

Tacoma Public Library, Documents Division, 1102 Tacoma Ave. South, Tacoma 98402, 206-591-5666

Whitman College, Penrose Memorial Library, 345 Boyer St., Walla Walla 99362, 509-527-5909

West Virginia

Bluefield State College, Hardway Library, Documents Dept., 219 Rock St., Bluefield 24701, 304-327-4053

Kanawha County Public Library, 123 Capitol St., Charleston 25301, 304-343-4646(26)

West Virginia Library Commission, Reference Library, Science and Cultural Center, Charleston 25305, 304-348-2045(314)

Marshall University, James E. Morrow Library, Government Documents Dept., 400 Halo Greer Blvd., Huntington 25755, 304-696-2342

West Virginia Institute of Technology, Vining Library, Fayette Pike, Montgomery 25136, 304-442-3734

West Virginia University Library, Government Documents Section, P.O. Box 6069, Morgantown 26506-6069, 304-293-3640

Sheperd College, Ruth Scarborough Library, Documents Dept., Sheperdstown 25443, 304-876-2511(412)

Wisconsin

Lawrence University, Seeley G. Mudd Library, Government Documents, Appleton 54912, 414-735-6755

Beloit College, Colonel Robert H. Morse Library, Serials Documents Dept., 731 College St., Beloit 53511, 608-365-2486

University of Wisconsin at Eau Claire, William D. McIntyre Library, P.O. Box 5010, Park and Garfield St., Eau Claire 54702-4004, 715-836-3247

University of Wisconsin at Green Bay, Library Learning Center, Government Publications Dept., 2420 Nicolet Dr., Green Bay 54301-7001, 414-465-2547

University of Wisconsin at La Crosse, Murphy Library, Documents Dept., 1631 Pine St., La Crosse 54601, 608-785-8513

Madison Public Library, 210 West Mifflin St., Madison 53703, 608-266-6310

State Historical Society of Wisconsin Library, Government Publication Section, 816 State St., Madison 53706, 608-262-2781

University of Wisconsin at Madison, Memorial Library, Documents Dept., 728 State St., Madison 53706, 608-262-9852

Milwaukee Public Library, Documents Division, 814 West Wisconsin Ave., Milwaukee 53233, 414-278-2167

University of Wisconsin at Milwaukee, Golda Meir Library, Documents Dept., 2311 East Hartford, Milwaukee 53201, 414-229-4659

Marquette University, Law Library, 1103 West Wisconsin Ave., Milwaukee 53233, 414-288-5352

Alverno College Library/Media Center, 3401 South 39th St., Milwaukee 53215, 414-382-6089

University of Wisconsin at Oshkosh, Forrest R. Polk Memorial Lib., Government Documents, 800 Algoma Blvd., Oshkosh 54901, 414-424-3347(1000)

University of Wisconsin at Plattevillee, Karrmann Library, Government Publications and Maps, One University Plaza, Platteville 53818, 608-342-1758

| | |
|---|---|
| | Ripon College Library, Government Documents, Box 248, 300 Seward St., Ripon 54971, 414-748-8330 |
| | University of Wisconsin at River Falls, Chalmer Davee Library, Government Documents Rm., River Falls 54022, 715-425-3874 |
| | University of Wisconsin at Stevens Point, Learning Resources Center, Documents Dept., Stevens Point 54481, 715-346-3726 |
| | University of Wisconsin at Superior, Jim Dan Hill Library, Government Documents, 1800 Grand Ave., Superior 54880, 715-394-8512 |
| | Marathon County Public Library, 400 First St., Wausau 54401, 715-847-5544 |
| | University of Wisconsin at Whitewater, Library and Learning Resources, Governments and Research Collections, 800 West Main St., Whitewater 53190, 414-472-5521 |
| Wyoming | Natrona County Public Library, 307 East 2nd St., Casper 82601, 307-237-4935 |
| | Department of Administration and Information, State Library, 2101 Capitol Ave., Cheyenne 82002-0650, 307-777-5919 |
| | University of Wyoming, Coe Library, Documents Division, P.O. Box 3334, Laramie 82071, 307-766-5532 |

## U.S. GOVERNMENT DEPOSITORY LIBRARIES

The U.S. government is a major publisher of information, and every library in the United States can select to receive any of its publications. In early 1993, there were over 1,350 U.S. Government Depository Libraries in the United States.

Each state has one Regional Depository Library, usually in or near the state capitol. In addition, there is usually at least one selective depository (the library selects the items for its collection) in each congressional district. Many districts have more than one selective depository.

Contact your local public library and ask for the location of the closest depository. Each depository carries those publications it selects, rather than all available publications. Each depository library *must* participate in an interlibrary loan program. If your organization needs a particular document, your local library can obtain it on loan from one of the 1,350 depository libraries in the United States.

## U.S. GOVERNMENT BOOKSTORES

The U.S. government operates bookstores in 23 cities in the United States. These bookstores stock the more popular government publications, those in regular or seasonal demand by the public. (The "Plum" book—the directory of federal jobs subject to appointment by the new administration—was a hot item soon after November 3, 1992.) Every publication of the U.S. government can be purchased through these bookstores. They will accept telephone orders, with payment by mail. Location of the bookstores, by state:

| *State* | *Location* |
|---|---|
| Alabama | O'Neill Bldg., 2021 Third Ave., North, Birmingham 35203, 205-731-1056 |
| California | Arco Plaza, 505 South Flower St., C Level, Los Angeles 90071, 213-239-9844 |
| | Federal Bldg., Rm. 1023, 450 Golden Gate Ave., San Francisco 94102, 415-252-5334 |
| Colorado | Federal Bldg., Rm. 117, 1961 Stout St., Denver 80294, 303-884-3964 |
| | Norwest Banks Bldg., 201 West 8th St., Pueblo 81003, 719-544-3142 |
| District of Columbia | U.S. Government Printing Office, 710 N. Capitol St., NW, Washington 20401, 202-512-0132 |
| | 1510 H St., NW, Washington 20005, 202-653-5075 |
| Florida | 100 West Bay St., Suite 100, Jacksonville 32202, 904-353-0569 |
| Georgia | First Union Plaza, 999 Peachtree St., NE, Suite 120, Atlanta 30309-3964, 404-347-1900 |
| Illinois | One Congress Center, 401 South State St., Suite 124, Chicago 60605, 312-353-5133 |
| Maryland | U.S. Government Printing Office, Warehouse Sales Outlet, 8660 Cherry Lane, Laurel 20707, 301-953-7974/792-0262 (will accept credit card orders and send by USPS or UPS) |
| Massachusetts | Thomas P. O'Neill Bldg., 10 Causeway St., Rm. 169, Boston 02222, 617-720-4180 |
| Michigan | Federal Bldg., Rm. 160, 477 Michigan Ave., Detroit 48226, 313-226-7816 |
| Missouri | 120 Bannister Mall, 5600 E. Bannister Rd., Kansas City 64137, 816-765-2256 |

| *State* | *Location* |
|---|---|
| New York | Federal Bldg., Rm. 110, 26 Federal Plaza, New York 10278, 212-264-3825 |
| Ohio | Federal Bldg., Rm. 1653, 1240 E. 9th St., Cleveland 44199, 216-522-4922 |
| | Federal Bldg., Rm. 207, 200 North High St., Columbus 43215, 614-469-6956 |
| Oregon | 1305 SW First Ave., Portland 97201-5801, 503-221-6217 |
| Pennsylvania | Robert Morris Bldg., 100 N. 17th St., Philadelphia 19103, 215-597-0677 |
| | Federal Bldg., Rm. 118, 1000 Liberty Ave., Pittsburgh 15222, 412-644-2721 |
| Texas | Federal Bldg., Rm. IC50, 1100 Commerce St., Dallas 75242, 214-767-0076 |
| | Texas Crude Bldg., Suite 120, 801 Travis St., Houston 77002, 713-228-1187 |
| Washington | Federal Bldg., Rm. 194, 915 Second Ave., Seattle 98174, 206-553-4270 |
| Wisconsin | Federal Bldg., Rm. 190, 517 E. Wisconsin Ave., Milwaukee 53202, 414-297-1304 |

# 5

# CHAMBERS OF COMMERCE AND CONSULATES

## FOREIGN CHAMBERS OF COMMERCE IN THE UNITED STATES

Each of the 12 EC member states are represented by one or more chambers of commerce in the United States. While these chambers do not necessarily receive direct home-government funding, they are closely associated with the home-country business community and the trade promotion activities of the home government.

In each instance, the chamber is a meeting ground for people and businesses with common interests in a particular country. These interests can be social, political, or business. The activities of the chambers are commercial in nature, as their mission is to foster an improved trade and investment environment between the home-country and the United States.

Large chamber organizations, such as the French American Chamber, may have publications similar to those produced by our American Chambers of Commerce abroad (see Part Two). Their publications support the home-country businessperson and company active in the United States.

| *Country* / *State* | *Location* |
|---|---|
| Belgium | Belgian American Chamber of Commerce |
| New York | Empire State Bldg., Suite 1322, 350 Fifth Ave., New York 10118 |
| Denmark | Danish American Chamber of Commerce |
| California | 419 Main St., # 208, Huntington Beach 92648 |
| | 11469 Baird Ave., Northridge 91326 |
| | 36 Pacheco Creek Dr., Novato 94949 |
| | 23 Orinda Way, Orinda 94563 |

| *Country*<br>*State* | *Location* |
|---|---|
| | 1640 Stanley Dollar Dr., # 1A, Walnut Creek 94595 |
| District of Columbia | 2100 M St., NW, Suite 305, Washington 20037 |
| Illinois | 1801 Marble Dr., Evanston 60201 |
| New York | 825 Third Ave., 32nd Fl., New York 10022 |
| Oregon | 395 N. State St., Lake Oswego 97034 |
| Washington | 1300 Tower Bldg., Seattle 98101 |
| European Community | |
| District of Columbia | European American Chamber in Washington, 801 Pennsylvania Ave. NW, Suite 950, Washington 20004 |
| New York | European American Chamber of Commerce, 520 Madison Ave., New York 10022 |
| France | French American Chamber of Commerce in the United States |
| California | 6380 Wilshire Blvd., Suite 1608, Los Angeles 90048 |
| | 425 Bush St., Suite 401, San Francisco 94108 |
| District of Columbia | 1129 20th St., NW, Suite 710, Washington 20036 |
| Florida | 141 Sevillia Ave., Coral Gables 33134 |
| Georgia | 999 Peachtree St., NE, Suite 2095, Atlanta 30309 |
| Illinois | 55 E. Monroe St., Suite 3418, Chicago 60603 |
| Louisiana | 2938 World Trade Center, 2 Canal St., New Orleans 70130 |
| Massachusetts | 15 Court Square, Suite 320, Boston 02108 |
| Michigan | 535 Griswold, Suite 1000, Detroit 48226 |
| Minnesota | 904 Forshay Tower, 821 Marquette, Minneapolis 55402 |
| New York | 509 Madison, Suite 1900, New York 10022 |
| Pennsylvania | 4000 Bell Atlantic Tower, 1717 Arch St., Philadelphia 19103-2713 |
| | 435 Sixth Ave., Pittsburgh 15219 |
| Texas | 3838 Oak Lawn Ave., 1430 Two Turtle Creek Village, Dallas 75219-4515 |
| | 2727 Kirby, Suite 501, Houston 77098-1201 |

| *Country*<br>*State* | *Location* |
|---|---|
| Washington | 400 East Pine St., Suite 210, Seattle 98122 |
| Germany | German-American Chamber of Commerce |
| California | 3250 Wilshire Blvd., Suite 2212, Los Angeles 90010 |
| | 465 California St., San Francisco 94104 |
| Georgia | 3475 Lenox Rd., NE, Suite 620, Atlanta 30326 |
| Illinois | 77 East Monroe St., Chicago 60603 |
| New York | 40 West 57th St., 31st Fl., New York 10019-4094 |
| Texas | 5555 San Felipe, Suite 1030, Houston 77056 |
| Greece | |
| New York | Hellenic American Chamber of Commerce, 960 Avenue of the Americas, Suite 1204, New York 10001 |
| Ireland | Ireland Chamber of Commerce in the United States, Inc. |
| | The ICCUSA offers a fax-based Ireland Info Hotline, 203-877-8131, an information retrieval system for information on Ireland. |
| Connecticut | 1305 Post Rd., Suite 305, Fairfield 06430 |
| Massachusetts | P.O. Box 1335, Marshfield 02050 |
| Missouri | 8182 Maryland Ave., St. Louis 63102 |
| New York | 551 Madison Ave., 11th Fl., New York 10022 |
| Italy | Italy America Chamber of Commerce |
| California | 11520 San Vicente Blvd., Suite 101, Los Angeles 90049 |
| Florida | 80 SW 8th St., Suite 2047, Miami 33130 |
| New York | 350 Fifth Ave., Suite 3015, New York 10118 |
| Pennsylvania | 2400 Eleven Penn Center, Philadelphia 19103-2962 |
| | 200 First Ave., 4th Fl., Pittsburgh 15222 |
| Luxembourg | |
| New York | Luxembourg-American Chamber of Commerce, 350 Fifth Ave., Suite 1322, New York 10118 |
| Netherlands | Netherlands Chamber of Commerce in the U.S. |
| Georgia | 233 Peachtree St., NE, Suite 404, Atlanta 30303 |
| Illinois | 303 E. Wacker Dr., Suite 412, Chicago 60601 |
| New York | 1 Rockefeller Plaza, 11th Fl., New York 10020 |

| *Country* *State* | *Location* |
|---|---|
| Portugal | |
| California | Portuguese Chamber of Commerce of Santa Clara Valley, 1115 E. Santa Clara St., San Jose 95116 |
| New York | Portugal-U.S. Chamber of Commerce, 590 Fifth Ave., New York 10036 |
| Spain | Spanish-U.S. Chamber of Commerce |
| Florida | 2655 Lejeune Rd., Suite 1108, Coral Gables 33134 |
| New York | 350 Fifth Ave., Suite 3514, New York 10118 |
| United Kingdom | British American Chamber of Commerce |
| California | 3991 MacArthur Blvd., Suite 300, Newport Beach 92660 |
| | 41 Sutter St., Suite 303, San Francisco 94111 |
| | 1640 Fifth Ave., Suite 203, Santa Monica 90401 |
| Colorado | British American Business Association, 3000 Youngfield St., Suite 370, Lakewood 80215 |
| District of Columbia | British American Business Association, P.O. Box 17482, Washington 20041 |
| Florida | 2655 LeJeune Rd., Suite 500, Coral Gables 33134 |
| | 515 Bay St., Tampa 33606 |
| Georgia | British American Business Group, 1199 Euclid Ave., Atlanta 30307 |
| Illinois | 303 E. Wacker Dr., Suite 2800, Chicago 60601 |
| Massachusetts | British American Business Association, Lewis Wharf, Suite 523, Boston 02110 |
| New York | 52 Vanderbilt Ave., 20th Fl., New York 10017 |
| Pennsylvania | 1234 Market St., Suite 1800, Philadelphia 19107-3718 |
| Texas | British American Commerce Association, P.O. Box 225628, Dallas 75222 |
| | British American Business Association, 601 Jefferson, Suite 320, Houston 77002 |

## FOREIGN INFORMATION AND TRADE OFFICES

Eleven of the 12 EC member states (the exception is Denmark) maintain one or more trade or information offices in the United States. These offices are concentrated in New York, California, and Illinois.

Information and trade offices exist to promote investment in their home country, to obtain market intelligence for use by home-country exporters and investors, to serve the needs of tourism groups (in support of the tourism functions of the consular offices), and lastly to provide information to U.S. firms that seek to export to the home country.

Each of these offices usually maintains a library of information about the home country. These libraries may include trade resource publications, such as trade show directories, trade association memberships, industry groups, and other market related information. Other libraries may be limited to cultural and social information.

If an inquiry regarding export potential is rebuffed or turned away, a personal visit to the trade or information office will be worthwhile. Export market information can be developed by pursuing a line of inquiry toward potential joint venture partners in the home country. This avenue of research is a fit with the responsibilities of the staff of each of these offices. They are paid to develop opportunities for home-country firms and to develop investment in the home country. Research to support a joint venture (of any type) is in most instances identical to the research one would undertake to investigate market potential generally.

| *Country*<br>*State* | *Organization and Location* |
|---|---|
| Belgium | |
| Florida | Belgian Trade Office, 4100 N. Miami Ave., Miami 33127 |
| Denmark | |
| Colorado | Danish Trade Office, 1777 South Harrison St., Denver 80210 |
| Florida | Danish Trade Office, 15450 New Barn Rd., Suite 303, Miami Lakes 33014-2169 |
| Georgia | Danish Trade Office, 229 Peachtree St., NW, Suite 1008, Atlanta 30303 |
| Washington | Danish Trade Office, 1402 Third Ave., Suite 220, Seattle 98101 |
| France | |
| California | French Trade Commission, 1801 Avenue of the Stars, Suite 925, Los Angeles 90067 |
| | French Trade Commission, 88 Kearney St., Suite 510, San Francisco 94108 |
| District of Columbia | French Trade Commission, 4101 Reservoir Rd., NW, Washington 20007 |
| Florida | French Trade Commission, 1 Biscayne Tower, 2 S. Biscayne Blvd., Suite 1710, Miami 33131 |

| *Country* *State* | *Location* |
|---|---|
| Georgia | French Trade Commission, 285 Peachtree Center Ave., Suite 2801, Atlanta 30303 |
| Illinois | French Trade Commission, 1 E. Wacker Dr., Suite 3730, Chicago 60601 |
| Massachusetts | French Trade Commission, 15 Court Square, Suite 240, Boston 02108 |
| Michigan | French Trade Commission, 100 Renaissance Center, Suite 1670, Detroit 48243 |
| New York | Invest in France Agency, 610 Fifth Ave., Suite 301, New York 10020 |
| | French Trade Commission, 810 Seventy Ave., 38th Fl., New York 10019 |
| Texas | French Trade Commission, 2727 Allen Parkway, Suite 925, Houston 77019 |
| Germany | |
| District of Columbia | Representative for German Industry and Trade, 1 Farragut Square S., Suite 600, Washington 20006 |
| New York | German Information Center, 950 Third Ave., New York 10022 |
| Greece | |
| New York | Greek Trade Office, 150 E. 58th St., Suite 1701, New York 10022 |
| Ireland | |
| California | Industrial Development Authority (Ireland), 50 W. San Fernando St., Suite 830, San Jose 95113 |
| | 1821 Wilshire Blvd., Suite 317, Santa Monica 90403 |
| Georgia | Industrial Development Authority (Ireland), P.O. Box 11727, Atlanta 30335 |
| Illinois | Industrial Development Authority (Ireland), 75 E. Wacker Dr., Suite 600, Chicago 60601 |
| | Irish Export Board, 75 E. Wacker Dr., Suite 600, Chicago 60601 |
| Massachusetts | Industrial Development Authority (Ireland), 2 Center Plaza, Suite 825, Boston 02108 |
| New York | Industrial Development Authority (Ireland), 140 E. 45th St., 41st Fl., New York 10017 |

| *Country* *State* | *Location* |
|---|---|
| | Irish Export Board, 880 Third Ave., Eighth Fl., New York 10022 |
| | Ireland-United States Council for Commerce and Industry, 460 Park Ave., 22nd Fl., New York 10022 |
| Italy | |
| California | Italian Trade Commission, 1801 Avenue of the Stars, Suite 700, Los Angeles 90067 |
| Georgia | Italian Trade Commission, 233 Peachtree St., NE, Atlanta 30303 |
| Illinois | Italian Trade Commission, 401 N. Michigan Ave., Suite 3030, Chicago 60611 |
| New York | Italian Trade Commission, Italian Trade Center, 499 Park Ave., New York 10022 |
| | Officio Italiano Cambi, One Wall St., Rm. 2918, New York 10005 |
| Texas | Italian Trade Commission, 3050 Post Oak Blvd., Suite 1090, Houston 77056 |
| Luxembourg | |
| New York | Luxembourg Board of Economic Development, 801 Second Ave., New York 10017 |
| Netherlands | Netherlands Foreign Investment Agency |
| California | 901 Mariner's Island Blvd., San Mateo 94404 |
| | 11755 Wilshire Blvd., Los Angeles 90025 |
| New York | 1 Rockefeller Plaza, New York 10020 |
| Portugal | |
| District of Columbia | Portuguese Trade Commission, 1900 L St. NW, Suite 401, Washington 20006 |
| New York | Portuguese Trade Commission, 590 Fifth Ave., 3rd Fl., New York 10036 |
| | Portuguese National Tourism Office, 548 Fifth Ave., New York 10036 |
| Spain | Spanish Commercial Office |
| California | 350 S. Figueroa St., Suite 946, Los Angeles 90071 |
| District of Columbia | 2258 Massachusetts, NW, Washington 20008 |
| Florida | 2655 Lejeune Rd., Suite 1114, Coral Gables 33134 |
| Illinois | 500 N. Michigan Ave., Rm. 1500, Chicago 60611 |

| *Country* *State* | *Location* |
|---|---|
| New York | 405 Lexington Ave., 44th Fl., New York 10174 |
| Puerto Rico | P.O. Box 3179, Hato Rey 00919 |
| United Kingdom | |
| New York | British Trade and Investment, 845 Third Ave., 11th Fl., New York 10022 |
| | British Information Services, 845 Third Ave., 9th Fl., New York 10022 |
| Texas | British American Business Association, 601 Jefferson St., Suite 320, Houston 77002 |
| | British Consulate Trade Mission, 813 Stemmons Tower West, 2730 Stemmons Freeway, Dallas 75207 |

## FOREIGN CONSULATES IN THE UNITED STATES

Each EC state has a number of government offices in the United States in addition to its Embassy in Washington DC. The consular offices provide an access point for information on the country, its culture, geographic and political environment, and to some extent its business environment.

The activities of each consular office vary but usually include tourism services, immigration (arrange entry into the country), visa services, and a range of business services generally associated with exports from the country or assistance with direct investments into the country. Some of these services closely parallel the services of the foreign trade and information offices listed in the previous section of this chapter.

Each consular office is usually involved in the business community of the region. Consular officers (official or honorary) participate in business associations, world trade clubs or associations, luncheon groups, and cultural associations. These officials are also active in forming and supporting sister city associations in their respective regions.

Consular offices are listed alphabetically by country by state. If a consular office of your target country is not located in your city or region, contact the closest office: each is assigned a territory that can encompass your city. Key to letters:

C = Consulate
CA = Consular Agency
CG = Consulate General
E = Embassy
HC = Honorary Consulate
HVC = Honorary Vice Consulate
VC = Vice Consulate

| *State* | *Country* | *Type* | *Address* |
|---|---|---|---|
| Alabama | Denmark | C | 1350 Dauphin St., P.O. Box 15, Mobile 36601 |
| | France | HC | 31 Inverness Center Parkway, Suite 100, Birmingham 35242 |
| | Germany | HC | SouthTrust Bank Bldg., Suite 1200, P.O. Box 2345, Mobile 36652 |
| | Italy | C | 3537 Bermuda Dr., Birmingham 35210 |
| | | VC | 4160 E. Shan Dr., Mobile 36693 |
| Alaska | Belgium | HC | 1031 W. 4th Ave., Suite 400, P.O. Box 107502, Anchorage 99510 |
| | Denmark | HC | 601 W. Fifth Ave., Suite 700, Anchorage 99501 |
| | Germany | HC | 425 G. St., Suite 650, Anchorage 99501 |
| | Italy | HC | 12301 Johns Rd., No. 3, Anchorage 99515 |
| Arizona | Belgium | HC | 8300 N. Hayden Rd., Suite 205, Scottsdale (Phoenix) 85258 |
| | Denmark | C | 241 N. Central Ave., P.O. Box 71, Phoenix 85001 |
| | France | HC | 8610 E. Hazelwood, Scottsdale (Phoenix) 85251 |
| | Italy | VC | 2901 N. Central Ave., Phoenix 85012 |
| California | Belgium | CG | 6100 Wilshire Blvd., Suite 1200, Los Angeles 90048 |
| | | HC | 1 Maritime Plaza, Suite 1300, San Francisco 94111 |
| | Denmark | CG | 3440 Wilshire Blvd., Suite 904, Los Angeles 90010 |
| | France | CG | 10990 Wilshire Blvd., Suite 300, Los Angeles 90024 |
| | | CG | 540 Bush St., San Francisco 94108 |

| State | Country | Type | Address |
|---|---|---|---|
| | Germany | CG | 6222 Wilshire Blvd., Suite 500, Los Angeles 90048 |
| | | HC | 6868 Nancy Ridge Dr., Suite 1, San Diego 92121 |
| | | CG | 1960 Jackson St., San Francisco 94108 |
| | Greece | CG | 3255 Wilshire Blvd., Los Angeles 90012 |
| | | CG | 2441 Gough St., San Francisco 94123 |
| | Ireland | CG | 655 Montgomery St., Suite 930, San Francisco 94111 |
| | Italy | VC | 1620 E. Brundage Lane, P.O. Box 1340, Bakersfield 93302 |
| | | VC | 2409 Merced St., Suite 3, Fresno 93721 |
| | | CG | 12400 Wilshire Blvd., Suite 300, Los Angeles 90025 |
| | | C | 3334 Webster St., Oakland 94609 |
| | | VC | 5347 Folsom Blvd., Sacramento 95819 |
| | | HC | 751 Seventh St., San Diego 92101 |
| | | CG | 2590 Webster St., San Francisco 94115 |
| | | C | 777 N. First St., Suite 600-D, San Jose 95112 |
| | | CA | P.O. Box 719, Santa Cruz 95061 |
| | Netherlands | CG | 3460 Wilshire Blvd., Suite 509, Los Angeles 90010 |
| | | C | 1 Maritime Plaza, Fifth Fl., San Francisco 94108 |
| | Luxembourg | HC | 516 Avondale Ave., Los Angeles 90049 |
| | | CG | 1 Sansome St., Suite 830, San Francisco 94104 |

| *State* | *Country* | *Type* | *Address* |
|---|---|---|---|
| | Portugal | C | 1801 Avenue of the Stars, Suite 400, Los Angeles 90067 |
| | | CG | 3298 Washington St., San Francisco 94115 |
| | Spain | CG | 6300 Wilshire Blvd., Suite 1530, Los Angeles 90048 |
| | | CG | 2080 Jefferson St., San Francisco 94123 |
| | United Kingdom | CG | 3701 Wilshire Blvd., Suite 312, Los Angeles 90010 |
| | | CG | 1 Sansome St., Suite 850, San Francisco 94104 |
| Colorado | Denmark | HC | 5353 W. Dartmouth, Suite 508, Denver 80227 |
| | Germany | HC | 350 Indiana St., Suite 400, Golden 80401 |
| | Italy | VC | 8820 W. 84th Ave., Arvada (Denver) 80005 |
| Connecticut | France | HC | Brightwood Rd., Bristol 06010 |
| | Italy | VC | 945 Wethersfield Ave., Hartford 06114 |
| | Portugal | C | 20 E. Main St., Waterbury 06702 |
| Delaware | France | C | 2006 Woodbrook Dr., Westwood Manor, Wilmington 19810 |
| District of Columbia | Belgium | E | 3330 Garfield St., Washington 20008 |
| | Denmark | E | 3200 Whitehaven St., NW, Washington 20008 |
| | France | CG | 4101 Reservoir Rd., NW, Washington 20007 |
| | Germany | E&C | 4645 Reservoir Rd., NW, Washington 20007 |
| | Greece | E | 2211 Massachusetts Ave., NW, Washington 20008 |
| | Ireland | E | 2234 Massachusetts Ave., NW, Washington 20008 |

| *State* | *Country* | *Type* | *Address* |
|---|---|---|---|
| | Italy | C | 1601 Fuller St., NW, Washington 20009 |
| | | E | 3339 Massachusetts Ave., NW, Washington 20008 |
| | Luxembourg | E | 2200 Massachusetts Ave., NW, Washington 20008 |
| | Netherlands | E&C | 4200 Linnean Ave., NW, Washington 20008 |
| | Portugal | CG | 2310 Tracy Place, NW, Washington 20008 |
| | | E | 2125 Kalorama Rd., NW, Washington 20008 |
| | Spain | E&C | 2700 15th St., NW, Washington 20009 |
| | United Kingdom | E&C | 3100 Massachusetts Ave., NW, Washington 20008 |
| Florida | Belgium | HC | 4100 N. Miami Ave., Miami 33127 |
| | Denmark | HC | 2655 Lejeune Rd., Suite 600, Coral Gables 33134 |
| | | HC | 801 E. Washington St., Tampa 33602 |
| | France | CG | 1 Biscayne Tower, Suite 1710, 2 S. Biscayne Blvd., Miami 33131 |
| | | HC | 522 E. Washington St., Orlando 32801 |
| | Germany | HC | 1510 Talleyrand Ave., P.O. Box 3, Jacksonville 32201 |
| | | CG | 100 N. Biscayne Blvd., 22nd Fl., Miami 33132 |
| | | HC | 440 Central Ave., St. Petersburg 33711 |
| | Italy | CA | 4107 NE 17th Terrace, Gainesville 32609 |
| | | CA | 5627 Atlantic Blvd., Suite 4, Jacksonville 32207 |
| | | CG | 2600 SW Third Ave., Suite 765, Miami 33129 |

| *State* | *Country* | *Type* | *Address* |
|---|---|---|---|
| | | CA | 102 Martinique Ave., Tampa 33606 |
| | Luxembourg | HC | 200 S. Biscayne Blvd., Suite 3240, Miami 33131 |
| | Netherlands | HC | 900 University Blvd. N., Suite 500 Jacksonville 32211 |
| | | HC | 2401 SW Coral Way, Suite 103, Miami 33129 |
| | | HC | 5486 Jetport Industrial Blvd., Tampa 33634 |
| | Portugal | HC | 1901 Ponce de Leon Blvd., Coral Gables 33134 |
| | Spain | CG | 151 Sevilla Ave., Second Fl., Coral Gables 33134 |
| Georgia | Belgium | CG | South Tower, Suite 800, 225 Peachtree St., NE, Atlanta 30303 |
| | Denmark | HC | 225 Peachtree St., NE, Suite 201, Atlanta 30303 |
| | France | CG | 285 Peachtree Center Ave., Suite 2800, Atlanta 30303 |
| | Germany | CG | 285 Peachtree Center Ave., Suite 901, Atlanta 30303 |
| | Greece | C | Tower Place, Suite 1670, 3340 Peachtree Rd., NE, Atlanta 30326 |
| | Italy | HVC | 1106 W. Peachtree St., NW, Atlanta 30309 |
| | | HC | 235 Kensington Dr., Savannah 31405 |
| | Netherlands | HC | 133 Peachtree St., NE, Atlanta 30303 |
| | United Kingdom | CG | 225 Peachtree St., NE, Suite 912, Atlanta 30303 |
| Hawaii | Belgium | HC | 700 Bishop St., Suite 400, Honolulu 96734 |
| | Denmark | HC | P.O. Box 88122, Honolulu 96815 |

| *State* | *Country* | *Type* | *Address* |
|---|---|---|---|
| | France | C | 2222 Kalakua Ave., Suite 601, Honolulu 96815 |
| | Germany | HC | 2003 Kalia St., Honolulu 96815 |
| | Italy | VC | 3660 Waialea Ave., Honolulu 96816 |
| | Netherlands | C | 345 Queen St., Suite 600, Honolulu 96813 |
| | Portugal | HC | 700 Bishop St., Suite 1012, Honolulu 96813 |
| Idaho | Italy | C | 2443 S. Mariner Way, Boise 83706 |
| Illinois | Belgium | CG | 333 N. Michigan Ave, Rm. 2000, Chicago 60601 |
| | | HC | 740 18th Ave., Moline 61265 |
| | Denmark | CG | John Hancock Center, Suite 3430, 875 N. Michigan Ave., Chicago 60611 |
| | France | CG | 737 N. Michigan Ave., 20th Fl., Chicago 60611 |
| | Germany | CG | 104 S. Michigan Ave., Chicago 60603 |
| | Greece | CG | 168 N. Michigan Ave., 11th Fl., Chicago 60601 |
| | Ireland | CG | 400 N. Michigan Ave., Suite 911, Chicago 60611 |
| | Italy | CG | 500 N. Michigan Ave., Suite 1850, Chicago 60611 |
| | Netherlands | CG | 303 E. Wacker Dr., Suite 410, Chicago 60601 |
| | Luxembourg | C | 180 N. La Salle, Suite 1400, Chicago 60601 |
| | Portugal | HC | 1955 N. New England Ave., Chicago 60635 |
| | Spain | CG | 180 N. Michigan Ave., Suite 1500, Chicago 60601 |
| | United Kingdom | CG | 33 N. Dearborn St., Ninth Fl., Chicago 60602 |

| *State* | *Country* | *Type* | *Address* |
|---|---|---|---|
| Indiana | Germany | HC | 2314 N. Meridian St., Indianapolis 46208 |
| | Italy | HC | 720 Van Buren St., South Bend 46616 |
| Iowa | Denmark | HC | 222 Equitable Bldg., Des Moines 50309 |
| Kansas | Germany | HC | 8014 State Line, Suite 203, Leawood 66208 |
| | Italy | HC | 206 Brotherhood Bldg., Kansas City 66101 |
| Kentucky | Belgium | HC | 1009 S. Fourth St., Louisville 40203 |
| | Germany | HC | 2700 Citizens Plaza, Louisville 40202 |
| | Italy | CA | 2501 Plantside Dr., P.O. Box 99738, Louisville 40299 |
| Louisiana | Belgium | HC | 1127 Bourbon St., New Orleans 70116 |
| | France | CG | Lykes Center, Suite 2105, 300 Poydras, New Orleans 70130 |
| | | HC | 905 Louisiana Tower, 401 Edwards St., Shreveport 71101 |
| | Greece | C | 2318 World Trade Center, New Orleans 70130 |
| | Italy | CG | 630 Camp St., New Orleans 70130 |
| | Luxembourg | VC | 8012 Oak St., New Orleans 70118 |
| | Netherlands | HC | 643 Magazine St., New Orleans 70130 |
| | Portugal | HC | 509 N. Carrollton Ave. P.O. Box 19385, New Orleans 70179 |
| | Spain | CG | 2102 World Trade Center, 2 Canal St., New Orleans 70130 |

| *State* | *Country* | *Type* | *Address* |
|---|---|---|---|
| | United Kingdom | HC | 321 St. Charles Ave., 10th Fl., New Orleans 70130 |
| Maryland | Belgium | HC | 33 S. Gay St., Baltimore 21202 |
| | Denmark | C | 717 Light St., Suite 400, Baltimore 21230 |
| | Italy | C | 222 N. Charles St., Suite 106, Baltimore 21201 |
| | Netherlands | HC | 250 W. Pratt St., 14th Fl., Baltimore 21201 |
| | Spain | HVC | 8117 Forest Hill Dr., Ellicott City (Baltimore) 21043 |
| Massachusetts | Belgium | HC | 10 Post Office Square, Suite 300, Boston 02109 |
| | Denmark | HC | 419 Boylston St., 8th Fl., Boston 02116 |
| | | HVC | 8 Pond Rd., Gloucester 01930 |
| | France | CG | 3 Commonwealth Ave., Boston 02116 |
| | Germany | CG | 3 Copley Place, Suite 500, Boston 02116 |
| | Greece | C | Statler Office Bldg., 20 Park Plaza, Boston 02116 |
| | Ireland | CG | 535 Boylston St., Boston 02116 |
| | Italy | CG | 100 Boylston St., Boston 02116 |
| | | CA | 100 Acushnet Ave., Springfield 01105 |
| | | CA | 172 Shrewsbury St., Worcester 01605 |
| | Netherlands | C | 6 St. James Ave., Boston 02116 |
| | Portugal | CG | 899 Boylston St., Boston 02115 |
| | Spain | CG | 545 Boylston St., Suite 803, Boston 02116 |

| *State* | *Country* | *Type* | *Address* |
|---|---|---|---|
| | United Kingdom | CG | 600 Atlantic Ave., 25th Fl., Boston 02210 |
| Michigan | Belgium | HC | 4600 Bellevue Ave., Detroit 48207 |
| | Denmark | HC | 4133 N. Woodward Ave., Royal Oak (Detroit) 48072 |
| | Germany | CG | 2100 Edison Plaza, 600 Plaza Dr., Detroit 48226 |
| | Italy | C | 1840 Buhl Bldg., 535 Griswold, Detroit 48226 |
| | Luxembourg | HC | 43043 W. Nine Mile Rd., Northville (Detroit) 48167 |
| | Netherlands | HC | 2000 Town Center, Suite 1200, Southfield (Detroit) 48075 |
| | | C | 3250 28th St., SE, Grand Rapids 49512 |
| | Spain | HVC | 611 Woodward Ave., Detroit 48226 |
| Minnesota | Denmark | HC | 7600 Parklawn Ave., Suite 444, Minneapolis 55435 |
| | Germany | HC | 1910 First Bank Plaza West., 120 S. Sixth St., Minneapolis 55402 |
| | Italy | VC | 24 Circle W., Edina (Minneapolis) 55436 |
| | Netherlands | C | 701 N. Lilac Dr., Minneapolis 55440 |
| Mississippi | Germany | HC | P.O. Box 1200, Jackson 39215 |
| | Italy | CA | P.O. Box 1689, Gulfport 39501 |
| Missouri | Belgium | HC | 1000 Walnut St., Suite 1600, P.O. Box 13127, Kansas City 64199 |
| | | HC | 24 Foreway Dr., St. Louis 63124 |
| | Denmark | C | 1700 W. 12th St., P.O. Box 4046, Kansas City 64101 |

| State | Country | Type | Address |
|---|---|---|---|
| | | C | 6515 Page Blvd., P.O. Box 31, St. Louis 63166 |
| | Germany | HC | 49 Orange Hill Dr., Chesterfield (St. Louis) 63017 |
| | Ireland | HC | 65 Broadview, St. Louis 63105 |
| | Italy | VC | 8803 Gravois Ave., St. Louis 63123 |
| | Luxembourg | CG | 1429 Atlantic St., N., Kansas City 64116 |
| | Netherlands | HC | 1 Ward Parkway, Suite 138, Kansas City 64112 |
| | | C | 562 N. Woodlawn, Kirkwood 63112 |
| | Spain | HC | 1156 W. 103rd St., Suite 215, Kansas City 64114 |
| | | HC | 5715 Manchester Ave., St. Louis 63110 |
| Montana | France | HC | 11 Greenbriar Dr., Missoula 59802 |
| Nebraska | Denmark | HC | 1500 Woodmen Tower, Omaha 68102 |
| Nevada | Germany | HC | 925 E. Desert Inn, Suite C, Las Vegas 89109 |
| | Italy | CA | 302 E. Carson, Suite 830, Las Vegas 89101 |
| | | C | 1810 Stardust St., Reno 89503 |
| New Jersey | Italy | VC | 744 Broad St., Suite 2800, Newark 07102 |
| | | VC | 359 Hamilton Ave., Trenton 08609 |
| | Portugal | C | 1180 Raymond Blvd., Suite 222, Newark 07102 |
| New Mexico | France | HC | P.O. Box B, Santa Fe 87504 |
| | Germany | HC | 5700 Harper Dr., NE, Suite 430, Albuquerque 87109 |
| | Italy | VC | 1712 Old Town Rd., NW, Albuquerque 87104 |

| *State* | *Country* | *Type* | *Address* |
|---|---|---|---|
| New York | Belgium | CG | 50 Rockefeller Plaza, Rm. 1120, New York 10020 |
| | Denmark | CG | 825 Third Ave., 32nd Fl., New York 10022 |
| | France | CG | 934 Fifth Ave., New York 10021 |
| | Germany | HC | 135 Delaware Ave., Buffalo 14202 |
| | | CG | 460 Park Ave., New York 10022 |
| | Greece | CG | 69 E. 79th St., New York 10021 |
| | Ireland | CG | 515 Madison Ave., 18th Fl., New York 10022 |
| | Italy | VC | 1366 Hertel Ave., Buffalo 14216 |
| | | CG | 660 Park Ave., New York 10021 |
| | | HC | 185 Empire Blvd., Rochester 14609 |
| | Luxembourg | CG | 801 Second Ave., 13th Fl., New York 10017 |
| | | HC | 641 Lexington Ave., P.O. Box 5268, New York 10022 |
| | Netherlands | HC | 21 Brantwood Rd., Snyder (Buffalo) 14226 |
| | | CG | 1 Rockefeller Plaza, 11th Fl., New York 10020 |
| | Portugal | CG | 630 Fifth Ave., Rm. 655, New York 10111 |
| | Spain | CG | 150 E. 58th St., 16th Fl., New York 10155 |
| | United Kingdom | CG | 845 Third Ave., Ninth Fl., New York 10022 |
| North Carolina | Germany | HC | 330 Eastover Rd., Charlotte 28207 |
| Ohio | Belgium | HC | 1800 Huntington Bldg., Cleveland 44115 |

| *State* | *Country* | *Type* | *Address* |
|---|---|---|---|
| | Denmark | HC | 3200 National City Center, Cleveland 44114 |
| | France | HC | 901 Lakeside Ave., Cleveland 44114 |
| | | HC | 3300 Indianola Ave., Columbus 42314 |
| | Germany | HC | 425 Walnut St., Suite 2310, Cincinnati 45202 |
| | | HC | 1100 Huntington Bldg., Cleveland 44113 |
| | | HC | 41 S. High St., 34th Fl., Columbus 43215 |
| | Italy | CA | 1569 Chase Ave., P.O. Box 23171, Cincinnati 45223 |
| | | VC | 403 Cleveland Plaza, 1127 Euclid Ave., Cleveland 44115 |
| | Luxembourg | HC | 400 First National Bank Bldg., Middleton 45042 |
| | | HC | 245 Gypsy Lane, Youngstown 44504 |
| | Netherlands | HC | 7350 Young Dr., Cleveland 44146 |
| | Spain | HC | 23 E. 77th St., Cincinnati 45216 |
| | United Kingdom | CG | 1650 Illuminating Bldg., 55 Public Square, Cleveland 44113 |
| Oklahoma | Germany | HC | 4700 Willard, Oklahoma City 73105 |
| | Italy | C | P.O. Box 1805, Stillwater 74074 |
| Oregon | Belgium | HC | Pacific Bldg., 520 SW Yamhill, Portland 97201 |
| | Germany | HC | 200 SW Market St., Suite 1695, Portland 97201 |
| | Netherlands | HC | 4555 N. Channel Ave., Portland 97217 |
| | United Kingdom | HC | 1028 Bank of California Tower, Portland 97205 |

| *State* | *Country* | *Type* | *Address* |
|---|---|---|---|
| Pennsylvania | Denmark | HC | Suite 956, Sixth & Chestnut St., Philadelphia 19106 |
| | France | HC | 3400 Centre Square West, 1500 Market St., Philadelphia 19102 |
| | Germany | HC | 1101 Core States Plaza, Fifth and Market St., Philadelphia 19106 |
| | | HC | 500 Grant St., Pittsburgh 15219 |
| | Italy | CG | 421 Chestnut St., Philadelphia 19106 |
| | | VC | 419 Wood St., Pittsburgh 15222 |
| | Luxembourg | HC | National Steel Center, 20 Stanwix St., Pittsburgh 15222 |
| | Netherlands | C | 3600 Market St., Philadelphia 19104 |
| | Portugal | HC | 2001 Welsh Rd., Philadelphia 19115 |
| | United Kingdom | HC | 226 Walnut St., Philadelphia 19106 |
| Puerto Rico | Belgium | CG | Banco de Ponce Bldg., Suite 713, 1250 Ponce de Leon Ave., Stop 18, Santurce (San Juan) 00907 |
| | Denmark | HC | 400 Commercio St., P.O. Box S-2467, San Juan 00903 |
| | France | CG | Mercantile Plaza, Suite 720, Ponce de Leon Ave., Hato Rey (San Juan) 00918 |
| | Germany | HC | P.O. Box 36746, San Juan 00926 |
| | Italy | VC | Urban Golden Gate, Calle Amatista 93, Guaynabo (San Juan) 00968 |
| | Portugal | HC | 421 San Jovino, Urban Sagrado Corazon, Rio Piedras (San Juan) 00926 |

| *State* | *Country* | *Type* | *Address* |
|---|---|---|---|
| | Spain | CG | Edificio Mercantil Plaza, No. 1101, Hato Rey (San Juan) 00919 |
| Rhode Island | Denmark | HC | 161 S. Main St., Providence 02903 |
| South Carolina | Denmark | HC | 28 Broad St., P.O. Box 993, Charleston 29402 |
| | Germany | HC | 290 Montgomery Dr., Spartanburg 29302 |
| Tennessee | Denmark | HC | Vanderbilt University Hospital, Radiology Dept., Nashville 37232 |
| | Germany | HC | 100 North Main Bldg., Suite 1234, Memphis 38103 |
| | Italy | VC | 296 Washington Ave., Memphis 38103 |
| Texas | Belgium | HC | N. Central Expressway, Suite 2000, Dallas 75206 |
| | | HC | 2929 Allen Parkway, Suite 222, Houston 77019 |
| | Denmark | HC | 4517 Baldwin Blvd., P.O. Box 4585, Corpus Christi 78469 |
| | | HVC | 3200 Trammell Crow Center, 2001 Ross Ave., Dallas 75201 |
| | France | HC | P.O. Box 12077, Team Bank Bldg., Amarillo 79101 |
| | | HC | 2300 Nations Bank Tower, P.O. Box 98, Austin 78767 |
| | | HC | 750 N. St. Paul, Suite 670, Dallas 75201 |
| | | HC | 2727 Allen Parkway, Suite 976, Houston 77019 |
| | | HC | Route 1, Box 229, Converse (San Antonio) 78109 |
| | Germany | HC | 5440 Old Brownsville Rd., P.O. Box 4897, Corpus Christi 78469 |

| *State* | *Country* | *Type* | *Address* |
|---|---|---|---|
| | | HC | 10110 N. Central Expressway, Suite 230, Dallas 75231 |
| | | CG | 1330 Post Oak Blvd., Suite 1850, Houston 77056 |
| | | HC | 1500 Alamo Bldg., 105 S. St. Mary St., San Antonio 78205 |
| | Greece | C | 1360 Post Oak Blvd., Suite 2480, Houston 77056 |
| | Italy | C | 2202 Mechanic St., Suite 4, Galveston 77550 |
| | | CG | 1300 Post Oak Blvd., Suite 660, Houston 77056 |
| | | C | 2255 W. Mistletoe, San Antonio 78201 |
| | Netherlands | CG | 2200 Post Oak Blvd., Houston 77056 |
| | Spain | HC | 3141 Hood St., Second Fl., Dallas 75219 |
| | | HC | 3816 Mattox, El Paso 79925 |
| | | CG | 1800 Bering Dr., Suite 660, Houston 77057 |
| | United Kingdom | CG | 1100 Milam, Suite 2260, Houston 77002 |
| Utah | Belgium | HC | 615 Northcrest Dr., Salt Lake City 84103 |
| | Denmark | HC | 231 Edison St., Salt Lake City 84111 |
| | Germany | HC | 455 E. Fourth South, Salt Lake City 84111 |
| | Italy | VC | 9580 S. 1784 West, South Jordan (Salt Lake City) 84065 |
| | Netherlands | HC | 1415 Roberta St., Salt Lake City 84115 |
| Vermont | Italy | CA | 49 Manor Woods, P.O. Box 2362, South Burlington 05403 |

| *State* | *Country* | *Type* | *Address* |
|---|---|---|---|
| Virginia | Belgium | HC | 508 N. Birdneck Rd., Virginia Beach (Norfolk) 23451 |
| | Denmark | HC | 1800 Sovran Center, Norfolk 23510 |
| | Germany | HC | 142 W. York St., Suite 218, Norfolk 23510 |
| | Italy | VC | 7737 Hampton Blvd., Norfolk 23505 |
| | Netherlands | HC | 1128 W. Onley Rd., Norfolk 23507 |
| | United Kingdom | HC | 4601 Mayflower Rd., Suite 1-D, Norfolk 23508 |
| Washington | Belgium | HC | 3214 W. McGraw, Suite 200, Seattle 98199 |
| | France | C | 400 E. Pine St., Suite 210, Seattle 98122 |
| | Germany | CG | 1 Union Square, 600 University St., Seattle 98101 |
| | | HC | Sheraton Spokane Hotel, 322 Spokane Falls Court, Spokane 99201 |
| | Italy | VC | 4720 32nd Ave., S., Seattle 98118 |
| | Netherlands | HC | 10051 NE 112th St., Kirkland (Seattle) 98104 |
| | United Kingdom | C | 999 Third Ave., Suite 820, Seattle 98104 |
| Wisconsin | Belgium | HC | 825 N. Jefferson St., Suite 500, Milwaukee 53202 |
| | Denmark | HC | 9015 W. Maple St., Milwaukee 53214 |
| | France | HC | 9240 N. Sleepy Hollow Lane, Milwaukee 53217 |
| Wyoming | France | HC | 227 H St., Rock Springs 89201 |

# 6

# WORLD TRADE CENTERS AND WORLD TRADE CLUBS/ASSOCIATIONS

## WORLD TRADE CENTERS

A World Trade Center is usually an office building/real estate project developed to bring together many of the services an international businessperson would use in the conduct of international trade. These include:

- Information services: Trade research, information on trade opportunities, world markets, government regulations, tariffs, and other business topics.
- Educational services: Seminars, language instruction, and other training programs relating to international business.
- Clubs: Lounge and dining facilities for members and guests.
- Exhibit facilities: Space and promotion for the display of export products from the region.
- Consumer services: Hotels, banks, restaurants, shops, and other services to support the requirements of the international businessperson and international company.
- Trade missions: Organized by the members of a center to accomplish a specific objective.
- Business travel services: Support visiting international business persons; translation and interpretation, office services (secretarial, telephone, fax) meeting and conference facilities, hosting, and negotiation facilitation.
- Trade messages: Exclusive to the World Trade Center organizations, their NETWORK is a computer based international trade lead, buy and sell, electronic bulletin board.

The World Trade Centers listed here provide a range of services noted by this key:

C World Trade Center Club
D Display and Exhibit Facilities
E Trade Education Services
G Group Trade Missions
H Hotel
I Trade Information Services
L International Trade Library
M Meeting Facilities
N WTC NETWORK Access
O Temporary Offices
S Secretarial Services
T Translating Services
V Video Conference Facilities

The headquarters of the World Trade Center organization is:

The World Trade Center Association (WTCA), One World Trade Center, Suite 7701, New York, NY 10048, 212-432-2640

One of the objectives of the WTCA is to make a WTC opportunity available to any interested community. Contact the WTCA to learn about new organizations forming near your place of business.

| *State* | *Location* |
|---|---|
| Alaska | World Trade Center, University of Alaska Anchorage, WTC Bldg., 4201 Tudor Center Dr., Suite 320, Anchorage 99508, 907-561-1615<br>ILNEM |
| Arizona | World Trade Center Phoenix, 34 West Monroe, Suite 900, Phoenix 85003, 602-495-6480<br>ILNEMGHST |
| California | World Trade Center-Irvine, 1 Park Plaza, Suite 150, Irvine 92714, 714-724-9822<br>INEMGOST |
| | Greater Los Angeles World Trade Center, One World Trade Center, Suite 295, Long Beach 90831-0295, 310-495-7070<br>ILNCEMGHOST |
| | Los Angeles World Trade Center, 350 South Figueroa St., Suite 172, Los Angeles 90071, 310-680-1888<br>INGET |
| | World Trade Center of San Francisco, Inc., 110 Sutter St., Suite 408, San Francisco 94104, 415-392-2705<br>INEGHST |

| State | Location |
| --- | --- |
| Colorado | Colorado Springs World Trade Center, P.O. Box 6539, Colorado Springs 80934, 719-633-9041 |
| | World Trade Center-Denver, 1625 Broadway, Suite 680, Denver 80202, 303-592-5760<br>ILNEMHOST |
| Connecticut | World Trade Center Bridgeport, 360 Fairfield Ave., Bridgeport 06604, 203-336-5353<br>INEMGH |
| Delaware | World Trade Center-Delaware, Inc., 1207 King St., P.O. Box 709, Wilmington 19899, 302-656-7905<br>ILNEMHST |
| Florida | World Trade Center, 1100 Lee Wagener Blvd., P.O. Box 13065, Ft. Lauderdale International Airport, Ft. Lauderdale 33315, 305-359-3615<br>ILNEMDGHOS |
| | World Trade Center Association, 3 Independent Dr., Jacksonville 32202, 904-366-6646<br>ILNEMGS |
| | World Trade Center Miami, One World Trade Center Plaza, Suite 1800, 800 SW 8th St., Miami 33130, 305-759-0064<br>INEMGHST |
| | World Trade Center Orlando, 201 South Orange Ave., Suite 901, Orlando 32801, 407-649-1899<br>INEGHOST |
| | World Trade Center Tampa Bay, 800 Second Ave. South, Suite 340, St. Petersburg 33701, 813-822-2492<br>INEHT |
| Georgia | World Trade Center Atlanta, 240 Peachtree St., NE, Suite 2200, Atlanta, GA 30303, 404-525-4144<br>INCEMDGH |
| Hawaii | World Trade Center Honolulu, 521 Ala Moana Blvd., Suite 110, Honolulu 96813, 808-599-3969 |
| Illinois | Illinois World Trade Center Chicago, 321 North Clark St., Suite 550, Chicago 60610-4714, 312-467-0550<br>INCEMDGHOST |
| Indiana | World Trade Center Indianapolis, 3905 Vincennes Rd., Suite 504, Indianapolis 46268, 317-871-6807 |

| *State* | *Location* |
|---|---|
| Iowa | Cedar Rapids World Trade Center, 312 8th St., Suite 200, Des Moines 50309, 515-246-6000<br>INEMDGOST |
| | Iowa World Trade Center, 3200 Ruan Center, 666 Grand Ave., Des Moines 50309, 515-245-2555<br>IMHOST |
| Kansas | World Trade Center Wichita, EPIC Center, 301 N. Main St., Suite 1860, Wichita 67202, 316-262-3232<br>ILNEMDGHOSTV |
| Kentucky | World Trade Center Lexington, 410 West Vine St., Suite 290, Lexington 40507, 606-258-3139<br>ILNEMGHOSTV |
| Louisiana | World Trade Center of New Orleans, 2 Canal St., Suite 2900, New Orleans 70130, 504-529-1601<br>NCEMDG |
| Maryland | The World Trade Center Baltimore, 401 East Pratt St., Suite 1355, Baltimore 21202, 301-576-0022<br>ILNCEMDGHOST |
| Massachusetts | World Trade Center Boston, Executive Offices, Suite 50, Boston 02210-2004, 617-439-5001<br>ILNCMDGHOSTV |
| Michigan | World Trade Center Detroit/Windsor, 1000 Buhl Bldg., World Trade Center, Detroit 48226, 313-965-6500<br>ILNCEMST |
| Minnesota | Minnesota World Trade Center, 400 Minnesota World Trade Center, 30 East 7th St., St. Paul 55101, 612-297-1580<br>INLEGMGHOSTV |
| Missouri | Greater Kansas City World Trade Center, 920 Main St., Suite 600, Kansas City 64105, 816-221-2424<br>ILNEMG |
| | World Trade Center St. Louis, 121 South Meramec, Suite 1111, St. Louis 63105, 314-854-6141<br>ILE |
| Nevada | Nevada World Trade Center, Las Vegas, 6330 S. Eastern Ave., Suite 7, Las Vegas 89119, 702-795-8487<br>IENGOST |
| New York | Buffalo World Trade Center, Triple Vision Group, Inc., 5340 Goodrich Rd., Buffalo 14031, 716-741-4101<br>NSR |

| *State* | *Location* |
|---|---|
| | World Trade Center New York, One World Trade Center, Suite 35 East, New York 10048, 212-435-2329<br>INCEMDGHOT |
| | World Trade Center Schenectady-Capital District, One Broadway Center, Suite 750, Schenectady 12305, 518-377-4904<br>INE |
| North Carolina | World Trade Center Charlotte, Box 220814, Charlotte 28222, 704-335-0000<br>NSR |
| | World Trade Center Piedmont Triad, Piedmont Triad Airport Authority, P.O. Box 35005, Greensboro 27425, 919-665-5600<br>NSR |
| | The Research Triangle World Trade Center, P.O. Box 13487, Research Triangle Park (Raleigh-Durham) 27709, 919-554-8689<br>ILNEMGHOST |
| | World Trade Center Wilmington, Greater Wilmington Chamber of Commerce, P.O. Box 330, Wilmington 28402, 919-726-3525<br>INEGHST |
| Ohio | World Trade Center Columbus, International Trade Development Office, Columbus Area Chamber of Commerce, 37 North High St., Columbus 43215, 614-225-6915<br>ILNEMG |
| | Toledo World Trade Center, 828 Prouty St., Toledo 43609-3220, 419-225-7226<br>INMOST |
| Oregon | World Trade Center Portland, One World Trade Center, Suite 250, 121 SW Salmon St., Portland 97204, 503-464-8888<br>ILNEMDGHOSTV |
| Pennsylvania | Greater Philadelphia WTC and Financial Center, Carl Marks & Co., Inc., 135 E. 57th St., 27th Fl., New York, NY 10022, 212-909-8400<br>NSR |
| | World Trade Center Pittsburgh, 441 Smithfield St., 2nd Fl., Pittsburgh 15222, 412-355-4344<br>NSR |

| State | Location |
|---|---|
| Rhode Island | World Trade Center of Rhode Island, Greater Providence, Bryant College, P.O. Box 61, Smithfield 02917, 401-232-6400<br>ILNEMDSTV |
| South Carolina | South Carolina World Trade Center, Charleston Trident Chamber of Commerce, 81 Mary St., P.O. Box 975, Charleston 29402, 803-557-2510<br>INEGT |
| | The Greenville-Spartanburg World Trade Center, The Jenkins Companies, 315 Old Boiling Springs Rd., Greer 29650, 803-297-8600<br>IGOS |
| Tennessee | World Trade Center Chattanooga, 1001 Market St., Chattanooga 37402, 615-752-4316<br>ILNEMDGHOST |
| Texas | The Alliance World Trade Center (Ft. Worth/Dallas), Hillwood Development Corporation, 12377 Merit Dr., Suite 1700, Dallas 75251, 214-788-3050<br>NSR |
| | Houston World Trade Association, 1100 Milan, 25th Fl., Houston 77002, 713-658-2401<br>ILNEMGHOST |
| | World Trade Center Rio Grande Valley at McAllen, One Park Place, Suite 670, McAllen 78503, 512-686-1982<br>NSR |
| | World Trade Center San Antonio, 118 Broadway, Suite 621, San Antonio 78205, 512-978-7601<br>INEMGHOST |
| Virginia | World Trade Center Washington, DC, One Prince St., Alexandria 22314, 703-684-6630<br>ILNCEMGHOST |
| Washington | Seattle World Trade Center, Greater Seattle World Trade Center Association, 1201 Third Ave., Suite 1700, Seattle 98101, 206-224-7450<br>INEMDGHOST |
| | World Trade Center Tacoma, 3600 Port of Tacoma Rd., Suite 309, Tacoma 98424, 206-383-9474<br>INCEMGST |

| *State* | *Location* |
|---|---|
| Wisconsin | Wisconsin World Trade Center-Madison, Inc., 8401 Greenway Blvd., Middleton 53562, 608-831-0666 INCEMDGHOSTV |
| | Wisconsin World Trade Center at Milwaukee, Pfister Hotel, 424 E. Wisconsin, Milwaukee 53202, 414-274-3840 INEMGHOST |

## WORLD TRADE CLUBS AND ASSOCIATIONS

World Trade Clubs and/or International Trade Associations differ from the World Trade Centers in two important aspects: (1) they are usually a not-for-profit association formed to provide information or networking facilities for its members, and (2) they do not own real estate projects.

These clubs and associations can be a good contact point for a company that seeks to expand its knowledge of certain aspects of international trade or investment, or contact others with similar interests. Each organization functions to meet the needs of its members. Two examples demonstrate the diversity of interests:

- Seattle, WA: 17 Country Forums meet regularly on their own schedule, to address issues and business practices indigenous to a country or region.
- Buffalo, NY: Produced a 30 minute video on "The Cultural Environment of International Business."

The listed clubs and associations are members of the Federation of International Trade Associations (FITA),* which can provide you with complete contact information.

| *State* | *Organization* |
|---|---|
| Alabama | Alabama World Trade Association, Birmingham, 205-323-5461 |
| | Northern Alabama International Trade Association, Huntsville, 205-532-3505 |
| Arizona | Arizona World Trade Association, Phoenix, 602-495-6480 |
| | Sunbelt World Trade Association, Tucson, 602-795-4119 |

* The Federation of International Trade Associations is located at 1851 Alexander Bell Drive, Reston, VA 22091. Telephone: 703-620-1588. The location information listed above is used with the permission of Mr. Nelson Joyner, Chairman of FITA.

| *State* | *Organization* |
|---|---|
| Arkansas | Arkansas World Trade Club, Little Rock, 501-682-7690 |
| | Mid-South International Trade Association, Little Rock, 501-374-1957 |
| | World Trade Club of Northeast Arkansas, Jonesboro, 501-932-0000 |
| California | California Council for International Trade Association, San Francisco, 415-788-4127 |
| | Foreign Trade Association of Southern California, Los Angeles, 213-627-0634 |
| | International Business Council, Los Angeles, 310-553-2222 |
| | International Business Association of the Long Beach Chamber of Commerce, Long Beach, 213-436-1251 |
| | International Marketing Association of Orange County, Tustin, 714-956-7743 |
| | International Trade Association of South Bay, Torrance, 213-540-5858 |
| | Monterey Bay International Trade Association, Santa Cruz, 408-464-8585 |
| | Oakland World Trade Association, Oakland, 510-272-1307 |
| | San Francisco Chapter, Women in International Trade of Northern California, San Francisco, 415-984-5000 |
| | Santa Clara Valley World Trade Club, Santa Clara, 408-986-1406 |
| | Valley International Trade Association, Canoga Park, 818-345-5620 |
| | Women in International Trade, Los Angeles, 213-826-8782 |
| | Women in International Trade, Northern California, Sacramento, 916-652-8263 |
| | Women in World Trade, Irvine, 714-852-6025 |
| | World Trade Association of San Diego, San Diego, 619-453-4605 |
| | World Trade Association of San Francisco, San Francisco, 415-392-4511 |

| *State* | *Organization* |
|---|---|
| | World Trade Council of San Mateo County, San Mateo, 415-345-8300 |
| Colorado | International Business Association of the Rockies, Wheat Ridge, 303-422-7905 |
| | International Trade Association of Colorado, Denver, 303-798-8586 |
| Connecticut | Connecticut Foreign Trade Association, Stratford, 203-966-1563 |
| | Connecticut International Trade Association, Hartford, 203-688-0799 |
| | Connecticut World Trade Association, Bridgeport, 203-336-5353 |
| | Westconn International Trade Association, Stamford, 203-324-5620 |
| District of Columbia | Washington International Trade Association, Washington, 202-2293-4193 |
| | Women in International Trade, Washington, 202-682-7098 |
| Florida | Florida Importers and Exporters Association, Miami, 407-242-2062 |
| | Ft. Lauderdale Area World Trade Council, Ft. Lauderdale, 305-832-0132 |
| | Metro Orlando International Business Council, Orlando, 407-422-7159 |
| | Space Coast World Trade Council, Melbourne, 305-724-5400 |
| | Tampa Bay International Trade Council, Tampa, 813-228-7777 |
| | World Trade Council of Northwest Florida, Inc., Pensacola, 904-453-3146 |
| | World Trade Council of Palm Beach, West Palm Beach, 407-833-4314 |
| Georgia | World Trade Club of Atlanta, Atlanta, 404-525-4144 |
| Hawaii | Pacific and Asian Affairs Council, Honolulu, 808-941-6066 |
| Idaho | Boise World Trade Committee (of Boise Chamber of Commerce), Boise, 208-344-5515 |
| Illinois | International Trade Club of Chicago, Chicago, 312-368-9197 |

| State | Organization |
|---|---|
| | International Trade Association of Greater Chicago, Elk Grove Village, 708-980-4109 |
| | Women in International Trade, Chicago, 312-641-1466 |
| | World Trade Council of Northern Illinois, Rockford, 815-987-8123 |
| Indiana | Michiana World Trade Club, South Bend, 219-236-2000 |
| | Tri-State World Trade Council, Evansville, 812-425-8147 |
| | World Trade Club of Indiana, Indianapolis, 317-264-6892 |
| Iowa | International Trade Bureau, Cedar Rapids, 319-398-5317 |
| | International Traders of Iowa, Des Moines, 515-245-5284 |
| | Iowa-Illinois International Trade Association, Davenport, 319-322-1706 |
| | Northeast Iowa International Trade Council, Cedar Falls, 319-266-3593 |
| | Siouxland International Trade Association, Sioux City, 712-255-7903 |
| | Southeast Iowa Inciation, Burlington, 319-752-6365 |
| Kansas | World Trade Council of Wichita, Wichita, 316-689-3176 |
| Kentucky | Bluegrass International Trade Association, Lexington, 606-272-6656 |
| | Kentuckiana World Commerce Council, Louisville, 502-937-7415 |
| | Northern Kentucky International Trade Association, Florence, 606-283-1885 |
| Louisiana | World Trade Club of Greater New Orleans, New Orleans, 504-525-7201 |
| Maine | Maine World Trade Association, Augusta, 207-622-0234 |
| Maryland | Maryland International Trade Association, BWI Airport, 301-577-1779 |
| | Suburban Maryland International Trade Association, Olney, 301-924-0234 |

| *State* | *Organization* |
|---|---|
| Massachusetts | International Business Council of New England, Inc., Boston, 617-439-5280 |
| | Western Massachusetts International Trade Association, Springfield, 413-737-7000 |
| | Women in World Trade, Boston, 617-734-1408 |
| Michigan | West Michigan World Trade Association, Grand Rapids, 616-771-0319 |
| | Women in International Trade-Detroit Chapter, Waterford, 313-596-0340 |
| | World Trade Club of Detroit, Detroit, 313-681-8772 |
| Minnesota | Southern Minnesota International Trade Group, Owatonna, 507-455-4100 |
| Mississippi | International Trade Club of Mississippi, Jackson, 601-981-5234 |
| Missouri | International Trade Club of Greater Kansas City, Kansas City, 816-221-1462 |
| | Ozarks International Trade Association, Springfield, 417-862-7021 |
| | World Trade Club of St. Louis, Inc., St. Louis, 314-725-9605 |
| Nebraska | Mid-West International Trade Association, Omaha, 402-556-4420 |
| Nevada | Nevada World Trade Council, Carson City, 702-885-4325 |
| New Hampshire | New Hampshire International Trade Association, Portsmouth, 603-431-6128 |
| New Jersey | International Trade Roundtable, Paramus, 201-447-7975 |
| | South New Jersey Exporters Trade Association, Marlton |
| | World Trade Association of New Jersey, South Orange, 201-761-1303 |
| New Mexico | International Trade Council of New Mexico, Albuquerque, 505-765-2205 |
| New York | Buffalo World Trade Association, Tonawanda, 716-877-1452 |
| | International Business Council, Rochester, 716-454-2220 |
| | International Trade Committee of the Chemung Chamber of Commerce, Elmira, 607-734-5137 |

| *State* | *Organization* |
| --- | --- |
| | Mohawk Valley World Trade Council, Utica, 315-433-0111 |
| | Southern Tier World Commerce Association, Binghampton, 607-777-2342 |
| | Tappan Zee International Trade Association, Pearl River, 914-735-7040 |
| | Women in International Trade, New York, 212-408-3361 |
| | World Trade Club of New York, Inc., New York, 212-435-8336 |
| | World Trade Club of Westchester, White Plains, 914-948-6444 |
| | World Trade Council of Long Island, Commack, Long Island, 516-499-4400 |
| North Carolina | Ashville Chapter, North Carolina World Trade Association, Tuxedo, 704-693-8585 |
| | Cape Fear Chapter, North Carolina World Trade Association, Wilmington, 919-794-4327 |
| | Charlotte Chapter, North Carolina World Trade Association, Charlotte, 919-794-4327 |
| | Coastal Plains Chapter, North Carolina World Trade Association, Greenville, 919-794-4327 |
| | North Carolina World Trade Association, Raleigh, 919-821-3700 |
| | Sandhills Chapter, North Carolina World Trade Association, Pinehurst, 919-692-4222 |
| | Triad Chapter, North Carolina World Trade Association, Greensboro, 919-275-00931 |
| | Triangle Chapter, North Carolina World Trade Association, Raleigh, 919-362-0043 |
| | Western Carolina Chapter, North Carolina World Trade Association, Statesville, 919-794-4327 |
| Ohio | Cleveland World Trade Association, Cleveland, 216-621-3300 |
| | Greater Akron Export Association, Akron, 216-379-3170 |
| | Greater Cincinnati World Trade Association, Cincinnati, 513-579-3100 |

| *State* | *Organization* |
|---|---|
| | North Central Ohio International Trade Association, Mansfield, 419-522-0022 |
| | Toledo Area International Trade Association, Toledo, 419-243-8191 |
| | World Trade Association, Columbus, 614-225-6951 |
| Oklahoma | Oklahoma City International Trade Association, Oklahoma City, 405-943-9513 |
| | Oklahoma Women in World Trade, Oklahoma City, 405-755-0228 |
| | Tulsa World Trade Association, Tulsa, 918-585-1201 |
| Oregon | Pacific Northwest International Trade Association, Portland, 503-228-4361 |
| Pennsylvania | International Business Forum, Inc., Philadelphia, 215-922-2900 |
| | International Trade Development Association, Philadelphia, 215-824-4954 |
| | The Women's International Trade Association, Philadelphia, 215-922-6610 |
| | World Trade Association of Philadelphia, Philadelphia, 215-988-0711 |
| | World Trade Club of Lehigh Valley, Trexlertown, 215-253-6272 |
| | York County International Network, York, 717-848-4000 |
| Rhode Island | World Trade Club of Rhode Island, Providence, 401-521-5000 |
| South Carolina | Midlands International Trade Association, Columbia, 803-765-3449 |
| | Pee Dee International Trade Club, Bennetsville, 803-479-3002 |
| | Western South Carolina International Trade Association, Greenville, 803-574-4400 |
| Tennessee | Memphis World Trade Club, Memphis, 901-523-3122 |
| | World Trade Council of Chattanooga, Chattanooga, 615-752-4302 |
| | World Trade Council of Middle Tennessee, Nashville, 615-385-1222 |
| Texas | Austin International Business Council, Austin, 512-322-5618 |

| *State* | *Organization* |
|---|---|
| | International Trade Association of Dallas/Ft. Worth, Dallas, 214-748-3777 |
| | San Antonio World Trade Association, San Antonio, 512-229-9036 |
| | Women in International Trade, Garland, 214-681-4635 |
| | World Trade Division of the Greater Houston Partnership, Houston, 713-658-2401 |
| Utah | World Trade Association of Utah, Salt Lake City, 801-974-5544 |
| Virginia | Hampton Roads Foreign Commerce Club, Norfolk, 804-627-6336 |
| | International Trade Association of Western Virginia, Roanoke, 703-857-7304 |
| | International Trade Association of Northern Virginia, Reston, 703-860-8795 |
| | Piedmont World Trade Council, Lunchburg, 804-384-3454 |
| | Richmond Export-Import Club, Richmond, 804-648-1234 |
| Washington | Inland Northwest World Trade Council, Spokane, 509-625-6190 |
| | World Trade Club of Seattle, Seattle, 509-448-8803 |
| Wisconsin | Central Wisconsin World Trade Association, Stevens Point, 715-423-1222 |
| | Madison International Trade Association, Madison, 608-222-5658 |
| | Milwaukee World Trade Association, Milwaukee, 414-273-3000 |
| | Northeastern Wisconsin World Trade Association, Neenah, 414-722-7758 |
| | South Central Wisconsin World Trade Association, Whitewater, 414-472-3217 |
| | Western Wisconsin World Trade Association, Eau Claire, 715-839-6301 |

# 7

# NONPROFIT AND BILATERAL TRADE ORGANIZATIONS

The international affairs organizations presented here are supported in part by the United States Information Agency (USIA), which supports over 100 exchange programs developed to foster closer understanding between peoples of foreign nations and the United States. These local organizations provide an access point for information and experience with foreign business, cultural, and political leaders.

## PRIVATE NONPROFIT ORGANIZATIONS

The USIA supports the activities of over 100 different exchange programs throughout the United States and abroad. One of these is the **International Visitors Program.** Each of the 102 organizations listed below participate to some extent in the USIA programs.

The International Visitors Program concentrates on bringing foreign leaders (current or emerging) to the United States to meet with and learn about U.S. business and political institutions. The focus has been on Europe and Africa. Past program participants include 138 current and former heads of government, and over 900 people in cabinet-level positions in their respective governments. Hundreds of others are leaders and managers in business, academia, and medicine.

Community organizations conduct some or all of the following activities with these foreign business and political leaders:

- Arrange and conduct professional meetings and seminars
- Provide language aid
- Provide local business and political information
- Arrange technical visits
- Arrange hotel accommodations
- Arrange multi-language tour opportunities, transportation, protocol materials, spouse and family programs, speakers, entertainment, and in-home hospitality.

Participation in this type of organization can be broad or tightly focused on a particular country, region, or topic. The format provides U.S. participants with the opportunity to meet socially and closely with selected future national leaders of nations throughout Europe. Organizations are listed alphabetically by state.

| *State* | *Organization* |
| --- | --- |
| Alabama | Huntsville-Madison County Council for International Visitors, Madison County Court House, Rm. 535, Huntsville 35801, 205-532-3559 |
| Arizona | World Affairs Council of Arizona, Ramada Valley Ho, 6850 Main St., Scottsdale 85251, 602-945-7750 |
| | Tucson Council for International Visitors, P.O. Box 42226, Tucson 85733, 602-795-0330 |
| Arkansas | Arkansas Council for International Visitors, University of Arkansas at Little Rock, 2801 South University Ave., Little Rock 72204, 501-569-3282 |
| California | University of California at Davis, International Visitors Office, Rm. 307, South Hall, Davis 95616-8624, 916-752-0464 |
| | International Student Service of Southern California, P.O. Box 83143, Los Angeles 90083, 213-641-5826 |
| | International Visitors Council of Los Angeles, Biltmore Court, 520 S. Grand Ave., Suite 680, Los Angeles 90071, 213-622-6835 |
| | University of California-Los Angeles Visitors Center, 1417 Ueberroth Bldg., 10945 LeConte Court, Los Angeles 90024, 213-825-4467 |
| | International Relations Council of Riverside, P.O. Box 2221, Riverside 92516, 714-686-0582 |
| | Sacramento Council for International Visitors, 7645 Eastgate St., Citrus Heights 95610, 916-966-1370 |
| | International Visitors Council of San Diego, 3800 Fifth Ave., San Diego 92103, 619-291-8105 |
| | International Visitors Center of the Bay Area, Inc., 312 Sutter St., Suite 402, San Francisco 94108, 415-986-1388 |
| | The Protocol Foundation of Orange County, 10 Civic Center Plaza, Santa Ana 92701, 714-834-5654 |

| State | Organization |
|---|---|
| | Bechtel International Center, Stanford University, Office of International Visitors, P.O. Box 5816, Stanford 94309, 415-723-1984 |
| Colorado | Boulder Council for International Visitors, P.O. Box 1285, Boulder 80306, 303-442-8818 |
| | Institute of International Education, 700 Broadway, Suite 112, Denver 80203, 303-837-0788 |
| | International Hospitality Center, Division of UNA, USA, 1245 East Colfax Ave., # 202, Denver 80218, 303-832-4765 |
| Connecticut | World Affairs Council, Inc., 770 Asylum Ave., Lower Level, Hartford 06105-2804, 203-549-7123 |
| | International Center, Inc., 442 Temple St., P.O. Box 94A, New Haven 06520, 203-549-7123 |
| | International Hospitality Committee of Fairfield County, P.O. Box 349, Westport 06880, 203-787-3531 |
| Delaware | Delaware Council for International Visitors, P.O. Box 831, Wilmington 19899, 302-656-9928 |
| Florida | Gainsville Council for International Friendship, Center for International Students and Scholars, University of Florida, 1504 W. University Ave., Gainsville 32608, 904-392-1345 |
| | International Resource Center of Jacksonville, Inc., 128 E. Forsyth St., Suite 502, Jacksonville 32202, 904-630-1750 |
| | Florida Spacecoast Council for International Visitors, P.O. Box 2621, Melbourne 32902-2621, 407-729-6387 |
| | Council for International Visitors of Greater Miami, Inc., 555 NE 15th St., Suite G-7, Miami 33132, 305-379-4610 |
| | International Visitors Council of Central Florida, 500 West Livingston St., Third Fl., Orlando 32801, 407-246-0849 |
| | Tampa Bay Council for International Visitors, 609 W. Horatio St., Tampa 33606, 813-251-4242 |
| Georgia | Georgia Council for International Visitors, 999 Peachtree St., Suite 770, Atlanta 30309-3918, 404-873-6170 |

| *State* | *Organization* |
|---|---|
| Illinois | International Visitors Center of Chicago, 520 N. Michigan Ave., Suite 522, Chicago 60611, 313-645-1836 |
| | International Fellowship Committee, 2849 North Flansburg Rd., Freeport 61032, 815-563-4619 |
| | Geneseo International Thanksgiving Fellowship Program, 607 S. Spring St., Geneseo 61254, 309-944-4486 |
| | International Thanksgiving Fellowship, RR# 1, Box 84, Kansas 61933, 217-948-5360 |
| | Springfield Commission on International Visitors, 109 North 9th St., Springfield 62701, 217-789-2362 |
| | Rock River Valley International Fellowship Committee, 15543 Highland Dr., Sterling 61081, 815-625-5896 |
| Indiana | Indiana International Council, Inc., P.O. Box 68466, Indianapolis 46268, 317-297-0502 |
| Iowa | The Des Moines Area Council for International Understanding, 1000 Walnut St., Suite 324, Des Moines 50309, 515-282-8269 |
| | Council for International Visitors to Iowa City, 120 International Center, Iowa City 52242, 319-335-0351 |
| Kansas | International Visitors Council of the Wichita Rotary Club, 106 W. Douglas, Wichita 67202, 316-262-4375 |
| Kentucky | Louisville International Cultural Center, 1311 South Third St., Louisville 40208, 502-636-3568 |
| Louisiana | Council for International Visitors of Greater New Orleans, Box 546, New Orleans 70148-0546, 504-286-7266 |
| | International Council of Louisiana, Inc., World Trade Center, Suite 1146, 2 Canal St., New Orleans 70130-1302, 504-525-1947 |
| Maine | World Affairs Council of Maine, University of Southern Maine, 96 Falmouth St., Portland 04103, 207-780-4551 |
| Maryland | International Visitors Center of Maryland, World Trade Center, Suite 1010, Baltimore 21202, 301-837-7150 |
| Massachusetts | Boston Center for International Visitors, 20 Park Plaza, Suite 1010, Boston 02116, 617-542-8995 |

| *State* | *Organization* |
|---|---|
| | Harvard University Marshal's Office, Wadsworth House, Cambridge 02138, 617-495-5724 |
| | Massachusetts Institute of Technology, Information Center, Rm. 7-121, 77 Massachusetts Ave., Cambridge 02139, 617-253-1875 |
| | World Affairs Council of Western Massachusetts, Inc., International Center, 1350 Main St., 3rd Fl., Springfield 01101-4234, 413-733-0110 |
| | International Center of Worcester, Inc., 22 Downing St., Worcester 01610, 508-752-8414 |
| Michigan | The International Center University of Michigan, 603 E. Madison St., Ann Arbor 48109-1370, 313-764-9310 |
| | International Visitors Council of Metropolitan Detroit, Inc., 200 Renaissance Center, Suite 627, Detroit 48243, 313-259-2680 |
| | Community Volunteers for International Programs, Center for International Programs, Rm. 101-A, Michigan State University, East Lansing 48823-1035, 517-353-1735 |
| | Flint Council for International Visitors, 806 Blanchard Ave., Flint 48503, 313-238-6722 |
| Minnesota | Minnesota International Center, 711 East River Rd., Minneapolis 55455, 612-625-4421 |
| | Worthington-Crailsheim International, Inc., 1914 Summit Ave., Worthington 56187, 507-372-2610 |
| Mississippi | The International Visitors Center of Jackson, 1400 J.R. Lynch St., P.O. Box 17103, Jackson 39217, 601-968-2043 |
| | Natchez Convention and Visitors Bureau, 311 Liberty Road, Natchez 39120, 601-446-6345 |
| Missouri | International Visitors Council of Greater Kansas City, 920 Main St., Suite 600, Kansas City 64105, 816-221-2424 |
| | World Affairs Council of St. Louis, 232 North Kingshighway Blvd., Suite 105, St. Louis 63108, 314-361-7333 |
| Montana | Montana Council for International Visitors, 104 East Main St., Suite 307, Bozeman 59715, 406-586-8030 |

| *State* | *Organization* |
| --- | --- |
| Nebraska | Council for International Visitors, P.O. Box 505, Grand Island 68802, 308-381-0114 |
| | Mayor's Committee for International Friendship, 129 North 10th St., Box 3, Lincoln 68508, 402-477-4355 |
| | Kiwanis Club of Omaha, Inc., Professional Tower, # 407, 105 S. 17th St., Omaha 68102, 402-345-9999 |
| Nevada | International Visitors Council of Northern Nevada, P.O. Box 41261, Reno 89504, 702-359-4689 |
| New Hampshire | New Hampshire Council on World Affairs, 11 Rosemary Lane, Durham 03824, 603-862-1683 |
| New Mexico | Albuquerque Council for International Visitors, Ramada Hotel Classic, Suite 227, 6815 Menaul Blvd., NE, Albuquerque 87110, 505-888-1867 |
| | Council on International Relations, P.O. Box 1223, Santa Fe 87504-1223, 505-982-4931 |
| New York | The International Center of the Capital Region, Inc., 8 Russell Rd., Albany 12206, 518-459-8812 |
| | Buffalo-Western New York Council for International Visitors, Inc., 140 North St., Suite 145, Buffalo 14201-1581, 716-883-5804 |
| | The International Center in New York, Inc., 119 West 40th St., 11th Fl., New York 10018-2505, 212-921-8205 |
| | International Visitors Program Service of the Rochester Association for the United Nations, 55 St. Paul St., Rochester 14604, 716-232-1080 |
| | Rochester International Friendship Council, 50 West Main St., RIT City Center, Rm. 6256, Rochester 14614, 716-262-3482 |
| | International Center of Syracuse, Hotel Syracuse, Suite 1141, 500 S. Warren St., Syracuse 13202, 315-471-1222 |
| North Carolina | The International House, 322 Hawthorne Lane, Charlotte 28204, 704-333-8099 |
| | The International Visitors Council, P.O. Box 12843, 10 Alexander Dr., Suite 104, Research Triangle Park 27709, 919-549-9191 |
| Ohio | Akron Area Network for International Friendship, 125 Sage Ave., Akron 44301-2028, 216-724-9771 |

| *State* | *Organization* |
|---|---|
| | Cincinnati International Visitors Center, Inc., 120 West 5th St., Suite 509, Cincinnati 45202, 516-241-7384 |
| | Cleveland Council on World Affairs, 1422 Euclid Ave., # 539, Cleveland 44115, 216-781-3730 |
| | International Visitors Council, Inc., Port Columbus International Airport, 4600 International Gateway, Suite 102D, Columbus 43219, 614-231-9610 |
| | International Institute of Greater Toledo, Inc., 2040 Scottwood Ave., Toledo 43620, 419-241-9178 |
| Oklahoma | International Visitors Council, Oklahoma City Convention & Visitors Bureau, Four Santa Fe Plaza, Oklahoma City 73102-9083, 800-225-5652 |
| | International Council of Tulsa, Inc., 616 South Boston Ave., Suite 401, Tulsa 74119, 918-584-4685 |
| Oregon | World Affairs Council of Oregon, 1 World Trade Center, Suite 320, 121 SW Salmon St., Portland 97204, 503-274-7488 |
| Pennsylvania | The International Visitors Council of Philadelphia, 34th St. and Civic Center Blvd. at the Civic Center Museum, Philadelphia 19104-4395, 215-826-7261 |
| | Pittsburgh Council for International Visitors, 413 Bellefield Hall, 315 Bellefield Ave., Pittsburgh 15260, 412-624-7800 |
| Rhode Island | Council for International Visitors, 85 Taylor Rd., Portsmouth 02871, 401-846-0222 |
| | World Affairs Council of Rhode Island, 72 Arcade Bldg., Providence 02903, 401-421-0401 |
| South Carolina | Columbia Council for Internationals, 1925 Madison Rd., Columbia 29204, 803-782-9520 |
| Tennessee | Knoxville Area International Council, 1515 Cumberland, Knoxville 37966-1700, 615-974-4453 |
| | Memphis Council for International Visitors, 169 N. Mid-America Mall, Suite 969, Memphis 38103, 901-576-4336 |
| | Nashville Council for International Visitors, 971 Davidson Dr., Nashville 37205, 615-352-2699 |
| Texas | International Hospitality Committee of Austin, Drawer A, University Station, 100 West 26th St., Austin 78713-7206, 512-471-1211 |

| *State* | *Organization* |
|---|---|
| | Dallas Committee for Foreign Visitors, 9417 Waterview Rd., Dallas 75218, 214-321-1163 |
| | El Paso Council for International Visitors, P.O. Box 619, El Paso 79968-0619, 915-747-5725 |
| | Greater Fort Worth Council on Foreign Affairs, 309 West 7th St., Suite 1800, Fort Worth 76102, 817-923-2964 |
| | IIE Volunteer Services, Southern Region, 515 Post Oak Blvd., Suite 150, Houston 77027-9407, 713-621-6300 |
| | San Antonio Council for International Visitors, 2227 Waverly Ave., San Antonio 78228, 512-225-3211 |
| Utah | International Visitors-Utah Council, 40 East South Temple, Suite 348, Salt Lake City 84111, 801-532-4747 |
| Vermont | The Vermont Council on World Affairs, Inc., Trinity College Administration Bldg., Colchester Ave., Burlington 05401-1480, 802-658-0337 |
| Washington | World Affairs Council of Seattle, 515 Madison St., Suite 501, Seattle 98104, 206-682-6986 |
| | Spokane International Exchange Council, 505 South Leta Rd., Spokane 99216, 509-924-8084 |
| | Yakima Valley Council for International Visitors, 821 West Barker Heights Rd., Wapato 98951, 509-924-8084 |
| Wisconsin | International Institute of Wisconsin, 2810 West Highland Blvd., Milwaukee 53208, 414-933-0521 |

## SISTER CITY ORGANIZATIONS*

President Eisenhower stated that the Sister Cities program "is an important resource to the negotiations of governments in letting the people themselves give expression of their common desire for friendship, goodwill, and cooperation for a better world for all." The concept was developed from a White House conference in 1956 and has evolved into a network of city-to-city and state-to-state relations involving 100 foreign countries, all 50 states, 915 U.S. and 1,464 foreign cities.

* Material adapted from directory information provided by Sister Cities International, 120 South Payne Street, Alexandria, VA 22314.

Sister City relationships offer the businessperson the opportunity to meet with other business, civic, and professional people who share a common interest in a particular foreign city or region. These relationships encompass the professions, cultural affairs, language and the arts, travel and tourism between cities or states, and the development of business relations between U.S. and foreign business persons.

Each Sister City organization receives some degree of recognition and support from the host city in each nation and state. Quasi-diplomatic communiques and greetings are exchanged between political leaders. Cultural and business tours and trade missions are a regular part of the agenda of each sister association. The Sister City format is a very good environment for exposure to a targeted foreign marketplace, to meet others with experience in that market (cultural, business, or political), and to join a network of people with a common and specific interest. From this beginning the businessperson can develop or take advantage of what opportunities might exist.

To participate in a Sister City association, contact the office of the Mayor of your target U.S. city, or contact Sister Cities International (703-836-3535).

| *State* / *City* | *Country/City* |
|---|---|
| Alabama | |
| Mobile | Spain/Malaga |
| | France/Pau |
| | Germany/Worms |
| | Greece/Zakinthos |
| Alaska | |
| Anchorage | England/Whitby |
| Arizona | |
| Glendale | Germany/Memmingen |
| Phoenix | Ireland/Ennis |
| | France/Grenoble |
| Tempe | Germany/Regensburg |
| Tucson | Greece/Trikkala |
| Arkansas | |
| Fort Smith | Italy/Cisterna |
| California | |
| Artesia | Netherlands/Koudekerke an-den Rijn |
| Beverly Hills | France/Cannes |
| Cupertino | Italy/Ivrea |
| Del Mar | England/Wisborough Green |
| Dinuba | Germany/Malsch |
| El Cajon | Germany/Sulzfeld |
| El Monte | France/Marcq-en-Baroeul |

| *State* / *City* | *Country/City* |
|---|---|
| Fresno | Germany/Munster |
| Gilroy | France/Saint-Clar |
| | Italy/Monticelli d'Ongina |
| Hayward | Portugal/Faro |
| Hemet | Denmark/Ebeltoft |
| Inglewood | Italy/Pedavena |
| Lafayette | France/Langeac |
| Los Angeles | Greece/Athens |
| | France/Bordeaux |
| Marin County | England/Devon County |
| Martinez | Scotland/Dunbar |
| | Italy/Milazzo |
| Menlo Park | Ireland/Galway |
| Monterey | Spain/Lerida |
| Nevada City | England/Penzance, Cornwall |
| Newark | England/Newark |
| Newport Beach | France/Antibes |
| Orange | France/Orange |
| Pacifica | Spain/Balaguer |
| Palo Alto | Netherlands/Enschede |
| Pasadena | Germany/Ludwigshafen am Rhein |
| Redlands | Scotland/Inverness |
| San Diego | Scotland/Edinburgh |
| San Francisco | Italy/Assisi |
| | Ireland/Cork |
| San Mateo | Denmark/Varde |
| Santa Barbara | Italy/Paterno |
| Santa Clara | Portugal/Coimbra |
| Santa Clara County | Italy/Florence Province |
| Santa Fe Springs | Germany/Tirschenreuth |
| Santa Maria | Spain/Santa Maria |
| S. San Francisco | Italy/Lucca |
| Tulare | Portugal/Angra do Heroismo, Azores |
| Vallejo | Italy/La Spezia |
| Visalia | Italy/Putignano |
| Walnut Creek | Italy/Noceto |
| Whittier | Germany/Freiburg im Breisgau |
| Colorado | |
| Arvada | Germany/Gerscher |
| Aspen | France/Chamonix |
| | Germany/Garmisch Partenkirchen |
| Boulder | Netherlands/Meppel |
| Broomfield | England/Broomfield |

| *State* / *City* | *Country/City* |
|---|---|
| Central City | France/Champagne-Vigny |
| Denver | France/Brest |
| | Italy/Potenza |
| Evans | England/Ashby de la Zouch |
| **Connecticut** | |
| Bristol | Greece/Kosani |
| Danbury | Portugal/Gouveia |
| Glastonbury | England/Glastonbury |
| Haddam | England/The Haddams |
| Hartford | Italy/Florida |
| | Greece/Thessaloniki |
| New Britain | Germany/Rastatt |
| New Haven | France/Avignon |
| Ridgefield | Germany/Ingelheim |
| Stratford | England/Stratford on Avon |
| Wallingford | England/Wallingford |
| **Delaware** | |
| Dover | Greece/Lamia |
| Lewes | England/Lewes |
| Newark | France/La Garde Freinet |
| Wilmington | England/Watford |
| **Florida** | |
| Boca Raton | Germany/Berlin-Spandau |
| Bradenton | Spain/Barcarrota |
| Clearwater | Greece/Kalamaria |
| Coral Gables | Spain/Granada |
| | Spain/el Puerto de Santa Maria |
| Dade County | Italy/Asti Province |
| Dunedin | Scotland/Stirling |
| Fort Lauderdale | Italy/Rimini |
| Gainsville | Scotland/Cumbernauld |
| Hollywood | France/Romorantin |
| Jacksonville | France/Nantes |
| Jacksonville Beach | Luxembourg/Ettelbruck |
| Madeira Beach | Portugal/Machico |
| Miami | Spain/Ibiza |
| | France/Nice |
| Mount Dora | Scotland/Forres |
| New Port Richey | France/Cavaliere sur Mer |
| St. Augustine | Spain/Cuitadella, Minorca |
| Tampa | Italy/Agrigento |
| | Spain/Oviedo |

| *State* / *City* | *Country/City* |
|---|---|
| Georgia | |
| Atlanta | Belgium/Brussels |
| | England/Newcastle on Tyne |
| | France/Toulouse |
| Helen | Germany/Fussen |
| Macon | France/Macon |
| Marietta | Germany/Linz am Rhein |
| Savannah | Greece/Patrai |
| Thomasville | Germany/Luneberg |
| Toccoa | Germany/Messtetten |
| Hawaii | |
| Hawaii County | Portugal/Sao Miguel |
| Honolulu County | France/Bruyeres |
| | Portugal/Funchal |
| Kauai County | England/Whitby |
| Maui County | Portugal/Funchal |
| | Portugal/Ponta Delgada, Azores |
| | Portugal/Sao Miguel |
| | Spain/Madrid |
| Idaho | |
| Ketchum | Italy/Lignano Sabbiadoro |
| | Germany/Tegernsee |
| Illinois | |
| Aledo | Spain/Aledo |
| Belleville | Germany/Paderborn |
| Belvidere | Germany/Schwieberdingen |
| Bloomington | NormalEngland/Canterbury |
| Bourbonnais | Germany/Stenheim |
| Chicago | Italy/Milan |
| Chicago Heights | Italy/San Benedetto del Tronto |
| Decatur | Germany/Seevetal |
| Deerfield | Germany/Ludinghausen |
| Des Plaines | Italy/Cremona |
| East Moline | Belgium/Maldegem-Adegem |
| Glen Ellyn | Spain/Calatayud |
| Hanover Park | Italy/Ravenna |
| Highland Park | Italy/Ferrara |
| Naperville | Spain/Alcala de Henares |
| Niles | Italy/Pisa |
| Quincy | Germany/Herford |
| Rolling Meadows | France/Henin-Beaumont |
| Schaumburg | Germany/Schaumburg |

| *State* / *City* | *Country/City* |
|---|---|
| Shelbyville | Italy/Frosinone |
| Tinley Park | Germany/Budingen |
| Waterloo | Germany/Porta Westfalica |
| Western Springs | England/Rudeley |
| Indiana | |
| Elkhart | England/Burton upon Trent |
| Evansville | Germany/Osnabruck |
| Goshen | Germany/Bexbach |
| Huntingburg | Germany/Schledehausen |
| Indianapolis | Germany/Cologne |
| Jasper | Germany/Pfaffenweiler |
| La Grange | Netherlands/Grijpskerk |
| La Porte | Scotland/Grangemouth |
| Mount Vernon | France/Peronne |
| New Harmony | Germany/Wiernsheim |
| Vincennes | France/Vincennes |
| Iowa | |
| Davenport | Germany/Kaiserslautern |
| Des Moines | France/St. Etienne |
| Emmetsburg | Ireland/Dublin |
| Kansas | |
| Great Bend | Germany/Villigen-Schwenningen |
| Hays | Germany/Newstadt an der Waldnaab |
| Hesston | France/Coex |
| Kansas City | Ireland/Cork |
| Lawrence | Germany/Eutin |
| Maple Hill | Scotland/Braemar |
| Shawnee | Belgium/Pittem |
| | Ireland/Listowel |
| Victoria | Germany/Kubelsteinstadt Schesslitz |
| Wichita | France/Orleans |
| Kentucky | |
| Bardstown | France/Billom |
| Campbellsville | Ireland/Buncana |
| Lexington | France/Deauville |
| | Ireland/County Kildare |
| Louisville | France/Montpellier |
| Radcliff | Germany/Munster |
| Louisiana | |
| Franklin | France/L'etang Sale, Reunion |
| Houma | France/Cambrai |
| Lafayette | Belgium/Namur |

| *State*<br>*City* | *Country/City* |
|---|---|
| Napoleonville | France/Pontivy |
| New Iberia | Belgium/Woluwest Pierre, Lex Bruxelles |
| Maine | |
| Calais | France/Calais |
| Maryland | |
| Annapolis | Wales/Newport |
| Anne Arundel County | England/Sussex County |
| Baltimore | Greece/Piraeus |
| | Italy/Genoa |
| | Netherlands/Rotterdam |
| Baltimore County | Italy/Grosetto Province |
| | Italy/Castel del Piano |
| Columbia, Howard County | France/Cergy-Pontoise |
| | Spain/Tres Cantos |
| Frederick | Germany/Morzheim |
| | Germany/Schifferstadt |
| Hagerstown | Germany/Wesel |
| Rockville | Germany/Pinneberg |
| Salisbury | England/Salisbury |
| Massachusetts | |
| Amherst | France/Arcachon |
| Andover | England/Andover |
| Billerica | England/Billericay |
| Boston | Italy/Padua |
| | France/Strasbourg |
| Cambridge | England/Cambridge |
| | Italy/Gaeta |
| | Portugal/Coimbra |
| Concord | France/St. Mande |
| Dartmouth | England/Dartmouth |
| Fall River | Portugal/Lagoa County, Azores |
| | Portugal/Ponta Delgada, Azores |
| | Portugal/Povoacao County, Azores |
| | Portugal/Ribeira Grande County, Azores |
| | Portugal/Villa Franca do Campo County, Azores |
| Fitchburg | Germany/Kleve |
| Gloucester | England/Gloucester |
| Haverhill | England/Haverhill |
| Hudson | Portugal/Vila do Porto, Azores |
| Marlborough | England/Marlborough |
| New Bedford | Portugal/Funchal |
| | Portugal/Horta, Azores |

| *State* / *City* | *Country/City* |
|---|---|
| Northampton | England/Northampton |
| Pittsfield | Italy/Cava de Tirreni |
| Southborough | England/Southborough |
| Taunton | England/Taunton |
| Truro | England/Truro |
| Waltham | France/Belfort |
| Wareham | England/Wareham |
| Weston | France/Rombas |
| Wilbraham | England/Great Wilbraham |
| Wincester | France/St. Germain-en-Laye |
| Michigan | |
| Ann Arbor | Germany/Tubingen |
| Bay City | Belgium/Malines |
| Belleville | Wales/Machynlleth |
| Coldwater | Germany/Soltau |
| Constantine | Germany/Dorfen |
| Dexter | Germany/Ofterdingen |
| Frankenmuth | Germany/Gunzenhausen |
| Greenville | Denmark/Haderslev |
| Hillsdale | Netherlands/Rhenen |
| Manton | Ireland/Enniscorthy |
| Midland | Germany/Marl |
| Muskegon | England/Hartlepool |
| Oak Park | Spain/Yecla |
| Oxford | England/Oxford |
| Plymouth | England/Plymouth |
| Saline | Wales/Brecon |
| Sturgis | Germany/Wiesloch |
| Warren | Italy/Terrasini |
| Ypsilanti | Greece/Navplion |
| Zeeland | Netherlands/Kapelle |
| Minnesota | |
| Fridley | France/Fourmies |
| New Ulm | Germany/New Ulm |
| | Germany/Ulm |
| Redwood Falls | Germany/Neusaess |
| St. Paul | Italy/Modena |
| Willmar | Belgium/Frameries |
| Worthington | Germany/Crailsheim |
| Missouri | |
| Kansas City | Spain/Sevilla |
| Lafayette County | France/Chavaniac |
| Liberty | Luxembourg/Diekirch |

| *State* <br> *City* | *Country/City* |
|---|---|
| N. Kansas City | Luxembourg/Diekirch |
| | Luxembourg/Esch-sur-Alzette |
| Springfield | France/Tours |
| St. Louis | France/Lyon |
| | Germany/Stuttgart |
| | Italy/Bologna |
| Washington | Germany/Marbach am Neckar |
| Nevada | |
| Sparks | Ireland/Longford |
| New Jersey | |
| Bayonne | France/Bayonne |
| Englewood | Netherlands/Maastricht |
| Hackensack | Germany/Passau |
| Margate | England/Margate |
| Montclair | England/Barnet |
| Princeton | France/Colmar |
| Randolph | England/Wisbech |
| Trenton | England/Stoke on Trent |
| New Mexico | |
| Albuquerque | Germany/Helmstedt |
| Santa Fe | Spain/Santa Fe |
| New York | |
| Albany | Netherlands/Nijmegen |
| Amityville | France/Lebourget |
| Buffalo | Germany/Dortmund |
| Elmira | Germany/Melsungen |
| Garden City | France/Aix en Provence |
| | Germany/Coburg |
| Greece | France/Vitre |
| Jamestown | Italy/Cantu |
| New Rochelle | France/La Rochelle |
| New York | Spain/Madrid |
| Rochester | France/Rennes |
| | Germany/Wurzburg |
| | Ireland/Waterford |
| | Italy/Caltanissetta |
| Saranac Lake | France/Entrains-sur-Nohain |
| Saratoga Springs | France/Vichy |
| Williamsville | Germany/Friolzheim |
| North Carolina | |
| Charlotte | Germany/Krefeld |
| Durham | England/Durham City |
| Greensboro | France/Montbeliard |

| *State* *City* | *Country/City* |
|---|---|
| Raleigh | England/Kingston-upon-Hull |
| | France/Compiegne |
| Ohio | |
| Botkins | Germany/Gottelfingen |
| Bowling Green | France/St. Cyr sur Loire |
| Centerville | Germany/Bad Zwischenahn |
| Cincinnati | Germany/Munich |
| Cleveland | England/Cleveland County |
| | Germany/Heidenheim |
| Columbus | Denmark/Odense |
| Dayton | Germany/Augsburg |
| Eaton | Germany/Rodental |
| Englewood | Germany/Billerbeck |
| Kettering | England/Kettering |
| Mansfield | England/Mansfield |
| Marietta | Germany/Kusel |
| Montgomery | France/Neuilly-Plaisance |
| Oakwood | France/Le Vesinet |
| Portsmouth | Germany/Zittau |
| Richfield | Germany/Wolfach |
| Toledo | Spain/Toledo |
| Vandalia | Germany/Lichtenfels |
| Oklahoma | |
| Stroud | England/Stroud |
| Oregon | |
| Astoria | Germany/Walldorf |
| Medford | Italy/Alba |
| Pennsylvania | |
| Berwick | England/Berwick upon Tweed |
| Charleroi | Belgium/Charleroi |
| Cheltenham | England/Cheltenham |
| Coatesville | Scotland/Greenock |
| Ephrata | Germany/Eberbach |
| Fryburg | Germany/Freiburg im Breisgau |
| Kennett Square | England/Kennett |
| Manheim | Germany/Mannheim |
| New Holland | France/Longvic |
| Norristown | Italy/Montella |
| Philadelphia | Italy/Florence |
| Pittsburgh | England/Sheffield |
| | Germany/Saarbrucken |
| | Spain/Bilbao |

| *State*<br>*City* | *Country/City* |
|---|---|
| Swathmore | Germany/Stade |
| Yardley | England/Laughton |
| York | France/Arles |
| | Germany/Leinfelden-Echterdingen |
| Rhode Island | |
| Coventry | England/Coventry |
| East Providence | Portugal/Ribeira Grande, Azores |
| Newport | Italy/Imperia |
| Warwick | England/Warwick |
| South Carolina | |
| Charleston | Italy/Spoleto |
| Greenville | Belgium/Kortrijk |
| | Italy/Bergamo |
| South Dakota | |
| Sioux Falls | Germany/Potsdam |
| Vermillion | Germany/Ratingen |
| Tennessee | |
| Brentwood | England/Brentwood |
| Brownsville | Germany/Regen |
| Chattanooga | Germany/Hamm |
| Dickson | Italy/Carmagnola |
| Lavergne | France/Lavergne |
| Nashville | France/Caen |
| Texas | |
| Arlington | Germany/Bad Koenigshofen |
| Castroville | France/Eguisheim |
| Corpus Christi | Spain/Toledo |
| Dallas | France/Dijon |
| D'Hanis | France/Nieder/Oberentzen |
| Farmer's Branch | England/Bassettlaw District |
| Fort Worth | Germany/Trier |
| | Italy/Reggio Emilia |
| Fredericksburg | Germany/Gluckstadt |
| Hondo | France/Geispolsheim |
| Houston | France/Nice |
| | Scotland/Grampian Region |
| | Spain/Huelva |
| Irving | England/Merton |
| | Germany/Baumholder |
| | Italy/Marino |
| New Braunfels | Germany/Braunfels |
| San Antonio | Spain/Santa Cruz de Tenerife |

| *State* / *City* | *Country/City* |
|---|---|
| Shiner | Germany/Winterlingen |
| Tyler | France/Metz |
| Utah | |
| Ogden | Germany/Hof |
| Park City | France/Courchevel |
| Vermont | |
| Barnet | England/Barnet |
| Colchester | England/Colchester |
| Virginia | |
| Abermarle County | |
| Charlottesville | Italy/Prato/Poggio a Cajano |
| Alexandria | Scotland/Dundee |
| Fredericksburg | France/Frejus |
| Hampton | England/Southampton |
| | France/Vendome |
| Herndon | England/Runnymede |
| Lexington | Germany/Eichstatt |
| Luray | France/Luray |
| Norfolk | England/Norfolk County |
| | France/Toulon |
| | Germany/Wilhelmshaven |
| Poquoson | France/Bar sur Loup |
| Portsmouth | England/Portsmouth |
| Richmond | England/Richmond upon Thames |
| Suffolk | England/Suffolk |
| York County | Germany/Zweibrucken |
| Washington | |
| Bingen-White Salmon | Germany/Bingen am Rhein |
| Kelso | Scotland/Kelso |
| Olympia | Greece/Olympia |
| Seattle | France/Nantes |
| | Ireland/Galway |
| Spokane | Germany/Lubeck |
| Wisconsin | |
| Beloit | Italy/Pinerolo |
| Dane County | Wales/Clwyd County |
| Horicon | France/Senonches |
| Kenosha | France/Douai |
| | Germany/Wolfenbuttel |
| Racine | Denmark/Alborg |
| | France/Montelimar |
| Sheboygan | Germany/Esslingen |

| *U.S. Sister States* | *Sister Country* |
|---|---|
| Arkansas | Bavaria, Germany |
| California | Catalonia, Spain |
| | Puglia Province, Italy |
| Colorado | Bavaria, Germany |
| Connecticut | Baden Wurttenburg, Germany |
| Hawaii | Azores, Portugal |
| Indiana | Baden Wurttenburg, Germany |

## OTHER ORGANIZATIONS

The Small Business Exporters Association
4603 John Tyler Court, Suite 203
Annandale, VA 20003
703-642-2490

This is a relatively new trade association focused on the needs and interests of emerging companies.

American Association of Exporters and Importers
11 West 42d St.
New York, NY 10036
212-944-2230

This 70-year-old trade association represents exporters and importers before regulatory agencies. It has a number of publications targeted to specific interest groups, principally importers:

*International Trade Alert:* Weekly update on legislation and rulings from Commerce, Treasury, the International Trade Commission, the Federal Maritime Commission, and others.

*International Trade Quarterly:* Analysis of international trade issues.

*Textile Quota Report:* Weekly customs reports on the status of all textile import quotas.

United States Council for International Business
1212 Avenue of the Americas
New York, NY 10036
212-354-4480

The council represents
American business interests (300 multinational corporations are the principal members) to the major international economic policy making institutions and to the Executive and Legislative branches of the federal government.

The council is the official U.S. member of: the International Chamber of Commerce, the Business and Industry Advisory Committee to the Organization for Economic Cooperation and Development (OECD), and the International Organization of Employees. It represents U.S. corporate interests to United Nations bodies, the World Bank, and GATT, to the OECD, and to the International Labor Organization (ILO).

The Council states that it expresses U.S. business views on issues before the European Community as a member of and as secretariat of the U.S. Industry Coordinating Group. The Council has a staff person assigned to manage its EC activities.

National Foreign Trade Council, Inc.
1625 K St., NW
Washington, DC 20006
202-887-0278

The Council was formed in 1914. It develops positions on international trade, investment, tax and export finance issues, and advocates these positions to Congress, the Administration, and others. NFTC committees deal with taxation, international trade, international investment, the European Communities, Russia and the NIS, export finance, the balance of payments, management resources, and immigration.

Chamber of Commerce of the United States
1615 H St., NW
Washington, DC 20062
202-463-5460

This is the world's largest voluntary business federation. It has an international division that analyzes, develops and implements Chamber recommendations on legislation and government policies on international economic issues. It has an international policy committee and four subcommittees covering market access, export promotion, import relief, and EC-1992 issues.

National Association of Manufacturers (NAM)
1331 Pennsylvania Ave., NW, Suite 1500 N
Washington, DC 20004-1703
202-637-3000

Founded in 1895, the NAM represents industrial and business firms. It is an active voice in international business and trade circles.

# 8

# LEGAL RESOURCES

There are thousands of lawyers and law firms in the United States. Most of these individuals and firms have only a passing acquaintance with international trade, international contracts, legal issues, or international law generally.

Many law firms in the United States are large or extremely competent, internationally known and respected. There are too many of these attorneys and firms to list in this book. This section directs the corporate manager or counsel to the right resources. Many small or regional firms are quite skilled on some aspects of international trade. Many are not; they must call on the services of other firms or attorneys, much as a small bank calls on the services of a larger correspondent for its international banking, trust, or investment services.

This guide also identifies principal members of a national Export Legal Assistance Network, dispute resolution organizations, and lists additional resources that can be used to locate lawyers or law firms with particular skills in specific geographic markets. This guide does not endorse or recommend any firm or individual attorney.

## EXPORT LEGAL ASSISTANCE NETWORK

The Export Legal Assistance Network (ELAN) is a cooperative program among the Federal Bar Association, the U.S. Department of Commerce, and the Small Business Administration. Participating firms have committed to provide initial consultations with exporters or prospective exporters free of charge to get these firms started on the best foot. ELAN attorneys devote time to respond to all manner of international business query: financing, trademarks, patents, copyrights, documentation, dispute settlements, and so on. The National Coordinator of the ELAN program is:

Judd L. Kessler, Partner, Porter, Wright, Morris & Arthur, 1233 20th St., NW, Suite 400, Washington, DC 20036-2395, 202-778-3080

The regional coordinators listed may handle all queries themselves, refer callers to others in the firm, or call on the assistance of other attorneys in the community with the required expertise. This is an excellent starting point for the corporate executive with a legal question relating to international trade or international business.

| *State* | *Regional Coordinator* |
|---|---|
| Alabama | James C. Wilson, Jr., Lange, Simpson, Robinson & Somerville, 1700 First Alabama Bank Bldg., Birmingham 35203, 205-250-5000 |
| Arizona | Harry A. Cavanagh, O'Conner, Cavanagh, Anderson, et al., 3003 North Central Ave., Suite 1800, Phoenix 85012, 602-263-3811 |
| California | Michael R. Doram, Politis, Pollack & Doram, 3255 Wilshire Blvd., Suite 1688, Los Angeles 90010, 213-386-1383 |
| | Mark F. Johannessen, Esq., 555 Capitol Mall, Suite 270, Sacramento 95814, 916-443-5292 |
| | Harold C. Pope, Pope & Dixson, 4275 Executive Square, Suite 800, La Jolla 92037, 619-546-2944 |
| | Harry B. Endsley, Harry B. Endsley & Associates, 465 California St., Suite 700, San Francisco 94104, 415-982-5454 |
| Colorado | Louise Aron, Esq., 1536 South Ingalls, Lakewood 80226-7016, 303-922-7687 |
| Connecticut | Philip Ettman, Esq., 6 Wilcox St., Simsbury 06070, 203-651-6161 |
| District of Columbia | Judd L. Kessler, Porter, Wright, Morris & Arthur, 1233 20th St., NW, Suite 400, Washington 20036, 202-778-3080 |
| | Margaret Png, Stewart & Stewart, 808 17th St., NW, Suite 300, Washington 20006, 202-785-4185 |
| Florida | Michael A. Pyle, P.O. Box 3096, Daytona Beach 32118-0096 |
| | Laurence J. Pino, Pino & Dicks, 25 South Orange Ave., Orlando 32802, 407-425-7831 |
| | Stanley F. Rose, 2110 Imperial Golf Course Blvd., Naples, 813-566-3511 |

| *State* | *Regional Coordinator* |
|---|---|
| | Thomas F. Morante, Cantor & Morante, P.A., Suite 3750, One Biscayne Tower, Two South Biscayne Blvd., Miami 33131, 305-374-3886 |
| | Lucius Dyal, Shackleford, Farrior, Stallings & Evans, P.A., P.O. Box 3324, Tampa 33601, 813-273-5000 |
| Georgia | William M. Poole, Chamberlain, Hrdlicka, White, et al., 1400 Harris Tower, 233 Peachtree St., NE, Atlanta 30303, 404-659-1410 |
| Hawaii | David L. Bourgoin, 100 Bishop St., Suite 1560, Honolulu 96813, 808-523-7779 |
| Idaho | Richard S. Christensen, Penland & Munther, 350 N. 9th St., Suite 500, Boise 83701 |
| Illinois | Paul H. Vishny, D'Ancona & Pflaum, 30 N. LaSalle St., Suite 2900, Chicago 60602, 312-580-2000 |
| Indiana | Eugene L. Henderson, Henderson, Daley, Withrow & Devoe, One Indiana Square, Rm. 2450, Indianapolis 46204, 317-639-4121 |
| Iowa | A. J. Greffenius, Davis, Hockenberg, Wine, et al., 666 Walnut St., Suite 2300, Des Moines 50309, 515-243-2300 |
| Louisiana | Sharon A. Perlis, 433 Metairie Rd., Suite 215, Metairie 70005, 504-834-3700 |
| Massachusetts | Robert W. Chmielinski, 36 Washington St., Suite 70, Wellesley Hills 02181, 617-235-8815 |
| Michigan | Roger H. Leemis, 29777 Telegraph Rd., Suite 2500, Southland 48034, 313-353-5060 |
| Minnesota | Philip R. Sherwood, Sherwood & McKenzie, Minnesota World Trade Center, Suite 950, St. Paul 55101, 612-297-6564 |
| Mississippi | Stephen M. Roberts, Watkins, Ludlam & Stennis, 633 N. State St., Jackson 39205 |
| Missouri | Jeffrey L. Michelman, Blumenfeld, Kaplan & Sandweiss, 168 N. Maraneck, Suite 400, St. Louis 63105, 314-863-0800 |
| | Ted J. Lickteig, 6900 College Blvd., Suite 430, Overland Park 66211, 913-451-1122 |
| Montana | Mae Nan Ellingson, Dorsey & Whitney, 127 East Front St., Suite 310, Missoula 59802, 406-721-6025 |

| *State* | *Regional Coordinator* |
|---|---|
| New Hampshire | Arthur W. Mudge, P.O. Box 986, Andover 03755, 603-795-4460 |
| New Jersey | Richard L. Abbott, 43 Foxcroft Dr., Princeton, 609-924-3484 |
| New Mexico | Alison K. Schuler, P.O. Box 90460, Albuquerque 87199, 505-842-5521 |
| New York | M. Barry Levy, Sharrets, Paley, Carter & Blauvelt, P.C., 67 Broad St., New York 10004, 212-425-0050 |
| | Paul A. Mitchell, Lippes, Kaminsky, Silverstein, et al., 28 Church St., Suite 700, Buffalo 14202, 716-853-5100 |
| | Bernard T. McCann, Hinman, Straub, Pigors & Manning, P.C., 71 Bay St., Glens Falls 12801-0018, 518-792-0598 |
| North Carolina | E. Thomas Watson, Parker, Poe, Thompson, et al., 2600 Charlotte Plaza, Charlotte 28244, 704-372-9000 |
| Ohio | Robert J. Watkins, Porter, Wright, Morris & Arthur, 250 East Fifth St., Suite 2200, Cincinnati 42502, 513-381-4700 |
| | Thomas Talcott or Daniel F. Gourash, Porter, Wright, Morris & Arthur, 925 Euclid Ave., Suite 1700, Cleveland 44115, 216-443-9000 |
| | Dixon F. Miller, Porter, Wright, Morris & Arthur, 41 South High St., Columbus 43215-3406, 614-227-2000 |
| Oregon | Pegi Groundwater, Perkins, Coie, Stone, et al., 111 SW Fifth Ave., Suite 2500, Portland 97204, 503-295-4400 |
| Pennsylvania | Robert Jones, Drinker, Biddle & Reath, 1000 West Lakes Dr., Suite 300, Berwyn 19312, 215-988-2710 |
| | David P. Hanson, School of Business Administration, Duquesne University, Pittsburgh 15282, 412-434-6238 |
| South Carolina | Timothy D. Scranton, Nelson, Mullins, Riley & Scarborough, 151 Meeting St., Suite 400, Charleston 29402, 803-853-5200 |
| | James V. Dunbar or George A. Folsom, Barry, Dunbar, Daniel, et al., 1310 Lady St., Fifth Fl., Columbia 29211-1645, 803-765-1030 |
| Tennessee | Thomas W. Bell, Jr., Armstrong, Allen, Prewitt, et al., 1900 One Commerce Square, Memphis 38103-2568, 901-523-8211 |

| *State* | *Regional Coordinator* |
|---|---|
| Texas | Jay M. Vogelson, Stutzman & Bromberg, 2323 Bryan, Suite 2200, Dallas 75201, 214-969-4900 |
| | Frank B. Burney, Martin, Drought & Torres, Inc., 300 Convent St., 25th Fl., San Antonio 78205, 512-227-7591 |
| | Arturo Torres, Martin, Drought & Torres, Inc., 1111 First City Bank Tower, McAllen 78501, 512-686-2348 |
| Utah | Lee Ford Hunter, Kirton, McConkie & Bushnell, 330 South Third St., Salt Lake City 84111, 801-521-3680 |
| Vermont | James D. Smiddy, Smiddy & Smiddy, 61 Central St., Woodstock 05091, 802-457-4867 |
| Washington | E. Charles Routh, Garvey, Schubert, Adams & Barer, 1011 Western Ave., 10th Fl., Seattle 98104, 206-464-3939 |
| Wisconsin | Thomas F. Clasen, Foley & Lardner, 777 East Wisconsin Ave., Milwaukee 53202, 414-271-2400 |

## LAW DIRECTORIES AND OTHER SOURCES

*Law Firms' Yellow Book: Who's Who in the Management of Leading U.S. Law Firms.* Monitor Publishing Co., 1993, 104 Fifth Ave., New York 10011.

Law firms are listed by name, address, communications information, general information, management, departments, administration, U.S. offices. There is a geographic index listing firms by country. Most leading law libraries have this book. This directory reports that the number of U.S. law firms with offices in EC countries are:

| | |
|---|---|
| Belgium | 38 U.S. Firms |
| France | 28 U.S. Firms |
| Germany | 26 U.S. Firms |
| Italy | 4 U.S. Firms |
| Netherlands | 2 U.S. Firms |
| Spain | 3 U.S. Firms |
| United Kingdom | 77 U.S. Firms |

Martindale Hubbell, *Bar Register of Preeminent Lawyers in the United States, Canada, and Other Countries,* 1989, the Bar Register, a division of Martindale Hubble Inc., a division of Reed Publishing (USA), Inc., P.O. Box 1001, Summit, NJ 07902-1001.

Published annually since 1917. "We know of no other publication in which the listings are so narrowly confined to the outstanding members of the Bar." One part of this directory lists lawyers selected by their peers. The remainder of the directory lists only those firms that subscribe.

This directory has sections on international listings, by type of legal services provided, e.g., Admiralty, Antitrust, Communications, Bond, Tax, Trademark, etc. The international section is organized by country, by city, by local firm, and by American firms in the city, with contact information. Most major law libraries carry this directory.

Martindale Hubbell, *International Law Directory 1992, Europe, Asia, Australia, Middle East and Africa,* 1991, Reed Publishing (USA) Inc., 121 Chanlon Rd., New Providence, NJ 07974.

The North America Directory lists over 600 U.S. law firms with specific international interests. It is very incomplete and should be used as a secondary or backup reference only. Many leading U.S. law firms with major international practices and leading practitioners are not listed. Most major law libraries carry this volume

*The International Law List 1992,* 1992, Cooper-Morduant & Co., 57 Fitzwardings House, 14 Portman Square, London, W1H 9HB, England.

This is another very incomplete listing, which includes only those firms and individuals that subscribe. It lists firms by city within a country. It lists the principal members of the firms or, for foreign firms, the resident counsel, with address and telephone numbers. It also reports the other offices of the listed firms. Users should look up the foreign country and city of interest, and from that information identify the U.S. firms which could be of use.

The American Bar, *The Professional Directory of the Lawyers of the World,* 1992, Foster Long Co., Sacramento, CA.

This directory lists firms and attorneys by state, by city, and by firm. The directory provides the names of the partners, the specialties practiced, and the foreign offices of each firm.

The international section is reported by country. Firms are listed within a country by city, by firm. Firm listings include specialties and foreign offices.

International Bar Association, *Directory of Members,* International Bar Association, 2 Harewood Place, Hanover Square, London W1R 9HB, England.

This directory, available to members only, covers the 14,000 members of the IBA. Entries include name, address, and other communications data, subject or committee affiliation, nationality, languages spoken.

The arrangement of the data is geographic. Corporate counsel should be able to obtain the use of this directory as required.

## Other Resources

Lex Mundi, a global association of independent law firms, publishes a directory of law firms that have affiliated to provide legal services across international borders. Titled *The Directory of Law Firm Alliances, Networks, Clubs, Associations and Other Affiliations,* it is available from the association. Contact the association for names of firms or affiliations headquartered outside the United States:

Lex Mundi, Mr. Stephen J. McGarry, President, 1800 West Loop South, Suite 1880, Houston, TX 77027, 713-626-9393

The U.S.-based members of Lex Mundi affiliations are:

Akin, Gump, Strauss, Hauer, & Feld, 4100 First City Center, 1700 Pacific Ave., Dallas, TX 75201-4618, 214-969-2800

Baker & McKenzie, One Prudential Plaza, 130 East Randopph, Chicago, IL 60601, 312-861-8800

Brobeck Hale & Door International, 1301 Avenue of the Americas, New York, NY 10019, 212-581-1600

Brobeck, Phleger, & Harrison, Spear St. Tower, One Market Plaza, San Francisco, CA 94105, 415-442-0900

Hale and Dorr, 660 State St., Boston, MA 02109, 617-742-9100

Chadbourne & Parke, 30 Rockefeller Plaza, New York, NY 10112, 212-408-5100

Coudert Brothers, 200 Park Ave., New York, NY 10166, 212-880-4400

Dewey Ballantine, 1301 Avenue of the Americas, New York, NY 10019-6092, 212-259-8000

Gibson Dunn & Crutcher, 333 South Grand Ave., Los Angeles, CA 90071-3197, 213-229-7000

- *Globex Member Firms*

Foley Lardner, First Wisconsin Center, 777 East Wisconsin Ave., Milwaukee, WI 53202-5367, 414-271-2400

Graham & James, One Maritime Plaza, San Francisco, CA 94111-3492, 415-954-0200

- *Interlex Member Firms*

Hopkins & Sutter, Three First National Plaza, Chicago, IL 60602, 312-558-6600

International Lawyers Network, Epstein Becker & Green, 250 Park Ave., New York, NY, 212-351-4500

- *Le Club Member Firms*

  Sidley & Austin, One First National Plaza, Chicago, IL 60603, 312-853-7000

- *Legal Network International Member Firms*

  Reisenfeld & Associates, 919 18th St., NW, Washington, DC 20006, 202-393-3503

  Hanson Bridgett, Marcus Vlahos, Rudy, 333 Market St., San Francisco, CA 94105-2173, 415-777-3200

  McDermott, Will & Emery, 227 West Monroe St., Chicago, IL 60606-5096, 312-372-2000

- *MNF International Legal Network Member Firms*

  Nutter, McClennen & Fish, One International Plaza, Boston, MA 02210-2669, 617-439-2000

  O'Melveny & Myers, 400 South Hope St., Los Angeles, CA 90071-2899, 213-669-6000

  Thelen, Marrin, Johnson & Bridges, Two Embarcadero Center, San Francisco, CA 94111, 415-392-6320

- *The Network Member*

  Gardere & Wynne, 1601 Elm St., Dallas, TX 75201, 214-979-4500

- *Terralex Member Firms*

  Paul Landy Beiley & Harper, 200 SE First St., Miami, FL 33131, 305-358-9300

  Weil, Gotshal & Manges, 767 Fifth Ave., New York, NY 10153, 212-310-8000

  Wintrhop, Stimson, Putnam & Roberts, One Battery Park Plaza, New York, NY 10004-1490, 212-858-1000

- *World Law Group Member*

  Fenwick & West, Two Palo Alto Square, Palo Alto, CA 94306, 415-494-0600

State and county bar associations throughout the United States maintain contact and specialty information on their members. Corporate managers that want to discuss a particular type of international business topic with an attorney, and are unable to get good or comforting direction from other sources, should telephone the state or county bar association and ask for the names and telephone numbers of attorneys in their locale that practice the required specialty.

Foreign embassies and consulates of the United States maintain lists of attorneys in their jurisdiction and will make this information available when asked. They do not endorse any firm or person. American banks and CPA firms will provide similar information.

## REFERENCE BOOKS

Corporate managers may want to review or acquire one or more reference publications that can assist in directing the efforts of legal counsel. The following is not a comprehensive list, but rather a sample of publications from three fields of international business where legal issues should be understood by corporate managers.

### International Trade Law

*U.S. International Trade Laws,* Alan M. Stowell, Ed., Bureau of National Affairs, Inc. 1231 25th St., NW, Washington, DC.

This is a compilation of key United States statutes dealing with imports and exports. It provides the full text of statutes that most directly affect the control of U.S. export and imports.

*International Trade for the Nonspecialist,* Paul H. Vishny, Ed., American Law Institute-American Bar Association Committee for Continuing Professional Education. 4025 Chestnut St., Philadelphia, PA 19104-3099.

This two-volume set was written by attorneys who practice in the field of international trade, for the benefit of attorneys that do not work regularly in the field of international trade.

*Schmitthoff's Export Trade: The Laws and Practices of International Trade,* 9th Ed., Clive M. Schmitthoff, Stevens & Sons, London, 1990. c/o Sweet & Maxwell Ltd., South Quay Plaza, 183 Marsh Wall, London, England.

Written from the British perspective, the author states his objective . . ." is to give an account of the law and practice of international trade. Written for lawyers and laymen alike, for use by businesspeople and their advisors." Its eight parts cover: sales, finance, insurance, transport, commercial disputes, long term contracts, and customs law.

### International Banking

*International Banking: A Legal Guide,* 1991, International Financial Law Review, Euromoney Publications, plc. Nestor House, Playhouse Yard, London, EC4V 5EX.

This rather thin volume seeks to clarify banking laws and regulations worldwide. It is written in 37 sections, with the section on EC written by the firm Norton Rose, Kempson House, Camomile Street, London, EC3A 7AN. The EC section, and sections on the laws of many of the EC countries, identify the legal issues and structures in banking and the securities markets.

## Arbitration

*The Arbitration Kit,* 1986, Laura F. Brown, Ed., Eastman Arbitration Library, American Arbitration Association, 140 West 51st St., New York, NY 10020.

This book provides source documents, commentary, reading lists and other information compiled to meet the needs of those interested in international arbitration. It includes basic documents that provide practical instruction and useful reference assistance.

## ARBITRATION

Arbitration is a cost effective and relatively quick way to resolve disputes in an international transaction, because many countries are signatories to one or more conventions or treaties that require the courts of the signatory countries to enforce an arbitration decision. Arbitration treaties are critical because indigenous laws are not enforceable outside the home country; there is no "international law" as such. There is only national law governing international transactions, and these national laws, absent treaties to the contrary, can be in conflict. (The World Court in The Hague, Netherlands, hears and rules on matters between nations or supranational organizations that have by agreement consented to be bound by the decisions of the World Court.)

The 10 Elements of a Good International Arbitration Clause include the following:*

1. Name a good institutional arbitration association or drafting a detailed addendum to your international contract that defines the procedural ground rules for an ad hoc arbitration.
2. Choose the number of arbiters that will decide a dispute and describe how they will be chosen if different than provided in the rules of the institutional arbitration association.
3. Name an appointing authority if a party should fail to act so that the arbitration can proceed even if one party is uncooperative.
4. Agree upon the language to be used in the arbitration proceeding.
5. Name the place (venue) where the arbitration will be held. (This is critical and important; one should consider the convenience of the site, the facilities and technical assistance available, the familiarity and reputation of the venue with respect to arbitration and the likely place of enforcement of the award.)
6. State that the arbitration shall be final and binding.
7. Use all-inclusive language such as "Any dispute, controversy, or claim arising out of or relating to this contract, or the breach, termination or invalidity thereof. . . ."

* From the newsletter *International Arena,* published by the law offices of Vincent E. Bryan III, Seattle, Washington.

8. Address which law will be applied in the arbitration including the substantive, procedural, and conflict of law as well as whether the arbitrator(s) can or should be given the power to make their decision ex aigne et bono (based on equity).
9. Allocate the costs of the arbitration or give the arbitrator authority to allocate costs in the award.
10. Provide a method to recover attorneys fees incurred as a result of the arbitration proceeding and enforcement.

## Arbitration and Mediation Associations

There are two leading arbitration organizations in the United States: United States Arbitration & Mediation, Inc. (USA&M), and the American Arbitration Association (AAA). They are listed by state and by city.

| *State* | *USA&M* | *AAA* |
|---|---|---|
| | National Office<br>Michael S. Gillie<br>601 Union Ave., Suite 4300<br>Seattle, Washington<br>98101-2327<br>800-933-6348 | National Affairs<br>Thomas R. Colosi<br>1730 Rhode Island Ave., NW,<br>Suite 512, Washington DC<br>202-331-7073 |
| AL | See Jackson, MS | |
| AK | Paul L. Davis<br>510 L St., Suite 270<br>Anchorage 99501<br>907-279-1681 | |
| AZ | Brice E. Buehler<br>7226 N. 16th St., Suite 200<br>Phoenix 85020<br>602-870-4400 | Harry Kaminsky<br>333 E. Osborne, Suite 310<br>Phoenix 85012-2365<br>602-234-0950 |
| | Brice E. Buehler<br>145 E. University Blvd.<br>Tucson 85705<br>602-798-3283 | |
| AR | James Ammel<br>Three Financial Center, # 300<br>Little Rock 72211<br>501-225-6942 | |
| CA | Patricia A. Doniger<br>11601 Wilshire Blvd., Suite 500<br>Los Angeles 90025<br>310-575-4801 | Lori S. Markowicz<br>2601 Main St., Suite 240<br>Irvine 92714-6220<br>714-474-5090 |

| *State* | *USA&M* | *AAA* |
|---|---|---|
| | Jennifer St. Thomas<br>1655 N. Mountain Ave., # 104<br>Upland 91786<br>714-931-0839 | Jerrold L. Murase<br>443 Shatto Place<br>Los Angeles 90020-0994<br>213-383-6516 |
| | Timothy J.W. Wise<br>1801 Oakland Blvd., Suite 210<br>Walnut Creek 94596<br>510-946-9696 | Dennis Sharp<br>525 C St., Suite 400<br>San Diego 92101-5278<br>619-239-3051 |
| | | Charles A. Cooper<br>417 Montgomery St.<br>San Francisco 94104-1113 |
| CO | See USA&M National | Mark Appel<br>1660 Lincoln St., Suite 2150<br>Denver 80264-2101<br>303-831-0823 |
| CT | W. LeMoult & B. Aaron<br>102 Highland Ave., # 200<br>Rowayton 06853<br>203-855-1906 | Karen M. Jalkut<br>111 Founders Plaza, Fl. 17<br>E. Hartford 06108-3240<br>203-289-3993 |
| DE | See USA&M National | |
| DC | Phyllis Hanfling<br>2 Wisconsin Circle, # 700<br>Washington 20815<br>202-686-0370 | Garylee Cox<br>1150 Connecticut Ave., Fl.6<br>Washington 20036-4104<br>202-296-8510 |
| FL | A. Nicholson, B. Lowlicht<br>28 W. Flagler, Suite 1010<br>Miami 33130<br>305-579-9990 | Rene Grafals<br>99 SE 5th St., Suite 200<br>Miami 33131-2501<br>305-358-7777 |
| | | Mark Sholander<br>201 E. Pine St., Suite 800<br>Orlando 32801-2742<br>407-648-1185 |
| GA | T. Tobin, L. Hoffspiegel<br>1201 Peachtree, NE, Suite 1501<br>Atlanta 30361<br>404-897-7077 | India Johnson<br>1360 Peachtree, NE, Suite 270<br>Atlanta 30309-3214<br>404-872-3022 |
| HI | Bradley A. Coates<br>900 Fort St. Mall, # 1400<br>Honolulu 96813<br>808-524-4854 | Keith W. Hunter<br>810 Richards St., Suite 641<br>Honolulu 96813-4714<br>808-531-0541 |

| *State* | *USA&M* | *AAA* |
|---|---|---|
| ID | Ed Litteneker<br>322 Main St.<br>Lewiston 83501<br>208-746-0806 | |
| IA | D. Stamatelos, G. Kenyon, R. Calkins<br>930 Grand Ave.<br>West Des Moines 50265<br>515-226-0100 | |
| IL | William J. Schaefle<br>800 Roosevelt Rd., Suite B-321<br>Glen Ellyn 60137<br>708-858-1760 | David Scott Carfello<br>225 N. Michigan St., Suite 2527<br>Chicago 60601-7601<br>312-616-6560 |
| IN | J. Abbott, L.R. Hesson<br>1601 E. Main St.<br>Plainfield 46168<br>317-839-9024 | |
| KS | See Kansas City, MO | |
| KY | Ted W. Spiegel<br>6040 Dutchmans Lane, # 130<br>Louisville 40205<br>502-459-9866 | |
| LA | L. Selig, R. Jenks, R. Larue<br>3748 N. Causeway Bl., # 201<br>Metairie 70002<br>504-831-2141 | Deann Gladwell<br>650 Polydras St., Suite 1535<br>New Orleans 70130-6101<br>504-522-8781 |
| ME | See Boston, MA | |
| MD | 9515 Deereco Rd., Suite 500<br>Timonium 21093<br>800-354-2478 | |
| MA | M.S. Pessin, C.P. Kauders<br>148 State St., 8th Fl.<br>Boston 02109<br>617-742-0064 | Richard M. Reilly<br>133 Federal St.<br>Boston 02110-1703<br>617-451-6600 |
| MI | J. Schavrien, P. Monicatti<br>25505 W. 12 Mile Rd., # 2713<br>Southfield 48034<br>313-350-3060 | Mary A. Bedikian<br>Ten Oak Hollow St., # 170<br>Southfield 48034-7405<br>313-352-5500 |
| MN | Helen Preddy<br>P.O. Box 240487<br>St. Paul 55124<br>612-893-9584 | James R. Deye<br>514 Nicollet Mall, Suite 670<br>Minneapolis 55402-1092<br>612-332-6545 |

| *State* | *USA&M* | *AAA* |
|---|---|---|
| MS | Robert W. Sneed<br>503 S. State St.<br>Jackson 39201<br>601-969-5580 | |
| MO | Richard L. Routman<br>P.O. Box 26064<br>Kansas City 64196<br>816-221-4079 | Lori A. Madden<br>1101 Walnut St., Suite 903<br>Kansas City 64106-2110<br>816-221-6401 |
| | Robert W. Crowe<br>915 Olive St., Suite 1101C<br>St. Louis 63101<br>314-231-4642 | Neil Moldenhauer<br>One Mercantile Center, # 2512<br>St. Louis 63101-1614<br>314-621-7175 |
| NE | F.S. Cassman, F. Pospishil<br>8712 W. Dodge Rd., Suite 300<br>Omaha 68114<br>402-392-1250 | |
| | Clare Galvin<br>5 Tomkins Dr.<br>South Sioux City 68776<br>402-494-4473 | |
| NV | Brice E. Buehler<br>626 S. 7th St.<br>Las Vegas 89101<br>800-235-3746 | |
| | Brice E. Buehler<br>400 Hill St.<br>Reno 89501<br>800-235-3746 | |
| NH | See Boston, MA | |
| NJ | Harris Gould<br>187 Arch St.<br>Ramsey 07446<br>201-529-0888 | Richard Naimark<br>265 Davidson Ave., Suite 140<br>Somerset 08873-4120<br>908-560-9560 |
| NM | Brice E. Buehler<br>365 Alda Rd., SE<br>Rio Rancho 87124<br>800-235-3746 | |
| | Brice E. Buehler<br>102 W. San Francisco St., #24<br>Santa Fe 87501<br>800-235-3746 | |

| *State* | *USA&M* | *AAA* |
|---|---|---|
| NY | James Baumann<br>4601 Henry Hudson Pkwy., A2<br>Riverdale 10471<br>212-548-4207 | Mark Resnick<br>666 Old Country Rd., Suite 603<br>Garden City 11530-2004<br>516-222-1660 |
| | Justin Vigdor<br>235 Park Ave.<br>Rochester 14607<br>716-442-7801 | Carolyn M. Penna<br>140 W. 51st St.<br>New York 10020-1203<br>212-484-4000 |
| | | Deborah A. Brown<br>205 South Salina St.<br>Syracuse 13202-1376<br>315-472-5483 |
| | | Marion J. Zinman<br>34 South Broadway<br>White Plains 10601-4485<br>914-946-1119 |
| NC | See Pittsburgh | Neil Carmichael<br>428 E. Fourth St., Suite 300<br>Charlotte 28202-2431<br>704-347-0200 |
| OH | William S. Clark<br>1580 Fishinger Rd.<br>Columbus 43221<br>614-459-1012 | Philip S. Thompson<br>441 Vine St., Suite 3308<br>Cincinnati 45202-2809<br>513-241-8434 |
| | | Audrey Mendenhall<br>17900 Jefferson Rd., Suite 101<br>Middleburg Heights 44130<br>216-891-4741 |
| OK | 5900 Mosteller Rd.<br>Oklahoma City 75112<br>405-842-6311 | |
| OR | Janis Sue Porter<br>1000 SW Broadway, Suite 1710<br>Portland 97205<br>503-223-2671 | |
| PA | Alvora Varin-Hommen<br>3637 Markham Dr.<br>Bensalem 19020<br>215-750-6970 | Kenneth Egger<br>230 S. Broad St., Fl. 6<br>Philadelphia 19102-4106<br>215-732-5260 |
| | R.A. Creo, Laurie Kraeuter<br>1807 Jancey St.<br>Pittsburgh 15206-1065<br>412-361-7914 | John F. Schano<br>Four Gateway Center, Rm. 419<br>Pittsburgh 15222-1207<br>412-261-3617 |

| *State* | *USA&M* | *AAA* |
|---|---|---|
| RI | See Boston, MA | Mark Bayliss<br>115 Cedar St.<br>Providence 02903-1082<br>401-453-3250 |
| SC | See Pittsburgh, PA | |
| SD | See Nebraska | |
| TN | See Kentucky | Sheila R. Barton<br>221 Fourth Ave. N.<br>Nashville 37219-2111<br>615-256-5857 |
| TX | D. Johnson, R. Pulitzer<br>12700 Park Central Dr., # 1705<br>Dallas 75251<br>214-490-6394 | Helmut O. Wolff<br>Two Galleria Tower, Suite 1440<br>Dallas 75240-6620<br>214-702-8222 |
| | R. Pendergraft, M.H. Jamison<br>909 Fannin St., Suite 1600<br>Houston 77010-1007<br>713-655-9011 | Therese Tilley<br>1001 Fannin St., Suite 1005<br>Houston 77002-6706<br>713-739-1302 |
| | 1777 NE Loop 410, Suite 600<br>San Antonio 78217<br>512-841-5711 | |
| UT | P. Sincock, J. Holbrook<br>201 S. Main St., Suite 900<br>Salt Lake City 84111<br>801-530-7450 | Diane Abegglen<br>645 S. 200 St. East, Suite 203<br>Salt Lake City 84111-3834<br>801-531-9748 |
| VT | See Boston, MA | |
| VA | See Philadelphia, PA | |
| WA | Michael S. Gillie<br>601 Union St., Suite 4300<br>Seattle 98101-2327<br>206-467-0793 | Neal M. Blacker<br>1325 Fourth Ave., Suite 1414<br>Seattle 98191-2511<br>206-622-6435 |
| WV | See Pittsburgh, PA | |
| WI | Daniel A. Noonan<br>2631 N. Downer Ave.<br>Milwaukee 11913<br>414-962-3502 | |

*International*

| | | |
|---|---|---|
| FR | Stephen J. Redner<br>Villantipolis No. 11<br>Route des Dolines<br>Park de Sophia Antipolis<br>33-93-65-41-30 | |

| *State* | *USA&M* | *AAA* |
|---|---|---|
| FRG | Dr. Peter H. Feuerstein<br>D-6200 Wiesbaden<br>Riederbergstrasse 73<br>49-611-521057 | |
| IRE | Brian MacMahon<br>Popular Square<br>Naas, County Kildare<br>353-045-97615 | |
| UK | Richard Schiffer<br>Three Quays, Tower Hill<br>London, EC3R 6DS<br>44-71-929-4675<br><br>36-38 Baldwin St.<br>Bristol BS1 1NR<br>44-27-225-2090 | |

# 9

# TRADE CONSULTING FIRMS

Consulting is a service field with unrestricted entry, and little in the way of well-established review or certification procedures. As such, selection of a consultant for any purpose can be a difficult process. International trade is fraught with the same perils. Bankers, salespeople, entrepreneurs, and others display the consultant banner and offer their brand of advice and counsel. Many of these can be quite good, many are lacking in the background, training, capacity, scope, and character required of a quality international trade consultant.

Some minimum criteria for selection of a trade consulting firm, small or large, include the following:

- Experience in the field and discipline at issue. This could be a country, a region, an issue such as finance or investment, or an element, such as shipment, insurance, logistics, site selection, dispute resolution, distributor selection, contract services.
- Training appropriate to the field.
- Scope and capacity. The size of the firm must be appropriate to your requirements.
- The character of the firm or individual can be difficult to verify, but is most critical. Is the work product and procedures of this person or firm consistently above reproach? Has this been verified by reports from a spread of earlier clients?
- Cost of the services of a trade consultant that meets the above criteria should be viewed in the context of the total cost and outcomes of the project at hand. Consultants are "hired guns" used to achieve a specific result and nothing more. They are not an addition to staff or corporate overhead. They are expendable. Use them as such.

Consultant directories abound. Consultants can be found in industry directories, geographic directories, and general business directories. Two directories that are published annually are:

*The American Export Register*, Thomas International Publishing Company, Inc., 250 West 34th St., New York, NY 10119, 212-290-7344

This directory lists over 110 management consultants, and approximately 60 marketing consultants (see p. 248) engaged in international trade.

*The Export Yellow Pages*
(a public-private initiative sponsored by the U.S. Department of Commerce Office of Export Trading Company Affairs)

This directory lists over 200 companies that offer international trade consulting in a number of fields. Contact the closest district office of the Department of Commerce (Chapter 1) to acquire a copy.

Any of the firms listed in the above directories may meet your requirements for a trade consultant. The directory information does not provide the potential contractor with information as to the qualifications or capacities of any listed firm. That may be useful information.

A leading association of management consultants is the Council of Consulting Organizations. It is the umbrella organization for ACME, The Association of Management Consulting Firms, and IMC, the Institute of Management Consultants. The address of each of these organizations is:

Council of Consulting Organizations, Inc., 521 Fifth Ave., New York, NY 10175-3598, 212-697-9693

Membership in either of these organizations is subject to written criteria and standards. While this alone does not assure quality, it provides a minimum level of comfort as to the competence of the member firms.

ACME membership is limited to firms that have been established a minimum of five years, and meet standards of professional practices based on the recommendation and endorsement of their peers. ACME members agree to a code of ethics that addresses client services, fees, and codes of conduct. ACME members consult in the disciplines of:

- Administrative services
- Finance and accounting
- General management
- Government administration
- Human resources
- Information technology and systems
- International operations
- Manufacturing administration
- Marketing
- Materials management
- Packaging
- Physical distribution/logistics

- Purchasing
- Research and development.

ACME members consult in for the following industries:

- Agriculture
- Forestry
- Fishing
- Communications
- Construction
- Finance
- Insurance
- Real estate
- Government
- Manufacturing
- Mining
- Services
- Transportation
- Utilities
- Wholesale and retail trade.

■ *The Association of Management Consulting Firms (ACME),* 521 Fifth Ave., New York, NY 10175-3598, 212-697-9693

AMCE members that consult in the field of international operations are:

The Alexander Consulting Group, 125 Chubb Ave., Lyndhurst, NJ 07071, 201-460-6600

Andersen Consulting, 69 West Washington St., Chicago, IL 60602, 312-580-0069

Bender Management Consultants, Inc., 2231 Crystal Dr., Arlington, VA 22202, 703-920-0407

Berenschot Group B.V., Bernadottelaan 13, 3527 GA Utrecht, The Netherlands, 31-30-916916

Roland Berger & Partner GmbH, Arabellastrasse 33, 8000 Munich 81, Germany, 49-89-9223-0

Caliper Corporation, 741 Mt. Lucas Rd., P.O. Box 2050, Princeton, NJ 08543-2050, 609-924-3800

Coopers & Lybrand, 1251 Avenue of the Americas, New York, NY 10020, 212-536-2000

Herbert W. Davis & Company, 111 Charlotte Place, Englewood Cliffs, NJ, 201-871-1760

EFS & Partners, EFS Unternehmensberatung GmbH, Ungargasse 59-61, A-1030 Vienna, Austria, 431-712-56-010

Ernst & Young, 787 Seventh Ave., New York, NY 10019, 212-773-3000

ICME International Management Consultants, Restelbergstrasse 49, 8044 Zurich, Switzerland, 41-1-366-5511

A.T. Kearney, Inc., 222 South Riverside Plaza, Chicago, IL 60606, 312-648-0111

Knight/Emerson Consultants, Inc., Brook 35 Park, 2130 Highway 35, Suite 121A, Sea Girt, NJ 08750, 908-974-9200

KPMG Peat Marwick, 767 Fifth Ave., New York, NY 10153, 212-909-5000

Management Partner GmbH, Heinestrasse 41 A, D-7000 Stuttgart 70, Germany, 49-711-76-83-0

Mecrastor Corp., Kimmeltie 1, 02110 Espoo, Finland, 358-97-46971

Mercer Management Consulting, Inc., 33 Hayden Ave., Lexington, MA 02173, 617-861-7580

Moran, Stahl, & Boyer, 355 Lexington Ave., New York, NY 10017, 212-661-4878

Kurt Salmon Associates, Inc., 1355 Peachtree St., Atlanta, GA 30309, 404-892-0231

Towers Perrin, 245 Park Ave., New York, NY 10167, 212-309-3400

Trebag International Management Consultants, Ismaniger Strasse 98, 8000 Munchen 80, Germany, 49-89-92-69-640

Twijnstra Gudde Management Consultants, P.O. Box 907, 3800 AX, Amersfoort, The Netherlands, 31-33-67777

Emanual Weintraub Associates, Inc., Polygon Plaza, 2050 Center Ave., Fort Lee, NJ 07024, 201-947-2404

Welling & Woodard, Inc., 1067 Broadway, San Francisco, CA 94133, 415-776-4500

■ *The Institute of Management Consultants (IMC)*, 521 Fifth Ave., New York, NY 10175-3598, 212-697-8262

The Institute of Management Consultants (IMC) is a principal certifying body for the consulting profession. It grants the appellation "CMC" that signifies a consultant is publicly committed to excellence and integrity. The certification assures that the consultant meets a rigorous standard of professional competence in the consulting profession. IMC members offer services in:

- Personnel/human resources
- Manufacturing administration

- Marketing
- Materials management
- Purchasing
- Packaging
- Physical distribution
- Research and development
- Other fields.

The IMC has a referral service to assist potential clients in their selection of an appropriate consultant/consulting firm.

## Other Resources

Management consultants in the EC form associations of mutual interest and support, just as the organizations noted earlier in this chapter. For information on management consulting firms active in your targeted EC member state, you may wish to contact:

European Federation of Management Consultants Associations
3, rue Leon Bonnat, F-75016 Paris, France, 33-1-524-4353

Their directory lists the 15 member associations of the Federation. The directory is updated annually.

# 10

# ACCOUNTING, FINANCE, AND INSURANCE

Accounting, finance, and insurance are service sectors that can be critical to the long-term success of every corporation's international activities. This chapter identifies the leading U.S. accounting firms that provide services in support of EC-based operations, the U.S. and foreign banks that service the EC and are active in the United States, and the property and casualty insurers that serve the international risk management needs of American corporations.

## ACCOUNTING

The nature of your international activity will dictate your accounting and financial management requirements. Export sales to unrelated distributors and resellers, branch offices, subsidiaries, joint ventures, or licensing arrangements have different management, reporting, tax, and control requirements. Effective accounting support is critical to managing this international activity. The firms listed here have offices in the EC or service arrangements in the EC.

There are two lists of accounting firms. The first list contains the larger U.S.-based accounting firms with offices in the EC. It includes the "Big 6" and other firms with a strong international presence.

The second list sets out smaller or regional firms that by association can also assist with audit, tax, and other services in the EC. These firms are members of ACPA International, Inc., which is described at the heading of the second list.

When you seek the assistance of an accounting firm for your activities in the EC, begin with your own CPA firm. Large national firms have significant resources in place in the EC. Smaller firms, whether local or regional, may be able to assist you through association with firms of similar size in your target country.

Do not discount the capabilities or contacts of your local CPA or accounting firm. Discuss your requirements with your account manager, determine the firms capacity, then begin the selection process. Identify and utilize the services appropriate to your long-term requirements. Interview at least three different firms to select the best fit for your company. This will not always be the large national firm.

## Major U.S. Firms with Offices in the EC[1]

*Arthur Andersen & Co.*, 69 West Washington, Chicago, IL 60602

This large firm provides audit, business advisory, tax, and special consulting services through the Arthur Andersen trade style, and Andersen Consulting offers strategic services, management consulting, systems integration, process and change management, and application software products. It has offices in each of the 12 EC member states. It has a number of publications that deal with Europe and the EC, including:

*Holding Companies in Europe*

*Guidelines for U.S. Investors in Real Estate*

*A Tax Guide to Europe*

*European VAT News*

*Refunds of VAT and GST*

*Treasury Management: A Comparison between Ireland, Belgium, the Netherlands, and Luxembourg*

*Grants and Other Assistance Available from Irish and European Community Bodies*

*Luxembourg Holding Companies*

*BDO Seidman*, 15 Columbus Circle, New York, NY 10023
212-765-7500

BDO Seidman is the U.S. member firm of the world's seventh largest accounting organization, BDO Binder. EC activities are directed from the organization's international office in Brussels, Belgium.

*International Executive Office*
BDO Hillen
Brussels, Belgium

*U.S. International Services*
BDO Seidman
15 Columbus Circle
New York, NY 10023
212-765-7500

In addition to accounting, audit, and tax services in each of the 12 EC member states, the firm provides location studies, assists with certification under ISO 9000, and provides start-up services for firms interested in opening operations in Europe. Their EC-related publications include:

[1] Professional Services Review, Bellevue, WA assisted in developing this listing.

*Doing Business in . . . .(each EC member state except Belgium, Luxembourg, Greece, and Italy)*

*VAT in the European Community*

*Indirect Taxation: A Guide to the EC Proposals for Change*

*Financial Statements for European Banks*

*Financial Statements Worldwide*

*Coopers & Lybrand,* 1251 Avenue of the Americas, New York, NY 10020

Coopers & Lybrand is the U.S. associate of Coopers & Lybrand (International), an association of professional accounting firms throughout the world. The firm has representation in 117 countries with over 700 offices. They have offices throughout the EC. The firm provides a full range of accounting services.

Their EC related publications include:

*A Guide for Businessmen and Investors* (various countries)

*International Tax News,* a regular newsletter

*Guide to Growing Your Business Internationally, an International Starter Kit*

*Accounting and Auditing in Germany*

*Serving the German Speaking Market*

*The German Banking System*

Various UK related publications

*EC Initiatives in Direct Taxation and the National Responses*

*Deloitte & Touche,* 10 Westport Rd., Wilton, CT 06897
203-761-3149

Deloitte & Touche is a major international accounting firm with offices throughout the EC. Internationally, the firm is known as Deloitte Touche Tohmatsu International. In each of the EC countries the firm provides the following services: audit, tax, consulting, evidentiary services, corporate finance, and special services.

*International Executive Office*

Deloitte Touche Tohmatsu International, 1633 Broadway, New York, NY 10019-6754
212-489-1600

Their EC related publications include:

*Your Guide to Raising Finance in the United Kingdom*

*International Tax and Business Guide(s)*

*Business Handbooks* (individual countries)

*European Update* (a monthly newsletter)

*European Newsletter* (a quarterly newsletter)

*Ernst & Young*, 787 Seventh Ave., New York, NY 10019
212-773-3000

Ernst & Young is a major international accounting, tax, consulting, and advisory services firm with offices in each of the EC member states. It is the largest professional services firm in the United States, and supports a European American Advisory Group to serve the needs of U.S. firms interested in doing business in the EC.

*International Executive Offices*

European American Advisory
787 Seventh Ave.
New York, NY 10019
212-773-5992

European Business Advisory Centre
Ave. Marcel Thiry 204
B-1200 Brussels
Belgium
32-2-774-9111

Their EC related publications include:

*Doing Business in . . .* (each EC member state)

*Manufacturing Investment Abroad Study*

*EC Brief* (newsletter series)

Video *"Guide to the European Single Market"*

*Value Added Tax in Europe*

*International Quality Studies* (various)

*Grant Thornton*, 800 One Prudential Plaza, Chicago, IL 60601, 312-856-0001

This major international accounting and advisory services firm has 128 offices in the EC member states, with a client list of over 40,000 names. The firm provides audit, accounting, tax, and strategic consulting services to firms interested in the EC.

*International Executive Offices*

Grant Thornton International, European Community Office, 227 rue de la Loi, B-10410 Brussels, Belgium, 32-2-231-0580

Their EC related publications include:

*The Month in Brussels* (a monthly newsletter)

*European Business Conspectus*

*Doing Business Guide . . .* (each member state)

*Kenneth Leventhal, & Company,* 2049 Century Park East, Suite 1700, Los Angeles, CA 90067, 310-277-0880

Kenneth Leventhal & Company is a member of Clark Kenneth Leventhal, an international association of independent accounting firms. With members in all of the EC member states except Greece and Portugal.

*International Executive Office*

25 New St. Square, London, EC4A 3LN, United Kingdom, 44-71-353-0508

The firm provides the following services to its domestic and international clients: accounting and audit, tax, corporate reorganization, strategic planning, investigative services, litigation support, capital access and financing, and consulting in the fields of human resources and MIS. Publications of the firm and its associates include:

*Finance from the European Community*

*International Business Letter* (a monthly newsletter)

*Client Newsletter, V.F. Nathan* (Ireland) (newsletter)

*KPMG Peat Marwick,* 767 Fifth Ave., New York, NY 10153, 212-909-5798

KPMG Peat Marwick is the world's largest firm of accountants and consultants. It has offices in each of the EC member states. It provides a full range of accounting and consulting services: accounting-audit, tax, and consulting; business strategy, information technology, financial management, and human resource management services.

*International Offices for the EC*

KPMG EC Centre
44, rue du Taciturne
B-1040 Brussels
Belgium
32-2-519-3177

KPMG International Office
World Trade Center
Strawinskylaan 957
1077 XX Amsterdam
Netherlands
31-20-750111

KPMG Peat Marwick publishes a number of books, brochures, and newsletters dealing with the EC. Some of them are:

*Europe 1992 and the Insurance Industry*

*Europe 1992 and the High Technology Industry*

*ITC Circular* (a newsletter of the International Tax Centre)

*Venture Capital in Europe, the Yearbook of the European Venture Capital Association*

*Disclosure of Company Documents in the European Community*

*Taxation of International Transfers of Technology*

*Taxation of Cross Border Mergers and Acquisitions*

*World* (a quarterly magazine on international business issues)

*Deal Watch* (tracks significant international M&A deals)

*The European Agenda* (a monthly that tracks EC legislation)

Other KPMG Peat Marwick publications are listed in Chapter 3.

*McGladrey & Pullen,* 102 West Second St., Davenport, IA 52801
319-326-5111

McGladrey & Pullen is a member of DRM, an association of independent accounting firms represented in 70 countries.

*International Executive Offices*

| | |
|---|---|
| 1133 Avenue of the Americas<br>New York, NY 10036<br>212-382-0493 | 186 City Rd.<br>London EC1V 2NU<br>44-71-865-2385 |

The DRM organization is represented in each of the 12 EC member states. McGladrey & Pullen has 111 offices in the United States.

The members of DRM publish *Doing Business in* . . . their country, e.g., *Doing Business in the UK* by Robson Rhodes, the U.K. member firm. These publications cover: the business environment, employment, business organization, finance, company taxation, personal taxation, and financial assistance and government grants. Other information is available from McGladrey & Pullen.

*Price Waterhouse,* 1251 Avenue of the Americas, New York, NY 10020, 212-819-5000

Price Waterhouse is a major U.S. accounting firm, with offices in each of the 12 EC member states. Price Waterhouse publishes an Information Guide *Doing Business in the European Community.*

*EC Service Office*, EC Services, Place St. Lambert 14, B-1200 Brussels, Belgium

## U.S. CPA Firms with Service Capacity in the EC

ACPA International Inc., the Affiliated Conference of Practicing Accountants, encompasses 63 (1993) smaller CPA firms in 26 countries, with over 1,700 total personnel. The average firm has a staff of 28, with 16 professionals and four para-professionals. In addition to tax and audit services, U.S. members offer their clients international tax, audit, and advisory services through affiliation with EC firms of similar size, interests, and relevant expertise. This is a list of the U.S. members of ACPA. Affiliates are located in Belgium, France, Germany, Ireland, Italy, Luxembourg, Netherlands, Portugal, Spain, and the United Kingdom (not represented in Denmark or Greece).

| | |
|---|---|
| California | Duitch & Franklin, 11601 Wilshire Blvd., 23rd Fl., Los Angeles 90025, 310-208-8600 |
| | Stadtler, Rosenblum & Saris, 2301 Market, Suite 200, San Francisco 94114, 415-864-0500 |
| Colorado | Bondi & Co., 44 Inverness Dr. East, Bldgs. A&B, Englewood 80112, 303-799-6826 |
| Connecticut | Konowitz, Kahn & Co., Inc., 116 Washington Ave., North Haven 06473, 203-239-6888 |
| Florida | Karpel & Co., P.A., 4770 Biscayne Blvd., Suite 1070, Miami 33137, 305-576-6200 |
| Illinois | Lipschultz Bros., Levin & Gray, 900 Skokie Blvd., Suite 104, Northbrook 60062, 708-272-5300 |
| Maryland/DC | Stegman & Co., 405 East Joppa Rd., Suite 200, Towson MD 21204, 410-823-8000 |
| | also Baltimore, MD<br>Columbia, MD |
| Massachusetts | Arron, Smith, Bergman, Gaffney & Rubinstein, P.C., 270 Benton Dr., East Longmeadow 01028, 413-525-0009 |
| | Gordon, Harrington & Osborn, P.C., 630 Turnpike St., North Andover 01845, 508-689-0601 |
| Michigan | Edwards, Koshiw, Melton & Company, P.C., 2855 Coolidge Highway, Suite 103, Troy 48084, 313-643-4545 |
| | also Ann Arbor |
| Minnesota | Baune, Dosen & Co., 601 Lakeshore Parkway, Suite 150, Minnetonka 55305, 612-473-2002 |
| | also Hibbing |
| New Jersey | Dorfman, Abrams, Music & Co., 11 Harristown Rd., Glen Rock 07452, 201-444-6700 |
| New York | Davidson, Fox & Company, 40 Chenango St., Binghamton 13901, 607-772-5386 |
| | also Syracuse |
| | Levine Mandelbaum Neider Wohl, 230 Park Ave., New York 10169, 212-949-0900 |
| | Lucker, Kennedy & Felmeden, 241 Main St., Suite 100, Buffalo 14203, 716-852-1470 |
| | Rander, Kimball & DeCicco, P.C., 103-111 Hurley Ave., Kingston 12401-0905, 914-331-5030 |
| Oregon | Jones & Roth, P.C., 260 East 11th Ave., Eugene 97401, 503-687-2320 |

| | |
|---|---|
| | also Springfield<br>Hillsboro<br>Forest Grove |
| Tennessee | Lattimore, Black, Morgan & Cain, P.C., 5203 Maryland Way, Suite 200, Brentwood 37024-1869 |
| Texas | Wallace Sanders & Co., 8131 LBJ Freeway, Suite 875, Dallas 75251, 214-690-6301 |

## U.S.-BASED BANKS (U.S. AND FOREIGN) SERVING THE EC

Trade, operating, and investment finance services for business in the EC are available from a number of different types of financial intermediaries: finance companies, leasing companies, factors, banks, and insurance companies. This section identifies the banks located in the United States that have on-site services in the EC, and EC-based banks that have offices in the United States. Contact your commercial lending officer or the international department of your local bank to learn how they may be able to assist you in your EC activities. Most U.S. banks rely on correspondent banks to serve the EC in-country needs of their domestic clients. Many local banks may offer certain export finance services (see the Eximbank Referral List in this section), and some public sector organizations have arrangements to work with Eximbank (see City/State Program in this section).

### U.S. Banks with Offices in the EC

| *EC Member State* | *U.S. Bank* | *Type of Office* |
|---|---|---|
| Belgium | Bank of America, SF | B |
| Denmark | none | |
| France | American Express Bank, NY | S |
| | Bankers Trust Co., NY | S |
| | Bank of New York, NY | R |
| | Bank of America, SF | B |
| | Chemical Bank, NY | S,R |
| | Chase Manhattan, NY | S |
| | Citibank, NY | B |
| | CoreStates Bank, PA | R |
| | First National Bank of Boston | B |
| | Manufacturers Hanover | S of Chemical, NY |
| | Morgan Guaranty Trust, NY | R |
| | NationsBank, TX | R |

| *EC Member State* | *U.S. Bank* | *Type of Office* |
|---|---|---|
| | Republic National Bank of NY, | S |
| | Riggs National Bank, DC | S |
| Germany | American Express, NY | S, B |
| | Bank of America, SF | B |
| | Bankers Trust, NY | B,S |
| | Bank of New York, NY | B |
| | Chase, NY | S |
| | Chemical, NY | B |
| | Citibank, NY | S |
| | First National Bank of Boston | B |
| | National Bank of Detroit | B |
| | State Street Bank & Trust, Boston | S |
| Greece | American Express Bank, NY | B |
| | Bank of America, SF | B |
| | Chase, NY | B |
| | Citibank, NY | B |
| Ireland | Bank of America, SF | B |
| | Chase, NY | S |
| | Citibank, NY | B |
| Italy | Bank of America, SF | R |
| | Bankers Trust, NY | B,S |
| | Bank of New York, NY | B |
| | Chase, NY | B |
| | Chemical Bank, NY | B |
| | Citibank, NY | B |
| | Continental Bank, Chicago | B |
| | CoreStates, PA | R |
| | Morgan Guaranty Trust, NY | R |
| | Republic National Bank, NY | B |
| Luxembourg | American Express Bank, NY | S |
| | Bank of America, SF | S |
| | First National Bank of Boston | S |
| | Chase, NY | S |
| | Citibank, NY | S |
| | Maryland National Bank | S |
| | Republic National Bank, NY | S |
| Netherlands | American Express Bank, NY | B |
| | Bank of America, SF | B |
| | Citibank, NY | B |
| | Morgan Guaranty Trust, NY | S |

| *EC Member State* | *U.S. Bank* | *Type of Office* |
|---|---|---|
| Portugal | Chase, NY | R |
| | Chemical Bank, NY | S |
| | Citibank, NY | B |
| Spain | Bank of America, SF | B,S |
| | Bankers Trust, NY | B,S |
| | Bank of New York, NY | R |
| | Chemical Bank, NY | B |
| | CoreStates, PA | R |
| United Kingdom | American Express Bank, NY | B |
| | Bankers Trust, NY | B,S |
| | Bank of America | B,S |
| | Bank of New York | B |
| | Bank of New England, Boston | B |
| | Chase, NY | B,S |
| | Chemical Bank, NY | B,S |
| | Citibank, NY | B,S |
| | Citizens & Southern, Savannah, GA | B |
| | Continental Bank, Chicago | B |
| | CoreStates, PA | B |
| | Fidelity Bank, PA | B |
| | Fiduciary Trust Co., NY | R |
| | First National Bank of Chicago | S |
| | First National Bank of Boston | B |
| | First National Bank of Chicago | B |
| | First National Bank of Maryland | B |
| | First National Bank of Boston | S |
| | First National Bank of Providence | B |
| | Greyhound Bank, PLC | S of Greyhound Dial |
| | Harris Trust & Savings Bank, Chicago | R |
| | Mellon Bank, PA | B |
| | Merrill Lynch International Bank | S of ML&Co, DE |
| | Morgan Guaranty Trust, NY | B |
| | NationsBank, Charlotte | S,B |
| | NationsBank, TX | B |
| | Northern Trust Co., Chicago | B |
| | PaineWebber International | S of PaineWebber, DE |
| | Republic Bank, NY | B |
| | Riggs National Bank, DC | S |
| | State Street Bank of Boston | B |

Key: R Representative office. Introductions, arrangements, support. No loan or deposit services

B Full, or limited, banking services. Deposits, loans, credits, payments, other services. Varies by location and by bank.

S Subsidiary bank or company. Formed to benefit from local law or tax regime. May offer banking services, corporate financing, M&A, and other services.

## EC-Based Banks with Offices in the United States

Foreign banks are permitted to operate in the United State in accordance with U.S. banking law. Banks in the United States are regulated by the Federal Reserve System, the Controller of the Currency, the Federal Deposit Insurance Corporation, and various state banking authorities. Jurisdictions overlap. Foreign banks select locations and forms of organization that meet the needs of their clients, or that meet the strategic needs of the bank at the time of the investment. Because of this, there are many different structures to the EC banks operating in the U.S. Foreign banking offices in the United States are usually structured as representative offices, branch, of subsidiary banks. The subsidiary may be a national bank, a state bank, or an agency.

| *Country of Parent* | *Name and Location of U.S. Bank* | *Type* |
|---|---|---|
| Belgium | ASLK-CGER Bank, New York | B |
| | Bank Bruxelles Lambert, SA, New York | B |
| | Generale Bank, New York | B |
| | General Investment Banking Corp., New York | NY |
| | Kreditbank, NV, New York | B |
| | Kreditbank, NV, Atlanta | A |
| Denmark | Aktivbanken A/S, Long Beach | A |
| | Den Danske Bank, New York | B |
| | National Bank of Long Beach | S of Aktivbanken,AS |
| | Unibank A/S, New York | B |
| France | Banque Nationale de Paris (BNP), New York | B |
| | Banque Nationale de Paris, Miami | A |
| | Banque Nationale de Paris, Chicago | B |
| | Banque Nationale de Paris, Houston | A |
| | Banque Nationale de Paris, Los Angeles | A |

| *Country of Parent* | *Name and Location of U.S. Bank* | *Type* |
|---|---|---|
| | Banque Nationale de Paris, San Francisco | A |
| | Bank of the West, San Francisco | S of BNP, Paris |
| | Banque Indosuez, New York | B |
| | Banque Indosuez, Houston | A |
| | Banque Indosuez, Los Angeles | B |
| | Banque Francaise du Commerce Exterieur, New York | B |
| | Banque Paribas, New York | B |
| | Banque Paribas, Chicago | B |
| | Banque Paribas, Houston | A |
| | Banque Paribas, Los Angeles | A |
| | Banque Sudameris, Miami | A |
| | BAII Banking Corporation, New York | NY |
| | Caisse Nationale de Credito Agricole, New York | B |
| | Caisse Nationale de Credito Agricole, Chicago | B |
| | Compagnie Francaise du Commerce Exterieur, NY | B |
| | Credit Commercial de France, New York | B |
| | Credit Lyonnais, New York | B |
| | Credit Lyonnais, Miami | A |
| | Credit Lyonnais, Atlanta | A |
| | Credit Lyonnais, Chicago | B |
| | Credit Lyonnais, Los Angeles | B |
| | Credit Lyonnais, San Francisco | B |
| | Credit National, New York | A |
| | Credit Local de France, New York | A |
| | Credit du Nord, New York | B |
| | French American Banking Corp., New York | NY |
| | Societe Generale, New York | B |
| | Societe Generale, Chicago | B |
| | Societe Generale, Dallas | A |
| | Societe Generale, Los Angeles | B |
| | United Bank for Africa, Ltd., New York | B |
| Germany | Bayerische Landesbank Girozentrale, New York | B |
| | Bayerische Hypotheken -und Wechsel Bank, New York | B |
| | Bayerische Vereinsbank AG, New York | B |

| Country of Parent | Name and Location of U.S. Bank | Type |
|---|---|---|
| | Bayerische Vereinsbank AG, Chicago | B |
| | Bayerische Vereinsbank AG, Los Angeles | A |
| | Berlin Handels -und Frankfurter Bank, New York | B |
| | Commerzbank AKT, New York | B |
| | Commerzbank AKT, Atlanta | A |
| | Commerzbank AKT, Chicago | B |
| | Commerzbank AKT, Los Angeles | B |
| | Deutsche Bank AG, New York | B |
| | Deutsche Bank AG, Chicago | B |
| | Deutsche Bank AG, Los Angeles | B |
| | Deutsche Genossenschaftsbank, New York | B |
| | Deutsche Genossenschaftsbank, Atlanta | A |
| | DG Bank-Deutsche Genossenschaftsbank, Los Angeles | B |
| | Deutsche Sudamerikanische Bank, AKT-SCH, Miami | A |
| | Dresdner Bank, New York | B |
| | Dresdner Bank, Chicago | B |
| | Dresdner Bank, Los Angeles | A |
| | Hessiche Landesbank Girozentrale, New York | B |
| | Norddeutsche Landesbank Girozentrale, New York | B |
| | Westdeutsche Landesbank Girozentrale, New York | B |
| Greece | Atlantic Bank of New York, New York | S |
| | National Bank of Greece, SA, Boston | B |
| | National Bank of Greece, SA, Cambridge | B |
| | National Bank of Greece, SA, West Roxbury | B |
| | National Bank of Greece, SA, Chicago | B |
| Ireland | Allied Irish Bank Limited, New York | B |
| | Governor & County Banks of Ireland, New York | B |
| Italy | Banca Commerciale Italiana, New York | B |

| *Country of Parent* | *Name and Location of U.S. Bank* | *Type* |
|---|---|---|
| | Banca Commerciale Italiana, Chicago | B |
| | Banca Commerciale Italiana, Los Angeles | A |
| | Banca Nazionale Dell Agricoltura, New York | B |
| | Banca Nazionale del Lavoro, New York | B |
| | Banca Nazionale del Lavoro, Miami | A |
| | Banca Nazionale del Lavoro, Atlanta | A |
| | Banca Nazionale del Lavoro, Chicago | B |
| | Banca Nazionale del Lavoro, Los Angeles | A |
| | Banco di Napoli SPA, New York | B |
| | Banco di Roma, New York | B |
| | Banco di Roma, Chicago | B |
| | Banco di Roma, Houston | A |
| | Banco di Roma, San Francisco | A |
| | Banca Populare di Milano, New York | B |
| | Banco di Santo Spirito SPA, New York | B |
| | Banco di Sicilia, New York | B |
| | Banco di Sicilia, Los Angeles | A |
| | Cassa di Risparmio delle Provincie Lombarde, NY | B |
| | Cassa di Risparimo di Torino, New York | B |
| | Credito Italiano, New York | B |
| | Credito Italiano, Los Angeles | A |
| | First Los Angeles Bank, Los Angeles | S |
| | Instituto Bancario San Paolo di Torino, New York | B |
| | Instituto Bancario San Paolo di Torino, Los Angeles | B |
| | Monte dei Paschi di Siena, New York | B |
| Netherlands | ABN-AMRO Bank NV, Boston | B |
| | ABN-AMRO Bank NV, New York | B |
| | ABN-AMRO Bank NV, Pittsburgh | B |
| | ABN-AMRO Bank NV, Miami | B |
| | ABN-AMRO Bank NV, Atlanta | B |
| | ABN-AMRO Bank NV, Chicago | B |
| | ABN-AMRO Bank NV, Los Angeles | B |
| | ABN-AMRO Bank NV, San Francisco | B |
| | ABN-AMRO Bank NV, Seattle | S |

| Country of Parent | Name and Location of U.S. Bank | Type |
|---|---|---|
| | ABN-AMRO Bank NV, Houston | A |
| | Amsterdam-Rotterdam Bank NV, New York | B |
| | Bank of Hillside, Hillside, NJ | S |
| | European American Bank, New York | S |
| | Internationale Nederlandsbank NV, New York | B |
| | Internationale Nederlandsbank NV, Dallas | A |
| | LaSalle Bank Lake View, Chicago | S |
| | LaSalle Bank Northwest, Chicago | S |
| | LaSalle Bank Northbrook, Northbrook | S |
| | LaSalle Bank Westmont, Westmont | S |
| | Rabobank Nederland, New York | B |
| | Rabobank Nederland, Dallas | A |
| Portugal | Banco Espirito Santo e Commercial, New York | B |
| | Banco Fonescas & Burnay | A |
| | Banco Portugues do Atlantico, New York | B |
| | Banco Portugues do Atlantico, Miami | A |
| | Banco Totta & Acores, New York | A |
| Spain | Banco Atlantico, New York | A |
| | Banco Atlantico, Miami | A |
| | Banco Bilbao Vizcaya, New York | B |
| | Banco Bilbao Vizcaya, Miami | A |
| | Banco Bilbao Vizcaya, SA, San Francisco | A |
| | Banco Central Hispano-Americano, SA, New York | B |
| | Banco Central Hispano-Americano, SA, Miami | A |
| | Banco Central Hispano-Americano, SA, San Francisco | A |
| | Banco de Santander, SA, New York | B |
| | Banco de Santander, Miami | A |
| | Banco Santander International, New York | E |
| | Banco Santander International, Miami | E |
| | Banco Central of New York, New York | S |
| | Banco Exterior de Espana, SA, Miami | A |
| | Banco Exterior de Espana, SA, Los Angeles | A |
| | Extebank, Stonybrook, NY | S |

| *Country of Parent* | *Name and Location of U.S. Bank* | *Type* |
|---|---|---|
| | Banco Espanol de Credito SA, New York | B |
| | Banco Espanol de Credito SA, Miami | A |
| | Banesto Banking Corporation, New York | NY |
| United Kingdom | Bank of Scotland, New York | B |
| | Barclays Bank PLC, Boston | B |
| | Barclays Bank PLC, New York | B |
| | Barclays Bank of New York, New York | S |
| | Barclays Bank PLC, Miami | A |
| | Barclays Bank International, PLC | B |
| | Barclays Bank PLC, San Francisco | A |
| | Coutts & Company (USA) International, Miami | E |
| | National Westminster Bank NJ, Jersey City | S |
| | National Westminster Bank USA, New York | S |
| | National Westminster Bank PLC, New York | B |
| | National Westminster Bank PLC, Chicago | B |
| | National Westminster Bank PLC, Dallas | A |
| | National Westminster Bank PLC, Los Angeles | A |
| | Midland Bank PLC, New York | B |
| | Royal Bank of Scotland PLC, New York | B |
| | Royal Bank of Scotland PLC, San Francisco | A |
| | Standard Chartered Bank PLC, New York | B |
| | Standard Chartered Bank PLC, Miami | A |
| | Standard Chartered Bank Ltd, Atlanta | A |
| | Standard Chartered Bank Ltd, Chicago | B |
| | Standard Chartered Bank UK, Houston | A |
| | Standard Chartered Bank, Los Angeles | B |
| | United Bank of Kuwait Ltd., New York | B |

Key:

A — Agency. Limited banking powers. Arranges loans or deposits, provides information and advisory services. Authority and services limited by state or federal law

B — Branch. Permitted under state or federal law to take deposits and make loans. Deposit and lending services focus on a specific market segment, often the larger corporations in the region served.

| | |
|---|---|
| S | Subsidiary, organized under the laws of the state or federal government. Authorized to engage in the business of banking in the United States as permitted by its state or federal license. |
| NY | A New York State licensed investment company. A bank subsidiary engaged in non-bank activities. |
| E | An Edge or Agreement Corporation (powers limited to international transactions or investments). |

## U.S. Banks That Deal with the Export-Import Bank of the United States (Eximbank Referral List)

The Export Import Bank of the United States (Eximbank) is a government corporation formed in 1945. It supports U.S. exports by making loans, issuing guarantees to bank and nonbank lenders, and issuing political and commercial risk insurance. The banks listed in this section have some form of working relationship with Eximbank. This relationship can range from simply being aware of Eximbank programs to actively working with Eximbank to develop new programs to finance exports. Each bank is different, in style, appetite for risk, and evaluation of export financing opportunities. U.S. and European banks on this list have some appetite for export financing transactions. Banks from other regions of the world have not been listed because their interest in U.S.-EC transactions is limited. Contact the international department of the selected bank.

| *State* | *Bank Contact Information* |
|---|---|
| Alabama | AmSouth Bank, NA, 1900 Fifth Ave. North, Birmingham 35203, 205-326-5491 |
| | AmSouth Bank, NA, P.O. Drawer 1628, Mobile 36633, 205-438-8207 |
| | SouthTrust Bank of Alabama, NA, P.O. Box 2554, Birmingham 35290, 205-254-5218 |
| | First Alabama Bank, P.O. Drawer 3527, Mobile 36622, 205-690-1245 |
| Arizona | First Interstate Bank of Arizona, P.O. Box 29744, Phoenix 85038-9744, 602-528-6568 |
| | Valley National Bank of Arizona, P.O. Box 13800, Tucson 85732, 602-792-7118 |
| Arkansas | First Commercial Bank, P.O. Box 1471, Little Rock 72203, 501-371-7340 |

| *State* | *Bank Contact Information* |
|---|---|
| | Worthen National Bank of Arkansas, 200 W. Capital Ave., 3rd Fl., Little Rock 72201, 501-378-1058 |
| California | Bank of La Costa, 7608 El Camino Real, Carlsbad 92009, 619-942-7634 |
| | Imperial Bank, 9920 S. La Cienega Blvd., Inglewood 90301, 213-417-5715 |
| | American International Bank, 624 S. Grand Ave., Los Angeles 90017-3379, 213-688-8628 |
| | Bank of America, 555 S. Flower St., 48th Fl., Los Angeles 90017, 213-228-9817 |
| | California Commerce Bank, 811 Wilshire Blvd., Los Angeles 90017, 213-488-2629 |
| | Citicorp-North America, Inc., 725 Figueroa, 6th Fl., Los Angeles 90017, 213-239-1748 |
| | General Bank, 201 S. Figueroa St., Los Angeles 90012, 213-972-4160 |
| | Lippo Bank, 711 West College St., Los Angeles 90012, 213-625-8688 |
| | National Westminster Bank, PLC, 400 S. Hope St., Suite 1000, Los Angeles 90071, 213-624-8555 |
| | Standard Chartered Bank, 707 Wilshire Blvd., Los Angeles 90017, 213-614-4062 |
| | Union Bank, 445 South Figueroa St., Los Angeles 90071, 213-236-5025 |
| | Westdeutsche Landesbank, 633 West Fifth St., Suite 6750, Los Angeles 90071, 213-623-0009 |
| | Wilshire State Bank, 3200 Wilshire Blvd., Los Angeles 90010, 213-387-3014 |
| | Community Bank, 100 E. Carson St., Pasadena 91103, 818-568-2046 |
| | Union Bank, 555 Capitol Mall Ave., Sacramento 95814, 916-321-3164 |
| | Bank of Commerce, 7980 Clairemont Mesa Blvd., San Diego 92111, 619-292-9004 |
| | First Interstate Bank, 401 B. St., Suite 2201, San Diego 92101, 619-699-3030 |
| | Banco Bilbao Vizcaya, 580 California St., Suite 1900, San Francisco 94104, 415-392-2530 |
| | Bank of America, 5629 South Van Ness, San Francisco 94103, 415-241-4678 |

| *State* | *Bank Contact Information* |
| --- | --- |
| | Bank of America, P.O. Box 3700, San Francisco 94137, 415-622-3958 |
| | Bank of California, 400 California St., San Francisco 94104, 415-765-3357 |
| | Bank of the West, 180 Montgomery St., San Francisco 94104, 415-956-0707 |
| | Banque Nationale de Paris, 180 Montgomery St., San Francisco 94104, 415-956-0707 |
| | First Interstate Bank, 345 California St., SF23-3, San Francisco 94104, 415-773-7056 |
| | Union Bank, 350 California St., 9th Fl., San Francisco 94104, 415-445-0616 |
| | Wells Fargo Bank, NA, 525 Market St., 25th Fl., San Francisco 94105, 415-396-7281 |
| | Union Bank, 99 Almaden Blvd., San Jose 95113, 415-445-0616 |
| | U.S. Bank, 999 Baker Way, Suite 120, San Mateo 94404, 415-358-0912 |
| | Bank of A. Levy, 2575 Vista Del Mar Dr., Ventura 93001, 805-656-2575 |
| Colorado | Colorado National Bank of Denver, P.O. Box 5168, Denver 80217, 303-892-4136 |
| | First Interstate Bank, 633 17th St., Denver 80270, 303-293-5299 |
| | Norwest Bank International, 1700 Broadway, Denver 80274-8685, 303-863-6428 |
| Connecticut | Connecticut National Bank, 777 Main St., Hartford 06115, 203-728-2060 |
| | First National Bank of Connecticut, One Commercial Plaza, Hartford 06103, 203-727-0700 |
| | Fleet Bank, NA, Constitution Plaza, Hartford 06115, 203-244-4976 |
| | Connecticut National Bank, 1 Landmark Square, Stamford 06904, 203-358-6175 |
| Delaware | Bank of New York (Delaware), 1105 North Market St., Wilmington 19801, 302-651-2010 |
| District of Columbia | Banque Nationale de Paris, 1819 H St., NW, Rm. 600, Washington 20006, 202-429-9218 |
| | Equator Bank, 1850 K St., NW, Suite 390, Washington 20006, 202-293-3275 |

| *State* | *Bank Contact Information* |
|---|---|
| | First American Bank, 740 15th St., NW, Washington 20005, 202-637-4344 |
| | Petra International Banking Corp, 1133 21st St., NW, Suite 200, Washington 20036, 202-293-2250 |
| | Riggs National Bank, 800 17th St., NW, Washington, 202-835-5037 |
| Florida | Popular Bank of Florida, Two Alhambra Plaza, Suite 100, Coral Gables 33134, 305-567-2265 |
| | Sun Bank/South Florida, NA, P.O. Box 8911, Ft. Lauderdale 33310-8911, 305-765-7606 |
| | Consolidated Bank, 900 West 49th St., Hialeah 33012, 305-364-9722 |
| | Barnett Bank of Jacksonville, 50 Laura St., Jacksonville 32202, 904-791-7579 |
| | ABN-AMRO Bank, NV, 1200 Brickell Ave., 5th Fl., Miami 33131, 305-372-1596 |
| | Atlantic Security Bank, 801 Brickell Ave., PH2, Miami 33131, 305-372-9014 |
| | Banco Nazionale del Lavoro, 1200 Brickell Ave., 18th Fl., Miami 33131, 305-374-5441 |
| | Banco Bilbao Vizcaya, 1 Biscayne Tower, Suite 3301, Miami 33131, 305-371-7544 |
| | Banco Exterior de Espana, 777 Brickell Ave., Suite 620, Miami 33131, 305-371-5008 |
| | Banco de Santander International, 1000 Brickell Ave., Miami 33131, 305-539-5900 |
| | Bank of Boston International, 800 Brickell Ave., Suite 1500, Miami 33131, 305-530-2400 |
| | BankAmerica International, 201 S. Biscayne Blvd., 28th Fl., Miami 33131, 305-530-4090 |
| | Barclays Bank PLC, 801 Brickell Ave., 16th Fl., Miami 33131, 305-579-8572 |
| | Barnett Bank of South Florida, 701 Brickell Ave., Miami 33131, 305-350-7126 |
| | Capital Bank, 1221 Brickell Ave., 4th Fl., Miami 33131, 305-536-1745 |
| | Citizens & Southern International Bank, 80 SW 8th St., 22nd Fl., Miami 33131, 305-995-5311 |
| | Deutsche-Suedamerikanische Bank, AG, 801 Brickell Ave., 7th Fl., Miami 33131, 305-530-0148 |

| *State* | *Bank Contact Information* |
|---|---|
| | Espirito Santo Bank of Florida, 1395 Brickell Ave., Miami 33131, 305-539-7716 |
| | First American International Bank, 1001 South Bayshore Dr., Suite 2800, Miami 33131, 305-536-3950 |
| | First Interstate Bank International, 701 Brickell Ave., Suite 1700, Miami 33131, 305-539-7791 |
| | First Union National Bank of Florida, 800 Brickell Ave., 2nd Fl., Miami 33131, 305-789-3948 |
| | International Bank of Miami, NA, 2121 Southwest Third Ave., Miami 33129, 305-864-8800 |
| | NCNB National Bank, 150 Southeast Third Ave., Miami 33131, 305-577-5744 |
| | NCNB of Florida, 250 SE 1st St., Miami 33131, 305-577-5417 |
| | Pacific National Bank, 1390 Brickell Ave., 5th Fl., Miami 33131, 305-539-7500 |
| | Riggs National Bank, 800 Brickell Ave., Suite 900, Miami 33131, 305-374-2405 |
| | Southeast Bank, NA, 800 Brickell Ave., 2d Fl., Miami 33131, 305-789-3946 |
| | Sun Bank/Miami, NA, 777 Brickell Ave., Miami 33131, 305-579-7445 |
| | Barnett Bank of Central Florida, P.O. Box 3200, Orlando 32801, 407-420-2781 |
| | Sun Bank, NA, 200 South Orange Ave., Orlando 32801, 407-237-4737 |
| | Barnett Bank of Tampa, NA, 101 East Kennedy Blvd., Tampa 33630, 813-225-8155 |
| | First Union National Bank of Florida, 100 South Ashley Dr., 10th Fl., Tampa 33602, 813-276-6502 |
| | Southern Commerce Bank, 5650 Breckenridge Dr., Suite 100, Tampa 33610, 813-621-2080 |
| | Sun Bank of Tampa/Sun Trust, 315 E. Madison St., 3rd Fl., Tampa 33601-3303, 813-224-2121 |
| Georgia | Banca Nazionale del Lavoro, 245 Peachtree St., 21st Fl., Atlanta 30303, 404-581-0143 |
| | Barclays Bank, PLC, 300 Galarie Parkway, NW, Suite 800, Atlanta 30339, 404-859-2400 |
| | First National Bank of Georgia, 34 Peachtree St., NW, Atlanta 30303, 404-584-1585 |

| *State* | *Bank Contact Information* |
|---|---|
| | NationsBank, 35 Broad St., Atlanta 30302-4899, 404-581-3306, |
| | Trust Company Bank, P.O. Box 4418, Atlanta 30302, 404-827-6671 |
| | Wachovia Bank of Georgia, 191 Peachtree St., NW, 27th Fl., Atlanta 30303, 404-332-5916 |
| Idaho | First Security Bank of Idaho, P.O. Box 7069, Boise 83730, 208-338-2118 |
| Illinois | Affiliated Bank, 758 W. North Ave., Chicago 60610, 312-335-5686 |
| | American National Bank & Trust Co, 33 N. LaSalle St., Chicago 60690, 312-661-6896 |
| | BankAmerica International-Chicago, 200 West Adams, 27th Fl., Chicago 60606, 312-269-4604 |
| | Barclays Bank, PLC, 200 W. Madison St., 37th Fl., Chicago 60606, 312-558-1125 |
| | Citicorp-North America, 200 S. Wacker Dr., 32nd Fl., Chicago 60606, 312-993-3101 |
| | Continental Bank, NA, 231 S. LaSalle St., Chicago 60697, 312-828-4021 |
| | First National Bank of Chicago, 1 N. Dearborn St., 9th Fl., Chicago 60670, 312-407-1722 |
| | Harris Trust & Savings Bank, 111 W. Monroe St., 9C, Chicago 60690, 312-461-3481 |
| | National Westminster Bank, 33 N. Dearborn St., 12th Fl., Chicago 60602, 312-621-1562 |
| | Northern Trust Co., 50 S. LaSalle St., Chicago 60675, 312-444-3450 |
| | American Midwest Bank & Trust, 1600 West Lake St., Melrose Park 60160-3890, 708-681-8600 |
| | Amcore Bank, NA, P.O. Box 1537, Rockford 61110-0037, 815-961-7018 |
| | First National Bank & Trust Co., 401 East State St., Rockford 61110-4900, 815-962-3771 |
| | Busey Bank, Race & Main Sts., Urbana 61801, 217-384-4511 |
| Indiana | Lincoln National Bank & Trust Co, P.O. Box 960, Ft. Wayne 46801, 219-461-6440 |
| | Bank One Indianapolis, NA, 111 Monument Circle, Suite 1801, Indianapolis 46277, 317-321-7947 |

| *State* | *Bank Contact Information* |
|---|---|
| | Indiana National Bank, One Indiana Square, Suite 1610, Indianapolis 46266, 317-266-5998 |
| | Merchants National Bank & Trust Co., One Merchants Plaza, Suite 770S, Indianapolis 46255, 317-267-6255 |
| | First Source Bank, P.O. Box 1602, South Bend 46634, 219-236-2617 |
| | Society Bank Indiana, P.O. Box 6, South Bend 46624, 219-237-5358 |
| Iowa | Firstar Bank Cedar Rapids, 222 2nd Ave., SE, Cedar Rapids 52401, 319-368-4708 |
| | Davenport Bank & Trust Co., NA, 203 W. Third St., Davenport 52801, 319-383-4990 |
| | Bankers Trust Co., 665 Locust St., Des Moines 50304, 515-245-2424 |
| | Norwest Bank International, 666 Walnut St., Des Moines 50304, 515-245-3397 |
| Kentucky | Citizens Fidelity Bank & Trust Co., Citizens Plaza, Louisville 40296, 502-581-3242 |
| | First National Bank of Louisville, P.O. Box 36000, Louisville 40233, 502-581-4086 |
| Louisiana | Jefferson Guaranty Bank, 3525 N. Causeway Blvd., Metairie 70002, 504-838-4520 |
| | Alerion Bank, 200 Carondelet St., New Orleans 70130, 504-525-7761 |
| | First National Bank of Commerce, 210 Barrone St., New Orleans 70160, 504-561-1313 |
| | Hibernia National Bank, 313 Carondelet St., New Orleans 70130, 504-585-5152 |
| | Whitney National Bank, 228 St. Charles, New Orleans 70161, 504-586-7305 |
| Maryland | First National Bank of Maryland, 25 South Charles St., 15th Fl., Baltimore 21201, 301-244-4853 |
| | Maryland National Bank, 10 Light St., 15th Fl., Baltimore 21201, 401-605-5000 |
| | Signet Bank/Maryland, 7 St. Paul St., Baltimore 21203, 410-332-5775 |
| Massachusetts | BayBank Boston, NA, 175 Federal St., Boston 02110, 617-482-1040 |

| State | Bank Contact Information |
|---|---|
| | First National Bank of Boston, 150 Federal St., Boston 02105, 617-434-5178 |
| | First National Bank of Chicago, One Financial Center, 27th Fl., Boston 02111, 617-457-2524 |
| | Fleet Bank of Massachusetts, 28 State St., MABO S33Crr, Boston 02109, 617-573-2593 |
| | Olympic National Bank & Trust Co., 303 Congress St., Boston 02210, 617-357-8000 |
| | Shawmut Bank, NA, One Federal St., OF 3307, Boston 02211, 617-457-3825 |
| | State St. Bank & Trust Co., 225 Franklin St., M2, Boston 02110, 617-654-3795 |
| | Multibank International/South Shore Bank, 1400 Hancock St., Quincy 02169, 617-847-3276 |
| Michigan | Manufacturers National Bank of Detroit, 100 Renaissance Center, 12th Fl., Detroit 48243, 313-222-3136 |
| | Michigan National Bank, 1300 Riverplace, Suite 6000, Detroit 48207, 313-568-3492 |
| | National Bank of Detroit, 611 Woodward Ave., Detroit 48226, 313-225-1017 |
| | Michigan National Bank, 27777 Inkster Rd., Farmington Hills 48334, 313-473-3217 |
| Minnesota | First Bank, NA, P.O. Box A1567, Minneapolis 55480, 612-370-4489 |
| | Norwest Bank Minnesota, NA, Sixth & Marquette, 5th Fl., Minneapolis 55479, 612-667-5869 |
| Mississippi | Bank of Mississippi, One Mississippi Plaza, Tupelo 38802, 601-680-2527 |
| Missouri | Boatman's First National Bank, P.O. Box 419308, Kansas City 64183, 816-691-7571 |
| | Commerce Bank of Kansas City, 1000 Walnut, 4th Fl., Kansas City 64141, 816-234-2608 |
| | Mercantile Bank of Kansas City, 1101 Walnut, Kansas City 64106, 816-871-2220 |
| | Boatman's National Bank of St. Louis, 1 Boatman's Plaza, St. Louis 63101, 314-466-6449 |
| | Mark Twain Bank, 8822 Ladue Rd., St. Louis 63124, 314-746-2661 |

| *State* | *Bank Contact Information* |
| --- | --- |
| | Mercantile Bank of St. Louis, NA, 721 Locust St., St. Louis 63101, 314-425-2857 |
| New Hampshire | Fleet Bank New Hampshire, 1 Indianhead Plaza, Nashua 03060, 603-594-5000 |
| New Jersey | United Jersey Bank, 800 Kings Highway, Cherry Hill 08034, 609-486-4187 |
| | Princeton Commercial Div./Chemical Bank, 399 Thornall St., Edison 08837, 908-603-5731 |
| | Midlantic National Bank, P.O. Box 600, Edison 08818, 908-321-8230 |
| | First Fidelity Bank of New Jersey, NA, 550 Broad St., Newark 07102, 201-565-3096 |
| | Midlantic National Bank North, P.O. Box 2177, Paterson 07509, 201-881-5282 |
| | National Community Bank, 385 Rifle Camp Rd., West Paterson 07424, 201-357-7651 |
| New York | Eastchester Savings Bank, 22 East 1st St., Mount Vernon 10551, 914-285-9600 |
| | ABN-AMRO Bank NV, 500 Park Ave., New York 10022, 212-466-4237 |
| | American Express Bank, Ltd., World Financial Center, 22nd Fl., New York 10285, 212-298-2518 |
| | Atlantic Bank of New York, 960 Avenue of the Americas, New York 10001, 211-714-7250 |
| | BHF Bank, 55 East 59th St., New York 10022, 212-756-5926 |
| | Banco Nazionale del Lavoro, 25 West 51st St., New York 10019, 212-581-0710 |
| | Banco Atlantico, SA, 62 William St., New York 10005, 212-422-3400 |
| | Banco Portugues do Atlantico, 2 Wall St., New York 10005, 212-306-7814 |
| | Bank of New York, One Wall St., 9th Fl., New York 10286, 212-635-7603 |
| | Bankers Trust Co., 280 Park Ave., 10W, New York 10017, 212-454-4588 |
| | Banque Indosuez, 1230 Avenue of the Americas, New York 10020, 212-408-5651 |
| | Banque Paribas, 787 7th Ave., 32nd Fl., New York 10019, 212-841-2600 |

| *State* | *Bank Contact Information* |
| --- | --- |
| | Barclays Bank, PLC, 222 Broadway, New York 10038, 212-412-2943 |
| | Bayerische Vereinsbank, AG, 335 Madison Ave., New York 10017, 212-210-0346 |
| | Chase Manhattan Bank, NA, 1 Chase Manhattan Plaza, 10th Fl., New York 10081, 212-552-5462 |
| | Chemical Bank, 270 Park Ave., New York 10017, 212-270-3345 |
| | Chemical Bank, 52 Broadway, 8th Fl., New York 10004, 212-701-4532 |
| | Citibank, NA, 153 East 53d St., New York 10043, 212-559-6788 |
| | Citicorp/Citibank, 399 Park Ave., 11th Fl., New York 10043, 212-207-4027 |
| | Continental Bank International, 520 Madison Ave., New York 10022, 212-605-2969 |
| | Credit Commercial de France, 450 Park Ave., 7th Fl., New York 10022, 212-848-0518 |
| | Credit Lyonnais, 1301 Avenue of the Americas, New York 10019, 212-261-7000 |
| | Credit Suisse, 100 Wall St., 14th Fl., New York 10005, 212-612-8000 |
| | Creditanstalt-Bankverein, 245 Park Ave., 28th Fl., New York 10167, 212-856-1000 |
| | Deutsche Genossenschafts Bank NY, 609 Fifth Ave., New York 10017, 212-745-1582 |
| | Extebank, 645 5th Ave., 11th Fl., New York 10022, 212-688-7500 |
| | First American Bank of New York, 350 Park Ave., New York 10022, 212-418-5490 |
| | First Chicago International, 153 West 51st St., 8th Fl., New York 10019, 212-373-1049 |
| | French American Banking Corporation, 499 Park Ave., New York 10022, 212-415-9651 |
| | Lloyds Bank, 199 Water St., New York 10038, 212-607-4965 |
| | Marine Midland Bank NA, 2 World Trade Center, 24th Fl., New York 10048, 212-912-2496 |
| | Morgan Guaranty Trust Co., 60 Wall St., New York 10260, 212-648-7235 |

| *State* | *Bank Contact Information* |
| --- | --- |
| | NMB Bank, 135 East 57th St., New York 10022, 212-446-1729 |
| | National Commercial Bank, 245 Park Ave., 37th Fl., New York 10167, 212-916-9008 |
| | National Westminster Bank, 515 7th Ave., New York 10018, 212-704-7091 |
| | National Westminster Bank USA, 175 Water St., 14th Fl., New York 10038, 212-602-2577 |
| | Rabobank Nederland, 245 Park Ave., New York 10167, 212-916-7941 |
| | Societe Generale, 50 Rockerfeller Plaza, 2nd Fl., New York 10020, 212-830-7091 |
| | Standard Chartered Bank, 160 Water St., New York 10038, 212-612-0517 |
| | Svenska Handelsbanken, 599 Lexington Ave., 38th Fl., New York 10022, 212-326-5133 |
| | Swiss Bank Corporation, 10 East 50th St., 19th St., New York 10022, 212-574-3317 |
| | Swiss Bank Corporation, 395 Church St. Station, New York 10008, 212-594-3317 |
| | Unibanco, 555 Madison Ave., 24th Fl., New York 10022, 212-207-9393 |
| | Union Bank of Switzerland, 299 Park Ave., 33d Fl., New York 10171, 212-715-3430 |
| | United Bank for Africa, PLC, 551 Madison Ave., New York 10022, 212-308-7222 |
| | Westdeutsche Landesbank Girozentrale, 1211 Avenue of the Americas, New York 10036, 212-852-6000 |
| | Z-Laenderbank Bank of Austria, AG, 767 Fifth Ave., New York 10153, 212-326-1897 |
| | Chase Lincoln First Bank, NA, One Lincoln First Plaza, Rochester 14643, 716-258-4262 |
| | Bank of New York, 123 Main St., 4th Fl., White Plains 10602, 914-684-5402 |
| North Carolina | First Union National Bank, 301 South Tyron St., T-7, Charlotte 28288, 704-374-5917 |
| | NationsBank of North Carolina, 1 NS Bank Plaza, T-21-3, Charlotte 28255, 704-386-8908 |

| *State* | *Bank Contact Information* |
|---|---|
| Ohio | First National Bank of Ohio, 106 South Main St., Akron 44308, 216-384-7128 |
| | Central Trust Co., NA, 201 East Fifth St., 7th Fl., Cincinnati 45202, 513-651-8564 |
| | Star Bank, NA, 425 Walnut St., Cincinnati 45202, 513-632-4134 |
| | The Fifth Third Bank, 38 Fountain Square Plaza, Cincinnati 45263, 513-579-4317 |
| | Ameritrust Company, NA, 900 Euclid Ave., Cleveland 44101, 216-737-3445 |
| | Bank One Cleveland, NA, 600 Superior Ave., Cleveland 44115, 216-781-4478 |
| | Citicorp-North America, Inc., 1300 East 9th St., 20th Fl., Cleveland 44114, 312-993-3000 |
| | Huntington National Bank, P.O. Box 5065, Cleveland 44101, 216-344-6223 |
| | National City Bank, 1900 East 9th St., Cleveland 44114, 216-575-2960 |
| | Society National Bank, 800 Superior Ave., 12th Fl., Cleveland 44114, 216-689-3684 |
| | Bank One Columbus, NA, 100 East Broad St., Columbus 43271, 614-248-5632 |
| | BankOhio National Bank, 155 East Broad St., Columbus 43251, 614-463-7528 |
| | Huntington National Bank, 41 South High St., HC 1245, Columbus 43216, 614-463-4086 |
| | Bank One Dayton, NA, Kettering Tower, Dayton 45401, 513-449-8777 |
| Oklahoma | Bank of Oklahoma, P.O. Box 24128, Oklahoma City 73124, 405-272-2196 |
| | First Interstate Bank of Oklahoma, P.O. Box 25189, Oklahoma City 73125, 405-272-4283 |
| | Security Bank & Trust Co., P.O. Box 311, Ponca City 74602, 405-765-4444 |
| | Stillwater National Bank & Trust, P.O. Box 1988, Stillwater 74076, 405-372-2230 |
| | Bank of Oklahoma, P.O. Box 2300, Tulsa 74192, 918-588-6886 |

| *State* | *Bank Contact Information* |
|---|---|
| | First National Bank & Trust Co., 15 East Fifth St., Tulsa 74193, 918-586-5879 |
| Oregon | Bank of America-Oregon, 121 SW Morrison, Suite 1700, Portland 97204, 503-275-1557 |
| | First Interstate Bank of Oregon, 1300 SW Fifth Ave., T-19, Portland 97201, 503-225-2501 |
| | Key Bank of Oregon, 1211 SW Fifth Ave., Suite 300, Portland 97204, 503-790-7548 |
| | U.S. Bank of Oregon, P.O. Box 6979, Portland 97228, 503-275-5504 |
| Pennsylvania | Meridian Bank, 51 South Duke St., Lancaster 17602, 717-295-8584 |
| | Meridian Bank, 1700 Arch St., 5th Fl., Philadelphia 19103, 215-854-3483 |
| | Philadelphia National Bank, Broad & Chestnut Sts., Philadelphia 19101, 215-973-7336 |
| | ABN-AMRO Bank, NV, One PPG Place, Suite 2950, Pittsburgh 15222, 412-566-2290 |
| | Mellon Bank, NA, One Mellon Bank Center, Rm. 4535, Pittsburgh 15258, 412-234-8871 |
| | Pittsburgh National Bank, Fifth & Wood Sts., 10th Fl., Pittsburgh 15265, 412-762-2585 |
| Rhode Island | Fleet National Bank, 111 Westminster St., 2nd Fl., Providence 02903, 401-278-5703 |
| | Old Stone Bank, 150 South Main St., Providence 02903, 401-278-2250 |
| Tennessee | First Tennessee Bank, 165 Madison Ave., 9th Fl., Memphis 38103, 901-523-4420 |
| | First American National Bank, First American Center, Nashville 37237, 615-748-2834 |
| | NationsBank-Tennessee, One Sovran Plaza, Nashville 37219, 615-749-3009 |
| Texas | Park National Bank, P.O. Box 1277, Bellaire 77402, 713-667-7000 |
| | First City, Texas, 1700 Pacific Ave., Dallas 75201, 214-939-7926 |
| | NationsBank of Texas, P.O. Box 830304, Dallas 75283, 214-508-3548 |
| | Texas Commerce Bank, 2200 Ross Ave., Dallas 75266, 214-922-2966 |

| *State* | *Bank Contact Information* |
|---|---|
| | Continental National Bank, Drawer 5050, El Paso 79953, 915-544-9000 |
| | El Paso State Bank, 114 East San Antonio, El Paso 79901, 915-532-4746 |
| | State National Bank, 221 N. Kansas, El Paso 79901, 915-546-4841 |
| | Banque Nationale de Paris, 333 Clay St., Suite 3400, Houston 77002, 713-951-1233 |
| | Bank One Texas, NA, 910 Travis, Houston 77002, 713-751-6126 |
| | Charter Bank Houston, P.O. Box 4525, Houston 77210, 713-522-8414 |
| | First City Texas-Houston, NA, 1001 Fannin St., 5th Fl., Houston 77002, 713-658-6640 |
| | First Interstate Bank of Texas, NA, P.O. Box 3326, Houston 77253, 713-221-2390 |
| | Independence Bank, NA, 6910 North Eldridge Parkway, Houston 77041, 713-644-7283 |
| | Lakewood National Bank, P.O. Box 15104, Houston 77220, 713-674-7661 |
| | Metrobank, 5075 Westheimer, Suite 1060, Houston 77056, 713-877-1666 |
| | NationsBank of Texas, 700 Louisiana St., 8th Fl., Houston 77002, 713-247-6213 |
| | Pacific Southwest Bank, 6828 Ranchester Dr., Houston 77036, 713-272-7700 |
| | Southwest Bank of Texas, NA, P.O. Box 27459, Houston 77241, 713-759-9086 |
| | Sterling Bank, 10260 Westheimer, Houston 77042, 713-952-6055 |
| | Sunbelt National Bank, 8580 Katy Freeway at Bingle, Houston 77024, 713-984-3723 |
| | Texas Commerce Bank, NA, P.O. Box 2558, Houston 77252, 713-236-4803 |
| | International Bank of Commerce, 1200 San Bernardo, Laredo 78040, 512-726-6696 |
| | Laredo National Bank, P.O. Box 59, Laredo 78042, 512-723-1151 |
| | Union National Bank, P.O. Box 699, Laredo 78042, 512-726-8307 |

| *State* | *Bank Contact Information* |
|---|---|
| | First State Bank, 107 West Taylor, Morton 79346, 806-266-5511 |
| | Frost National Bank, 100 W. Houston St., San Antonio 78205, 512-220-4238 |
| | San Benito Bank & Trust Co., P.O. Box Drawer 1911, San Benito 78586, 512-399-1326 |
| Utah | First Security Bank of Utah, NA, 15 East & 100 South, Salt Lake City 84111, 801-350-5604 |
| | Zions First National Bank, One South Main St., Salt Lake City 84111, 801-524-4916 |
| Virginia | Central Fidelity Bank, P.O. Box 27602, Richmond 23261, 804-697-6861 |
| | Crestar Bank, 919 East Main St., Richmond 23219, 804-782-7478 |
| | NationsBank, NA, 111 East Main St., Richmond 23219, 804-788-2732 |
| Washington | Bank of Grays Harbor, P.O. Box 1826, Aberdeen 98520, 206-533-8870 |
| | Bank of California, 910 Fourth Ave., Suite 602, Seattle 98164, 206-587-3665 |
| | First Interstate Bank of Washington, P.O. Box 160, Seattle 98111, 206-292-3345 |
| | Seattle First National Bank, P.O. Box 24146, Seattle 98124, 206-358-3088 |
| | U.S. Bank of Washington, P.O. Box 720, Seattle 98111, 206-344-4589 |
| Wisconsin | Bank One Milwaukee, NA, P.O. Box 975, Milwaukee 53201, 414-765-2642 |
| | First Bank (NA) Milwaukee, 201 West Wisconsin Ave., Milwaukee 53259, 414-227-5430 |
| | First Wisconsin National Bank of Milwaukee, 777 E. Wisconsin Ave., Milwaukee 53202, 414-765-5452 |
| | Marshall & Ilsley Bank, 770 N. Water St., Milwaukee 53202, 414-765-7623 |

## Eximbank City/State Program

Eximbank has formed cooperative arrangements with state and local finance and development agencies, to help small or emerging firms make more effective use of Eximbank programs. City/state partners are listed by state. The services offered by these agencies vary, from counseling, loan packaging and referral, to financing and insurance services. Contact the selected agency and ask them to specify the services they provide, their charges, and their success ratio. Some of these agencies have carried out very effective self-promotion campaigns, but have no verifiable successes.

Eximbank has a City/State Coordinator assigned to work with these programs. Contact the coordinator at Eximbank in Washington, DC.

Marketing Division, Export Import Bank of the United States, 811 Vermont Ave., NW, Washington, DC 20571, 202-566-4490

| *State* | *Organization* |
|---|---|
| Arizona | Tucson Local Development Corp., P.O. Box 27210, Tucson 43221, 614-645-6171 |
| California | California Export Finance Office, 107 South Broadway, Suite 8039, Los Angeles 90012, 213-897-3997 |
| Florida | Florida Department of Commerce, 107 West Gaines, # 366, Tallahassee 32399-2000, 904-488-5287 |
| Georgia | Georgia Department of Industry, Trade & Tourism, Trade Division, 285 Peachtree Center Ave., Suite 1100, Atlanta 30303, 404-656-3571 |
| Hawaii | International Business Center of Hawaii, City Financial Tower, Suite 1510, 201 Merchant St., Honolulu 96813, 808-587-2797 |
| Maine | International Commerce Division, Maine Office of Business Development, State House Station, # 59, Augusta 04333, 207-289-5700 |
| Maryland | Maryland Industrial Development Financing Authority, The World Trade Center, 7th Fl., 401 East Pratt St., Baltimore 212020-3042, 301-333-8189 |
| Massachusetts | Massachusetts Industrial Finance Agency, 75 Federal St., Boston 02110, 617-451-2477 |
| Michigan | Michigan Export Development Authority, Michigan International Office, Department of Commerce, 525 West Ottowa, 5th Fl., Lansing 48909, 517-373-1054 |
| Nevada | Nevada State Development Corp., 350 South Center, Suite 310, Reno 89501, 702-323-3625 |
| New Hampshire | Department of Resources and Economic Development, Office of International Trade, P.O. Box 856, Concord 03302-0856, 603-271-2591 |

| *State* | *Organization* |
|---|---|
| New York/ New Jersey | Port of New York/New Jersey, Xport Trading Co., One World Trade Center, 35N, New York 10048, 212-435-2313 |
| Ohio | Columbus County-Wide, 941 Chatham Lane, Suite 207, Columbus 43221, 614-645-6171 |
| Oklahoma | Oklahoma Department of Commerce, Export Finance Program, 6601 Broadway, Oklahoma City, 73126-0980, 405-841-5142 |
| Pennsylvania | Pennsylvania Department of Commerce, Officer of International Development, 486 Forum Bldg., Harrisburg 17120, 717-787-7190 |
| Texas | Texas Department of Commerce, Finance Division, P.O. Box 12728, Austin 78711, 512-320-9662 |
| Utah | Division of Business and Economic Development, 324 S. State St., Suite 200, Salt Lake City 84111, 801-538-8786 |
| Vermont | Vermont Department of Economic Development, 109 State St., Montpelier 05609, 802-828-3221 |
| Virginia | Virginia Small Business Financing Authority, 1021 East Cary St., Richmond 23206-0798, 804-371-8255 |
| Washington | Export Assistance Center of Washington, 2001 Sixth Ave., Seattle 98121, 206-464-7123 |
| West Virginia | West Virginia Economic Development Authority, Building 6, Rm. 525, Capitol Complex, Charleston 25305, 304-558-3650 |

## PROPERTY AND CASUALTY INSURERS

International business—export, import, or investment on any scale—exposes the corporation and its assets to new and varied risks. The previous sections identified organizations that can assist in the mitigation of accounting, tax, management, and financing risks. Tangible and intangible assets are exposed to additional risks which can be managed by a well conceived and effective insurance program.

Amelioration of international business and transaction risks requires a comprehensive insurance program developed in cooperation with a quality insurance company. The companies listed in this section are members of the American Institute of Marine Underwriters.[2] They

[2] Source: American Institute of Marine Underwriters, New York, NY.

represent over 100 insurance and reinsurance companies that write over 90 percent of the marine insurance cover provided to U.S. corporations. Some of these same firms are among the few that provide political and commercial risk insurance to protect tangible, personal, and intangible assets abroad.

Your present property and casualty insurer may not be listed. Do not hesitate to contact one of the listed firms to discuss the nature of the business risks you will encounter in exporting to, importing from, or investing in the EC.

Aetna Life & Casualty, 151 Farmington Ave., Hartford, CT 06156, 203-273-0123

Allendale Insurance/Allendale Group, Allendale Park, P.O. Box 7500, Johnston, Rhode Island 02919, 401-275-3000

American International Group*, 70 Pine St., 18th Fl., New York, NY 10270, 212-770-7000

American Re-Insurance Co., 555 College Rd. East, Princeton, NJ 08543-5241, 609-243-4200

The Atlantic Mutual Companies, Three Giralda Farms, Madison, NJ 07940, 201-408-6000

Chubb & Son, Inc.*, Chubb Group of Companies, 15 Mountain View Rd., Warren, NJ 07061-1615, 908-580-2000

CIGNA Corp. Insurance Company of North America*, CIGNA Group, 1601 Chestnut, Philadelphia, PA 19192, 215-761-1000

Employers Reinsurance Corp., 5200 Metcalf Ave., Overland Park, KS 66201, 913-676-5200

Fireman's Fund Insurance Companies, 777 San Marin Dr., Novato, CA 94998, 415-899-2000

Generali-U.S. Branch, One Liberty Plaza, New York, NY 10006, 212-602-7600

General Reinsurance Corp., 695 East Main St., Stamford, CT 06904-2530, 203-328-5000

GRE Insurance Group, 61 Broadway, 33rd Fl., New York, NY 10006, 212-208-4100

Great American Insurance Companies* **, 580 Walnut St., Cincinnati, OH 45201-2575, 513-369-5000

Home Insurance Co., 59 Maiden Lane, New York, NY 10038, 212-530-7000

* These companies are the principal U.S.-based insurers of international business risks, including political risk insurance.

** Great American is the principal carrier for the political risk insurance vendor FCIA Management Company, Inc., New York, NY. FCIA Management Company, Inc., is the successor to FCIA, the former servicing agent for export credit insurance offered by the Eximbank.

International Marine Underwriters, Commercial Union Insurance Companies, One Beacon St., Boston, MA 02108, 617-725-6000

ITT Hartford Insurance Group, Hartford Plaza, Hartford, CT 06115, 203-547-5000

Kemper National Insurance Companies, Long Grove, IL 60049, 708-540-2000

Marine Office of America Corp., 1 Continental Dr., Cranberry, NJ 08570-0009, 609-395-2602

Wm. H. McGee & Co., Inc., 4 World Trade Center, New York, NY 10048, 212-775-1300

Munich Reinsurance Group, 560 Lexington Ave., New York, NY 10022, 212-310-1800

The Nippon Fire & Marine Insurance Co., Ltd.-U.S. Branch, One Tower Square, Hartford, CT 06183-7040, 203-954-1720

North American Reinsurance Corp., 237 Park Ave., New York, NY 10017, 212-9007-8000

Reliance Insurance Corp., Reliance Insurance Group, 4 Penn Center Plaza, Philadelphia, PA 19103, 215-864-4000

Royal Insurance Company of America, 9300 Arrowpoint Blvd., Charlotte, NC 28273-8135, 704-522-2000

Somerset Marine Group, 123 William St., New York, NY 10038, 212-349-1600

St. Paul Fire & Marine Insurance Co., Ltd., 385 Washington St., St. Paul, MN 55102, 612-221-7911

The Sumitomo Marine & Fire Insurance Co., Ltd.-U.S. Branch, 1 World Trade Center, # 9035, New York, NY 10048, P.O. Box 4602, Warren, NJ 07059, 212-297-6600

The Tokio Marine & Fire Insurance Co., Ltd.-U.S. Branch, 101 Park Ave., New York, NY 10178-0095, 212-797-6600

Trygg-Hansa Insurance Co., Ltd.-U.S. Branch, 29 Smith St., Nanuet, NY 10954, 914-624-7780

Washington International Insurance Co., 1930 Thoreau Dr., Suite 101, Schaumburg, IL 60173, 708-490-1850

The Yasuda Fire & Marine Insurance Company of America, Two World Trade Center, 43rd Fl., New York, NY 10281, 212-416-1200

*Subscriber Members*

English American Insurance Corp., 26 Main St., Chatham, NJ 07928, 201-635-4000

Phoenix Reinsurance Co., 80 Maiden Lane, New York, NY 10038, 212-837-9520

Underwriters Reinsurance Co., 22801 Ventura Blvd., Woodland Hills, CA 91364, P.O. Box 4030, Woodland Hills, CA 91365, 818-225-1000

*Associate Members-Brokers*

Alexander & Alexander Services, Inc., 1211 Avenue of the Americas, New York, NY 10036, 212-840-8500

Jardine Insurance Brokers, 333 Bush St., San Francisco, CA 94104, 415-391-2600

Johnson & Higgins, 125 Broad St., New York, NY 10004, 212-574-7000

Marsh & McLennan, Inc., 1166 Avenue of the Americas, New York, NY 10036, 212-345-5000

McGriff, Seibels, & Williams, P.O. Box 10265, Birmingham, AL 35202, 205-252-9871

Rollins Hudig Hall, 261 Madison Ave., New York, NY 10016, 212-952-1200

Willis Corroon, Wall St. Plaza, New York, NY 10005, 212-363-4100

## Insurance/Risk Management Consultants

A recommended approach to the management of international asset and operational risks is to use the services of a qualified risk management consultant. Most risks a corporation encounters in international business—such as risks involved in shipment, storage, handling, loss of goods, loss of use, risks to the personal safety of personnel, and others—can be managed and insured to protect the value for the corporation.

There are a few risk management consultants that are not attached to or dependent on a major carrier and can therefore provide independent counsel. A qualified risk manager can achieve the optimum mix of protection and cost in achieving specified corporate objectives.

# 11

# INTERNATIONAL MARKETING ORGANIZATIONS

Marketing services can be provided by advertising agencies and market research organizations (market research, product promotion) and by companies engaged in the export marketing of goods and services. This chapter lists the latter type of company, and resources that can be used to contact other international trade marketing organizations.

In 1982, Congress passed the Export Trading Company Act, which has the potential for significant impact on the international marketing of American products. The intended users (banks) are not interested in the Act or the opportunities; however, over 90 Export Trading Companies have been formed under the auspices of the Act and enjoy its benefits. The primary beneficial title of the Act, Title III, provides the American business community with the opportunity to obtain an *antitrust preclearance* for export activities. This preclearance, referred to as an "Export Certificate of Review," is issued by the Department of Commerce with Justice concurrence and *provides specific protection from U.S. antitrust liability.* Any U.S. corporation or partnership, any resident individual, or any state or local entity may apply for a Certificate of Review. Export conduct certified to date includes: establishment of export prices; exclusive arrangements with domestic suppliers; joint export production/marketing arrangements among domestic competitors; allocation of markets, territories, or customers; refusals to deal; exchange of business information and business technology. (The act improves corporate flexibility.)

Certified ETCs are engaged in the manufacture and distribution of seafood, linerboard, rice, fruit, forest products, manufactured goods, tools, film and entertainment products, and other diverse industries. These are international marketing organizations formed under the single U.S. law that encourages and supports competitive international marketing strategies and activities.

## CERTIFIED EXPORT TRADING COMPANIES

| | |
|---|---|
| Alabama | Irrigation Components International (V.I.), P.O. Box 1348, Mobile 36633 |
| Alaska | Sealaska Timber Corporation, 2030 Sealevel Dr., Suite 202, Ketchikan 99901 |
| | Wrangell Forest Products, Ltd., P.O. Box 5380, Ketchikan 99901 |
| California | American Film Marketing Association, 12424 Wilshire Blvd., Suite 600, Los Angeles 90025 |
| | Farmers' Rice Cooperative, P.O. Box 15223, Sacramento 95831 |
| | California Cherry Export Association, P.O. Box 877, Lodi 95241 |
| | California Kiwifruit Commission, 1540 River Park Dr., Suite 110, Sacramento 95815 |
| | Comet Rice, Inc., 10990 Wilshire Blvd., Suite 1800, Los Angeles 90024 |
| | International EXIM Corp., 2091 Business Center Dr., # 100, Rm. 35, Irvine 92715 |
| | National Geothermal Association, P.O. Box 1350, Davis 95617 |
| | Strand International, 17155 Von Karmen Ave., Suite 105, Irvine 92714 |
| | Streamline Shippers Association, Inc., 970 East 3rd St., Los Angeles 90013 |
| | Trade Development Corp. of Chicago, 2049 Century Park East, Suite 480, Los Angeles 90067 |
| | United Export Trading Co., 13315 Washington Blvd., Suite 200, Los Angeles 90066 |
| | U.S. Export & Trading Co., 848 Harding St., Escondido 92027 |
| | Wheeling, John J., 11117 Sunglow Dr., Moreno Valley 92557 |
| | World International Investments Corp., 4400 MacArthur Blvd., 9th Fl., Newport Beach 92660 |
| | World-Wide Sires, Inc., 16032 10th Ave., Hanford 93232 |
| Connecticut | U.S. Bus. & Ind. Dev. Service, P.O. Box 141, Easton 06612 |

| | |
|---|---|
| Delaware | Sun International Trading, Ltd., P.O. Box 2230, Wilmington 28402 |
| | U.S. Shippers Association, 1209 Orange St., Wilmington 19801 |
| District of Columbia | Aerospace Industry Association of America, 1250 I St., NW, Washington 20005 |
| | International Trading Organization, 1330 Connecticut Ave. NW, Suite 300, Washington 20036 |
| | Miller's National Federation, 600 Maryland Ave. NW, Suite 305W, Washington 20024 |
| | National Association of Energy Service Companies, 1350 New York Ave. NW, Suite 615, Washington 20005 |
| | National Hydropower Association, 555 13th St., NW, Suite 900-E, Washington 20004 |
| | Trust International Services, Inc., 1250 4th St., Suite 505, Washington 20005 |
| | The Ferrous Scrap Export Association, Washington |
| | TWP Company Inc., 1235 Kenilworth Ave., NE, Washington 200109 |
| | U.S. Hide, Skin, & Leather Association, 1700 N. Moore St., Suite 1600, Washington 22209 |
| | Valve Manufacturers Association of America, 105 17th St., NW, Suite 701, Washington 20036 |
| Florida | Demick International & Association, 4550 NW 9th St., # 118E, Miami 33126 |
| | Gate Group, U.S.A., Inc., 2890 N. Andrews Ave., Ft. Lauderdale 33311 |
| | Olde South Traders, Inc., 101 N. Monroe St., Tallahassee 32301 |
| | Southeastern Fisheries Association, Inc., 312 E. Georgia St., Tallahassee 32301 |
| | Watsand International, Ltd., 101 Krandon Blvd., # 377, Key Biscayne 33149 |
| Georgia | Barlar International, Inc., P.O. Box 708, Alpharetta 30239 |
| | Georgia Wood Export Marketing Cooperative, 600 Park Ave., Statesboro 30458 |
| | Savannah Sales Corp., P.O. Box 10204, Savannah 31412 |

| | |
|---|---|
| Idaho | Great Agassiz Basin Export Trading Co., P.O. Box 3455, Boise 83703 |
| Illinois | Basler Electric Co., P.O. Box 269, Route 143, Highland 62249 |
| | Brass & Bronze Ingot Manufacturers, 300 West Washington St., Suite 1500, Chicago 60606 |
| | EXILL Trading Co., 321 North Clark St., Suite 550, Chicago 60610 |
| | Micro Products Co., 20 North Wacker Dr., Chicago 60606 |
| | Non-Ferrous Founders' Society, 455 State St., Suite 100, Des Plaines 60016 |
| | Stone Export Trading Co., 360 N. Michigan Ave., Chicago 60601 |
| Indiana | Carpenter Body Works, Inc., 1500 West Main St., Mitchell 47446 |
| Iowa | AEON International Corp., 360 Seventh Ave., Marion 52302 |
| Kansas | Opti-Copy, Inc., 10930 Lackman Rd., Lenexa 66219 |
| | SOR, Inc., P.O. Box 591, 11705 Blackbob Rd., Olathe 66061 |
| Kentucky | Kentucky World Trade Center, Lexington, 410 W. Vine St., Suite 290, Lexington 40507 |
| Louisiana | Gerhardt's, Inc., 819 Central Ave., Jefferson 70181 |
| Maine | North America Blueberry Export Corp., P.O. Box 100, Milbridge 04658 |
| Maryland | East-West Trade Association, Inc., 15207 Frederick Rd., Rockville 20850 |
| | National Tooling and Machinery Association, 9300 Livingston Rd., Mt. Washington 20744 |
| Michigan | Airborne Business Cargo, Inc., P.O. Box 67, Lawrence 49064 |
| | CherreX Corp., 2220 University Park Dr., Suite 200, Okemos 48854 |
| | Michigan Export Development Authority, State of Michigan, P.O. Box 30017, Lansing 48909 |
| Mississippi | International Continental Agri-Tech, Inc., Route 2, P.O. Box 8-A, Florence 39073 |
| | Quality Exporters, Inc., P.O. Box 1051, Highway 51 South, Grenada 38901 |

| | |
|---|---|
| Missouri | International Trailer Sales, Inc., 1126 Swift, North Kansas City 64116 |
| Montana | Port of Montana Port Authority, P.O. Box 3741, Butte 59702 |
| New York | Apparatex International Trading Co., 350 Fifth Ave., Rm. 4920, New York 10118 |
| | Calcined Petroleum Coke, 230 Park Ave., Suite 2717, New York 10017 |
| | Custom Business Solutions, Inc., 120 Corporate Woods, Suite 180, Rochester 14623 |
| | Fleetwood International, Inc., 61 Broadway, New York 10065 |
| | Harmerl-Davis International, Inc., 140 East 28th St., Suite PHA, New York 10016 |
| | NEXCO-National Association of Export Companies, 475 Park Ave. South, 26th Fl., New York 10016 |
| | The Port Authority of New York & New Jersey, One World Trade Center, New York 10048 |
| | U.S.A. Book Expo, Inc., 86 Millwood Rd., Millwood 10546 |
| North Carolina | American Textile Export Co., P.O. Box 66, Gastonia 28053 |
| North Dakota | Mutual Trade Services, P.O. Box 2611, Fargo 58108 |
| Ohio | Fabiano & Associates, 21 East State St., Suite 700, Columbus 43215 |
| | Forging Industry Association, 25 Prospect Ave. West, Suite 300, Cleveland 44115 |
| | CISA Export Trade Group, Inc., 6990 Rieber St., Worthington 43805 |
| | N.B. Carson & Co., Inc., 4636 Broadway, Cleveland 44127 |
| Oklahoma | McChris International, 6722 S. Lewis, # 906, Tulsa 74136 |
| Oregon | American Wood Chip Export Association, 900 SW Fifth Ave., 23rd Fl., Portland 97204 |
| | Crann Corporation, P.O. Box 567, Beaverton 97075 |
| Pennsylvania | Chlor/Alkali Producers International, P.O. Box 2111, Pittsburgh 15230 |
| | EXIM International, 1100 Liberty Ave., Suite 817, Pittsburgh 15222 |

| | |
|---|---|
| | Wood Machinery Manufacturers of America, 1900 Arch St., Philadelphia 19103 |
| South Carolina | Carolina Western, Inc., P.O. Box 2524, Greenville 29602 |
| | FEXCORP, Inc, Highway 64 & I-95, Walterboro 29488 |
| Tennessee | Abdullah Diversified Marketing, Inc., P.O. Box 24479, Nashville 37202 |
| Texas | Intex International Trading Co., 11807 Demia Court, Suite II, Stafford 77477 |
| | KIAD International Trading Co., Inc., 7501 Chesterfield Place, Suite 1424, Dallas 75237 |
| Virginia | Air Conditioning and Refrigeration Institute, 4301 North Fairfax Dr., Suite 425, Arlington 22203 |
| | Association for Manufacturing Technology (NMTBA), 7901 Westpark Dr., McLean 22102 |
| | International Development Institute, 1900 Mt. Vernon Ave., Alexandria 22301 |
| | Outdoor Power Equipment Institute, 341 South Patrick St., Alexandria 22314 |
| | Safety Equipment Export Trading Co., 1901 N. Moore St., Suite 501, Arlington 22209 |
| | The Aries Group, Ltd., 1745 Jefferson Davis Highway, Arlington 22202 |
| | Vextrac, Ltd., 101 N. 8th St., 5th Fl., Richmond 23219 |
| Washington | First International Shippers Association, 821 Second Ave., Suite 1400, Seattle 98104 |
| | Grays Harbor Exporting-Importing Co., P.O. Box 1462, Aberdeen 98520 |
| | Northwest Gourmet Foods, Inc., East 491 St. Thomas Moore Way, Spokane 99208 |
| | Northwest Fruit Exporters, 1005 Tieton Dr., Yakima 98902 |
| | Pacific Northwest Fish Export Association, 4200 Seattle First National Bank Bldg., Seattle 98154 |
| | U.S. Apple and Pear Marketing Board, P.O. Box 70548, Seattle 98107 |
| | United States Surimi Commission, 4200 First Interstate Center, Seattle 98104 |
| Wisconsin | Construction Machinery Manufacturers Association, 111 East Wisconsin Ave., Suite 940, Milwaukee 53202 |

DMT World Trade, Inc., W299, N2494 Highway 164, Waukesha 53186

## RESEARCH CENTERS AND INSTITUTIONS

Many international marketing research organizations across the United States operate in conjunction with colleges or universities. The following is a list of some of the more prominent of these organizations, that place an emphasis on international marketing.

| | |
|---|---|
| Alaska | Alaska Center for International Business, 4201 Tudor Center Dr., Suite 120, Anchorage 99508 |
| Arizona | Arizona State University, Center for Financial Systems Research, Tempe 85287-4406 |
| California | California State University at Northridge, Division of Business and Industry Services, 18111 Nordhoff St., Northridge 91330 |
| Colorado | Center for the New West, 600 World Trade Center, 1625 Broadway, Boulder 80202 |
| District of Columbia | Georgetown University, Center for International Business and Trade, 1242 35th St., NW, Suite 501, Washington 20057 |
| Iowa | Midwest Agribusiness Trade Research and Information Center, 578 Heady Hall, Ames 50011-1070 |
| Massachusetts | International Marketing Institute, 314 Hammond St., Suite 52, Chestnut Hill 02167 |
| | Marketing Science Institute, 1000 Massachusetts Ave., Cambridge 02138 |
| North Carolina | University of North Carolina at Chapel Hill, Center for International Marketing, Carroll Hall, CB 3490, Chapel Hill 27514-3490 |
| Ohio | University of Toledo, International Business Institute, 1040 Stranahan Hall, 2801 W. Bancroft, Toledo 43606 |
| | World Trade Education Center, 1983 E. 24th St., Cleveland 44115 |
| Oklahoma | Oklahoma State University, Center for International Trade Development, Hall of Fame & Washington, Stillwater 74078 |
| Washington | University of Washington, Center for International Trade in Forest Products, College of Forest Resources, Seattle 98195 |

| | |
|---|---|
| | Washington State University, International Marketing Program for Agricultural Commodities and Trade Center, Pullman 99164 |

## COMPUTERIZED DATABASES

A number of organizations publish computerized data bases of information on international markets and international marketing. The more prominent among these international marketing information resources are those listed herein.

| | |
|---|---|
| California | Dialog Information Services, Inc., 3460 Hillview Ave., Palo Alto 94304, 415-858-2700 |
| | SRI International, Inc., World Business Division, 333 Ravenswood Ave., Menlo Park 94025-3493 |
| Colorado | Standard & Poor's Compustat Services, Inc., 7400 S. Alton Ct., Englewood 80112, 303-771-6510 |
| District of Columbia | The Bureau of National Affairs, Inc., 1231 25th St., NW, Washington 20037, 202-452-4132 |
| | German Technology Exchange, Inc., 1 Farragut Square S., Suite 600, Washington 20006, 202-347-0247 |
| | U.S. Bureau of Economic Analysis, Washington 20230, 202-523-0777 |
| | U.S. Department of Agriculture, Economic Research Service, 1301 New York Ave., NW, Washington 20005-4788 |
| | U.S. Department of Commerce, Bureau of the Census, Washington 20233, 301-763-4100 |
| | U.S. Department of Commerce, International Trade Administration, Office of Commercial Information Management Systems, 14th & Constitution Ave., NW, Washington 20230, 202-582-4203 |
| | U.S. Small Business Administration, Office of Procurement Assistance, 1411 L St., NW, Washington 20416, 202-653-6635 |
| Massachusetts | DRI/McGraw Hill, Data Products Division, 24 Hartwell Ave., Lexington 02173, 617-863-5100 |
| New Jersey | S.J. Rundt & Associates, Inc, P.O. Box 1797, Montclair 07042, 212-838-0141 |
| New York | Citicorp, 77 Water St., 2nd Fl., New York 10043, 212-898-7425 |

| | |
|---|---|
| | Dow Jones & Co., Inc, 200 Liberty St., New York 10281, 212-416-2758 |
| | FIND/SVP, Inc., 625 Avenue of the Americas, New York 10011, 212-645-4500 |
| | Global Finance Information, Inc., 270 Lafayette St., Suite 1305, New York 10012, 212-925-2300 |
| | Journal of Commerce, Inc., Trade Information Service, 120 Wall St., New York 10005, 212-425-1616 |
| | Reuters Information Services, Inc., 40 E. 52nd St., New York 10022, 212-593-5500 |
| | Strategic Intelligence Systems, Inc., 404 Park Ave., Suite 1301, New York 10016-8403, 212-725-4550 |
| | Political Risk Services, 407 University Ave., Suite 107, Syracuse 13210, 315-472-1224 |
| Ohio | Penton Publishing Co., 1100 Superior Ave., Cleveland 44114, 216-696-7000 |
| | Predicasts, 11001 Cedar Ave., Cleveland 44106, 216-795-3000 |
| Wisconsin | AgriData Resources, Inc., 330 Kilbourn Ave., Milwaukee 53202, 414-278-7676 |

## DIRECTORIES

| | |
|---|---|
| Georgia | International Directory of Market Research Organizations, Market Research Society, 15 Northburgh St., London, EC1V 0AH, England c/o MacFarland & Co., Inc., 1 Park Place, 1900 Emery St., NW, Suite 450, Atlanta 30318, 404-352-2290 |
| Michigan | European Directory of Marketing Information Sources, Euromonitor Publications, Ltd., 87-88 Turnmill St., London, EC1M 5QU, England c/o Gale Research Co., Book Tower, Detroit 48226, 800-223-4253 |
| New Jersey | Principal International Businesses: The World Marketing Directory, Dun's Marketing Services, 3 Sylvan Way, Parsippany 07054-3896, 800-526-0651 |
| New York | International Directory of Marketing Research Companies and Services, New York Chapter, American Marketing Association, 310 Madison Ave., New York 10017, 914-761-0199 |

| | |
|---|---|
| Ohio | Predicasts Source Directory, Predicasts, Inc., 11001 Cedar Ave., Cleveland 44106, 800-321-6388 |
| Virginia | Bradford's Directory of Marketing Research Agencies and Management Consultants in the United States and the World, Bradford's Directory of Marketing Research Agencies, P.O. Box 2300, Centerville 22020-2300, 703-830-5303 |

## TRADE FAIR AND EXHIBITION ORGANIZERS

Trade fairs and international trade exhibitions are an important part of the international marketing formula. European firms allocate a major portion of their annual purchasing budget to trade shows and exhibitions. It is important that U.S. firms become familiar with this activity; it is very different in Europe than in the United States because it is transaction oriented. Relationships are established, distributors, dealers, representatives, and agents are signed, and significant sales are written.

A leading directory of these fairs and exhibitions is

M + A Messesplanner International: Schedule of Fairs and Exhibitions Worldwide, M + A Verlag fur Messen, Ausstellungen und Kongresse GmbH, Mainzer Landstrasse 251 D-6000 Frankfurt am Main 1, Germany, Fax: 69-75951280

*Tradeshow Week* is a leading U.S.-based source of news and information on the Tradeshow industry.

*Tradeshow Week*, 121 Chanlon Rd., New Providence, NJ 07974, 800-521-8110

### European Fair Authorities and Related U.S. Offices

| | |
|---|---|
| Belgium | Ministere des Affaires Economiques, Admin. du Commerce "Expositions", Rue J.A. Demot 24-26, B-1040 Brussels |
| | Belgian-American Chamber of Commerce in the United States, 50 Rockefeller Plaza, Suite 1003-1005, New York, NY 10020 |
| Denmark | |
| Copenhagen | Bella Center A/S, Center Blvd., DK-2300 Copenhagen S. |
| | Danish American Chamber of Commerce, 825 Third Ave., 32nd Fl., New York, NY 10022-7519 |
| Herning | Exhibition Center Herning, Vardevej 1, Postbox 524, DK-7400 Herning |

| | |
|---|---|
| Odense | Messecenter Fyns Forum A/S, Orbaekvej 350, DK-5200 Odense |
| France | AFSS, 22 Ave. Franklin Roosevelt, 75008 Paris |
| General | International Trade Exhibitions in France, 2300 Clarendon Blvd., Suite 310, Arlington, VA 22201 |
| Bordeaux | Foire International de Bordeaux, Parc des Expositions, B.P. 55, 33030 Bordeaux Cedex |
| Grenoble | Chambre de Commerce et d'Industrie de Grenoble, 1 Place Andre Malraux, B.P. 297, 38016 Grenoble |
| Lyon | S.E.P.E.L., B.P. 87, 69683 Chassieu Cedex |
| Montpellier | Foire International de Montpellier, B.P. 1056, 34006 Montpellier Cedex |
| Germany General | AUMA (The German Council for Trade Fairs and Exhibitions), Lindenstrasse 8, 5000 Koeln 1 |
| Berlin | AMK Berlin, Austellungs-Messe-Kongress-GmbH, Messedam 22, 1000 Berlin 19 |
| | AMK Berlin, 101 West Grand Ave., Suite 601, Chicago, IL 60610 |
| Cologne | Koelnmesse, Messe-und Anstellungs GmbH, Messeplatz 1, Postfachs 210760, 5000 Koln 21 |
| | German-American Chamber of Commerce, Trade Fairs Department, 666 Fifth Ave., New York, NY 10019 |
| Dusseldorf | Duesseldorfer Messegesellschaft MbH, Postfach 32 02 03, 4000 Duesseldorf 30 |
| | Dusseldorf Trade Shows, Inc., 150 No. Michigan Ave., Suite 2920, Chicago, IL 60601 |
| Essen | Messe Essen GmbH, Messehaus Norbertstrasse 56, Postfach 100165, 4300 Essen 1 |
| Frankfurt | Messe Frankfurt GmbH, Postfach 970126, 6000 Frankfurt 1, GACC, Trade Fairs Department, NY |
| Hamburg | Hamburg Messe und Congress GmbH, Messehaus, Jungiusstrasse 13, Postfach 302480, 2000 Hamburg 36 |
| Hanover | Deutsche Messe AG Messegelaende, 3000 Hanover 82 |
| | Hannover Fairs USA, Inc., P.O. Box 7066, Carnegie Center, Princeton, NJ 08540 |
| Munich | Muenchener Messe-und Austellungsgesellschaft mbH, Postfach 12 01009, 8000 Muenchen 12 |
| | Kallman & Associates, 5 Maple Court, Ridgewood, NJ 07450 |

| | |
|---|---|
| Nuremberg | Nuernbergmesse, NMA (Nuermberger Messe und Austellungsgellschaft mbH), 8500 Nuernberg 50 |
| | Salk International, 2950 Airway Ave., Suite D1, Costa Mesa, CA 92626 |
| Stuttgart | Stuttgarter Messe-und Kongress GmbH, Postfach 103252, Am Kochenhof 15, 7000 Stuttgart 10 |
| | World Access Corp., 15 Bemis Rd., P.O. Box 171, Wellesley Hills, MA 02181 |
| Greece General | American Hellenic Chamber of Commerce & Industry, 16 Kanari St., GR-106 74 Athens |
| Athens | Athens Chamber of Commerce, 7-9 Akademias St., GR-106 71 Athens |
| Thessaloniki | Thessaloniki Fair Authority, (HELEXPO), 154 Egnatias St., GR-156 21 Thessaloniki |
| Ireland | Board Failte Eirann, Baggot St., Ballsbridge, Dublin 2 |
| Italy | Italian Trade Commission, 499 Park Ave., New York, NY 10022 |
| Bari | Fiera del Levante, Lungomare Starita, 70123 Bari |
| Genoa | Fiera International di Genova, P. le J.F. Kennedy 1, 16129 Genova |
| Milan | E.A. Fiera Milano, Largo Domodossalai, 20145 Milano |
| Padua | E.A. per le Fiere di Padova, Via N. Tommaseo 59, 31531 Padova |
| Parma | Ente Autonomo Fiere de Parma, Via Fortunato Rizzi 3, C.P. 411, 43031 Banganzola/Parma |
| Rome | Ente Autonomo Fiera di Roma, Via dell'Arcadia 2, 00147 Roma |
| Luxembourg | Foires International de Luxembourg, Plateau du Kirchberg, 2088 Luxembourg |
| | Board of Economic Development, 801 Second Ave., New York, NY 10017 |
| | Board of Economic Development, One Sansome St., Suite 830, San Francisco, CA 94104 |
| Netherlands General | The Netherlands Chamber of Commerce, One Rockefeller Plaza, New York, NY 10020 |
| Amsterdam | RAI, Europaplein 8, 1078 GZ Amsterdam |
| Utrecht | Royal Netherlands Industries Fair, Jaarsbeursplein, Postbus 8500, 3503 RM Utrecht |

| | |
|---|---|
| Portugal | Associacao Industrial Portuguese, Fiera International de Lisboa (FIL), Praca das Industrias, 1399 Lisboa Codex |
| | Portugal-U.S. Chamber of Commerce, 5 West 45th St., New York, NY 10036 |
| Spain General | Spain-U.S. Chamber of Commerce, 500 Fifth Ave., Rm. 4220, New York, NY 10036 |
| Barcelona | Feria de Barcelona, Av. Reina Maria Cristina, s/n, 08004 Barcelona |
| Bilbao | Feria International de Bilbao, Apartado 468, 48080 Bilbao |
| Madrid | Institucion Ferial de Madrid, (IFEMA), Avda. de Portugal, s/n, 28011 Madrid |
| Valencia | Feria Muestrario International de Valencia, Avda. de las Ferias, s/n, Apartado 476, 46080 Valencia |
| Zaragoza | Feria de Muestros de Zaragoza, Apartado 108, 5008D Zaragoza |
| United Kingdom General | Industrial & Trade Fairs, Ltd., 23 St. James Square, London SW1 4JH |
| | British American Chamber of Commerce, 10 E. 40th St., Rm. 2805, New York, NY 10016 |
| Birmingham | NEC Exhibition Division, National Exhibition Centre, Birmingham B40 1NT |
| Edinburgh | Scottish Tourist Board, 23 Ravelston Terrace, Edinburgh EH4 3EU |
| London | London Exhibition Venues Association, Information Bureau, 137 Sheen Rd., Richmond, Surrey TW9 1YJ |

## U.S.-Based International Trade Fair Associations

International Association of Fairs & Expositions, P.O. Box 985, Springfield, MO 65801

International Exhibitors Association, Backlick Rd., Suite 200, Springfield, VA 22151

## Other Marketing and Market Information Resources

The Department of Commerce and eight internationally active service organizations provide a fax-based export market information retrieval system called *The Export Hotline.* Market information is available on over 68 countries and 49 industry sectors, in addition to general documents on trade and investment issues, contacts, shipping requirements, and news/advisories. The corporate sponsors are: AT&T, Berlitz International, Delta Air Lines, DHL Airways, KPMG Peat Marwick, Cahners Publishing Company, Reed Exhibition Companies, and The Journal of Commerce. Call 800-872-9767 to get an application form and menu of information.

The Office of Western Europe, International Trade Administration, U.S. Department of Commerce published a guide to European trade fairs in April 1991. Contact the Office of Western Europe (see Chapter 1) and request a copy of *European Trade Fairs: A Key to the World for U.S. Exporters.*

Other publications that provide guidance on international marketing include:

*International Public Relations: How to Establish Your Company's Product, Service and Image in Foreign Markets.* J. Wonters, NY: Amacom, 1991.

*Handbook of International Direct Marketing.* UK, J. Dillon, Ed., Maidenhead, Berkshire: McGraw-Hill, 1976.

*Bacon's International Publicity Checker, Guide to Western European PR Markets.* IL: Bacon's Information International Ltd., 1990.

## U.S. BASED INTERNATIONAL MARKETING CONSULTANTS

In addition to the international marketing consultants listed in the American Export Register and the Export Yellow Pages (see Chapter 3), the following firms provide international marketing services to one or more industry sectors with a focus on Europe and the European Community. This list is not comprehensive. It is not a recommendation of any firm or organization.

| | |
|---|---|
| California | Modern Management, P.O. Box 10777, Beverly Hills 90213 |
| | E.J. Associates, Ltd., 20074 Beatty Ridge Rd., Los Gatos 95030 |
| | Johansson Export-Import Marketing, 8300 Manitoba St., Suite 306, Playa Del Rey 90293 |
| | Ag Resources International, 4025 23rd St., San Francisco 94114 |
| | Marcon International, 1094 Robbea Dr., Sunnyvale 94087 |
| | IMC, 1332 Bell Ave., Suite 2F, Tustin 92680 |
| Colorado | J and M Marketing, 5735 Arapaho, Boulder 80303 |

| | |
|---|---|
| Connecticut | Fisher International, 16 S. Main St., South Norwalk 06854 |
| | International Management & Export Development Corp., P.O. Box 355, Southport 06490 |
| | Schneider-Sohn and Associates, Inc., P.O. Box 5237, Westport 06881 |
| District of Columbia | Kramer Associates, Inc., 2100 M. St., NW, Washington 20037 |
| Georgia | Howard M. Hoffman & Associates, 3169 Holcomb Bridge Rd., Norcross 30071 |
| Illinois | R.B. Johnson and Associates, 175 Lake Blvd., Buffalo Grove 60090 |
| | A.T. Kearney, Inc., 222 S. Riverside Plaza, Chicago 60606 |
| Maryland | MacPherson Marketing, Inc., 807 S. Charles St., Baltimore 21203 |
| Massachusetts | Strategic Marketing and Communications, Inc., 10 High St., # 630, Boston 02110 |
| | Technical Marketing Associates Inc., 124 Boston Post Rd., Sudbury 01776 |
| New Jersey | Erop Distributors, 81 Partridge Lane, Cherry Hill 08003 |
| | DRC Associates, 452 Hudson Terrace, Englewood Cliffs 07632 |
| New York | Intermanagement Technology Co., 51 Harbor Park Dr., Centerport 11721 |
| | Statistikon Corp., P.O. Box 246, East Norwich 11732 |
| | Demby and Associates, Inc., 141 E. 44th St., Suite 310, New York 10017 |
| | Contact Systems Corp., 200 Madison Ave., New York 10016 |
| | International Book Marketing, Ltd., 210 S. 5th Ave., New York 10010 |
| | IRM (USA), Inc., The Plaza, 2 59th St., New York 10019 |
| | Leon Fleischer, 245 E. 25th St., New York 10010 |
| | Marketing & Planning Group, Inc., 160 W. 77th St., New York 10024 |
| | Rossman, Graham Associates, 201 E. 17th St., 17th Fl., New York 10003 |

| | |
|---|---|
| North Carolina | Access Management Corporation, 7 Woodlawn Green, Suite 212, Charlotte 28217 |
| Ohio | Datafinders, 2843 Ash Dr., Springfield 45504 |
| Texas | C. Clarke Straughan & Associates, 3304 Western Dr., Austin 78745 |
| | Teksources International, Route 2, Box 32, Edinburg 78539 |
| | IKR, 1032 Hercules Ave., Houston 77058 |
| Virginia | Marketing & Contract Management, 1338 Butter Churn Dr., Herndon 22070 |
| | HCI Corp., P.O. Box 936, Lexington 24450 |
| Washington | Smart Decisions, Inc., 18604 SE 58th St., Issaquah 98027-8511 |

# 12

# TRANSLATION SERVICES AND OTHER LANGUAGE AND TRAVEL SERVICES

The foreign language requirements of companies active in international markets are directly dependent on the nature of their activities. Exporters may require the translation of promotional, sales, service, warranty, and agreement documents. Contractors may require translation of contracts, agreements, and performance documents. Corporate investors—those firms with branches, subsidiaries, or other investments—have different requirements. Each translation requirement should be performed by a professional translator, a person skilled in the translation process, knowledgeable about the industry or industry sector, and current in the practical usage of the foreign language.

Many colleges, universities, and foreign nationals offer translation services, often at fees that are lower than professional services. Users are cautioned on their consideration of these institutional or casual translation resources. The ability to translate—exchange a word in one language for the word or words in another—may be present, however, the ability to provide a translation that is relevant in context, meaning, and nuance to the situation at hand may be lacking.

Larger corporations may have internal translation departments or divisions. Translation companies or agencies are available nationwide. These translation companies bring together the freelance translators and those firms that require particular translation skills. A good translation company will also be able to provide services for the odd language and subject combinations that arise from time to time. They can also arrange for overload services (temporary language services if you will).*

Translations are provided by type and, in business situations, an appreciation of situational requirements is paramount. Literal translation

* From *The Translator's Handbook*. London, Aslib, The Association for Information Management, 2d ed, 1989. Catriona Picken, Ed.

has its place in the classroom and academia. It is more important for the translator to bring the proper emphasis and meaning to the translated work, in the context of the user culture—the foreign text must be understood *as intended* inside the receiving culture. An incorrect or inept translation can cause significant market and financial costs for the user organization. The types of translation include:

- *Promotional and instructional material.* This category includes all nonliterary texts translated for publication, from advertising slogans to user instructions.
- *Advertising copy.* Translations must address how the message is received and interpreted by the intended audience. Differences in national culture and psychology can cause problems or create opportunities.
- *Publicity and sales literature.* This product type is a mix of the medium and the message. The audience forms an opinion of the firm by the "feel" and quality of the presentation material in addition to the content and presentation of the translated message.
- *Captions.* Translators must capture the correct nuance in the caption, so the message of picture and words are relevant within the context of the target culture.
- *Signs and notices.* These messages must capture the meaning of the message in the context of the readers language and culture. Dates and times must be in correct form.
- *Instructional material.* Translators must put the content at the appropriate level of language for the intended user, the appropriate level of technicality. The correct use of jargon and words-of-the-trade will increase user confidence in the material and extend to the product.
- *Instructions on forms.* Like the forms themselves, the instructions should be clear, clean, and culturally congruent.
- *Legal and official documents.* These documents usually must be translated in strict adherence to the form of the original. Ambiguities in the original documents will be danger points in the translated material. Excessive care must be taken with this type of translation.
- *Contracts and tenders.* These documents usually require absolute precision in the wording, in order to eliminate the potential for future conflict.
- *National and international standards.* The EC has developed and applies a series of product and performance standards that must be met by foreign firms. Translations must accurately convey the intent and the requirements of the relevant standards; the translation of the words must not obscure the meaning.

These categories demonstrate the diversity inherent in the translation of business communications.

The American Translators Association has over 4,000 members in the United States. Its *Translation Services Directory* is biennial and is restricted to active members of ATA. The directory includes three sections: Language/Subject Area, Translator Profiles, and Advertising. The ATA suggests seven signs of a good translator.

1. Good translators speak and write well. They communicate with you in the way you would communicate with your colleagues and customers.
2. Good translators know where to find the information they will need in order to provide an accurate translation, and have invested in other essential resources that enable them to work quickly and efficiently.
3. Good translators take their work and their customers seriously, and present themselves in a businesslike manner. They are experienced and can provide professional credentials and references.
4. Good translators can give you an estimate of how long a job will take to translate, and how much it will cost (provided you let the translator know exactly what the job entails).
5. Good translators are versatile and eager to learn. They are willing to invest time and energy in learning more about a new field.
6. Good translators are aware of their own capabilities and limitations. They will not take on a job if they cannot do it completely and will instead refer you to a colleague who can offer the best possible service.
7. Good translators ask questions. This does not mean they are ignorant; it means they know when to consult you about concepts or terminology that only you can explain.

## U.S. AND EC MEMBERS OF THE INTERNATIONAL FEDERATION OF TRANSLATORS

The ATA is a U.S. based translation resource. In the EC, managers should contact one of its national counterparts. There is an international association of translators called the *Association Internationale des Traducteurs de Conference* or International Federation of Translators.

| | |
|---|---|
| Belgium | Chambre Belge des Traducteurs, Interpretes et Philologues-Belgische, Albertlaan 250, 1180 Brussels, Federlingua, Chaussee de Wavre 564, 1040 Bruxelles |
| Denmark | Translatorforeningen, Bornholmsgade 1, DK-1266 Kobenhaven K |

| | |
|---|---|
| France | Societe Francais des Traducteurs (SFT), 11 rue de Navarin, 75009, Paris, BP 295 09, 75425 Paris Cedex 09 |
| | Association des Traducteurs Litteraires de France (ATLF), 99 rue de Vaugirard, 75006 Paris |
| Germany | Bundesverband der Dolmetscher und Ubersetzer e.V. (BDU), Rudigerstrasse 79a, D-5300 Bonn 2 |
| | Verband Deutschsprachiger Ubersetzer Literarischer und Wissenschaftlicher Werke e.V., Soatspad 18, D-4172 Straelen |
| Greece | Hellenic Association of Literary Translators, 7 Tsakona St., Pal. Psychiko, 15453 Athens |
| | Panhellenic Association of Translators, 26 Tsimiski St., 54624 Thessalonika |
| Italy | Associazione Italiana Traduttori e Interpreti (AITI), via B. d'Alviano 75, 20146 Milan |
| Netherlands | Nederlands Genootschap van Vertalers, Prinsessestraat 2, 2012 LR Haarlem |
| | Vereniging van Letterkundigen-Vakbond van Schrijvers, Huddestraat 7, 1018 HB Amsterdam |
| Spain | Asociacion Profesional Espanola de Traductores e Interpretes (APETI), Calle de Recoletos 5-3 Izqda, 28001 Madrid |
| United Kingdom | Institute of Translation and Interpreting (ITI), 318a Finchley Rd., London NW3 5HT |
| | Translators Association, 84 Drayton Gardens, London SW10 9SB |
| United States | American Translators' Association (ATA), 1735 Jefferson Davis Highway, Suite 903, Arlington, VA 22202-3413, 703-892-1500<br>4000+members, monthly newsletter, directory |
| | Also, chapters of the ATA are located in |
| | Colorado<br>Missouri<br>Washington, DC<br>New York City<br>Cleveland<br>San Francisco<br>Los Angeles |
| | Association of Professional Translators, c/o Mellon Bank, 3 Mellon Bank Center, Pittsburgh, PA 15259, 412-234-5751<br>100 members, monthly newsletter, directory |

## DIRECTORIES

Association Internationale des Traducteurs de Conference-Annoyer, International Association of Conference Translators, 15, Route des Morillons, Grand Saconnex, CH-1218 Geneva, Switzerland

Lists approximately 120 translators willing to work at international conferences or for international organizations.

Directory of International Business Centers, M. Worsley, Investment Bankers, Brokers and Consultants, c/o Standard Chartered Bank, Bandar Seri Begawan, Brunei

Lists over 1,900 firms in 126 countries that provide office services, including interpreting and translating.

## OTHER RESOURCES

In addition to translation services, international activities require that company personnel travel and live in different cultures. This can be challenging, stressful, and exciting, all at the same time. Preparation for the travel or living experience includes language training, acculturation training, and information on the business environment in the target country or region. Resources are available for each of these needs.

### ■ Language Training

The best known of the language training programs is probably Berlitz. They operate language training centers across the United States. Other language training programs include:

*Schau ins Land* a monthly "audiomagazine" in German, accompanied by a transcript, a glossary, and a study guide. It is suitable for those with some ability in the language seeking to maintain or improve their proficiency. The program is available from:

Schau ins Land, P.O. Box 158067, Dept. MGO, Nashville, TN 37215-8067, 800-824-0829

*Champs-Elysees* is the French language version of the above. Same mailing address and telephone. Dept. MJF

*Acquerello italiano* is the Italian language version of the above. Same mailing address and telephone. Dept. MIT.

Professional Cassette Center offers CD or cassette language programs composed of 32 cassettes and study materials, in Spanish,

French, German, and Italian, among others. Information is available from:

Professional Cassette Center. 408 South Pasadena Ave., Suite 4, Pasadena, CA 91105, 800-852-8346

Language Assistant Series from Microtac Software is a computer based bidirectional sentence by sentence translation program, with dictionaries, on-line reference tools, grammar and character utilities. The programs are available in French, German, Italian, and Spanish. Information is available from:

Microtac Software, 4655 Cass St., Suite 214, San Diego, CA 92109, 800-366-4170

Other language translation software products are offered by:

Systran Translation Systems, La Jolla, CA

Finalsoft Corp., Miami, FL

Linguistic Products, Woodlands, TX

Globalink, Inc., Fairfax, VA

This list is not exhaustive but suggests alternatives available in the marketplace.

## Acculturation

Acculturation is the process of acquiring empathy, understanding, and appreciation for another culture, another sociopolitical system, another people. This is a key component for the personal satisfaction and minimization of stress on personnel traveling through or living in a different cultural environment.

Leading colleges and universities offer excellent seminars and short courses in this field. Cross cultural consultants are available in every major city. Some programs are available on videotape. One of the many cultural training resources is *Going International,* a four film series to help orient Americans to cultural difference around the world. For information on the series contact:

Griggs Productions, 302 23rd Ave., San Francisco, CA 94121, 415-668-4200

## Environmental Information

Volumes are written on travel, business conditions, cultural practices, health tips, and other pertinent aspects of a foreign business environment. Data are available in desk calendars from *The Economist, American Express, The Financial Times,* and others. Business environment information is comprehensively available in *The Exporter's Encyclopedia* and *The Export Reference Manual.* There are few publications or products that provide relevant and comprehensive information in a compact, readily portable, and relevant form.

One of the leading vendors of this type of information is Austin House. Their *Business Travel Organizer*—Europe is a compact and comprehensive resource on the business environment in all EC states. Approximately the size of a thick small pocket diary, it contains the following types of information:

A Summary and overview of the EC

Currency and exchange

Electricity and adapters required by country

How to call to the U.S. from within any EC country

International clothing sizes

International telephone codes

Worldwide weather by city by season

A business vocabulary in English, French, German, and Spanish

Country briefs on each EC member state and 11 other nations. These country briefs include:

Social and cultural history

Structural information on: government, area, population, languages, religions, ethnic groups, principal business cities, currency, public holidays

Travel information

Business brief on: GDP, natural resources, agriculture, industry, trade, workforce, business hours, radio and telephone communications

Business information on: economy and commerce, business approaches, language, communication, courtesy

Data on principal cities: maps, trade fairs, hotels, tours and nightlife

Useful addresses for: embassies and consulates, ministries, chambers of commerce, banks, translators, travel offices.

The value of this type of travel resource is in its coverage, detail, size, and relevance. This information is all available from other sources, that are listed elsewhere. This guide puts it all in one place, so it is convenient for use in the office, on a plane, a cab, or any other location. For information contact:

Austin House, P.O. Box 117, Station B, Buffalo, NY 14207, 800-268-5157

P.O. Box 1051, 2388 Spears Rd., Oakville, Ontario, Canada L6J 5E9

Other resources of this type may be available.

# 13

# SHIPPING AND LOGISTICS

International trade enjoys the participation of a broad range of service providers that support and facilitate the movement of goods from one country to another. This chapter identifies these service providers by type. All are engaged in the logistics process—the movement of goods or services from a supplier to a potential consumer. The concept of logistics includes all of the functions within a company that control, time, and monitor the flow of goods from raw materials to finished products.

This chapter deals with the shipping and logistics services from the point of manufacture or supply to the destination. These include: freight forwarders, air carriers, ocean carriers, NVOCCs, and port authorities. Two other factors that are very important to users of imported parts or components are the Free Trade Zone and Drawback.

## INTERNATIONAL FREIGHT FORWARDERS

A freight forwarder is a firm or individual providing intermediary services for the domestic and/or international shipment of goods by various transportation modes. A forwarder may be an Ocean Freight Forwarder licensed by the Federal Maritime Commission, or an Air Freight Forwarder usually endorsed by IATA, the International Air Transport Association. Freight forwarders provide some or all of the following services:

1. Perform or provide pick-up and/or delivery
2. Perform or provide for crating, binding, shrink-wrapping, and so on
3. Provide packing, marking, and labeling advice with regard to carrier, customs requirements, or destination country requirements
4. Prepare documents or provide advice on document preparation
5. Provide routing and carrier choice
6. Negotiate carrier rates
7. Book freight space and coordinate intermodal transport
8. Provide insurance advice

9. Prepare letters of credit, drafts, and other financial arrangements
10. Track and trace shipments
11. Arrange for customs clearance services
12. Provide assembly or distribution services
13. Provide specialized services to purchasing departments
14. Provide warehouse or consolidation facilities and services
15. Offer advice on special finance or trade requirements of foreign countries
16. Perform general problem solving or analysis of distribution needs.

Freight forwarders often specialize in a particular foreign market or region. Because of this specialization, they may develop an expertise in one or more product sectors.

Selection of an international freight forwarder should be based on:

1. Your corporate requirements and capacity to do the work in-house
2. The forwarders reputation in your community and with your product type
3. Forwarder capacity to serve your document and service requirements in your target destinations. Does the forwarder have an office, a branch, a subsidiary, or a correspondent in the target country?
4. Forwarder capacity to interface with ports, carriers, truckers, and U.S. Customs. This means the forwarder utilizes Electronic Data Interchange (EDI) and has the appropriate computer interfaces with U.S. Customs.
5. Forwarder management is interested in your company and its success
6. The forwarder is financially strong and has a history of strength
7. The forwarder is more than a one-person shop. Many capable and successful forwarder companies are a one-person shop; the drawback is quickly apparent—when this person is sick or on holiday, your goods don't move.

There are hundreds of highly qualified freight forwarder firms, many with offices across the United States and abroad. In addition, the major European forwarders have moved into the United States in force. Three leading European forwarders with offices across the United States are:

Schenkers Internationa
Hellman International
Kuehne & Nagel, Inc.

Major U.S.-based international freight forwarders include:

Tower Group (a McGraw-Hill subsidiary)
Expeditors International, Inc.

Arthur J. Fritz & Co., Inc.
Norman G. Jensen, Inc.
Harper Robinson & Co.
F. W. Myers, Inc.
Panalpina Airfreight, Inc.

This list is an indication only. It presents only a few of the thousands of freight forwarders serving the international business community across the United States. Your local forwarder will be pleased to discuss its service capabilities and scope of operation.

## AIR CARRIERS

Approximately 80 international air carriers serve end points in the United States and one or more of the EC member states. Most of these are passenger carriers that also carry freight; some are freight only services. 19 major U.S. airlines or air carriers are represented by the Air Transport Association, the industry's voice in Washington and elsewhere. ATA members that serve EC end points are noted with an asterisk after their name. Another air carrier trade association represents six airlines and four associates that specialize in low-cost scheduled and charter services for passenger and cargo operations (American Trans Air and Evergreen are on this end-point listing). Carriers are listed alphabetically by airline, with their principal U.S. office and notations as to countries served. Many of these companies have sales, service, or cargo offices in major airports across the United States.

| | *Countries Served* | | | | | | | | | | | |
|---|---|---|---|---|---|---|---|---|---|---|---|---|
| *Airline* | *Bel* | *Den* | *Fr* | *Ger* | *Gre* | *Ire* | *Ita* | *Lux* | *Neth* | *Por* | *Spa* | *UK* |
| Aer Lingus<br>122 E. 42nd St.<br>New York, NY 10168<br>800-223-7660 | | X | X | X | | X | X | | X | | X | X |
| Aeroflot<br>224 N. Michigan Ave.<br>Chicago, IL 60601<br>312-819-2350 | X | X | X | X | X | | X | X | X | X | | X |
| Aerolineas Argentina<br>JFK International Airport<br>Cargo Bldg. 78,<br>Jamaica, NY 11430<br>718-632-1737 | | | X | | | | X | | X | | | X |

| | *Countries Served* | | | | | | | | | | | |
|---|---|---|---|---|---|---|---|---|---|---|---|---|
| *Airline* | *Bel* | *Den* | *Fr* | *Ger* | *Gre* | *Ire* | *Ita* | *Lux* | *Neth* | *Por* | *Spa* | *UK* |
| Air Afrique Cargo<br>One Cross Island Plaza<br>Rosedale, NY 11422<br>718-723-5699 | | | X | | | | X | | | | | X |
| Air Canada*<br>500 Rene Levesque Blvd.<br>West Montreal, Quebec<br>H2Z 1X5<br>514-879-6174 | X | X | X | X | X | | | | X | | | X |
| Airborne Express<br>3101 Western Ave.<br>Seattle, WA 98111<br>206-245-4600 | X | X | X | X | X | X | X | X | X | X | X | X |
| Air China<br>45 E. 49th St.<br>New York, NY 10017<br>212-371-9898 | | | | | | | X | | | | | |
| Air France<br>One Cross Island Plaza<br>Rosedale, NY 11422<br>718-712-0591 | X | X | X | X | X | | X | | X | X | | X |
| Air India<br>JFK International Airport<br>Cargo Bldg. 86<br>Jamaica, NY 11430<br>718-632-0132 | | X | X | X | X | | X | | X | | X | X |
| Air Lanka<br>8133 San Fernando Rd.<br>Sun Valley, CA 91352<br>800-421-9898 | | | X | X | X | | X | | X | | | X |
| Alitalia<br>666 Fifth Ave.<br>New York, NY 10103<br>212-903-3300 | X | X | X | X | X | X | X | X | X | X | X | X |
| All Nippon<br>5701 West Imperial<br>Highway, Suite 101<br>Los Angeles, CA 90045<br>213-646-4186 | | | | | | | | | | | | X |
| American Airlines*<br>P.O. Box 619616<br>Dallas/Ft.Worth Airport<br>Texas, 75261-9616<br>817-967-2400 | | | X | X | | | X | | X | | | X |

| | Countries Served | | | | | | | | | | | |
|---|---|---|---|---|---|---|---|---|---|---|---|---|
| *Airline* | *Bel* | *Den* | *Fr* | *Ger* | *Gre* | *Ire* | *Ita* | *Lux* | *Neth* | *Por* | *Spa* | *UK* |
| American Trans Air*<br>Box 51609<br>Indianapolis Int'l Airport<br>Indianapolis, IN 46251 | X | X | X | X | X | X | X | X | X | X | X | X |
| America West<br>4000 E. Skyharbor Blvd.<br>Phoenix, AZ 85034<br>800-228-7862 | | | X | | | | | | | | | X |
| Ansett<br>9841 Airport Blvd., Suite 418<br>Los Angeles, CA 90045<br>213-338-8183 | | | | X | | | | | | | | X |
| Arrow Air<br>P.O. Box 026062<br>Miami, Fl 33102-6062<br>305-526-0900 | | | | X | | | | | | | | |
| Austrian Airlines<br>Cargo Bldg. 15<br>JFK International Airport<br>Jamaica, NY 11430<br>718-481-4650 | X | X | | X | X | | X | | X | | X | X |
| Balkan-Bulgarian<br>41 E. 42nd St., Suite 606<br>New York, NY 10017<br>212-573-5530 | X | X | X | X | X | | X | X | | | | X |
| British Airways<br>Cargo Bldg. 66<br>JFK International Airport<br>Jamaica, NY 11430<br>718-917-5000 | X | X | X | X | X | X | X | X | X | X | X | X |
| CSA-Czechoslovakia<br>Bldg. 54<br>JFK International Airport<br>Jamaica, NY 11430<br>718-656-8439 | | X | X | X | X | | X | X | X | | | X |
| Canadian Airlines*<br>840 Malcolm Rd.<br>Burlingame, CA 94010<br>415-877-5936 | | | | X | | | X | | X | X | | X |
| Cargolux<br>Bldg. 2200<br>Miami, FL 33152<br>305-871-2414 | X | X | X | X | | | X | X | X | X | X | |

| | *Countries Served* | | | | | | | | | | | |
|---|---|---|---|---|---|---|---|---|---|---|---|---|
| *Airline* | *Bel* | *Den* | *Fr* | *Ger* | *Gre* | *Ire* | *Ita* | *Lux* | *Neth* | *Por* | *Spa* | *UK* |
| Cathay Pacific<br>11001 Aviation Blvd.<br>Los Angeles, CA 90045<br>310-348-9789 | | X | X | X | X | | X | | X | | | X |
| China Airlines<br>11201 Aviation Blvd.<br>Los Angeles, CA 90045<br>213-646-4293 | | | X | X | | | X | X | X | | | X |
| Continental*<br>Gateway 2, Suite 300<br>15333 JFK Blvd.<br>Houston, TX 77032<br>713-987-6730 | | | X | X | | | | | X | | | X |
| DHL Airways*<br>333 Twin Dolphin Dr.<br>Redwood City, CA 94065<br>800-225-5345 | X | X | X | X | X | X | X | X | X | X | X | X |
| Delta Airlines*<br>Hartsfield Atlanta Int'l Airport<br>Atlanta, GA 30320<br>404-714-8600 | X | X | X | X | X | X | X | | X | | | X |
| EAS Cargo<br>340 North Belt, Suite 260<br>Houston, TX 77060<br>713-448-6442 | X | | | | | | X | | X | | | X |
| Eastern*<br>Bradley International Airport<br>Windsor Locks, CT 06096<br>203-627-3520 | | | | X | | | | | X | | | |
| Egyptair<br>159-11 Rockaway Blvd.<br>Jamaica, NY 11434<br>718-656-8627 | X | X | X | X | X | | X | | X | | | X |
| El Al<br>Cargo Bldg. 83<br>JFK International Airport<br>Jamaica, NY 11430<br>718-244-3169 | X | | X | X | X | | | | X | X | | X |
| Emirates<br>8135 San Fernando Rd.<br>Sun Valley, CA 91352<br>800-228-1376 | | X | | | | | | | | | | X |

| | *Countries Served* | | | | | | | | | | | |
|---|---|---|---|---|---|---|---|---|---|---|---|---|
| *Airline* | *Bel* | *Den* | *Fr* | *Ger* | *Gre* | *Ire* | *Ita* | *Lux* | *Neth* | *Por* | *Spa* | *UK* |
| Evergreen International<br>3850 Three Mile Lane<br>McMinnville, OR 97128<br>503-472-0011 | | | | X | | | | | | | | |
| Federal Express*<br>P.O. Box 727<br>Memphis International Airport<br>Memphis, TN 38194<br>800-238-5355 | X | | X | X | | X | X | X | X | | | X |
| Finnair Cargo<br>Hanger 10<br>JFK International Airport<br>Jamaica, NY 11430<br>718-656-7663 | X | X | | X | X | | X | X | X | | | X |
| Garuda Indonesia<br>5600 West Century Blvd.<br>Los Angeles, CA 90045<br>310-337-1610 | X | | X | X | | | X | | X | | | |
| Gulf Air<br>420 Lexington Ave., Suite 2626<br>New York, NY 10170<br>212-986-3950 | | | X | X | X | | X | | X | | | X |
| Heavylift Cargo<br>301 E. 51st St.<br>Kansas City, MO 64112<br>816-753-3337 | | | | | | | | | | | | X |
| Iberia Airlines<br>Cargo Bldg. 76<br>JFK International Airport<br>Jamaica, NY 11430<br>718-632-1258 | X | X | X | X | X | | X | | X | X | X | X |
| Icelandair<br>Cargo Bldg. 84<br>JFK International Airport<br>Jamaica, NY 11430<br>718-917-0661 | X | X | X | | | | X | | X | | | X |
| JAL<br>655 Fifth Ave.<br>New York, NY 10022<br>212-310-1459 | X | X | X | X | X | | X | | X | | X | X |

| | *Countries Served* | | | | | | | | | | | |
|---|---|---|---|---|---|---|---|---|---|---|---|---|
| *Airline* | *Bel* | *Den* | *Fr* | *Ger* | *Gre* | *Ire* | *Ita* | *Lux* | *Neth* | *Por* | *Spa* | *UK* |
| JAT-Yugoslavia<br>630 Fifth Ave.<br>New York, NY 10111<br>212-765-4050 | X | X | X | X | X | | X | | X | | X | X |
| KLM-Royal Dutch<br>565 Taxter Rd.<br>Elmsford, NY<br>10523-2312<br>800-klm-9000 | X | X | X | X | X | X | X | | X | X | X | X |
| Korean Air<br>6101 Imperial Highway<br>Los Angeles, CA 90045<br>800-262-1553 | | | X | X | X | | X | | X | | | X |
| Kuwait Airways<br>Cargo Bldg. 263<br>JFK International Airport<br>Jamaica, NY 11430<br>800-221-6727 | | X | X | X | X | | X | | X | | X | X |
| Lan Chile<br>9700 S. Dixie Highway<br>Miami, FL 33156<br>800-736-5526 | | | | | | | | | X | | X | |
| Lineas Aereas Paraguay<br>6445 NW 25th St.<br>Miami, FL 33126<br>305-526-6784 | | | | X | | | | | | | | |
| LOT Polish<br>Bldg. 263<br>JFK International Airport<br>Jamaica, NY 11430<br>718-656-2674 | X | X | | X | X | | X | | X | | | X |
| Lufthansa<br>1640 Hempstead Turnpike<br>E. Meadow, NY 11554<br>516-296-9421 | X | X | X | X | X | X | X | X | X | X | X | X |
| Malaysian Airline<br>5933 West Century Blvd.,<br>Suite 506<br>Los Angeles, CA 90045<br>800-421-8641 | | | X | X | | | | | | | | X |
| Malev-Hungarian<br>630 Fifth Ave., Suite<br>1900<br>New York, NY 10111<br>212-757-6480 | X | X | X | X | X | | X | | X | | | X |

| | *Countries Served* | | | | | | | | | | | |
|---|---|---|---|---|---|---|---|---|---|---|---|---|
| *Airline* | *Bel* | *Den* | *Fr* | *Ger* | *Gre* | *Ire* | *Ita* | *Lux* | *Neth* | *Por* | *Spa* | *UK* |
| Martinair Holland<br>1165 Northern Blvd.<br>Manhasset, NY 11030<br>516-365-6146 | | | | X | | | | | X | | X | X |
| Middle East Air<br>680 Fifth Ave., 5th Fl.<br>New York, NY 10019<br>212-664-7300 | X | X | X | X | X | | X | | | | | X |
| Nigeria Airways<br>120-65 168th St.<br>Jamaica, NY 11434<br>781-917-6060 | X | | X | X | | | X | | | | | X |
| Nippon Cargo<br>Bldg. 69, Rm. 229<br>JFK International Airport<br>Jamaica, NY 11430<br>718-244-6836 | | | | | | | | | X | | | |
| Norwest Airlines*<br>5101 Northwest Dr.<br>St. Paul, MN 55111<br>612-626-7474 | | | X | X | | | X | | X | | | X |
| Olympic Airways<br>647 Fifth Ave.<br>New York, NY 10022<br>212-735-0273 | X | | X | X | X | | X | | X | | | X |
| Pakistan Int'l<br>Cargo Bldg. 86<br>JFK International Airport<br>Jamaica, NY 11430<br>800-221-6024 | X | X | X | X | X | | X | | X | | | X |
| Pan American*<br>Cargo Bldg. 67<br>JFK International Airport<br>Jamaica, Ny 11430<br>800-421-5330 | X | | X | X | X | | X | | X | | X | X |
| Philippine Airlines<br>447 Sutter St.<br>San Francisco, CA 94108<br>415-877-4841 | | | X | X | X | | X | | X | | | X |
| Qantas Airways<br>Cargo Bldg. 632<br>San Francisco International Airport<br>San Francisco, CA 94128<br>415-877-3861 | | X | X | X | X | | X | | X | | | X |

| | Countries Served | | | | | | | | | | | |
|---|---|---|---|---|---|---|---|---|---|---|---|---|
| *Airline* | *Bel* | *Den* | *Fr* | *Ger* | *Gre* | *Ire* | *Ita* | *Lux* | *Neth* | *Por* | *Spa* | *UK* |
| Royal Air Maroc.<br>Cargo Bldg. 261<br>JFK International Airport<br>Jamaica, NY 11430<br>800-221-4752 | X | | | X | X | | X | | X | X | | X |
| Royal Jordanian<br>Cargo Bldg. 89<br>JFK International Airport<br>Jamaica, NY 11430<br>800-221-0746 | | | | X | | X | | | X | | | X |
| SAS-Scandinavian<br>138-02 Queens Blvd.<br>Jamaica, NY 11435<br>800-221-7897 | X | X | X | X | X | X | X | | X | X | | X |
| Sabena Belgian<br>1155 Northern Blvd.<br>Manhasset, NY 11030<br>516-562-9600 | X | X | X | X | X | X | X | X | X | X | | X |
| Saudia<br>747 3rd Ave., 29th Fl.<br>New York, NY 100107<br>212-758-4774 | X | X | X | X | X | | X | | X | | | X |
| Singapore Airlines<br>P.O. Box 90831<br>Los Angeles International Airport<br>Los Angeles, CA 90009<br>310-646-6200 | X | X | X | X | X | | X | | X | | | X |
| South African Air<br>900 3rd Ave., 9th Fl.<br>New York, NY 10022<br>212-826-0995 | X | X | X | X | X | | X | | X | X | X | X |
| Swissair<br>Bldg. 15<br>JFK International Airport<br>Jamaica, NY 11430<br>800-221-4740 | X | X | X | X | X | X | X | X | X | X | X | X |
| Syrianair<br>see Royal Jordanian | | X | X | X | X | | X | | | | | |
| Tap Air Portugal<br>Bldg. 263<br>JFK International Airport<br>Jamaica, NY 11430<br>800-221-7890 | X | X | X | X | X | | X | | X | X | X | X |

| | *Countries Served* | | | | | | | | | | | |
|---|---|---|---|---|---|---|---|---|---|---|---|---|
| *Airline* | *Bel* | *Den* | *Fr* | *Ger* | *Gre* | *Ire* | *Ita* | *Lux* | *Neth* | *Por* | *Spa* | *UK* |
| Tarom-Romanian<br>342 Madison Ave., Suite 819<br>New York, NY 10173<br>212-687-6013 | | X | X | | | | X | | | | | |
| Thai Airways<br>720 Olive Way, Suite 1400<br>Seattle, WA 98101<br>800-421-2109 | X | X | X | X | | | X | | X | | X | X |
| Trans World Air*<br>100 S. Bedford Rd.<br>Mt. Kisco, NY 10549<br>914-242-3253 | | X | X | X | X | X | X | | X | X | X | X |
| UTA-Union de Tr<br>71 Stevenson St., Suite 1400<br>San Francisco, CA 94105<br>415-227-4411 | X | | X | X | | | X | | X | | | X |
| United Airlines*<br>Box 66100<br>Chicago, IL 60666<br>800-631-1500 | X | | X | X | | | | | X | | | X |
| United Parcel*<br>601 West 43d St.<br>New York, NY 10036<br>212-695-7500 | X | X | X | X | | X | X | | X | | X | X |
| USAIR Cargo*<br>2345 Crystal Dr.<br>Arlington, VA 22227<br>703-418-7106 | | X | X | | | | | | | | | X |
| Varig-Brazilian<br>5600 West Century Blvd., Suite 1<br>Los Angeles, CA 90045<br>213-646-4724 | X | X | X | X | X | | X | | X | X | X | X |
| VIASA<br>Cargo Bldg. 263<br>JFK International Airport<br>Jamaica, NY 11430<br>718-656-7092 | | | X | X | | | X | | X | X | X | X |
| Virgin Cargo<br>1983 Marcus Ave.<br>Lake Success, NY 11042<br>516-775-2600 | | | | | | | | | | | | X |

| | *Countries Served* | | | | | | | | | | | |
|---|---|---|---|---|---|---|---|---|---|---|---|---|
| *Airline* | *Bel* | *Den* | *Fr* | *Ger* | *Gre* | *Ire* | *Ita* | *Lux* | *Neth* | *Por* | *Spa* | *UK* |
| ZAS Airlines-Egypt<br>181 S. Franklin Ave.<br>Valley Stream, NY 11581<br>516-791-5580 | | X | X | X | | | | | X | | | X |

* ATA Associate member status

## OCEAN CARRIERS

Ocean freight service to the member nations of the EC are by conference or agreement carriers, non-conference or independent carriers, and by NVOCCs (Non-Vessel Operating Common Carriers). Each provides a service that is suitable to different types of shippers (exporters or importers), whose needs vary by volume, size of shipment, frequency, reliability of schedule, and type of equipment required. Freight forwarders and transportation management firms can assist in the selection of ocean services, or assist the corporate transportation and logistics managers in their work. This section presents scheduled carriers, both conference and nonconference, then NVOCCs.

### Carriers Serving the United States and the European Community

The companies listed are the principal carriers that provide scheduled ocean marine transportation services between U.S. ports and EC ports. To arrange for service from any company, contact the listed telephone number and ask for their local agent or representative. Alternatively, look in the yellow pages of your telephone book under *Steamship Companies.* If you want to use the services of a freight forwarder, look under that heading. Information on steamship services (routes, dates of service, contact information) is available in three leading publications:

- *The New York Journal of Commerce SHIPCARDS,* updated every business day. The Journal of Commerce, Inc., Two World Trade Center, New York, NY 10048, 800-221-3777
- *Pacific Shipper,* published weekly with information on all ports in the U.S. K-III Information Co., 582 Mission St., Suite 601, San Francisco, CA 94105, 800-221-5488
- *Shipping Digest,* updated weekly with information on ship movements at all ports. Geyer-McAllister Publications, Inc., 51 Madison Ave., New York, NY 10010

ABC Container Line, Deepsea Marketing, 212-481-9240

Atlantic Container Line, New Jersey, 800-ACL-1313

Balt Gulf Line, Rice, Unruh, Reynolds Co., 115 Chestnut St., Philadelphia, PA 19106, 215-629-1711

Cho Yang Line, CY Agency, Inc., New Jersey, 908-412-3430

CMA, Compagnie Maritime D'affretement, 17 Battery Blvd., Suite 1128, New York, NY 10004, 800-CMA-USA9

Contship Containerlines Ltd., Contship Agencies, Inc., 95 Christopher Columbus Dr., 13th Floor, Jersey City, NJ 07032, 201-435-0450

DNOL MED Service, Columbus Lines, Inc., Plaza 2, Jersey City, NJ 07311, 201-432-0900

DSR-Lines, 7950 W. Joliet Rd., McCook, IL 60525, 708-447-2828

Eimskip USA, Inc., P.O. Box 3698, Norfolk, VA 23510, 804-627-4444

Ellerman, Southern Steamship Agencies, 50 Cragwood Rd., South Plainfield, NJ 07080, 212-406-2433

Evergreen America Corp., One Everthrust Plaza, Jersey City, NJ 07302, 201-915-3200

Farrell Lines, Inc., 1 Whitehall St., New York, NY 10004, 212-440-4645

Forest Lines, Gulf & Eastern Steamship, 120 Wall St., New York, NY 10005, 212-269-2800

Hapag-Lloyd (America), 1 Edgewater Plaza, Staten Island, NY 10305, 800-522-1720

HUAL, Hoegh-Ugland Autoliners A/S, Autoliners, Inc., 500 N. Broadway, Jericho, NY 11753, 516-935-2604

Independent Container Line, 2333 Morris Ave., Suite B8, Union, NJ 07083, 800-525-4499

Italia Line, 300 Warren St., 11th Fl., Jersey City, NJ 07302, 800-424-8252

Lykes Lines, Lykes Bros. Steamship, 17 Battery Place, 27th Fl., New York, NY 10004, 212-943-6363

Maersk, Inc., Giralda Farms, P.O. Box 880, Madison, NJ 07940-0880, 800-833-8569

Massan Shipping Line, Massan Shipping Industries, 6575 West Loop S., #425, Bellaire, TX 77401, 713-661-8898

Mediterranean Shipping Co., Containership Agency, Inc., 96 Morton St., 4th Fl., New York, NY 10014, 212-627-5300

Mexican Line, Transportacion Maritima Mexicana S.A. de C.V., Oceans International Corp., 5005 Mitchelldale, Suite 121, Houston, TX 77092, 800-497-4682

Nordana Agencies, 29 Broadway, Suite 1800, New York, NY 10006, 212-943-4406

Ocean World Lines, 9 Murray St., 12th Floor, New York, NY 10007, 800-851-7447

OOCL (Orient Overseas Container Line), 4141 Hacienda Dr., Pleasanton, CA 94588, 415-4577-6700

P&O Container Line, P&O Containers (Agencies), Inc., One Meadowlands Plaza, East Rutherford, NJ 07073, 201-896-6200

Polish Ocean Lines, Gdynia America Line, Inc., 1001 Durham Ave., South Plainfield, NJ 07080, 908-412-6000

President Container Lines, Ltd., 40 Parker Rd., Elizabeth, NJ 07207, 908-354-2220

RTM Line, Ltd., 233 Broadway, New York, NY 10279, 800-847-SHIP

Sea-land Service, 379 Thornall St., P.O. Box 800, Iselin 08830, NJ, 800-SEA-LAND

Shipping Services Italia, 212-619-8551

Star Shipping a/s, 16 Threadneedle Lane, Stamford, CT 06902, 203-965-0600

Tecomar S.A., Phoenician International Shipping, 2350 Adrthbelt East, Houston, TX 77032, 713-590-1500

Transatlantica Spanish Line, Trasatlantica Agency (USA), Inc., 99 Hudson St., New York, NY 10013, 212-925-3838

Wallenius Lines North America, Inc., 188 Broadway, P.O. Box 1232, Woodcliff, NJ 07675-1232, 201-307-1300

ZIM Container Service, One World Trade Center, 16th Fl., New York, NY 10048, 800-444-2000

## NVOCC Services between the United States and the European Community

NVOCCs are regulated by the Federal Maritime Commission to provide freight consolidation and shipping service. NVOs, like steamship lines, issue their own bills of lading to shippers, and provide service under their own published tariffs. NVO services are often more attractive for shippers of smaller volumes or for infrequent shippers. Each of these situations does not merit favorable rate negotiations with a scheduled carrier. Because NVOs contract for bulk space (container slots) over a period of time, they receive volume discounts that can be passed on to these smaller or less frequent shippers. The drawback to NVO service is that in high-traffic or high-demand seasons NVO shipments are often loaded or served last by the scheduled carrier because higher revenue traffic is available, and will receive priority treatment.

The following is a select list of NVOs that serve U.S.-EC end points on a regular basis. There are hundreds of NVOs in the United States; entry is easy and inexpensive. NVOs in your market will be listed in the yellow pages under Steamship companies. They will also be known to the marketing departments of the closest ocean or marine port.

American Export Lines
310-523-2300

ATE/OEC Group
714-994-4780

Brennan International Transport
310-637-7000

Cargo Speedline, Inc.
310-568-8818

Direct Express
310-608-2100

Euro Transport Connections
310-216-0556

Independent Cargo Express
708-344-7878

Jaguar Intermodal Transport
800-899-4548

Keihin Ocean Line
213-604-1444

Richard Boas & Co.
310-495-7233

Samson Transport
310-641-9929

Scanfreight
201-997-7700

Shipco Transport, Inc.
201-216-1500

Votainer Consolidation Services
800-442-5848

## Port Authorities

The American Association of Port Authorities is the trade association for ocean ports. Member ports are listed by state. Also noted is the country in which a port has an EC office. To benefit from these foreign offices or from the shipping and handling services available from port districts, contact the marketing department of that port.

| *State* | *Port/Foreign Office (if any)* |
|---|---|
| Alabama | Mobile 205-690-6113 |
| Alaska | Anchorage 907-272-1531 |
| | Cordova 907-424-6400 |
| | Dutch Harbor 907-581-1254 |
| | Homer 907-235-3160 |
| | Kenai 907-283-7535 |
| | Kodiak 907-486-5789 |
| | Matanuska-Susitna 907-745-9831 |
| | St. Paul 907-546-2331 |
| | Seward 907-224-2231 |
| | Valdez 907-835-4313 |
| | Whittier 907-472-2330 |
| California | Hueneme 805-488-3677 |

| *State* | *Port/Foreign Office (if any)* |
|---|---|
| | Humboldt Bay 707-443-0801 |
| | Long Beach 213-437-0041 |
| | Los Angeles 310-519-3400 |
| | England |
| | Denmark |
| | Oakland 510-272-1100 |
| | Netherlands |
| | Redwood City 415-365-1316 |
| | Richmond 510-214-4600 |
| | Sacramento 916-371-8000 |
| | San Diego 619-291-3900 |
| | San Francisco 415-274-0400 |
| | Stockton 209-946-0246 |
| Connecticut | New London 203-443-3856 |
| Delaware | Wilmington 301-571-4600 |
| Florida | Cape Canaveral 407-783-7831 |
| | Jacksonville 904-630-3000 |
| | Key West 305-292-8161 |
| | Manatee County 813-722-6621 |
| | Miami 305-371-7678 |
| | England |
| | Nassau County 904-261-0098 |
| | Palm Beach 407-842-4201 |
| | Panama City 904-763-8471 |
| | Pensacola 904-435-1870 |
| | Ft. Lauderdale 305-523-3404 |
| | St. Petersburg 813-893-7654 |
| | St. Lucie County 407-461-7899 |
| | Tampa 813-248-1924 |
| Georgia | Savannah 912-964-3811 |
| | Greece |
| Hawaii | Honolulu 808-587-1927 |
| Illinois | Chicago 312-646-4400 |
| | Waukegan 312-244-3133 |
| Indiana | Indianapolis 317-232-9200 |
| Louisiana | Baton Rouge 504-342-1660 |
| | Greater Lafourche 504-632-6701 |
| | Lake Charles 318-439-3661 |
| | New Orleans 504-522-2551 |
| | Plaquemines 504-682-0081 |

| State | Port/Foreign Office (if any) |
|---|---|
| | St. Bernard 504-277-8418 |
| | South Louisiana 504-652-9278 |
| Maine | Eastport 207-853-4614 |
| | Portland 207-773-1613 |
| Maryland | Baltimore 410-385-4700 |
| | Belgium<br>England |
| Massachusetts | Boston 617-973-5354 |
| | Fall River 508-674-5707 |
| Michigan | Detroit 313-841-6700 |
| | Monroe 313-241-6480 |
| | St. Joseph 616-983-7111 |
| Minnesota | Duluth 218-727-8525 |
| Mississippi | Gulfport 601-865-4300 |
| | Pascagoula 601-762-4041 |
| New Hampshire | Portsmouth 603-436-8500 |
| New Jersey | Delaware River 609-963-6420 |
| | Belgium |
| | South Jersey 609-541-8500 |
| New York | Albany 518-463-8763 |
| | New York & New Jersey 212-466-7000 |
| | England |
| | Ogdensburg 315-393-4080 |
| | Oswego 315-343-4503 |
| North Carolina | Wilmington 919-763-1621 |
| | England |
| Ohio | Ashtabula 216-992-8428 |
| | Cleveland 216-241-8004 |
| | Conneaut 216-593-1300 |
| | Fairport Harbor 216-352-0801 |
| | Huron 419-433-2141 |
| | Lorain 216-244-2269 |
| | Toledo 419-243-8251 |
| Oregon | Astoria 503-325-4521 |
| | Coos Bay 503-267-PORT |
| | Newport 503-265-7758 |
| | Portland 503-231-5000 |
| | St. Helens 503-397-2888 |
| Pennsylvania | Philadelphia 215-928-9100 |
| | Erie 814-455-7557 |

| *State* | *Port/Foreign Office (if any)* |
|---|---|
| Rhode Island | Providence 401-781-4717 |
| South Carolina | Charleston 803-723-8651 |
| | England |
| Texas | Beaumont 409-835-5367 |
| | Freeport/ Brazos 409-233-2667 |
| | Brownsville 512-831-4592 |
| | Calhoun County 512-987-2813 |
| | Corpus Christi 512-882-5633 |
| | Galveston 409-765-9321 |
| | Houston 713-670-2400 |
| | Orange 409-883-4363 |
| | Port Arthur 409-983-2011 |
| | Port Isabel 512-943-7826 |
| Virginia | Chesapeake 804-436-4121 |
| | Richmond 804-743-PORT |
| | Norfolk 804-683-8000 |
| | Belgium |
| Washington | Anacortes 206-293-3134 |
| | Bellingham 206-676-2500 |
| | Everett 206-259-3164 |
| | Grays Harbor 206-533-9528 |
| | Kalama 206-673-2325 |
| | Longview 206-425-3305 |
| | Olympia 206-586-6150 |
| | Netherlands |
| | Port Angeles 206-457-8527 |
| | Seattle 206-728-3000 |
| | Tacoma 206-383-5841 |
| | Vancouver 206-693-3611 |
| Wisconsin | Green Bay 414-448-4290 |
| | Milwaukee 414-278-3511 |
| | Superior 715-394-0335 |

## ■ Ports in the EC

| *Country* | *Port* |
|---|---|
| Belgium | Antwerp |
| Denmark | Aarhus, Copenhagen |

| *Country* | *Port* |
|---|---|
| France | Bordeaux, Fos, Le Havre, Marseille, Sete |
| Germany | Bremen, Bremerhaven, Frankfurt, Hamburg, Mainz |
| Greece | Piraeus, Salonika, Thessaloniki |
| Ireland | Cork, Dublin, Waterford |
| Italy | Genoa, La Spezia, Leghorn, Milan, Monfalcone, Naples, Palermo, Salerno, Savona, Turin |
| Netherlands | Amsterdam, Rotterdam |
| Portugal | Leixoes, Lisbon, Oporto |
| Spain | Algeciras, Alicante, Barcelona, Bilbao, Cadiz, Cartegena, Valencia, Vigo |
| United Kingdom | England: Felixstowe, Hull, Leeds, Liverpool, London, Manchester, Southampton, Thamesport |
| | Northern Ireland: Belfast |
| | Scotland: Glasgow, Grangemouth, Leith |

## FOREIGN TRADE ZONES

Foreign trade zones (zones or FTZs) in the United States are restricted access sites in or near ports of entry, which are licensed by the Foreign Trade Zones Board and operated under the supervision of the U.S. Customs Service. The Board grants authority to establish a zone to qualified corporations.

Zones operate as a public utility. Grantees usually contract with private firms to operate facilities and provide services to zone users. Zones have a public policy mission, to encourage employment in the United States which, for Customs duty avoidance reasons, might have been carried out abroad. This objective is accomplished when zones serve the needs of exporters and re-exporters, and when goods arrive in unfinished condition for processing in the zone.

Foreign and domestic merchandise may be moved into zones for legal operations of storage, exhibition, assembly, manufacture, and other processing. Formal customs entry and duties are not filed *unless and until* the good(s) enter into the United States for domestic consumption. Importers usually have the choice at that time to pay duty on the original foreign material or on the finished product. Quota restrictions do not usually apply to goods stored in zones. Domestic goods moved into a zone for export are usually considered exported for purposes of excise or inventory taxes and drawback. Subzones are special purpose arrangements approved by the Board, for operations by specific firms under certain conditions.

FTZs offer benefits to exporters and importers. The benefits are enhanced cash flow by deferral of duties, quicker capture of drawback (see next section), ease of operation and freedom from import and export paperwork on pass-through shipments. At least one Japanese car maker quickly identified the benefits of our FTZ legislation—the company applied for and received FTZ status for its central U.S. manufacturing plant. Duty on imported parts, components and assemblies is not paid until the finished automobile moves into the commerce of the United States. In addition, imported and domestic inventory is not subject to state excise taxes while within the confines of the FTZ.

Local Customs directors can assist with questions about FTZs, and direct you to the FTZ operators in your region. Further information can be obtained from: Executive Secretariat, Foreign Trade Zone Board, at 202-482-2862. Local offices of the Department of Commerce may have FTZ information in their libraries, and leading Customshouse Brokers and Freight forwarders will be knowledgeable on the local FTZ situation.

Of our 50 states, 47 have at least one FTZ, and the U.S. total is 174 and growing. The most active users of the FTZ legislation are: Texas—24 zones, New York—13 zones, Florida—10 zones, and Washington—9 zones.

## Drawback

Drawback is the refund of up to 99 percent of the duties paid to U.S. Customs on merchandise that is imported and subsequently exported from the U.S. or destroyed. Drawback is intended to assist U.S. corporations in foreign markets by eliminating the import duty cost component of export product costs.

Drawback is one of the oldest laws of our republic, enforced through the Customs service since 1789. In 1992 Customs paid out over US$2 billion in drawback, and industry experts report that up to US$4 billion was unclaimed in that year alone.

An exporter, importer, or manufacturer can make one drawback claim per shipment. There are 15 types of drawback. The three most common types are:

1. *Manufacturing drawback.* The refund of duties on exportation of articles produced in the United States with the use of imported goods.
2. *Same condition drawback.* The refund of customs duties on imported goods that are exported prior to use in the United States or destroyed under Customs supervision.
3. *Rejected merchandise drawback.* The refund of customs duties on imported goods that are exported because they do not conform to sample, specs, or are shipped without orders.*

The start up costs of an in house drawback program can be significant. However, once an in-house program is in place, the information

* Adapted in part from information provided by Mr. Joel Junker, Duty Recovery Services Group, Inc., Seattle, Washington 98101-2390.

capture and drawback reporting process is straightforward. Some freight forwarders, accountants, and law firms have developed drawback services as a separate profit center.

U.S. Customs will assist corporations in the drawback process, because they are required to do so. Training aids are also available from a few international trade training organizations.*

## APPENDIX A: NATIONAL TRADE DATA BANK DOCUMENTS

This is the detail on the contents of the documents, reports, and data available within each disk on the National Trade Data Bank (referenced on page 9). Data are updated on a monthly, quarterly, or annual schedule.

*Central Intelligence Agency*

Handbook on Economic Statistics (current year)

A reference aid that provides statistics for select non-Communist countries and all Communist countries. In general, the data in the Handbook are for 1960, 1965, 1970, 1975, 1980, and for the period 1984–92. Data are adjusted for comparability purposes and are obtained from public sources, including international organizations.

The World Factbook (current year)

Provides geographic, political, economic, and demographic information about countries and geographic areas of the world.

*Department of Agriculture, Foreign Agricultural Service*

Foreign Production Supply & Distribution of Agriculture Commodities

Estimates and forecasts by commodity specialists for: beginning stocks, production, imports, exports, domestic use, and ending stocks, for many commodities by country. Latest annual Data.

*Department of Commerce, Bureau of Export Administration (BXA)*

BXA Today

An informational pamphlet describing the Bureau of Export Administration, it mission, organization and various programs.

Bureau of Export Administration Annual Report FY (current year)

The fiscal year annual report of the Bureau of Export Administration. Contents include Export Administration Overview;

* Global Training Center, Inc., Dayton, Ohio is a national trainer in the field of international trade practices. They offer training programs in Drawback.

Export Licensing; National Security Controls; Foreign Policy Controls; Foreign Availability; Short Supply Controls; Export Enforcement; Antiboycott Compliance; Industrial Resource Administration; and several appendices.

Export Licensing Information

Several informational pamphlets on export licensing procedures and regulations.

*Department of Commerce, Bureau of the Census*

Exports from Manufacturing Establishments

Estimated shipments and employment related to manufactured exports for states by industry group [3-digit Standard Industrial Classification (SIC) level]. 1987 Data.

Merchandise Trade—Imports by Commodity

Merchandise trade data for imports by 10-digit Harmonized Tariff System (HTS) commodity codes. The top hundred 10-digit commodities are shown for each country; all 2-digit items and a grand total are also presented. CIF value, customs value, and quantity are currently provided for the last three full years, year-to-date this month last year, and year-to-date this month this year.

Merchandise Trade—Exports by Commodity

Merchandise trade data for exports by 10-digit Schedule B commodity codes. Shippers Export Declarations are summarized by 10-digit Harmonized System commodity codes and country of destination. FAS value and quantity are given for: each of the last five full years, year-to-date this month last year, and year-to-date this month this year.

Merchandise Trade—Imports by Country

Merchandise trade data for imports by 10-digit HTS commodity codes. CIF value, customs value, and quantity are currently provided for the last three full years, year-to-date this month last year, and year-to-date this month this year.

Merchandise Trade—Exports by Country

Merchandise trade data for exports by 10-digit Schedule B commodity codes. Shippers Export Declarations are summarized by 10-digit and 2-digit harmonized commodity codes by destination country. FAS value and quantity are given for: each of the last five full years, year-to-date this month last year, and year-to-date this month this year.

Total Mid-year Population & Projections Through 2050

Annual Census Bureau mid-year population estimates for 206 countries from 1950 to 1990, annual projections to 2050.

Trade & Employment

Quarterly report of data that measures changes in U.S. imports and domestic exports and related domestic employment. These data are presented in terms of a commodity classification based on the 1978 Standard Industrial Classification (SIC) at the 3-digit level. Data beginning with I–IV 1990.

*Department of Commerce, Bureau of Economic Analysis*

Fixed Reproducible Tangible Wealth Estimates

Annual estimates of gross and net stock in current-cost and constant-cost valuations for fixed private capital by industry, fixed nonresidential private capital by legal form, residential capital by tenure, government-owned fixed capital by government and durable goods owned by consumers by type of goods. Estimates for fixed private capital are for 2-digit SIC industries (1987 basis) for the years 1947–1990. All other estimates are for years starting in 1929 through 1990.

Foreign Direct Investment in the United States: BoP Basis

Country-by-industry estimates of the foreign direct investment position in the United States on a historical-cost basis and of balance of payments transactions between U.S. affiliates and their foreign groups for calendar years 1980–90. (updated annually). The balance of payments transactions consists of capital inflows and its components ( equity capital inflows, reinvested earnings, and intercompany debt inflows); income; royalties and license fees; and charges for other services.

International Services

U.S. balance of payments transactions in services and on sales of services by foreign affiliates of U.S. companies and by U.S. affiliates of foreign companies. 1987–1991 data available.

National Income & Product Accounts, Annual Series

The production and distribution of goods and services in the United States. Detailed tables that comprise the accounts can be viewed as components and elaborations of five principal accounts: (1) national income and product, (2) personal income and outlays, (3) government transactions, (4) foreign transactions, and (5) savings and investment. 1929–1990 Data.

National Income & Product Accounts, Quarterly Series

The production and distribution of goods and services in the United States. Detailed tables that comprise the accounts can be viewed as components and elaborations of five principal accounts: (1) national income and product, (2) personal income and outlays, (3) government transactions,

(4) foreign transactions, and (5) savings and investment. Official quarterly estimates from 1964 to 1992.

Operations of U.S. Affiliates of Foreign Companies
Data on financing and operations including income statements, balance sheets, employment and employee compensation, merchandise trade, sales of goods and services, and selected data by State. 1988 Data.

Operations of U.S. Parent Companies & Their Foreign Affiliates
Data on the financing and operation, including income statements, balance sheets, employment and employee compensation, merchandise trade, and sales of goods and services. 1987 Fiscal Year Data.

U.S. Assets Abroad & Foreign Assets in the United States
Component details for the international investment position of the U.S. provide details on the stocks of outstanding U.S. assets abroad and foreign assets in the U.S.. Major types of assets and liabilities covered are those of U.S. and foreign monetary authorities, those of (claims) of the U.S. Government on other than official foreigners, and securities, and bank and nonbank transactions. 1976–1990. Annual Data.

U.S. Businesses Acquired & Established by Foreign Direct Investors
New foreign direct investment in the United States, covering (1) existing U.S business enterprises in which foreign investors acquired at least 10 percent ownership interest and (2) new U.S. business enterprises established by foreign direct investors or their U.S. affiliates. 1987–90. Annual Data.

U.S. Direct Investment Abroad: Position, Capital, Income
Country-by-industry estimates of the U.S. direct investment position abroad on a historical-cost basis and of balance of payments transactions between U.S. parent companies and their foreign affiliates for calendar years 1982–90. The balance of payments transactions consist of capital outflows and its components (equity capital outflows, reinvested earnings, and intercompany debt outflows); income; royalties and license fees; and charges for other services.

U.S. Expenditures for Pollution Abatement & Control (PAC)
U.S. expenditures for PAC in current and constant dollars and selected fixed-weighted price indexes. Annual data are by type (e.g., air, water) and by expenditure category (e.g., sector). 1972–90 Data.

U.S. International Transactions (Balance of Payments)
A comprehensive view of economic transactions between the U.S. and foreign countries. Major types of transactions covered are merchandise trade; travel; transportation; other

private services; income on international investment; U.S. Government military and other services; private remittances; foreign aid; private capital flows including direct investment, securities, banking and nonbanking transactions; and changes in foreign official assets in the U.S. and U.S. official reserve assets. 1978–92 Quarterly Data.

U.S. Merchandise Trade (Balance of Payments Basis)

Comprehensive view of the movement of goods by selected end-use category and between the U.S. and foreign countries. These estimates are on a balance of payments basis, which excludes military trade of U.S. defense agencies and reflects adjustments for timing, coverage, and valuations to the trade data reported by the Census Bureau on the f.a.s.-customs valuation basis. 1979–92 Quarterly Data.

*Department of Commerce, Office of Business Analysis*

National Trade Data Bank (NTDB) BROWSE Manual

Comprehensive manual for using the NTDB BROWSE software. Includes examples of retrieving, copying and printing documents as well as a troubleshooting section.

Sources of Trade Information & Contacts

A series of telephone directories for government agencies providing information on international trade and exporting issues. Also a listing of all Federal Depository Libraries receiving the National Trade Data Bank CD-ROM.

*Department of Commerce, International Trade Administration (ITA)*

Business America

The Department of Commerce's bi-weekly publication that provides developments in international trade for the purpose of helping American companies sell their products overseas. Each issue has trade leads, marketing advice, export tips, descriptions of U.S. trade programs, general status of trade negotiations, and country trade outlooks. 12 Months of Back Issues.

A Basic Guide to Exporting

The publication provides information needed to export. It provides a thorough introduction to exporting and serves as a reference to obtain information on particular topics. 1992 Version.

Computer Markets—Sources of Information

Sources of information reports provide information on international computer hardware and software markets. The reports list market research reports available from the Department of Commerce and information on trade promotion events, intellectual property rights, tariffs and other taxes, U.S. export controls, and contacts.

Domestic and International Coal Issues & Markets

Analysis of the Coal market in 60 countries, including names and addresses of companies prominent in the overseas markets.

Eastern Europe Looks for Partners

A bi-weekly bulletin designed to help U.S. businesses locate partnership opportunities in the rapidly expanding East European market. The opportunities are compiled from Eastern European and U.S. public and private sources.

EC 1992: A Commerce Dept. Analysis of EC Directives, Vols I, II & III

A joint U.S. DOC/Industry Trade Associations' analysis of EC directives and regulations on 1992 to assess their impact on U.S. market access to the European Community.

Europe Now: A Report

A quarterly publication covering issues in the European Community.

Export Promotion Calendar

Calendar of world-wide trade events maintained by the interagency Trade Promotion Coordinating Committee (TPCC).

Export Programs: Directory of U.S. Government Resources

The guide provides an overview of U.S. Government export assistance programs and contact points for further information and expertise in utilizing these programs. April 1992 Version.

An Exporter's Guide—Export Trading Company Matchmaking Program

The Matchmaking Program run by the U.S. and Foreign Commercial Service (US&FCS) Pittsburgh District Office is an essential service that matches small-to-medium sized U.S. exporters with export trading companies from across the country based on specific criteria, including company size, regional interest, type of commodity, and industry. In addition to matchmaking companies, the Pittsburgh District Office Matchmaking Program provides crucial support and counseling services to ensure that partnerships between companies in the program prove successful.

Foreign Direct Investment in the United States—Annual Transactions

An annual report that identifies specific foreign direct investment transactions in the Untied States, analyzes recent trends in such investment, and provides data and related information on significant transactions. 1989, 1990 Data.

Foreign Traders Index

Names of foreign companies, organizations, government entities, banks, associations and institutes in selected countries served by the U.S. & Foreign Commercial Service which have some interest in importing goods or services from the U.S. Entries cover the entities' name, address telephone, cable, key contact, products, business interest, bank reference, year established, size, number of employees, and other data.

Investment Guides

A series of guidebooks detailing the climate for investing in particular countries and providing sources for more detailed information.

Lexicon of Trade Terms

The Lexicon is a collection of trade acronyms and definitions which was assembled by the Office of Management and Organization based on available publications,informal papers, and canvassing among program staff.

Market Research Reports

Country Marketing Plans, Industry Sector Analyses, Foreign Economic Trends Market Research covering individual countries, industries, and industry sub-sectors offering potential for U.S. exports. Material is provided by in-country market research firms or embassy research personnel. Reports are 2-to-90 pages long and provide information on market size, competitors, end-users, distribution channels, market access, best prospect products, economic factors and trends, business practices, and other data.

North American Free Trade Agreement (NAFTA) Information

Several documents containing basic information about the proposed North American Free Trade Agreement.

Software International

Software International is a quarterly newsletter that discusses intellectual property rights, export licensing, upcoming Department of Commerce trade promotion events, and other issues related to exporting computer hardware and software. Its primary goal is to provide U.S. vendors with information that will facilitate international sales.

Trade Opportunity Program

Sales opportunities and leads from U.S. embassies abroad for specific products, projects, government tenders, representation, joint ventures, and barter arrangements being sought by foreign companies, governments, or organizations from

U.S. suppliers. Records include name address, contact, HS or HTS code, description of the opportunity, and other pertinent data—(this data is on the Economic Bulletin Board-Call the office of Business Analysis).

Understanding U.S. Foreign Trade Data

Comprehensive publication providing an introduction to merchandise trade data for the occasional user of aggregate trade data and a more technical description for users of complex trade data series.

U.S. Foreign Trade Highlights

The U.S. Foreign Trade Highlights is an annual publication of the International Trade Administration that provides data on U.S. merchandise trade. Emphasis is on aggregate exports and imports, U.S. commodity and country/regional trade balances, and shifts in the commodity composition of U.S. exports and imports.

U.S. Foreign Trade Update—Monthly Analysis

Monthly analysis of U.S. foreign trade trends, including comparative trade statistics. November 1991-present.

U.S. Industrial Outlook—1992

Business reference book providing forecasts for and information concerning over 350 U.S. industries, generally, by SIC categories.

U.S. Manufacturers Trade Performance—Quarterly Report

Quarterly report containing text and tables which outline manufacturers trade performance on a variety of topics. 4th Quarter 1991.

Export Yellow Pages

This database contains the name, address, telephone and fax number, products/services, and key contact for 12,000 U.S. companies that are either producers of goods and services available for export or that provide export services.

*Department of Commerce, National Institute for Standards and Technology (NIST)*

GATT Standards Code Activities of NIST

Report describes the GATT Standards Code activities conducted by the Standards Code and Information Program, National Institute of Standards and Technology (NIST). NIST responsibilities include operating the U.S.GATT inquiry point for information on standards and certification activities and the technical office for non-agricultural products; notifying the GATT Secretariat of proposed U.S. Federal Government standards-based rules that might significantly affect trade; assisting U.S. industry with standards-related trade problems;

and responding to inquiries about proposed foreign and U.S. regulations.

Organizations Conducting Standards-Related Activities

Directory contains information on international and regional organizations which conduct standardization, certification, laboratory accreditation, or other standards-related activities. It describes their work in these areas, the scope of each organization, national affiliations of members, U.S. participants, restrictions on membership, as well as the availability of any standards in English.

Standards, Certification and Metric Information Program

The report describes the Center's program of providing information on U.S., foreign, and international voluntary standards, regulations and rules of certification for non-agricultural products.

*Department of Energy*

International Energy Database

Current data and trends for production, consumption, stocks, prices, imports, and exports of primary energy commodities in more than 190 countries and jurisdictions.

*Department of Labor, Bureau of Labor Statistics*

International Labor Statistics

Labor force, employment, unemployment rates, indexes of manufacturing productivity, labor costs, consumer price indexes, work stoppage statistics and related measures for 10–15 countries.

International Price Indexes

Import and export price indexes by SITC, BEA end-use and SIC-based code; special export price comparison (U.S., West Germany, Japan) and international service price indexes (selected categories); exchange rate indexes by SITC code.

*Department of State, Bureau of Public Affairs*

Background Notes

Brief, factual summaries concerning the people, history, government, economy, and foreign relations of about 170 countries (excluding the United States) and of selected international organizations.

Country Reports on Economic Policy and Trade Practices—1992

These reports on individual country economic policy and trade practices were prepared by the Department of State in accordance with section 2202 of the Omnibus Trade and Competitiveness Act of 1988. Modeled on the State Department's annual reports on country human rights practices, the reports are intended to provide a single, comprehensive and comparative analysis of the economic policies and trade practices of each country with which the United States has an economic or trade relationship.

Industrial Outlook for Petroleum and Natural Gas

These country specific reports consist of detailed studies of the petroleum and natural gas sectors of selected producer and consumer countries. Topics include hydrocarbon reserves and production, pipelines, natural gas, refining and petrochemicals, exports, domestic market and the investment market.

Key Officers of Foreign Service Posts

The Key Officers Guide lists key officers at Foreign Service posts with whom American business representatives would most likely have contact. All embassies, missions, consulates general, and consulates are listed.

Resource Guide to Doing Business in Central and Eastern Europe

A resource guide for U.S. businesses seeking market opportunities in Central and Eastern Europe. Information on U.S. Government Initiatives, Enhancing Private-Sector Opportunities, Support in CEE Countries as well as sources to contact for further information. April 1991 Publication.

*Export-Import Bank of the United States*

Export-Import Bank of the United States, Quarterly Report

A quarterly report that provides information on Bank programs by country and industry. 2nd Quarter 1990–2nd Quarter 1992 Data.

*Board of Governors of the Federal Reserve System*

Foreign Spot Exchange Rates

Spot exchange rates for 30 foreign countries based on averages of certified noon buying rates in New York for cable transfers. Units are either foreign currency per U.S. dollar or U.S. cents per unit of foreign currency. 1971–92 Monthly Data.

Foreign Three-Month Interest Rates

Interest rates for 3-month interbank loans for the foreign G-10 countries except for Canada, Finance Company Paper; Belgium, 3-month treasury bills; and Japan, Gensaki rate. Rates are averages of daily figures expressed on an annual basis. 1979–92 Monthly Data.

Stock Price Indices for the G-10 Countries

Stock price indices for the G-10 countries by week. Construction and sources of indices vary across countries. 1989–92 Data.

U.S. 3-Month CD Interest Rates

U.S. 3-month Certificate of Deposit (CD) interest rates (percent per annum). The rate on CDs is a simple average of dealer rates on negotiable CDs nationally trade in the secondary market. 1964–92 Monthly Data.

Weighted Average Exchange Value of the Dollar

Weighted average exchange value index (March 1973 = 100) of the U.S. dollar against currencies of 10 foreign industries countries. Weights are based on the 1972–76 average world trade of each country compared to the total of all ten countries. Series revised as of August 1978. 1979–92 Monthly Data.

*U.S. International Trade Commission*

Trade Between the U.S. & Non-Market Economy Countries

This series of reports by the United States International Trade Commission monitors imports from and exports to certain non-market economy countries (NMEs). These reports present data on the effect, if any, of imports from NMEs on the production of like or directly competitive articles in the U.S. and on employment within industries producing those articles.

*Overseas Private Investment Corporation*

OPIC Program Summaries

The report provides an overview of OPIC's programs of insuring U.S. investment projects abroad and financing investment projects through direct loans and loan guarantees.

*Small Business Administration*

Small Business and Export Information System

A description of the Small Business Administration and its Export Information System.

*Office of the U.S. Trade Representative*

National Trade Estimate Report on Foreign Trade Barriers

Congressional report required by Section 1304 of the Omnibus Trade and Competitiveness Act of 1988. It provides significant foreign tariffs and trade barriers to and distortions of trade. Provides an inventory of trade barriers affecting goods, services, investment, and intellectual property rights of major U.S trading partners.

North American Free Trade Agreement

This document contains a synopsis of the August 12, 1992 proposed North American Free Trade Agreement. Officials of Canada, Mexico, and the United States have been directed to complete work on the final agreement as soon as possible. The final text will be made public when completed.

Trade Projections Report to the Congress

Joint publication of United States Trade Representative and Secretary of Treasury required under the 1988 Trade Act (Section 1641) containing a review and analysis of economic developments in major U.S. trading partner countries.

*University of Massachusetts, MISER*

State of Origins of Exports

Year end totals and quarterly data according to 2-digit SIC numbers for each state showing where commodities began their export journey. The data do not show where exports were grown, mined or manufactured. They show the origin of the export journey. 1989–91 Year-end Totals; 1990–1992 1st QTR, Quarterly Data.

# PART TWO

# European Resources

## EUROPEAN TELEPHONES

Telephoning Europe, whether from the United States, from other European countries, or from one side of a European city to the other can sometimes be daunting. However, this directory tries to make the telephone listings in the directory as easy as possible to understand and use.

First, European numbers usually do not conform to the standard American three-digit area code followed by a seven-digit number. The number of digits in telephone numbers varies from country to country, and sometimes from city to city within countries.

Unless otherwise noted, the European telephone numbers have been listed the way they typically appear on Europeans' business cards—with the regional or city code, if applicable, but not the national code needed for calling from the United States.

The U.S. Embassy in Britain, for example, is listed as (071) 499-9000. The 071 is the code for central London; if telephoning the Embassy from another part of central London, the caller would merely dial the seven local digits: 499-9000. If calling from somewhere else in Britain, including the outer sections of London that use the 081 code, the caller would dial the full 10 numbers, starting with 071.

Calling Europe from the United States can be relatively straightforward. To reach one of this book's listed European numbers from the United States, first dial 011 for an international line. Then dial the two-digit or three-digit country code (44 for Britain, for example), which is listed for the EC countries with the respective statistical background at the beginning of each chapter.

The country code is followed by the regional or city code, which typically is anything from one to four digits. For London, again, the central city code is 071. When calling from outside Britain, however, the 0 in the city code is dropped. For example, the number to dial from the United States for the U.S. Embassy in London would be 011-44-71-499-9000.

Some countries have their own wrinkles for internal calls. In France, there is only one area code, the 1 for Paris; the rest of the country survives without an area code. In Spain, the national trunk line for calling one Spanish city from another is accessed by dialing 9, even though this is rarely shown in phone numbers printed within Spain.

Regarding telefaxes, most European companies and agencies readily provide fax numbers for contacts, and those that do are listed in this directory. However, fax numbers were not available for some entries. To find out if a listing has acquired a fax machine, call the main number listed.

Finally, those who encounter European telephone difficulties can always get straightened out quickly—almost always, anyway—by contacting the local or international operators.

## EXCHANGE RATES TABLE

| | | | | |
|---|---|---|---|---|
| BELGIUM | Nov '88 | Mar '90 | Apr '92 | July '93 |
| $1/BFr | 36.34 | 34.99 | 33.8 | 34.9 |
| DENMARK | Nov '88 | Mar '90 | Apr '92 | July '93 |
| $1/DKr | 6.69 | 6.44 | 6.39 | 6.51 |
| FRANCE | Nov '88 | Mar '90 | Apr '92 | July '93 |
| $1/FFr | 5.92 | 5.69 | 5.58 | 5.72 |
| GERMANY | Nov '88 | Mar '90 | Apr '92 | July '93 |
| $1/DM | 1.73 | 1.68 | 1.64 | 1.70 |
| GREECE | Nov '88 | Mar '90 | Apr '92 | July '93 |
| $1/DR | 144 | 161 | 191 | 230 |
| IRELAND | Nov '88 | Mar '90 | Apr '92 | July '93 |
| $1/Ir£ | 0.64 | 0.63 | 0.61 | 0.70 |
| ITALY | Nov '88 | Mar '90 | Apr '92 | July '93 |
| $1/L | 1,284 | 1,244 | 1,241 | 1,543 |
| LUXEMBOURG | Nov '88 | Mar '90 | Apr '92 | July '93 |
| $1/LFr | 36.3 | 34.9 | 33.8 | 34.9 |
| NETHERLANDS | Nov '88 | Mar '90 | Apr '92 | July '93 |
| $1/Fl | 1.95 | 1.90 | 1.85 | 1.90 |
| PORTUGAL | Nov '88 | Mar '90 | Apr '92 | July '93 |
| $1/Esc | 144 | 149 | 142 | 161 |
| SPAIN | Nov '88 | Mar '90 | Apr '92 | July '93 |
| $1/Pta | 113 | 108 | 104 | 131 |
| UNITED KINGDOM | Nov '88 | Mar '90 | Apr '92 | July '93 |
| £1/USD | 1.69 | 1.61 | 1.73 | 1.50 |

# 14

# BELGIUM

## GENERAL INFORMATION

Area: 11,782 square miles
Capital: Brussels
Languages: French, Dutch, German
Population: 10 million
Currency: Belgian Franc (BFr)
Exchange Rate (June 1993): $1/BFr = 34.9
International Trade*: $200 billion
Telephone Country Code: 32

Brussels is the home of the European Community's (EC) sprawling headquarters and 15,000 EC employees, including the 3,000 policymaking Eurocrats who set, interpret, and enforce the trade rules of the single market. Brussels is also the capital.

While Brussels admittedly does not share the style of Milan, the excitement of Paris, or the status of London, the rise of the EC has made the Belgian capital a key international crossroads. In recent years, law firms and other professional advisers and consultants, along with many leading corporations, have established offices in Brussels for easier access to the EC and the Eurocrats.

Belgium, the EC headquarters, sometimes makes people forget about Belgium, the promising trade partner. In recent years, however, about two-thirds of Belgium's GNP has come from exports, making it one of the most successful trading nations in the world.

Dress is conservative and business is conducted in a more formal style than in most other EC countries. Business cards are exchanged routinely. Small gifts, such as flowers, may be expected for hosts or hostesses when dinner is at a business contact's home. But the Eurocrats operate under the same sort of ethical rules that prohibit even small gifts to federal employees in the United States. Indeed, some people regard Brussels as an EC version of Washington, except that Belgium has perhaps more business

* This number represents total exports and imports.

regulation and less politics, even though it is also home of the headquarters of NATO.

The most sensitive political issue within Belgium itself is the north-south cultural divide that is most evident in the use of language. The northern Flemish prefer to speak English with visiting businesspeople, even those who speak good French.

The southern Walloons, on the other hand, may speak English but prefer French. About 55 percent of the population speaks primarily Flemish and 45 percent French. Both are official languages.

## BELGIAN AGENCIES IN THE UNITED STATES

Embassy of Belgium, 3330 Garfield St., NW, Washington, DC 20008
(202) 333-6900; Fax: (202) 625-7567

Belgian Consulate General, 229 Peachtree St., NE, Suite 2306, Atlanta, GA 30303
(404) 659-2150; Fax: (404) 659-8474

Belgian Consulate General, 333 North Michigan Ave., Suite 2000, Chicago, IL 60601
(312) 263-6624; Fax: (312) 263-4805

Belgian Consulate General, 6100 Wilshire Blvd., Suite 1200, Los Angeles, CA 90084
(213) 857-1244; Fax: (213) 936-2564

Belgian Consulate General, 50 Rockefeller Plaza, Suite 1104, New York, NY 10020
(212) 586-5110; Fax: (212) 582-9657

Belgian-American Chamber of Commerce, Empire State Bldg., 350 Fifth Ave., Suite 703, New York, NY 10018
(212) 967-9898; Fax: (212) 629-0349

Belgian-American Chamber of Commerce (Southern Chapter), 3333 Peachtree St., NE, South Tower, Suite 222, Atlanta, GA 30326
(404) 231-5985; Fax: (404) 233-6828

## U.S. AGENCIES IN BELGIUM

U.S. Embassy, 27 Boulevard du Regent, Brussels 1000
(02) 513 38 30; Fax: (02) 511 27 25

U.S. Consulate, Rubens Center, Nationalestraat 5, Antwerp 2000
(03) 225 00 71; Fax: (03) 234 36 98

Belgian Ministry of Foreign Trade, Rue Quatre-Bras 2, Brussels 1000
(02) 516 83 11; Fax: (02) 514 30 67

Belgian Foreign Trade Office, Boulevard Emile Jacqmain 162-Bte 36, Brussels 1210
(02) 219 44 50; Fax: (02) 217 61 23

Belgian Business Federation, Rue Ravenstein 4, Brussels 1000
(02) 515 08 11; Fax: (02) 515 09 99

Brussels Business Federation (UEB), Rue Botanique 75, Brussels 1210
(02) 219 32 23; Fax: (02) 218 56 06

INTRADIV - Association of International Traders in Flanders, Brouwersvliet 15 Antwerp 2000

## BANKS AND FINANCIAL INSTITUTIONS

Banque DeGroof, Rue de L'Industrie 44, Brussels 1040
(02) 233 85 11; Fax: (02) 233 85 68
Services: corporate, commercial banking

Banque Europ Amerique Latine, SA, Rue de L'Association 59, Brussels 1000
(02) 219 00 15; Fax: (02) 217 67 57
Services: corporate, commercial banking

Citibank Belgium, SA, Rue du Trone 60, Brussels 1050
(02) 519 15 11; Fax: (02) 519 15 39
Services: corporate, commercial banking

IPPA Bank, NV, Brusselstraat 45, Antwerp 2018
(03) 247 72 11; Fax: (03) 216 95 95
Services: corporate, commercial banking

Kredietbank, NV, Arengbergstraat 7, Brussels 1000
(02) 517 56 72; Fax: (02) 517 42 09
Services: corporate, commercial banking

Paribas, SA, Boulevard Emile Jacmain 162-Bte 2, Brussels 1210
(02) 220 41 11; Fax: (02) 218 51 42
Services: corporate, commercial banking

Shizuokla Bank Europa, SA, Avenue Louise 283, Box 13, Brussels 1050
(02) 646 04 70; Fax: (02) 646 24 62
Services: corporate, commercial banking

The Fuji Bank, Ltd., SA, Rue Guimard 6–8, Brussels 1040
(02) 234 01 11; Fax: (02) 230 93 66
Services: corporate, commercial banking

## LAW FIRMS

Arthur Flieger, Mechelsesteenweg 82, Antwerp 2018
(03) 216 03 14; Fax: (03) 216 18 44
Services: commercial, business, and military law

Baker & McKenzie, Crousse, DeKeyser, Hinnekens, Boulevard du Regent-Regentlan 40, 5th Fl., Brussels 1000
(02) 512 38 50; Fax: (02) 511 62 80

Coudert Brothers, Tour Louise, Box 8, Avenue Louise 149, Brussels 1050
(02) 539 35 35; Fax: (02) 537 27 10

Gleiss, Lutz, Hootz, Hirsch, & Partners, Avenue Louise 475-Bte 13, Brussels 1050
(02) 647 63 74; Fax: (02) 640 92 31
Services: EC and international law

Loeff & Van der Ploeg, Kortenberglann 66, Brussels 1040
(02) 736 13 84; Fax: (02) 733 01 13
Services: international law

McKenna & Co., Avenue de Cortenberg 66, Box 10, Brussels 1040
(02) 735 38 36; Fax: (02) 735 77 43
Services: EC, international trade, intellectual property, and internal market law

Skadden, Arps, Slate, Meagher, & Flom, Avenue Louise 523, Box 30, Brussels 1050
(02) 648 76 66; Fax: (02) 640 30 32

Thieffry & Associes, Avenue de Tervueren 100, Brussels 1040
(02) 733 97 15; Fax: (02) 733 97 16
Services: EC, competition, and arbitration law

## ACCOUNTING FIRMS

Arthur Andersen, Avenue des Arts 56, Brussels 1040
(02) 510 42 11; Fax: (02) 513 08 62

Blaekaert, Missorten, Sonck, Spaenhoven, & Co., Meiseselaan 71, Brussels 1020
(02) 268 08 35; Fax: (02) 268 39 87

Coopers & Lybrand, Avenue de Tervuren, 270–272 Bte 8, Brussels 1150
(02) 771 21 50; Fax: (02) 771 23 99

C.V. Claeys de Maeyer & Co., Rue de l'Autonomie 9, Brussels 1070
(02) 521 45 25; Fax: (02) 520 82 32

Deloitte & Touche Consultants, SA, Boulevard Saint-Michel 83, Brussels 1040
(02) 736 00 65; Fax: (02) 735 31 57

Haller, Joos, Waeterloos, & Partners, Avenue de Tervueren 62, Brussels 1040
(02) 735 00 58; Fax: (02) 733 68 39

Grant Thornton International, Rue de la Loi 227, Brussels 1040
(02) 231 05 80; Fax: (02) 230 22 49

S.P.R.L. Nevens Reviseurs D'Enterprises, Rue Perc Eudore Devroye 86 Bte 8, Brussels 1050
(02) 762 75 50; Fax: (02) 762 90 24

## INSURANCE AGENCIES

AG Group, Boulevard Emile Jacqmain 53, Brussels 1000
(02) 214 81 11; Fax: (02) 214 81 50

Assubel Leven, NV, Lakenstraat 35, Brussels 1000
(02) 214 61 11; Fax: (02) 214 62 74

Boels & Begault - Outshoorn, Meir 30, Antwerp 2000
(03) 220 79 11; Fax: (03) 220 79 82

Corona, SA, NV, Place J. Jacobs 11, Brussels 1000
(02) 517 71 11; Fax: (02) 514 13 55

Fidelitas Verzekeringsmy, NV, Van Eyckelei 14, Antwerp 2018
(03) 221 05 11; Fax: (03) 234 19 22

Generali Belgium, SA, NV, Avenue Louise 149, Brussels 1050
(02) 537 60 70; Fax: (02) 538 40 56

Royale Belge, SA, Boulevard du Souverain 25, Brussels 1170
(02) 661 61 11; Fax: (02) 611 93 40

Winterthur Europe Groep, Avenue des Arts 56, Brussels 1040
(02) 519 74 11; Fax: (02) 513 72 84

## ADVERTISING AND MARKETING AGENCIES

Associate Lowe Troost, Lentestraat 50–54, Brussels 1050
(02) 640 49 24; Fax: (02) 640 96 31

BSB Brussels, SA, Rue de Geneve 6, Brussels 1140
(02) 244 46 11; Fax: (02) 244 46 13
Services: international advertising

Grey, SA, Woluwelaan 58 Bte 3, Brussels 1200
(02) 773 17 11; Fax: (02) 771 26 90
Services: advertising, marketing

Information Publicitaire Benelux (IPB), Avenue Lloyd George 11, Brussels 1050
(02) 643 22 31; Fax: (02) 343 22 00

Media, SA, Avenue Louise 284, BP 7, Brussels 1050
(02) 640 20 25; Fax: (02) 640 30 55
Services: corporate advertising, marketing

Oglivy & Mather Worldwide Media, SA, Avenue Louise 489, Brussels 1050
(02) 649 21 60; Fax: (02) 648 14 29
Services: international advertising, marketing

Publicis, SCB, Avenue de la Couronne, Brussels 1050
(02) 645 35 11; Fax: (02) 646 34 56
Services: advertising, marketing, public relations

Young & Rubicam, SA, Boulevard Dieweg Bte 3, Brussels 1180
(02) 648 88 80; Fax: (02) 375 88 43

## TRANSLATING AND INTERPRETING SERVICES

Adintra All Language Services, Rue du la Revolution 12, Brussels 1000
(02) 218 01 45; Fax: (02) 217 79 96

Alltrans, 47–49 Rue Molstraat, Antwerp 2018
(03) 238 03 19; Fax: (03) 237 07 64

Berlitz, Kunstlaan 36, Brussels 1040
(02) 513 92 72; Fax: (02) 512 22 36

BIL International, Rue Ferme du Mansir 2, Floreffe 5150
(081) 43 46 00; Fax: (081) 43 43 75

CPAB, Chemin d'Ixelles 29–31, Brussels 1050
(02) 511 01 09; Fax: (02) 512 51 39

Groupe Moerman Deneve, SA, Avenue Louise 43–45, Brussels 1050
(02) 537 22 75; Fax: (02) 534 15 49

Lexitech, St. Pieterssteenweg 119, Brussels 1040
(02) 640 03 85; Fax: (02) 640 93 68

Mendez Translations, Avenue Franklin D. Roosevelt 8, Brussels 1050
(02) 647 27 00; Fax: (02) 647 55 50

## TRANSPORTATION AND DISTRIBUTION COMPANIES

Dolisy, SPRL, Avenue des Etats Unis 7, Gosselies 6041
(071) 37 20 34; Fax: (071) 37 27 33

Edmond Depaire, NV, Pourbusstraat, Antwerp 2000
(03) 237 78 50; Fax: (03) 237 78 54

Halbart Continental, SA, Avenue du Port 104, Brussels 1210
(02) 422 25 10; Fax: (02) 422 22 65

Intertrans, SA, Rue D. Lefvre 160, Brussels 1020
(02) 427 61 03

M&M Express Transport, NV, Durmakker 13, Evergem 9940
(091) 54 07 11; Fax: (091) 53 77 77

Otri, SA, Avenue du Port, Brussels 1020
(02) 427 37 47; Telex: 21161

Straps, SPRL, Rue de Namur 61–63, Liege 4000
(041) 52 26 27; Fax: (041) 52 36 94

Universal Express, SA, Avenue du Port 104, Brussels 1210
(02) 424 29 00; Fax: (02) 424 29 00

Verhaeghe Alice, Le Val d'Oise 17, Macquenoise 6593
(060) 51 15 61; Fax: (060) 51 27 30

## TRADE CONSULTANTS

ARA Consult, Avenue du Chateau 16BS, Brussels 1080
(02) 425 78 64; Fax: (02) 425 80 14

Boyden International, NV, Avenue Winston Churchill, Brussels 1180
(02) 344 65 45; Fax: (02) 346 14 61

Brains Trust International, NV, Boulevard Brand Whitlocklaan 24, Brussels 1200
(02) 735 81 40; Fax: (02) 735 20 75

Delville Stuckens & Partners, Avenue Franklin D. Roosevelt 103, Brussels 1050
(02) 660 30 07; Fax: (02) 673 45 41

Eurostandard, NV, Spastraat 67, Brussels 1040
(02) 230 02 15; Fax: (02) 230 92 20

Korn Ferry International, Avenue Louise 523, Brussels 1050
(02) 640 32 40; Fax: (02) 640 83 82

Quadrus, Vilain XIII Straat 19, Brussels 1050
(02) 640 26 73; Fax: (02) 640 59 18

Sema Group Belgium Sobemap, Marsveldplein 5B40, Brussels 1050
(02) 508 52 11; Fax: (02) 512 14 99

## TRADE SHOWS AND EXHIBITIONS

International Motorcar, Motorbike, & Bicycle Show, Brussels International Trade Fair, Place de Belgique, Brussels 1020
(02) 477 04 77; Fax: (02) 478 80 23
Description: biennial (January) exhibit of cars, motorbikes, and bicycles

International Week of Agriculture, Brussels International Trade Fair, Place de Belgique, Brussels 1020
(02) 477 04 77; Fax: (02) 478 80 23
Description: biennial (February) exhibit of agricultural produce and equipment

Eurotech—Trade Show for the Technical Equipment of Enterprises, Brussels International Trade Fair, Place de Belgique, Brussels 1020
(02) 477 04 77; Fax: (02) 478 80 23
Description: biennial (April) exhibit of latest technical equipment

# 15

# DENMARK

## GENERAL INFORMATION

Area: 16,632 miles
Capital: Copenhagen
Language: Danish
Population: 5.1 million
Currency: Kroner (DKr)
Exchange Rate (June 1993): $1/DKr 6.51
International Trade*: $55 billion
Telephone Country Code: 45

Denmark is a part of the European Community, but it has perhaps an even stronger identity as part of Scandinavia. Going into the single market of 1993, Denmark remained the only Scandinavian country in the EC—though Sweden and Finland are applying for membership, and Norway and Iceland may follow.

Part of the attraction is the growing economic power and influence of the EC. The Scandinavian non-members realize that to maintain their high standards of living and their access to the trade and financial markets of the larger neighbors to the south, they must avoid being on the outside looking in.

Another reason that the other Scandinavian countries are following Denmark into the EC is the way Denmark has succeeded in retaining its distinctive Scandinavian characteristics within the EC framework. Like its Nordic sisters, Denmark is a trading nation, heavily dependent on exports of both agriculture and manufacturing. Its people have been dealing cross-border since the days of Vikings, and they are among the most "international" on earth. Most Danes speak impeccable English, are familiar with American culture, and know how to do business with Americans.

* This number represents total exports and imports.

Conservative dress is expected for formal business meetings, but Danes and other Scandinavians frequently dress more casually than their counterparts in neighboring Germany. Business entertaining in restaurants is common; indeed, Denmark and other parts of Scandinavia are so expensive that virtually the only diners in finer restaurants are people on corporate expense accounts.

Punctuality is expected for all appointments, and Danes, like all Scandinavians, are known for their distaste of small talk to open business discussions. When a negotiating session is scheduled, you walk in at the appointed minute and get down to brass tacks almost immediately.

## DANISH AGENCIES IN THE UNITED STATES

Embassy of Denmark, 3200 Whitehaven St., NW, Washington, DC 20008-3683
(202) 234-4300; Fax: (202) 328-1470

Consulate General, 825 Third Ave., New York, NY 10022-7519
(212) 223-4545; Fax: (212) 754-1904

Consulate General, John Hancock Center, Suite 3430, 875 N. Michigan Ave., Chicago, IL 60611-1901
(312) 787-8780; Fax: (312) 787-8744

Consulate General, 3440 Wilshire Blvd., Suite 904, Los Angeles, CA 90010-2183
(213) 387-4277; Fax: (213) 387-9456

Danish Trade Office, Suite 1008, 229 Peachtree St. NE, Atlanta, GA 30303
(404) 588-1588; Fax: (404) 588-1589

Danish Trade Office, 19120 Detroit Rd., Cleveland, OH 44116
(216) 331-0550; Fax: (216) 331-6138

Danish Trade Office, Silverado Center II, Suite 500, 1777 South Harrison St., Denver, CO 80210
(303) 692-9090; Fax: (303) 756-0678

Danish Trade Office, Arbor Place, 15450 New Barn Rd., Suite 303, P.O. Box 5517, Miami Lakes, FL 33014-2169
(305) 556-5666; Fax: (305) 556-8715

Danish Trade Office, Joseph Vance Bldg., Suite 220, 1402 Third Ave., Seattle, WA 98101
(206) 624-9638; Fax: (206) 682-8914

Danish-American Chamber of Commerce, 825 Third Ave., 32nd Fl., New York, NY 10022
(212) 980-6240; Fax: (212) 754-1904

## U.S. AGENCIES IN DENMARK

U.S. Embassy, Dag Hammarskjold Alle 24, 2100 Copenhagen 0
(31) 42 31 44; Fax: (35) 43 02 23

Danish Ministry of Foreign Affairs, Investment Secretariat, 2 Asiatisk Plads, 1448 Copenhagen K
(33) 392 00 00

Export Service Center, Ministry of Foreign Affairs, Asiatisk Plads 2, 1448 Copenhagen K
(33) 92 05 00; Fax: (33) 92 17 73
Services: foreign company assistance, export company listings, import duties, and restrictions information

Danish Industry Ministry, Information Office for Foreign Investment, 25 Sondergade, 8600 Silkeborg
(86) 82 56 55

Chamber of Commerce of Denmark, Borsen, 1217 Copenhagen K
(33) 91 23 23

Federation of Danish Industries, H.C. Andersens Boulevard 18, 1596 Copenhagen V
(33) 15 22 33

## BANKS AND FINANCIAL INSTITUTIONS

Amagerbanken, A/S, Amagerbrogade 25, 2300 Copenhagen S
(31) 58 93 33; Fax: (31) 54 45 34
Services: corporate banking

Amtssparekassen, Vestre Stationsvej 7, 5100 Odense C
(66) 14 04 74; Fax: (65) 91 01 10
Services: foreign exchange, money market dealing, import and export financing, foreign collection and international collections

Bikuben, International Division, 8 Silkegade, 113 Copenhagen K
(33) 12 01 33
Services: international payments, documentary business, trade finance, export guarantees, and foreign currency exchange

Den Danske Bank, International Branch, 8 Laksgade, 1092 Copenhagen K
(33) 44 19 00; Fax: (31) 18 58 73
Services: corporate banking

Jyske Bank, International Division, Vesterbrogade 9, Postbox 298, 1501 Copenhagen
(31) 21 22 22; Fax: (31) 24 41 22
Services: corporate banking

Kreditforeningen Danmark, Jarmers Plads 2, 1590 Copenhagen V
(33) 12 53 00; Fax: (33) 14 35 48
Services: corporate banking

Nykredit, Otto Monsteds Plads 11, 1790 Copenhagen V
(33) 91 34 34; Fax: (33) 15 97 34
Services: corporate banking

Unibank, Sparekassen Nordjylland, A/S, 9100 Aalborg
(98) 18 73 11; Fax: (98) 18 56 77
Services: corporate banking

Viking Capital, A/S, Storegade 88, Postbox 222, 6100 Haderslev
(74) 52 74 40; Fax: (74) 52 86 06
Services: investment banking, project development, acquisitions, financing

## LAW FIRMS

Advokaterne i Toldkammeret, A/S, Ostre Stationsvej 43, 5100 Odense C
(66) 11 00 04; Fax: (66) 11 78 44
Services: commercial and corporate

Advokaterne i Vingardshus, Postbox 863, Vingardsgade 22, 9100 Aalborg
(98) 13 13 00; Fax: (98) 13 96 77
Services: commercial and corporate

Advokatfirmaet Lars Christensen, 4 Jernbanegade, 5100 Odense
(66) 11 78 11; Fax: (66) 14 43 28
Services: commercial and corporate

Erling Steffen & Thjelle Ehrenskjold, Vestergade 1, 1456 Copenhagen K
(33) 93 68 88; Fax: (33) 93 65 55
Services: commercial and corporate

Hjejle, Gersted, & Mogensen, Amagertorv 24, 1160 Copenhagen K
(33) 13 42 62; Fax: (33) 11 12 50
Services: commercial and corporate

Hvidkjaer & Partners, Lille Strandstrede 20, 1254 Copenhagen K
(33) 11 81 51
Services: corporate, commercial, banking, mergers, acquisitions, tax, real estate, industrial property rights, international transactions

Kromann & Munter, Radhuspladsen 14, 1550 Copenhagen V
(33) 11 11 10; Fax: (33) 11 80 28
Services: commercial and corporate

Ole Olsen, Barrister, & Solicitor, 59 Radhuspladsen, 1550 Copenhagen V
(33) 12 12 71; Fax: (33) 13 20 92
Services: commercial and corporate

Pontoppidan, Philip, & Partners, Frederiksgade 1, 1265 Copenhagen K
(33) 13 11 12; Fax: (33) 32 80 45
Services: commercial and corporate

Reumert & Partners, Bredgade 26, 1260 Copenhagen K
(33) 93 39 60; Fax: (33) 93 39 50
Services: commercial, corporate, intellectual property, construction, transport, energy, bankruptcy, EC, litigation, and international arbitration

## ACCOUNTING FIRMS

BDO Scanrevision, A/S, Postbox 1037, 7400 Herning
(97) 12 33 88; Fax: (97) 22 47 46

Bjerre-Poulsen, Frederiksberggade 25, 1459 Copenhagen K
(33) 14 33 88; Fax: (33) 93 01 88

Jensen/Coopers & Lybrand, KG, Postbox 2152, 1016 Copenhagen K
(33) 93 13 65

Lundgaard, Andersen, & Glud, A/S, Postbox 201, 2000 Copenhagen-Frederiksberg
(38) 33 34 00

Mortensen & Beierholm, A/S, Vester Sogade 10, 1601 Copenhagen V
(33) 12 68 11

Price Waterhouse/Seier-Petersen, Aboulevarden 70, 8000 Arhus C
(86) 13 07 88

## INSURANCE AGENCIES

A. Jessen & Co., EFTF, Meldahlsgade 5, 1613 Copenhagen
(33) 14 11 12; Fax: (33) 14 11 15
Services: international insurance brokers, marine, risk management

ABIM, APS, Kastelsvej 11, 2100 Copenhagen OE
(31) 26 20 24; Fax: (31) 26 13 26
Services: international insurance brokers, construction and product liability, leasing, exports and political risks, risk management

OLE HJORTH ASSURANCE, Kirke Vaerlosevej 38, 3500 Vaerlose
(42) 48 30 33; Fax: (42) 48 21 05
Services: international insurance brokers, marine, risk management

## ADVERTISING AND MARKETING AGENCIES

ATOPOS, Jens Benzons Gade 54, 5100 Odense C
(66) 12 71 72; Fax: (66) 12 74 76
Services: corporate advertising

H.C. Gruppen Horsens, A/S, Sondergade 10, 8700 Horsens
(75) 61 11 44; Fax: (75) 61 11 52
Services: corporate advertising

International Reklame and Marketing, APS, Klostervej 3 A, 8900 Randers
(86) 49 55 58; Fax: (86) 49 47 17
Services: marketing and corporate advertising

Kruhoffer Reklame OG Marketing, Kirkegardsvej 1, 8000 Arhus C
(86) 20 27 33; Fax: (86) 40 31 31
Services: marketing and corporate advertising

Maersk Flex, Thager Larsensvej 10, 9200 Aalborg SV
(98) 18 84 88; Fax: (98) 18 80 89
Services: corporate advertising

Samfunds-Kontakt, A/S, Osterbro 28, 5000 Odense C
(66) 17 78 58; Fax: (66) 17 74 42
Services: marketing and corporate advertising

EXPO Marketing, Skovlytoften 4, 2840 Holte

FINCO, Emdrupvej 28 A, 2100 Copenhagen O

Result Management Systems, Dronningensgade 23, Dronningegarden, 5000 Odense C

DTO, Danish Technical Information Service, Rygaards Alle 131 A, 2900 Hellerup
Services: market research

## TRANSLATING AND INTERPRETING SERVICES

Alpha Lingua, Kattesundet 12 A, 1458 Copenhagen K
(33) 14 66 26; Fax: (33) 32 07 50

Hopstock Professioneller Sprachendienst, Hestemollestraede 3, 1464 Copenhagen K
(33) 13 22 34; Fax: (33) 93 22 16

Interverbum Denmark, A/S, Sjaelsovej 49, Postbox 98,
3460 Birkered
(42) 81 84 44; Fax: (42) 81 48 21

## TRANSPORTATION AND DISTRIBUTION COMPANIES

Atlas Spedition, A/S, Belvedere Kajen, Elvaerksvej 11, 2450
Copenhagen SV
(31) 21 90 00; Fax: (31) 21 55 99

Baltic Transport Arhus, APS, Sindalsvej 42 B, Postbox 2194,
8240 Risskov
(86) 21 61 11; Fax: (86) 21 62 55

Dantransport, A/S, Kornmarksvej 12-20, Postbox 318,
2600 Glostrup
(33) 14 16 88; Fax: (43) 48 19 99

EAC Transport Agencies, Liner Agents/ Liner Agency,
Vermundsgade 38, 2100 Copenhagen 0
(39) 27 12 14; Fax: (39) 27 12 10

Fairplay Shipping, A/S, Oversea Shipping Consultants,
Industriholmen 7, 2650 Hvidovre
(36) 77 17 00; Fax: (36) 77 12 30

HR-Spedition, A/S, International Transport OG Spedition,
Plantagevej 14, 6330 Padborg
(74) 67 02 34; Fax: (74) 67 39 77

Leman International System Transport, A/S, Tjaeregade 2,
Postbox 453, 1790 Copenhagen V
(33) 13 16 00; Fax: (33) 13 70 69

N.E. Kock International, Spedition, A/S, Lejrvej 8, 6330 Padborg
(74) 67 15 35; Fax: (74) 67 09 35

Thor Jorgensen, A/S, Ostbanegade 55, 2100 Copenhagen O
(31) 26 33 33

Trans-World Shipping, APS, Graham BellsVej 18, Postbox 3035,
8200 Arhus N
(86) 78 44 66; Fax: (86) 10 13 22

## TRADE CONSULTANTS

Carl Bro. International, A/S, Consulting Engineers & Planners,
Granskoven 8, 2600 Glostrup
(42) 96 80 11; Fax: (42) 96 00 55
Services: energy, industries, rural development,
telecommunications, transportation, water supply,
sanitation, development economics

COWIconsult, Consulting Engineers & Planners, AS, Parallelvej 15, 2800 Lyngby
(45) 97 22 11; Fax: (45) 97 22 12
Services: building, industry, transportation, environment, water supply energy, offshore, rural development, urban development

Denconsult, International Development Consultants, Digtervejen 11, 9200 Aalborg, SV
(98) 18 73 66; Fax: (98) 18 73 22
Services: energy, environmental planning, engineering, industrial, and institutional development

Giersing Rose, A/S, Amagertorv 29, 1160 Copenhagen K
(33) 32 61 25; Fax: (33) 93 56 77
Services: civil engineering, fish-farming, and mining

Rasmussen & Schiotz, Datavej 36, 3460 Birkerod
(42) 81 99 11; Fax: (42) 81 51 41
Services: property development, design planning, project management, financing, property management and sales

## TRADE SHOWS AND EXHIBITIONS

International Agriculture Exhibition (AGROMEK), Contact: exhibition manager, Agromeks, Hojholvej 24, 8210 Arhus V
(86) 15 68 22; Fax: (86) 15 19 51
Description: annual (January, Exhibition Centre Herning) exhibit of agricultural mechanization, cattle, and pigs

Rail & Lorry Exhibition (EUROMODAL), Contact: exhibition manager, The Bella Centre, A/S, Center Boulevard, 2300 Copenhagen S
Description: annual (March) exhibit of combined rail and road transport systems

Cable & Pipe Exhibition, Contact: exhibition manager, Exhibition Centre Herning, 7400 Herning
Description: annual (May) exhibit of cable and pipe products

International Furniture Fair Denmark, Contact: exhibition manager, Exhibition Centre Herning
(86) 15 81 11; Fax: (86) 15 02 20
Description: annual (August) exhibit of home and office furniture

KONTOR & DATA International Business Exhibition, Contact: exhibition manager, The Bella Center, Center Boulevard, 2300 Copenhagen S
Description: annual (September) exhibit of business data systems

# 16

# FRANCE

## GENERAL INFORMATION

Area: 211,208 square miles
Capital: Paris
Language: French
Population: 58.4 million
Currency: French franc (FF)
Exchange Rate (June 1993): $1/1 FF 5.72
International Trade*: $400 billion
Telephone Country Code: 33

France is one of the most regulated bureaucratic societies in the world. Civil servants often seem to bend the rules to their own whims, and the rules themselves can be quite daunting. Office meetings are typically formal, with the "Monsieur-Madame" usage preferred to first names, and the French may want to know why something must be done a certain way even if it does not directly concern them or affect the deal.

The three-course business lunch is an institutionalized part of virtually every working day, and the French often want and expect to continue business, though typically not formal negotiations, over long and leisurely evening meals, too. Handshakes are standard, and dress for business occasions is conservative; American-style "power" dressing may look out of place.

The French are notoriously sensitive to American cultural colonization. Imported American television programs, fast food and concepts such as EuroDisneyland, located in the Paris suburbs, are sore spots for some French. Small talk is important, but not personal questions. Asking about someone's family can be considered overly familiar, and even questions about companies' finances can make the French uncomfortable. Business trips to France during the vacation period, particularly

* This number represents total exports and imports.

during August, can be frustrating because so many people take off the entire month or more.

Only minor functionaries try to make foreigners feel ashamed of not speaking French or speaking it badly. It is fine to dust off high school French for casual conversations, such as in restaurants, after apologizing for mangling French and vowing to learn to speak it better. It is bad form, however, to start a formal business discussion in French and then expect the conversation to switch to English at your convenience.

## FRENCH AGENCIES IN THE UNITED STATES

French Embassy, 4101 Reservoir Rd., NW, Washington, DC 20007-2173
(202) 944-6330

French Consulate, 285 Peachtree Center Ave., Suite 2800, Marquis Two, Atlanta, GA 30303
(404) 522-4226; Fax: (404) 880-9408

French Consulate, 3 Commonwealth Ave., Boston, MA 02116
(617) 266-9413; Fax: (617) 354-0566

French Consulate, 737 North Michigan Ave., Olympia Center, Suite 2020, Chicago, IL 60611
(312) 787-5359; Fax: (312) 664-4196

French Consulate, 1000 Renaissance Center, Suite 1670, Detroit, MI 48243
(313) 567-0510

French Consulate, 2 Waterfront Plaza, Suite 300, 500 Moana Blvd., Honolulu, HI 96813
(808) 599-4458; Fax: (808) 599-4751

French Consulate General, Wortham Tower, Suite 976, 2727 Allen Parkway, Houston, TX 77019
(713) 528-2181

French Consulate General, 3305 St. Charles Ave., New Orleans, LA 70115
(504) 897-6381; Fax: (504) 897-1647

French Consulate General, 8350 Wilshire Blvd., Suite 310, Beverly Hills, Los Angeles, CA 90211
(213) 653-3120; Fax: (213) 655-5546

French Consulate General, 1 Biscayne Tower, Suite 1710, 2 South Biscayne Blvd., Miami, FL 33131
(305) 372-9724; Fax: (305) 577-1069

Consulate General, 934 Fifth Ave., New York, NY 10021
(212) 606-3688; Fax: (212) 606-3620

Consulate General, 540 Bush St., San Francisco, CA 94108
(415) 397-4330

Consulate General, Mercantile Plaza, Suite 720, Ponce de Leon, Stop 27, 1/2 Hato-Rey, San Juan, Puerto Rico 00918
(809) 753-1700

French Trade Commission, Center Marquis Two Tower, Suite 2801, 285 Peachtree Center Ave., Atlanta, GA 30303
(404) 522-4843

French Trade Office, 810 Seventh Ave., 38th Fl., New York, NY 10019
(212) 307-8800

French Commercial Consulor, East Wacker Dr., Suite 3730, Chicago, IL 60601
(312) 661-1880

French Industrial Development Agency, 610 Fifth Ave., Suite 301, New York, NY 10020
(212) 757-9340

French-American Chamber of Commerce, 509 Madison Ave., Suite 1900, New York, NY 10022
(212) 371-4466; Fax: (212) 371-5623

French-American Chamber of Commerce, 999 Peachtree St., NE, Suite 2095, Atlanta, GA 30309
(404) 874-2602; Fax: (404) 875-9452

French-American Chamber of Commerce, McCormack Station, P.O. Box 3680, Boston, MA 02101
(617) 523-4438

French-American Chamber of Commerce, 55 East Monroe St., Suite 3710, Chicago, IL 60603
(312) 263-7668; Fax: (312) 263-7860

French-American Chamber of Commerce, 4144 North Central Expressway, Dallas, TX 75204
(214) 821-7475; Fax: (214) 828-1693

French-American Chamber of Commerce, 2727 Kirby, Suite 501, Houston, TX 77002
(713) 529-9578; Fax: (713) 529-2059

French-American Chamber of Commerce, 6380 Wilshire Blvd., Suite 1608, Los Angeles, CA 90048
(213) 651-4741; Fax: (213) 651-2547

French-American Chamber of Commerce, c/o Ronald Levitt, Relations Associates, Inc., 141 Sevilla Ave., Coral Gables, FL 33134
(305) 443-3223

French-American Chamber of Commerce, Foshay Tower, Suite 904, 821 Marquette Ave., Minneapolis, MN 55402
(612) 338-7750

## U.S. AGENCIES IN FRANCE

American Chamber of Commerce in France, 21 Avenue George V, 75008 Paris
(1) 47 23 70 28; Fax: (1) 47 20 18 62

French National Center for Foreign Commerce, 10 Avenue d'Iena, 75016 Paris
(1) 40 73 30 00

U.S. Embassy, 2 Avenue Gabriel, 75382 Paris
(1) 42 96 12 02

U.S. Consulate General, 22 Cours du Marechal Foche, 33080 Bordeaux Cedex
56 52 65 95

U.S. Consulate, 7 Quai General Sarrail, 69454 Lyon
78 24 68 49

U.S. Consulate, 12 Boulevard Paul Peytral, 13286 Marseille
91 54 92 00

U.S. Consulate, Avenue d'Alsace, 67082 Strasbourg
88 35 31 04

## BANKS AND FINANCIAL INSTITUTIONS

Banque de France, 39 Rue Croix des Petits Champs, 75001 Paris
(1) 42 92 42 92; Fax: (1) 42 96 04 23

Barclays Bank, 33 Rue de 4 September BP 24X, 75460 Paris Cedex 2
(1) 42 06 85 85; Fax: (1) 47 42 78 99

BCEN Eurobank, 79/81 Boulevard Haussmann, 75382 Paris Cedex 08
(1) 42 06 43 21; Fax: (1) 40 06 43 15

Chase Manhattan Bank, 18 Boulevard Malesherbes, 75008 Paris BP 456
(1) 40 70 13 00; Fax: (1) 40 17 15 34

Credit Industriel et Commercial de Paris, 66 Rue de la Victoire BP 207, 75452 Paris Cedex 09
(1) 45 96 96 96; Fax: (1) 45 96 96 66

L'Europeenne de Banque, 21 Rue Laffitte, 75428 Paris Cedex 09
(1) 42 47 82 47; Fax: (1) 42 47 82 52

Financiere Internationale de Gestion et de Conseil, Rue Vernet 2, 75008 Paris
(1) 40 70 07 07; Fax: (1) 47 20 98 55

Helvetia Compagnie Suisse D'Assurances, 2 Rue Sainte Marie, 92400 Courbevoie
47 89 90 00; Fax: 47 89 90 12

Nationale Suisse, 79/81 Rue de Clichy, 75009 Paris
(1) 40 82 40 82; Fax: (1) 40 82 40 99

Rhone Mediterranee, 7 Rue Bailli de Sufferen BP 1824, 13221 Marseille Cedex 01
91 54 92 16; Fax: 91 54 36 56

## LAW FIRMS

Bourgoing Durmonteil, 19 Rue de Lille, 75007 Paris
(1) 45 55 90 45; Fax: (1) 45 55 94 04
Services: international contracts, commercial, corporate, tax, arbitration, foreign investment

Clifford Chance, 36 Rue Brunel, 75850 Paris Cedex 17
(1) 45 74 96 60; Fax: (1) 45 74 58 55
Services: international law

J. et B. Cremades et Associes, 51 Avenue Georges Mandel, 75116 Paris
(1) 45 53 55 50; Fax: (1) 45 53 55 49
Services: commercial, corporate, tax, investment, licensing, insurance, banking, finance, oil and gas, real estate, patent, aeronautical, EC, arbitration

Lamy Veron Ribeyre et Associes, 40 Rue President Edouart Herriot BP 1214, 69202 Lyon Cedex 01
78 28 10 80; Fax: 78 39 26 73
Services: commercial, corporate, labor, industrial property

SCP Lebas Chaillet Tressa, 51 Rue Halevy, 5900 Lille
20 93 52 43; Fax: 20 09 19 20
Services: corporate, commercial, banking, financial, labor, construction, leasing, foreign investment, contract, creditors rights, bankruptcy

Maryan Green, 1 Bis Avenue Foch, 75116 Paris
(1) 45 01 71 12; Fax: (1) 45 00 60 99
Services: commercial, company, insurance, industrial, maritime

SCP Renard Allemand Tassy, 27 Cours Pierre-Puget, 13006 Marseille
91 37 74 30; Fax: 91 53 71 51
Services: admiralty, arbitration, commercial, EC, bankruptcy, labor

Shearman et Sterling, 21 Avenue George V, 75008 Paris
(1) 47 23 55 48; Fax: (1) 47 20 00 29
Services: international law

Thieffry et Associes, 23 Avenue Hoche, 75008 Paris
(1) 45 62 45 54; Fax: (1) 42 25 80 07
Services: arbitration, bankruptcy, tax, antitrust, EC, franchise, international contracts, foreign investment, labor, environmental, product liability, licensing, technology transfer, transportation, banking, finance

Sylvie J. Volnay, 44 Rue des Belles Feuilles, 75116 Paris
(1) 45 53 19 19; Fax: (1) 47 55 17 85
Services: commercial, corporate, contract, EC, unfair competition, trademark, copyright, international antitrust, economic regulations

## ACCOUNTING FIRMS

Booz Allen et Hamilton, 112 Avenue Kleber Trocadero BP 165, 75770 Paris Cedex 16
(1) 44 34 31 31; Fax: (1) 44 34 30 00
Services: accountancy management

Calan Ramolino et Associes, SA, 2 Rue Paul Cezanne, 75008 Paris
(1) 40 76 60 60; Fax: (1) 42 89 26 25
Services: taxation consultants, domiciling holding companies, auditing

CGI Informatique, 30 Rue du Chateau des Rentiers, 75640 Paris Cedex 13
(1) 40 77 20 00; Fax: (1) 40 77 22 22
Services: industrial accounting, accommodation management

CKL Europe, SA, 29 Rue des Pyramides, 75001 Paris
(1) 42 86 09 41; Fax: (1) 42 86 80 25
Services: taxation consultants, auditing

Fiduciaire Expertises Conseils, SA, 217 Rue du Faubourg St. Honore, 75008 Paris
(1) 45 63 81 50
Services: taxation consultants, auditing

GETECOM, SA (Societe), 24 Rue de Seine, 75008 Paris
(1) 42 65 32 99; Fax: (1) 42 66 45 75
Services: taxation consultants, auditing

Ouromoff Audit (CEA), 67 Avenue Kleber, 75116 Paris 16E
(1) 45 53 17 98; Fax: (1) 45 53 26 49
Services: auditors

Sogetic International, 1 Bis Rue Jean Mermoz, 75008 Paris
(1) 42 61 80 88
Services: taxation specialists

## INSURANCE AGENCIES

AGF Assurances, 87 Rue Richelieu, 75002 Paris
(1) 42 44 04 44; Fax: (1) 42 44 05 95

Becquet de Megille Guy, 59 Rue Dunkerque, 59200 Tourcoing
20 26 00 09; Fax: 20 43 07 51

Bidault et de Bardy, SNC, 36 Rue Buffon, 7600 Rouen
35 98 26 46; Fax: 35 98 32 58

Faugere et Jutheau, SA, 13 Rue Ville l'Eveque, 75008 Paris
(1) 42 68 15 00; Fax: (1) 42 68 06 71

GAN Assurances, 2 Rue Tillet, 75448 Paris Cedex 09
(1) 42 47 50 00; Fax: (1) 42 47 50 12

Geiss Alain Courtier, 7 Rue Gantelet, 51000 Chalons sur Marne
26 68 45 33; Fax: 26 65 42 37

Sant & Co., 8 Rue Malevy, 75009 Paris
(1) 47 42 79 44; Fax: (1) 42 66 95 05

Societe d'Affaires Rhone Alpes, 19 Rue Duquesne, 69006 Lyon
78 93 31 11; Fax: 78 94 96 34

Zurich, SA, 14 Boulevard Poissonniere, 75426 Paris Cedex 09
(1) 42 47 12 24; Fax: (1) 42 46 53 21

## ADVERTISING AND MARKETING AGENCIES

AGENA, SA, 16 Rue des Mouettes, 74000 Annecy le Vieux
50 23 55 23; Fax: 50 27 83 48
Services: marketing, commercial advertising

Binome-Communications, Rue du General Leclerc, 78000 Versailles
39 51 76 77; Fax: 39 51 11 74
Services: public relations, commercial advertising

Cible Publicite, 7 Boulevard Sarrail, 3400 Montpelier
67 66 32 40; Fax: 67 60 60 27
Services: commercial advertising

ID Traduction, 7 Impasse Charles Petit, 75011 Paris
(1) 43 48 67 78; Fax: (1) 43 71 87 69

Interface Conseil, 10/12 Boulevard Jules Favre, 69006 Lyon
78 52 99 90; Fax: 78 52 96 80

ISIT Institut Superieur D'Interpretation et de Traduction, 21 Rue d'Assas, 75270 Paris Cedex 06
(1) 42 22 33 16; Fax: (1) 45 44 17 67

KSM, 8 Rue St. Marc, 75002 Paris
(1) 42 33 66 56; Fax: (1) 42 36 63 79

Lexitech, 14 Boulevard St. Martin, 75010 Paris
(1) 42 39 60 00; Fax: (1) 42 39 62 13

Scientra Traducteurs Conseils, 33 Rue Fortuny, 75017 Paris
(1) 42 67 43 05; Fax: (1) 42 27 52 80

Trad'essonne, 19 Rue du Lieutenant Gayot, 91220 Bretigny sur Orge
60 84 76 63; Fax: 60 84 09 58

## TRANSPORTATION AND DISTRIBUTION COMPANIES

AVEKA, 4 Rue Jean Millot BP 24, 67017 Strasbourg Cedex
88 61 93 67; Fax: 88 61 20 80
Services: inland water transport

Brittany Ferries Truckline, Port de Bloscon BP 72, 29688 Roscoff Cedex
98 29 28 00; Fax: 98 29 27 00
Services: maritime transport

Jules Benoist et Cie, 2 Ro
(1) 43 25 94 49; Fax: (1) 46 34 65 57

Faroult Transit et Transports Gabriel, 16 Boulevard des Belges BP 287, 76004 Rouen Cedex
35 71 74 86; Fax: 35 70 71 01

France Ship Management, 4 Boulevard du Sanitat, 44040 Nantes Cedex 01
40 44 23 23; Fax: 40 73 68 67

Intramar, 19 Traverse Mardirossian, 13015 Marseille
91 69 90 01

Mondia Kirwan, SA, 9 Rue du Havre BP 127, 67028 Strasbourg Cedex
88 84 90 00; Fax: 88 84 65 60
Services: long-distance product transport

Navalsa, 11 Rue de Dunkerque BP 54, 67017 Strasbourg Cedex
88 61 50 23; Fax: 88 60 63 50

Tansso Alfred Balguerie, Rue Gaston Chevrolet BP 252, 21201 Beune Cedex
80 22 30 28; Fax: 80 22 57 31

## TRADE CONSULTANTS

AIDExport, 35 Avenue de Paris, 45000 Orleans
38 54 53 52; Fax: 38 54 09 09

AMD International, 13 Rue de Montholon BP 166, 01005 Bourg en Bresse Cedex
74 21 14 06; Fax: 74 21 95 14

ASCO International, La Ragnere-Aurin, 31570 Lanta
61 83 80 15

Assistex, Le Petit Montana-La Ronde, 79380 La Foret sur Sevre
49 72 72 08

Berlin International, 2 Mail des Charmilles BP 194, 10000 Troyes
25 80 54 19; Fax: 25 73 11 84

Degut International, 10 Rue Raymond Poincare, 54520 Laxou
83 27 51 91; Fax: 83 27 54 75

## TRADE SHOWS AND EXHIBITIONS

Paris World Tourism Travel Show (SMTV), 17 Rue d'Uzes, Paris
(1) 40 39 16 60; Fax: (1) 40 36 20 60
Description: annual (February) exhibition of tourism for travel industry

Lyon International Environmental Trade Fair (POLLUTEC), Techno Expo, 8 Rue de la Michodiere, Paris
(1) 47 42 92 56
Description: International Sporting Goods and Leisure Equipment Exhibition

55 Quai Alphonse Le Gallo BP 317, Billancourt Cedex, Boulogne
49 09 60 99; Fax: 49 09 61 06
Description: annual (September) exhibit of sport and leisure clothing and equipment

Paris International Motor Show (EQUIP-AUTO), 3 Avenue de President Wilson, Paris
(1) 47 23 59 40; Fax: (1) 47 23 06 30
Description: annual (October) exhibit of cars and accessories

Paris International Funeral Arts Trade Exhibition (FUNERAIRE), 22 Avenue Franklin Roosevelt, Paris
(1) 40 76 45 00; Fax: (1) 45 63 78 24
Descriptions: biennial exhibit of tombstones, funeral transportation and supplies

# 17

# GERMANY

## GENERAL INFORMATION

Area: 137,777 square miles
Capital: Berlin
Language: German
Population: 79.5 million
Currency: Deutsche marks (DM)
Exchange Rate (June 1993): $1/DM 1.70
Telephone Country Code: 49

Large areas of Germany, particularly the newer suburbs, look much like comparable neighborhoods in the United States. Similarly, in the international business community, Germans are perhaps the Europeans that most resemble middle-class, white Americans in appearance, with their somber suits and heavy briefcases. Many Germans, and particularly those doing business with Americans, are likely to speak good English.

But the similarities are only superficial. Germans are uncomfortable with typical American informality; even people who have worked together for years still refer to each other as "Herr" or "Frau," and wouldn't dream of moving past the formal "Sie" to the more familiar "Du" form of address until they had become friends outside the office. Germans love to shake hands, and it is standard practice in many offices for everyone to shake hands with everyone else in the morning and upon departing in the afternoon.

German meetings and talks are often conducted formally, with little give and take or challenge to the edicts being handed down from the top. Going to meetings in shirtsleeves can be bad form, and many Germans take off their jackets only in their own offices with the door closed. The closed door is, in effect, a "do not disturb" sign, and many Germans prefer that even co-workers make appointments through their secretaries instead of just knocking and popping in.

Many German offices clear out promptly at five o'clock, despite the country's much-vaunted work ethic. Few Germans take work home every night or every weekend. Visitors should try to make appointments well in advance because Germans often pride themselves on having full calendars, and they often prefer to have meetings early in the mornings, but at the office instead of over breakfast. Punctuality, almost to the minute, is expected.

Small talk, including superficial inquiries about families, is expected, but does not necessarily delay getting down to business the way it does in some southern European countries. In conversation, Germans are sensitive to criticism of the reunification process with the former East Germany, and probing about the country's political future can be unsettling to Germans. Business is often continued informally over lunch or a post-work beer. Instead of doing their business entertaining in restaurants, however, many Germans prefer to invite foreign visitors to their homes to eat and drink.

## GERMAN AGENCIES IN THE UNITED STATES

German Embassy, 4645 Reservoir Rd., NW, Washington, DC 20007-1998
(202) 298-4000; Fax: (202) 298-4249

German Consulate, 1000 Peachtree Center Cain Tower, 229 Peachtree St., NE, Atlanta, GA 30303-1618
(404) 659-4760

German Consulate, Three Copley Place, Suite 500, Boston, MA 02116
(617) 536-4414; Fax: (617) 536-8573

German Consulate, 104 South Michigan Ave., Chicago, IL 60603
(312) 263-0850; Fax: (312) 853-1940

German Consulate, Edison Place, Suite 2100, 660 Place Dr., Detroit, MI 48226
(313) 962-6526; Fax: (313) 962-7345

German Consulate, 1330 Post Oak Blvd. South 1850, Houston, TX 77056-3018
(713) 627-7770; Fax: (713) 627-0506

German Consulate, 6222 Wilshire Blvd., Suite 500, Los Angeles, CA 90048
(213) 930-2703; Fax: (213) 930-2805

German Consulate, 100 North Biscayne Blvd., Miami, FL 33132
(305) 358-0290; Fax: (305) 358-0307

German Consulate, 460 Park Ave., New York, NY 10022
(212) 308-8700; Fax: (212) 308-3422

German Consulate, 1960 Jackson St., San Francisco, CA 94109
(415) 775-1061; Fax: (415) 775-0187

German Consulate, 1617 IBM Bldg. 1200 5th Ave., Seattle, WA 98101
(206) 682-4312; Fax: (206) 682-3724

German Industry & Trade Office, 1 Farragut Square South, Washington, DC 20006
(202) 347-0247

German Information Center, 950 Third Ave., New York, NY 10022
(212) 888-9840; Fax: (212) 752-6691

German-American Chamber of Commerce, 666 Fifth Ave., 21st Fl., New York, NY 10103
(212) 974-8830; Fax: (212) 974-8867

## U.S. AGENCIES IN GERMANY

U.S. Embassy, Deichmanns Aue 29, 5300 Bonn 2
(0228) 339 93 391; Fax: (0228) 33 92 125

U.S. Consulate General, Siesmayerstrasse 21, 6000 Frankfurt
(069) 75 350; Fax: (069) 74 89 38

U.S. Consulate General, Alsterufer 27/28, 2000 Hamburg 36
(040) 41 17 10; Fax: (040) 41 06 598

U.S. Consulate General, 8000 Munich 22
(089) 28 881; Fax: (089) 28 30 47

U.S. Consulate General, Urbanstrasse 7, 5000 Koln 1
(0221) 20 571

U.S. Consulate General, 7000 Stuttgart
(0711) 21 450; Fax: (0711) 64 94 786

U.S. Agricultural Trade Office, Grosse Theaterstrasse 42, VI, 2000 Hamburg 36
(040) 34 12 07; Fax: (040) 34 12 00

American Chamber of Commerce in Germany, Rossmarkt 12, 6000 Frankfurt/M. 1
(069) 28 34 01; Fax: (069) 28 56 32

## BANKS AND FINANCIAL INSTITUTIONS

Bankenverband Baden-Wuttemberg, eV, Theodor-Heuss-Strasse 3, 7000 Stuttgart I
(0711) 29 45 03; Fax: (0711) 29 07 60
Services: investment, consulting

Bankenverband Hamburg, eV, Adolphsplatz 7, 2000 Hamburg 11
(040) 37 17 79; Fax: (040) 36 32 51
Services: commercial

Bankenverband Hessen, eV, Rossmarkt 18, 6000 Frankfurt AM 1
(069) 28 43 92; Fax: (069) 21 42 166
Services: investment, corporate

Bankenverband Niedersachsen, eV, Georgsplatz 20, 3000 Hannover 1
(0511) 32 05 88
Services: commercial

DEG-Deutsche Investitions-und Entwicklungsgesellschaft, mbH, Belvederestrasse 40, 5000 Koln 41
(0221) 49 860; Fax: (0221) 49 86 290
Services: corporate, investment

Deutsche Augleichsbank, AdoR, Kronprinzenstrasse 10, 5300 Bonn 2
(0228) 83 10; Fax: (0228) 83 12 55
Services: investment, corporate

Kreditanstalt fur Wiederaufbau, Palmengartenstrasse 5-9, 6000 Frankfurt AM II
(069) 74 310; Fax: (069) 41 52 560
Services: finance and investment consulting

Landwirtschaftliche Rentenbank, Hochstrasse 2, 6000 Frankfurt AM I
(069) 21 070; Fax: (069) 21 07 444
Services: commercial

Staatsbank Berlin, KdoR, Charlottenstrasse 33-33a, 0-1086 Berlin
(372) 23 34 414; Fax: (372) 23 34 602
Services: commercial, investment

## LAW FIRMS

Boden, Oppenhoff, Rasor, Schneider, & Schiederman, Furstenbergerstrasse 10-12, Postbox 180369, 6000 Frankfurt AM Main
(069) 55 07 27; Fax: (069) 597 8209
Services: EC market, antitrust, banking, high tech and telecommunications

Bottcher & Zapf, Morianstrasse 45, 5600 Wuppertal I
(0202) 45 00 05; Fax: (0202) 45 24 85
Services: commercial, aliens, road traffic

Fielder & Partner, Brienner Strasse 12, 8000 Munich 2
(089) 23 980; Fax: (089) 239 8259
Services: EC market, corporate, mergers and acquisitions, tax, arbitration, debt collection

Gleiss, Lutz, Hootz, Hirsch, & Partner, Birkenwaldstrasse 149, 7000 Stuttgart I
(0711) 25 025; Fax: (0711) 25 30 78
Services: international, EC market

Lange, Lotz, & Partner, Siesmayerstrasse 3, 6000 Frankfurt AM Main I
(069) 74 79 96; Fax: (069) 74 26 45
Services: international, construction, and business

Dr. Manfred Nopper and Partner, Olgastrasse 33, 7000 Stuttgart I
(0711) 24 04 55; Fax: (0711) 23 29 77
Services: company, commercial, unfair competition, industrial property rights, claims and damages

Dr. Pollmann & Partner, Pelmanstrasse 46, 4300 Essen I
(0201) 78 20 61; Fax: (0201) 78 12 57
Services: international, commercial, and company, German tax, mergers and acquisitions, antitrust and fair trade

Scholz, Kraatz, Dittman, & Partner, Postbox 200745, Konigsallee 1000, 4000 Dusseldorf
(0211) 38 10 21; Fax: (0211) 37 36 78
Services: corporate, tax, finance, banking, unfair competition, labor, commercial litigation, trademark, and licensing

Schurman & Partners, Postbox 111633, Friedrich-Ebert-Anlage 14, 6000 Frankfurt AM Main I
(069) 75 400; Fax: (069) 75 49 290
Services: company, commercial, tax, real estate, customs, foreign investment

Westphal and Voges, Esplanade 41, 2000 Hamburg 36
(040) 35 17 96; Fax: (040) 35 17 90
Services: international, commercial, maritime, public, shipbuilding, tax, environment

## ACCOUNTING FIRMS

Adig Allegmeine Deutsche-Investment, GmbH, Postbox 100108, 8000 Munich I BY
(089) 23 960
Services: corporate administration, auditing

Alusuisse-Lonza, GmbH, Postbox 724, 7700 Singen/Hohentwiel, BW
(07731) 83 020
Services: corporate administration

Bayerische Vereinsbank, AG, Postbox 10 01 01, 8000 Munich I BY
(089) 21 321

Deutscher Investment Trust, Postbox 110443, 6000 Frankfurt/Main I, HS
(069) 26 440
Services: corporate and wealth administration

Geka Verwaltungs, GmbH, Friedrich-Ebert-Strasse 34, 5600 Wuppertal I NW
(0202) 30 20 88
Services: real estate, corporate and home administration, auditing

Grohe Verwaltungs, GmbH, Postbox 1361, 5870 Hemer NW
(02372) 531
Services: corporate administration, auditing

IVG-Transport, GmbH, Postbox 200751, 5300 Bonn 2 NW
(0228) 84 40
Services: wealth and corporate administration

Scholz KG, Learing-Gesellschaft Walter, Postbox 269, 1000 Berlin 15 BL
(030) 881 6051
Services: estimates, wealth and corporate administration

Stadtische Werke Nurnberg, GmbH, Postbox 810220, 8500 Nurnberg 81 BY
(0911) 2710
Services: corporate administration

## INSURANCE AGENCIES

Allianz Versicherungs-Aktiengesellschaft, Konigstrasse 28, Postbox 440124, 8000 Munich 44 BY
(089) 38 000; Fax: (089) 38 00 34 35
Services: capital, pension, accident, disability, and property damage

Barmer Ersatzkasse (BEK), Untere Lichtenplatzer Strasse 100-102, Postbox 200108, 5600 Wuppertal 2 NW
(0202) 56 80; Fax: (0202) 56 81 459
Services: corporate health insurance

CIGNA Insurance Company of Europe, SA, NV, Erlenstrasse 2-6, 6000 Frankfurt/Main 1 HS
(069) 75 61 30; Fax: (069) 74 61 93
Services: foreign transactions, investment goods, fire and explosion

Hamburg-Mannheimer Versicherung, AG, Uberseering 45, Postbox 601060, 2000 Hamburg 60 HH
(040) 63 760; Fax: (040) 63 76 33 02
Services: capital, pension, accident, and disability

Schleswig-Holsternische Brandgilde von 1691, AG, Kieler Strasse 86, Postbox 2300, 2300 Kronshagen
(0431) 58 90 11; Fax: (0431) 58 97 04
Services: insurance consultants

Schunck, KG, Oskar, Leopoldstrasse 20, Postbox 440264, 8000 Munich 44 BY
(089) 38 17 70; Fax: (089) 34 60 99
Services: property damage, capital, and investment goods

Securitas Gilde Lebensversicherung, AG, Am Wall 121, Postbox 107807, 2800 Bremen I BR
(0421) 30 850; Fax: (0421) 30 85 300
Services: capital, pension, health, fire, and explosion

Volksfursorge Deutsche Sachversicherung, AG, Besenbinderhof 43, Postbox 106429, 2000 Hamburg I HH
(040) 28 650; Fax: (040) 28 65 25 15
Services: capital, investment goods

## ADVERTISING AND MARKETING AGENCIES

Allwi Allg. Werbe-Institut Schneider, KG, Frankfurter Strasse 30, 5000 Koln 80
(0221) 61 22 66; Fax: (0211) 61 22 27
Services: corporate advertising

Baums, Mang und Zimmermann Werbeagentur, GmbH, Schirmestrasse 76, 4000 Dusseldorf 1
(0211) 16 870; Fax: (0211) 16 87 100
Services: marketing, consulting

Ernst & Partner Werbeagentur, GmbH, Jan Wellem Platz 1, 4000 Dusseldorf 1
(0211) 88 930; Fax: (0211) 88 93 127
Services: corporate advertising

Huch D.K. Werbeagentur, 20 Dixbaume, 4300 Essen 15
(0201) 48 60 88; Fax: (0201) 48 60 80
Services: advertising

Nohren Aussenwerbung, GmbH, Papenreve 22, 2000 Hamburg 61
(040) 55 42 160; Fax: (040) 55 42 16 16
Services: corporate advertising

Publicis Werbeagenthur, GmbH, Lindemannstrasse 75, 4000 Dusseldorf 1
(0211) 68 770; Fax: (0211) 68 77 267
Services: public relations, marketing

Saatchi & Saatchi Advertising, GmbH, Werbeagentur, GWA, Wiesenau 38, 6000 Frankfurt 1
(069) 71 421; Fax: (069) 71 42 284
Services: marketing, corporate advertising, public relations

Wensauch, DDB, Needham Worldwide, GmbH, Schadowstrasse 48, 4000 Dusseldorf 1
(0211) 36 600; Fax: (0211) 36 60 328
Services: marketing, corporate advertising, public relations

Wilkens Ayer, GmbH, An der Alster 42, 2000 Hamburg 1
(040) 28 810; Fax: (040) 28 81 270
Services: corporate advertising

## TRANSLATING AND INTERPRETING SERVICES

APL-Agentur fur Personal Leasing, GmbH, Habsburgerring 24-26, 5000 Koln I NW
(0221) 23 66 61; Fax: (0221) 24 14 13

Fix-Betriebe, Mockebergstrasse 11, 2000 Hamburg 1 HH
(040) 33 82 78; Fax: (040) 33 82 70

GSD Gerber Servicegesellschaft fur Datenkommunikation, Muthmannstrasse 4, 8000 Munich 45 BY
(089) 32 37 090; Fax: (089) 32 37 09 29

Industrie-Ubersetzungen Inbudo & Co., GmbH, Grabenstrasse 32/2, 7320 Goppingen BW
(07161) 71 025; Fax: (07161) 71 027

International Business-Verks, GmbH, Markstrasse 3-5, 4440 Rheine NW
(05971) 50 316; Fax: (05971) 66 920

Intra-1 Fachubersetzergenossenschaft, eG, Charlottenplatz 17, Postbox 102423, 7000 Stuttgart 1 BW
(0711) 22 74 00; Fax: (0711) 22 74 008

Kuhn Sehreibburo, Gerda, St.-Anton-Strasse 3, 8900 Augsburg BY
(0821) 71 18 47

Teletex Translation Service, GmbH, An der Alster 26, 2000 Hamburg I HH
(040) 24 07 81

## TRANSPORTATION AND DISTRIBUTION COMPANIES

Balsam & Lange, GmbH, Gottfried-Hagen-Strasse 68, 5000 Koln 91 NW
(0221) 83 30 54; Fax: (0221) 83 047
Services: international and domestic product distribution

DPD Deutscher Paket Dienst, GmbH, Otto-Hahn-Strasse 5, 4750 Unna NW
(02303) 88 40; Fax: (02303) 88 436
Services: product distribution

Heinrich Baum-Koln, Siegburgerstrasse 122/124, 5000 Koln 21
(0221) 88 20 21; Fax: (0221) 88 29 79
Services: product distribution

InterRent Europcar Autovermietung, GmbH, Tangstedter Landstrasse 81, 2000 Hamburg 62 HH
(040) 52 01 80; Fax: (040) 52 01 84 52
Services: long-distance transport

Klaus E.H. Zapf Transporte, GmbH, Kopenicker Strasse 18-20, Postbox 620240, 1000 Berlin 36 BL
(030) 61 061; Fax: (030) 61 06 234
Services: furniture, live fish transport

Panalpina Welttransport, GmbH, Hafenstrasse 19, 6700 Ludwigshafen RH
(0621) 56 10 10; Fax: (0621) 56 20 43
Services: international and domestic product distribution

Transfracht Deutsche Transportgesellschaft, mbH, Gutleutstrasse 160-164, Postbox 111931, 6000 Frankfurt AM Main 1 HS
(069) 23 890; Fax: (069) 23 17 64
Services: furniture, international distribution

Westermann Spedition, GmbH, Fuggerstrasse 7, 4400 Munster NW
(02501) 80 030; Fax: (02501) 80 31 90
Services: forwarding agents, international distribution

## TRADE CONSULTANTS

Host F.G. Angermann, GmbH, Beichenbrucke 9 (Bleichenhof), Postbox 300140, 2000 Hamburg 36 HH
(040) 3 49 140; Fax: (040) 3 49 14 144
Services: export and management consultants

Arthur D. Little International, Gustav-Stresemann-Ring 1, 6200 Wiesbaden HS
(06121) 71 480; Fax: (06121) 70 21 57
Services: export, marketing, investment, operations research, management and technology consultants

BAO BERLIN Berliner Absatz-Organisation, GmbH, Hardenbergstrasse 16-18, 1000 Berlin 12 BL
(030) 3 15 100; Fax: (030) 3 15 10 316
Services: export, marketing, mercantile, computer services and management consultants

Booz Allen and Hamilton, Inc., Konigsallee 98a, 4000 Dusseldorf NW
(0211) 37 10 94; Fax: (0211) 37 10 02
Services: export, management, economic analysis, mercantile and operations research consultants

Condat DV-Beratung Organisation Software, GmbH, Alt-Moabit 91d, 1000 Berlin 21 BL
(030) 3 90 940; Fax: (030) 3 90 94 300
Services: export, management, office rationalisation, computer and economical analysis consultants

DBM V. Rundstedt & Partner, GmbH, Grunstrasse 5, 4000 Dusseldorf 1 NW
(0211) 13 10 91; Fax: (0211) 13 43 22
Services: export, computer analysis, and operations research consultants

Gesellschaft fur Wirtschaftsforderung Nordrhein-Westfalen, mbH, Kavalleriestrasse 8-10, Postbox 200309, 4000 Dusseldorf 1 NW
(0211) 13 00 00; Fax: (49211) 1 30 00 54
Services: export consultants

INTERCONTACT Unternehmensberatungsgesellschaft, mbH, 4600 Dortmund 1 NW
(0231) 52 82 08; Fax: (0231) 54 19 279
Services: export, management, marketing, acquisition and merger consultants

Interfinanz Gesellschaft fur internationale Finanzberatung, mbH, 4000 Dusseldorf 1 NW
(0211) 1 68 020; Fax: (0211) 35 78 57
Services: export, marketing, operations research, hotel and stock consultants

Team Trading Management, GmbH, Dusterhaupstrasse 12, 100 Berlin 28
(030) 40 26 056; Fax: (030) 40 24 097

## TRADE FAIRS AND EXHIBITIONS

Berlin International Food Agricultural Fair, Messedamm 22, Kongressgmbh, 1000 Berlin
(030) 30 38 20 28; Fax: (030) 30 38 23 25
Description: biannual (January) exhibit of food industry, agriculture and horticulture

International Tourism Exchange, AMK Berlin Ausstellungs-Messe-Kongress, GmbH, Messedamm 22, 1000 Berlin
(030) 30 380; Fax: (030) 30 38 23 5
Description: annual (January) exhibit of food industry, agriculture, forestry, gardening, German wines

Munich International Building Materials Trade Exhibition, Postbox 121009, Messedelande, Munich
(89) 51 07 230; Fax: (89) 51 07 171
Services: biennial (January) exhibit of outdoor and sanitary installations, chemical building products, insulation and other building materials and products

International Trade Fair for Consumer Goods, Messe Frankfurt, GmbH, Postbox 970126, 6000 Frankfurt 1
(069) 75 750; Fax: (069) 75 75 64 33
Description: two annual exhibits, one in January for paper products, stationery, cosmetics and toiletries, and one in February for kitchen and household goods, arts and crafts and jewelry

Frankfurt International Trade Fair Consumer Goods, Postbox 970126 AM Main 1, Messe Frankfurt, GmbH, 6000 Frankfurt
(069) 75 750; Fax: (069) 75 75 64 33
Description: semi-annual (February/August) exhibit of glass, china, fine metalware, ceramics, arts, lighting fixtures, small furniture and other consumer goods

Munich International Sporting Goods Spring & Fall (ISPO), Postbox 121009, Messegelande, Munich
(89) 51 07 218; Fax: (89) 51 07 173
Services: semi-annual (February/September) exhibit of winter and summer sports articles and equipment

Munich International Watch Clock Jewelry Precious Stones Silverware Fair, Postbox 121009, Messegelande, Munich
(89) 51 07 218; Fax: (89) 51 07 173
Services: semi-annual (February/September) exhibit of clocks, watches, jewelry, precious stones and technical equipment

Hanover Office Information Telecommunications Technology (CEBIT), Hanover Fairs USA, Inc., 103 Carnegie Center, Suite 207, Princeton, New Jersey 08540
(609) 98 71 202; Fax: (609) 98 70 092
Description: annual (March, Hanover Fairgrounds) exhibit, trade show for telecommunications

Hanover Industry Fair, Messegelande, Hanover
(609) 98 71 202
Description: annual (April) exhibit

International Trade Fair for Clothing and Textiles, Messe Frankfurt, GmbH, Postbox 970126, 6000 Frankfurt 1
(069) 75 750; Fax: (069) 75 75 64 33
Description: biannual (April/October) exhibit of textiles for all types of clothing, linings and facings, accessories, fibres and yarns

Berlin International Pharmaceutical Medico-Technical Exhibition, Klingsorstrasse 21, 1000 Berlin
(030) 79 13 901; Fax: (030) 79 13 094
Description: annual (June) exhibit of medico-technical instruments, pharmaceuticals and trade publications

International Audio & Video Fair, AMK Berlin Ausstellungs-Messe-Kongress, GmbH, Messedamm 22, 1000 Berlin
(030) 30 380; Fax: (030) 30 38 23 5
Description: annual (August/September) exhibit of consumer, communication and information electronics

Computer & Communications Exhibition (Nordburo), Jungiusstrasse, Postbox 302480, Hamburg
(040) 35 690; Fax: (040) 35 69 21 80
Description: biennial (September) exhibit of computer and communications technology

Dortmund International Electro Technical Trade Exhibition, Rheinlanddamm 200, Postbox 104444, Dortmund
(0231) 12 04 521; Fax: (0231) 12 04 678
Description: annual (September) exhibit of plumbing, industrial electronics, technical lighting, workshop equipment and tools and computers

Frankfurt Book Fair, Ausstellungs-undMesse-GmbH des Borsenvereins des Deutschen Buchhandels, Postfach 100116, 6000 Frankfurt 1
(069) 21 02 218; Fax: (069) 21 02 227
Description: annual (September/October) exhibit of books and periodicals from all over the world

International Trade Fair Plastics and Rubber, Dusseldorfer Messegesellschaft, mbH, NOWEA, Postbox 320203, 4000 Dusseldorf 30
(0211) 45 60 01; Fax: (0211) 45 60 668
Description: annual (October/November) exhibit of raw materials, semi-finished and finished products, engineering components, machinery, molds and accessories

# 18

# GREECE

## GENERAL INFORMATION

Area: 51,217 square miles
Capital: Athens
Language: Greek
Population: 10.1 million
Currency: Drachma (Dr)
Exchange Rate (June 1993): $1/Dr 230
International Trade*: $25 billion
Telephone Country Code: 30

Greece is one of the poorest of the EC countries, which also means that it is one of the EC countries with the most potential for rapid economic growth in the single market, particularly in terms of trade outside the community.

Greece's relatively low living standards and relatively unsophisticated economic development often put the country in conflict with its larger, more prosperous northern EC sisters. For example, Greece traditionally has argued that it needs more relaxed rules—on everything from currency movements to minimum wages to pharmaceutical testing—in order to provide incentives for the growth required to catch up with its richer northern EC neighbors. If Greece suddenly had to conform to Danish rules on employment conditions, literally tens of thousands of small Greek businesses would die overnight.

The northern EC countries, on the other hand, provide considerable economic assistance to Greece through many EC programs, but don't want to risk losing business to what they view as unfair competition when special rules are applied to Greece and other poorer member nations. After all, the idea of the EC single market, at least in theory, is to encourage growth through straightforward open-market competition.

Personally and socially, Greeks are among the friendliest people in Europe. Most of them genuinely like Americans. Dress is less formal

* This number represents total exports and imports.

than in much of northern Europe, though the usual suits are expected for formal business meetings.

Economically, Greece is one of the most farm-dependent countries in Europe, with about half the population working in agriculture. Because of its smaller, less developed economy, and the fact that so many businesses are small family-oriented enterprises, not many Greek companies have exploited the single market by expanding throughout the EC; a company with that kind of economy of scale is rare in Greece. In recent years, however, EC membership has helped spur industrial growth throughout Greece, particularly in fields such as textiles and apparel, chemicals, and building materials.

## GREEK AGENCIES IN THE UNITED STATES

Embassy of Greece, 2221 Massachusetts Ave., NW, Washington, DC 20008
(202) 667-3168; Telex: 0023/440287

Greek Consulate, Tower Place, Suite 1670, 3340 Peachtree Rd., NE, Atlanta, GA 30026
(404) 261-3391; Telex: 0023/549544

Greek Consulate General, 168 North Michigan Ave., Chicago, IL 60601
(312) 372-5356; Telex: 0023/255128 GREEK CONS CGO

Greek Consulate, World Trade Center, 2 Canal St., Suite 2318, New Orleans, LA 70130
(504) 523-1167; Telex: 0023/58291 GREEK CONS NLN

Greek Consulate, 69 East 79th St., New York, NY 10021
(718) 988-5500; Telex: 0023/9668508 CONS NYK

Greek Consulate, 2441 Gough St., San Francisco, CA 94123
(415) 775-2102; Telex: 0023/34255 GREEK CONS SFO

Hellenic-American Chamber of Commerce, 960 Avenue of the Americas, 12th Fl., New York, NY 10001
(212) 629-6380

## U.S. AGENCIES IN GREECE

U.S. Embassy, 91 Vassilissis Sophias Blvd., Athens 10160
(01) 723 97 05; Fax: (01) 646 34 50

U.S. Consulate, 49 Leoforos Nikis, 54622 Thessaloniki
(031) 266 121

American-Hellenic Chamber of Commerce, 16 Kanari, Athens 10671
(01) 361 83 85; Telex: 223063 AMCH GR

Chamber of Commerce of Athens, 7 Akadimias St., Athens 10671
(01) 362 73 37; Fax: (01) 360 78 97

Greek Export Promotion Organization, 1 Mitropoleos, Athens 10557
(01) 324 70 10; Telex: 220201 HOPE GR

Hellenic Organization of Small & Medium Size, Industries & Handicrafts, Xenias & Evrou, Athens 11528
(01) 770 11 01; Telex: 218819 HMIH GR

Union of Chambers of Commerce & Industry in Greece, 7-9 Akadimias, Athens 10671
(01) 362 40 60; Telex: 215707 EBEA GR

## BANKS AND FINANCIAL INSTITUTIONS

Commercial Bank of Greece, SA, 11 Sofocleous St., Athens, 10559
(01) 321 09 11; Telex: 216545

ETEVA National Investment Bank for Industrial Development, 14 Amalias Ave., Athens 10557
(01) 324 26 51; Telex: 216113 NBD GR

General Hellenic Bank, SA, 9 Panepistimiou St., Athens 10564
(01) 322 25 80; Telex: 219841 GHB GR

Hellenic Industrial Development Bank, SA (OETBA), 18 Panepistimiou St., Athens 10672
(01) 323 0771; Telex: 214246 ETVA GR

Ionian & Popular Bank of Greece, SA, 45 Panepistimiou St., Athens 10564
(01) 324 65 23; Fax: (01) 323 67 39

Midland Bank, PLC, 1 A Sekeri St., Athens 10671
(01) 364 74 10; Fax: (01) 364 43 01

National Bank of Greece, 86 Eolou St., Athens 10559
(01) 321 04 11; Telex: 215386

National Westminster Bank, 24 Stadious St., Athens 10564
(01) 325 09 24; Fax: (01) 322 29 51

## LAW FIRMS

Panayotis J. Economou, 26 Asklipiou St., Athens 10679
(01) 360 38 24; Fax: (01) 363 99 73

George A. Georgiades, 24 Omirou St., Athens 10672
(01) 361 31 24; Telex: 223819 LAZA

A. Iatrou Law Offices, 44 El. Venizilou (OPanepistimiou) Ave., Athens 10679
(01) 262 13 63; Fax: (01) 363 57 22

Kyriakides & Partners, 6 Queen Sophia Ave., Athens 10674
(01) 724 30 72; Telex: 216075 KYRI GR
Services: foreign investment, shipping, banking, tax, labor, patents, international and corporate law

Law Offices of Spiro D. Lekkas, 44a Aiantos St., 62 Old Faliron, Athens 10674
(01) 982 32 63; Fax: (01) 922 66 43
Services: debt collection, business, civil and commercial law

Nicolaus Pipilis, 8 Goura St., Athens 10558
(01) 362 64 40; Fax: (01) 322 80 34

Dr. Leon D. Pleionis, 51 Solonos St., Athens 10672
(01) 362 85 21; Fax: (01) 364 58 07
Services: EC, international transactions, foreign investment, corporate and commercial law

Anastasia Samara-Krispis, 10 Merlin St., Athens 10671
(01) 361 07 52; Fax: (01) 362 46 32

## ACCOUNTING FIRMS

Alexander, Young, & Co., Russell & Co., Russell, Nicolaou, & Co., 2 Mesogion Ave., Athens 11527
(01) 775 97 80; Fax: (01) 775 9790
Services: accounting, management consultants

Coopers & Lybrand, Abacus House, 9 Semitelou St., Athens 11528
(01) 771 01 12; Fax: (01) 777 73 90
Services: accounting, management consultants

Costouris Michaelides & Co., OE/Grant Thornton, 14 Filikis Eterias St., 2nd Fl., Athens 10675
(01) 722 89 87; Fax: (01) 722 57 62
Services: accounting

Deloitte Haskens & Sells, 23 Irodotou St., Athens, 10674
(01) 729 13 83; Fax: (01) 723 00 09
Services: accounting, management consultants

Hermes Accountants, Ltd., 93 Akti Miaouli St., Piraeus 18538
(01) 452 36 64; Telex: 212390 INNO GR
Services: accounting, management consultants

Kolokotronis-Papakyriacou & Co., 27-31 Hatzikyriakou Ave., Piraeus 18538
(01) 452 32 12; Fax: (01) 452 97 55
Services: accounting, management consultants

Touche Ross, M. Hadjipavlov, N. Sofianos, & Co., OE, P.O. Box 75195, 180 Syngrou Ave., Athens 17671
(01) 956 66 55; Fax: (01) 956 97 36
Services: accounting, management consultants

## INSURANCE AGENCIES

Apostolou-Svoronous Co., Ltd., 53-55 Akti Miaouli St., Piraeus 18536
(01) 452 2708; Telex: 212186 NAPO GR

Carver Marine Insurance, Ltd., 70 Syngrou & Dracou 2 St., Athens 11742
(01) 922 60 77; Fax: (01) 922 98 59

ETEBA General Insurance Co., SA, 12 Amalias Ave., Athens 10557
(01) 322 04 80; Fax: (01) 322 33 69

Ilios Greek Insurance Co., SA, 10 Mavromichali St., Athens 10679
(01) 360 64 10; Fax: (01) 360 17 41

International Insurance Brokers & Consultants Co., Ltd., 245 Syngrou Ave., Athens 17122
(01) 943 04 10; Telex: 214046

Nasco Hellas, Ltd., 247 Syngrou Ave., Athens 17122
(01) 942 50 94; Fax: (01) 941 19 19

J. D. Paleologo Insurance Group, 2-4 Mesogion Ave., Athens Tower B, Athens 11527
(01) 775 53 01; Telex: 216448 JDP GR

A. Zographos, Ltd., 310 Syngrou Ave., Athens 17673
(01) 956 62 18; Telex: 219210 AZAT GR

## ADVERTISING AND MARKETING AGENCIES

Freelance Unlimited, 50 Papadiamantopoulou St., Athens 15771
(01) 775 90 59; Telex: 218344 IBS GR (frlance)
Services: promotions, public relations

Gulf & Mediterranean Advertising Co., EPE, 45 Michalakopoulou St., 4th Fl., Athens 11528
(01) 721 2415; Fax: (01) 723 2990
Services: promotions, public relations

Marad Hellas, Ltd., 30 Marni St., Athens 10433
(01) 524 53 08
Services: advertising

Market Analysis, Ltd., 190 Syngrou Ave., Athens 17671
(01) 959 09 54; Fax: (01) 959 00 97
Services: market research, promotion

Market Focus, Ltd., 52 Vas. Sofias Ave., Athens 11528
(01) 724 43 33; Telex: 222116 MAFC GR
Services: advertising

Marketing Research Center, 24 Ippadamou, Platira Square, Athens 11635
(01) 701 80 82; Telex: 218602 KEME GR

Taylor Tomsche, Ltd., 29 Michalakopoulou St., Athens 11528
(01) 722 67 71; Fax: (01) 724 00 89
Services: promotions, public relations

Topaloglou S., M. Laboura, & Co., 9 Peloponnisou St., 18344 Moschato, Athens
(01) 481 19 75
Services: public relations

## TRANSLATING AND INTERPRETING SERVICES

ICAP Group of Services, 64 Vassilissis Sophias Ave., Athens 11528
(01) 724 78 84; Fax: (01) 722 02 55
Services: translating, interpreting, business referral, and consulting

## TRANSPORTATION AND DISTRIBUTION COMPANIES

Baxevanides International, 97 Syngrou Ave., Athens 11745
(01) 923 21 46; Telex: 218146
Services: transportation, warehousing

Gellatly Morphy, SA, 26-28 Akti Kondyli St., Piraeus 18545
(01) 412 21 71; Fax: (01) 412 95 15
Services: marine cargo distribution

Omega International Transport, SARL, P.O. Box 18010, 22 Vas Georgiou B. St., Athens 11635
(01) 724 11 01; Telex: 216208 MEGA GR
Services: transportation, warehousing

Orphec Beinoglou International Forwarders, Syngrou Ave. and 2 Evripidou St., 17674 Kallithea, Athens
(01) 943 19 55; Fax: (01) 943 10 21
Services: international transportation, warehousing

Overseas Maritime Consultants, EPE, 57 Notara St., Piraeus 18535
(01) 413 10 97; Fax: (01) 413 08 65
Services: maritime transportation

Sealandair Hellas, Ltd., 24 Kapodistriou St., Piraeus 18531
(01) 411 74 18; Telex: 213381 SLA GR
Services: international transportation, warehousing

Tzimitras, Priamos, 9 Alitheias St., Athens 11362
(01) 411 99 09
Services: maritime transportation

Venus International Forwarding Co., 253 Syngrou Ave., Athens 17122
(01) 942 28 62; Telex: 222240
Services: transportation, warehousing

## TRADE CONSULTANTS

Boudourakis, Theodossis, 350 Syngrou Ave., 17680 Kallithea, Athens
(01) 943 04 39

ICAP Hellas, SA, 64 Vas. Sofias Ave., Athens 11528
(01) 724 78 84

Lekkas, Spiros D., 44 Aiandos St., 17562 Palio Faliro, Athens
(01) 981 65 59; Telex: 220250 LEKS GR

Moscholios, Nicholas, 18 Valaoritou St., Athens 10671
(01) 361 98 00; Telex: 221657 MOSC GR

Remaco, SA, 6 Karneadou St., Athens 10675
(01) 721 61 46

Stedima, EPE, 29 Michalakopoulou St., Athens 11528
(01) 724 55 41; Fax: (01) 724 95 08

Theodorou Associates, EPE, 19-20 Kolonaki Square, Athens 10673
(01) 360 64 56; Telex: 214575

Top Management, J. Fourlas-A. Bouzas Co., 8 Diocharous St., Athens 11528
(01) 722 54 86; Telex: 221809 GET GR

## TRADE SHOWS AND EXHIBITIONS

International Exhibition of Building Materials, Heating, Air-Conditioning, Insulating and Solar Energy Technology, Helexpo, 154 Egnatia St., 54636 Thessaloniki, Greece
(031) 23 92 21; Fax: (031) 22 91 16
Description: annual (February) exhibit of building materials, heating, air-conditioning, insulating and solar energy

Exhibition of Greek Footwear, Leather Goods, Helexpo, 154 Egnatia St., 54636 Thessaloniki, Greece
(031) 23 92 21; Fax: (031) 22 91 16
Description: annual (May) exhibit of footwear, leather goods

Euromode Hellenic Fashion Fair, Helexpo, 154 Egnatia St., 54636 Thessaloniki, Greece
(031) 23 92 21; Fax: (031) 22 91 16
Description: semi-annual (May/December) exhibit of fashionwear

International Exhibition of Information Systems, Helexpo, 154 Egnatia St., 54636 Thessaloniki, Greece
(031) 23 92 21; Fax: (031) 22 91 16
Description: annual (September) exhibit of information technology systems

Jewelry, Precious Stones, Machinery and Equipment Exhibition, Helexpo, 154 Egnatia St., 54636 Thessaloniki, Greece
(031) 23 92 21; Fax: (031) 22 91 16
Description: annual (November) exhibit of jewelry, precious stones, machinery and equipment

# 19

# IRELAND

## GENERAL INFORMATION

Area: 27,137 square miles
Capital: Dublin
Languages: English, Gaelic
Population: 3.6 million
Currency: Irish Pound (Ir£)
Exchange Rate (June 1993): US$/£1 0.70
International Trade*: $50 billion
Telephone Country Code: 353

Ireland remains one of the most rural, agriculture-dependent and poor countries of Western Europe—a factor that can work both ways for Americans doing business in Ireland or with the Irish. Many Irish deserve their reputation for being canny in business, but at the same time, the relatively undeveloped, unsaturated, and in some ways unsophisticated markets can offer the import-export entrepreneur or corporate re-locator more opportunities than adjacent Britain.

Despite the apparent backwardness of Ireland, especially in the rural villages that seem to have changed little in half a century, the country has one of the highest literacy rates in the world. A number of U.S. companies have built factories or established administrative offices in Ireland in recent years because of the many well-educated, trainable young people who are eager to stay in Ireland—for wages that are among Western Europe's lowest—instead of following the traditional path of advancement to London or New York.

Along with their literacy, the Irish love the spoken word. They love to talk, and they truly like Americans. Business visitors to Ireland, whether in the cities or in farming villages, never fail to marvel at how friendly the Irish are, or how welcome they make foreigners feel.

There are some topics, however, that can be sensitive. Many Irish remain resentful of centuries of British influence on their country, and

* This number represents total exports and imports.

particularly the continued British rule of the six counties of Ulster that make up Northern Ireland. Ireland is 90 percent Catholic, and people often take time off around the Christmas holidays.

## IRISH AGENCIES IN THE UNITED STATES

Embassy of Ireland, 2234 Massachusetts Ave., NW, Washington, DC 20008
(202) 462-3939; Fax: (202) 232-5993

Irish Consulate General, 515 Madison Ave., 18th Fl., New York, NY 10022
(212) 319-2555; Fax: (212) 980-9475

Irish Consulate General, 535 Boylston St., Boston, MA 02116
(617) 267-9330; Fax: (617) 267-6375

Irish Consulate General, 400 North Michigan Ave., Chicago, IL 60611
(312) 337-1868

Irish Consulate General, 655 Montgomery, Suite 930, San Francisco, CA 94111
(415) 392-4214

Irish Industrial Development Authority, 2 Grand Central Towers, 140 East 45th St., New York, NY 10166
(212) 972-1000

Irish Industrial Development Authority, 75 East Wacker Dr., Suite 600, Chicago, IL 60601
(312) 236-0222

Irish Industrial Development Authority, 2 Center Plaza, Suite 825, Boston, MA 02108
(617) 367-8225

Irish Industrial Development Authority, 1821 Wilshire Blvd., Suite 317, Santa Monica, CA 90403
(213) 829-0081

Irish Chamber of Commerce, 551 Madison Ave., 11th Fl., New York, NY 10022
(212) 248-0008

## U.S. AGENCIES IN IRELAND

American Chamber of Commerce, 20 College Green, Dublin 2
(01) 67 93 733; Fax: (01) 67 93 402

U.S. Embassy, 42 Elgin Rd., Ballsbridge, Dublin
(01) 68 87 77; Fax: (01) 68 99 46

## BANKS AND FINANCIAL INSTITUTIONS

AIB Group, Bankcentre, Postbox 452, Ballsbridge, Dublin 4
(01) 60 03 11; Fax: (01) 68 25 08
Services: corporate and investment banking

Anglo-Irish Bank Corp., PLC, Stephen Court, 18-21 St. Stephen's Court, Dublin 2
(01) 76 01 41; Fax: (01) 61 19 81
Services: corporate, personal finance, insurance premium finance, leasing, treasury services

Bank of Ireland, Lower Baggot St., Dublin 2
(01) 61 59 33; Fax: (01) 61 51 01
Services: corporate and investment banking, insurance finance, treasury services

The Investment Bank of Ireland, Ltd., 26 Fitzwilliam Place, Dublin 2
(01) 61 64 33; Fax: (01) 61 66 88
Services: investment services, corporate finance

National Irish Bank, Ltd., 7-8 Wilton Terrace, Dublin 2
(01) 78 50 66; Fax: (01) 61 41 65
Services: corporate banking

UDT/First Southern Group, 13-16 Fleet St., Dublin 2
(01) 71 33 11; Fax: (01) 71 36 13
Services: commercial, insurance, vehicle and equipment leasing

Ulster Investment Bank, 2 Hume St., Dublin 2
(01) 61 34 44; Fax: (01) 76 30 21
Services: investment, fund management, corporate banking, treasury services

Woodchester Bank, Woodchester House, Golden Lane, Dublin 8
(01) 78 42 99; Fax: (01) 75 66 81
Services: consumer finance, industrial mortgages

## ACCOUNTING FIRMS

Arthur Andersen & Co., 49 St. Stephen's Green, Dublin 2
(01) 76 58 21; Fax: (01) 76 78 21
Services: tax advice, auditing, receiverships and liquidations

Bradley Austin, 6 Cook St., Cork
(021) 27 60 22
Services: auditing, tax advice, auditing, receiverships and liquidations

Costello Boyle & Co., 112 Pembroke Rd., Ballsbridge, Dublin 4
(01) 68 87 26; Fax: (01) 68 80 00
Services: auditing, tax advice, receiverships and liquidations

Fay McMahon & Co., 23 Harcourt St., Dublin 2
(01) 75 81 01; Fax: (01) 78 33 04
Services: auditing, tax advice, receiverships and liquidations

Keane Agnes & Co., Capital Buildings, 64/65 Catherine St., Limerick
(061) 49 411
Services: auditing, tax advice, receiverships and liquidations

O'Gorman Brannigan Purtill & Co., 3-4 Dr. Croke Place, Clonmel, County Tipperary
(052) 22 044; Fax: (052) 25 131
Services: auditing, tax advice, receiverships and liquidations

Smyth Lawlor & Co., Marlborough House, 21 Marlborough Rd., Donnybrook, Dublin 4
(01) 68 97 60; Fax: (01) 68 97 78
Services: auditing, tax advice, receiverships and liquidations

Whiteside Cullinan & Co., Molesworth House, 1/2 South Frederick St., Dublin 2
(01) 77 81 85; Fax: (01) 79 28 54
Services: auditing, tax advice, receiverships and liquidations

## INSURANCE AGENCIES

Church & General Insurance, PLC, 15 Marlborough St., Dublin 1
(01) 73 51 11; Fax: (01) 73 51 11
Services: capital redemption, air and marine cargo, commercial contractors (all risks), contract guarantee, libel, employers liability, riot, civil commotion and natural disaster

Eagle Star Shield Insurance Co., Shield House, 45/47 Pembroke Rd., Dublin 4
(01) 68 39 43; Fax: (01) 68 48 97
Services: capital redemption, air and marine cargo, commercial contractors (all risks), contract guarantee, libel, employers liability, riot, civil commotion and natural disaster

Hiberman Insurance Company, Ltd., Haddington Rd., Dublin 4
(01) 60 82 88; Fax: (01) 60 84 13
Services: marine and air cargo, riot, civil commotion and natural disaster, product liability

PMPA Insurance, Wolfe Tone House, Wolfe Tone St., Dublin 1
(01) 72 64 44; Fax: (01) 72 46 52
Services: riot, civil commotion and natural disasters, product liability

Royal Insurance (UK), Ltd., 50 Dawson St., Dublin 2
(01) 67 98 555; Fax: (01) 67 98 123
Services: pensions, reinsurance capital redemption

Sheridan Assurance Association, 53 Adelaide Rd., Dublin 2
(01) 61 54 66; Fax: (01) 61 81 38
Services: pensions, endowment mortgages, annuities

Standard Life Assurance Co., 90 St. Stephen's Green, Dublin 2
(01) 75 74 11; Fax: (01) 75 19 03
Services: pensions, endowment mortgages, annuities

Sun Alliance & London Insurance, PLC, 13/17 Dawson St., Dublin 2
(01) 77 18 51; Fax: (01) 71 76 25
Services: capital redemption, air and marine cargo, commercial contractors (all risks), contract guarantees, libel, employers liability, riot, civil commotion and natural disasters

## TRANSPORTATION AND DISTRIBUTION COMPANIES

DFDS Transport, 72-80 North Wall Quay, Dublin 1
(01) 78 73 99; Fax: (01) 72 68 11
Services: national and international distribution, brokers, customs clearance, freight consolidators, container roll on/roll off

Killeen Freight Services, Ltd., 1B Kylemore Industrial Estate, Killeen Rd., Dublin 10
(01) 62 66 36; Fax: (01) 62 67 310
Services: national and international transportation, distribution, brokers, customs clearance, freight consolidators, container roll on/roll off

LEP International, Ltd., 11/15 Tara St., Dublin 2
(01) 77 18 61; Fax: (01) 77 17 60
Services: national and international transportation, distribution, brokers, customs clearance, freight consolidators, container roll on/roll off

Metro Express (Ireland), Ltd., Dublin Industrial Estate, 144A Slaney Close
(01) 30 81 11; Fax: (01) 30 88 57
Services: freight transportation, customs clearance, freight consolidators, container roll on/roll off

Schenkers, Ltd., 11-15 Tara St., Dublin 2
(01) 77 17 77
Services: national and international transportation, distribution

Seagroup Agencies, Unit 1B, Kylemore Industrial Estate, Killeen Rd., Dublin 10
(01) 26 73 16; Fax: (01) 26 73 10
Services: national and international transportation, distribution

TNT Express, Eklad Industrial Estate, Coolock, Dublin 5
(01) 47 37 99; Fax: (01) 47 56 92
Services: national and international transportation, distribution

Uniroad International Freight (Ireland), Unit 88, Baldoyle Industrial Estate, Baldoyle, Dublin 13
(01) 39 37 36; Fax: (01) 39 34 72
Services: national and international transportation, distribution

## TRADE CONSULTANTS

Arthur Andersen & Co., 49 St. Stephen's Green, Dublin 2
(01) 76 58 21; Fax: (01) 76 78 21

Bastow Charleton, Marine House, Clanwilliam Court, Dublin 2
(01) 76 09 51; Fax: (01) 60 91 08

Coopers & Lybrand, Fitzwilton House, Wilton House, Dublin 2
(01) 61 03 33; Fax: (01) 60 17 82

Craig Gardner/Price Waterhouse, Gardner House/Wilton Place, Dublin 2
(01) 60 67 00; Fax: (01) 60 76 38

Freaney Oliver & Co., 43/45 Northumberland Rd., Dublin 4
(01) 68 86 44; Fax: (01) 68 97 55

Garland Thomas & Partners, Royal Liver House, Grand Parade, Dublin 6
(01) 96 43 22; Fax: (01) 96 47 25

Stokes Kennedy Crowley, 1 Stokes Place, St. Stephen's Green, Dublin 2
(01) 70 81 000; Fax: (01) 70 81 122

## TRADE SHOWS AND EXHIBITIONS

Ireland Brighter Homes & Do It Yourself Exhibition, John Palmer Exhibitions, Ltd., 3 Woodbine PK, Stillorgan, Dublin
(01) 69 40 22; Fax: (01) 69 22 95
Description: annual (March) exhibit of goods for home improvement

Ireland Computex (IBETA), SDL Exhibitions, Ltd., 18 Main St., Rathfarnham, Dublin
(01) 90 06 00; Fax: (01) 90 89 34
Description: annual (March) exhibit of computers, business and office equipment

Ireland International Electronics Show (ITRON), SDL Exhibitions, Ltd., 18 Main St., Rathfarnham, Dublin
(01) 90 06 00; Fax: (01) 90 89 34
Description: annual (October) exhibit of electronics industry

# 20

# ITALY

## GENERAL INFORMATION

Area: 116,303 square miles
Capital: Rome
Language: Italian
Population: 57.6 million
Currency: Italian lire (L)
Exchange Rate (June 1993): $1/L 1,543
International Trade*: $350 billion
Telephone Country Code: 39

Italians are proud of their economic success in recent years and are happy to argue that their country is now richer than Britain, at least in terms of GNP per capita.

This growth is particularly impressive in view of Italy's scant natural resources. Because of its reliance on exporting and the international appeal of so many of its products from food to fashion, Italy has become increasingly important to the United States as a trading partner.

For many Italians, the devotion to the family means rarely missing a lunch at home. Many Italian civil servants and other government officials do not take appointments in the afternoons, and some businesspeople don't, either. Many public offices are closed to the public after 3 P.M., even if the officials inside are still working.

In general, the pace of life, and business, is slower in Italy. While we live to work, the saying goes, Italians work to live. As much or more than other Europeans, Italians are interested in establishing long-term business relationships; they are less transaction-oriented and less attuned to the immediacy of the bottom line, which often hampers business dealings with Americans. Italian accounting methods often seem to compete with Italian government regulations to throw up the biggest roadblocks to doing business in Italy.

Business dress is stylish but conservative and fairly formal.

* This number represents total exports and imports.

## ITALIAN AGENCIES IN THE UNITED STATES

Italian Embassy, 16 Fuller St., NW, Washington, DC 20009
(202) 328-5500; Fax: (202) 483-2187

Italian Consulate General, 100 Boylston St., Suite 900, Boston, MA 02116
(617) 542-0483; Fax: (617) 542-3998

Italian Consulate General, 500 North Michigan Ave., Suite 1850, Chicago, IL 60611
(312) 467-1550

Italian Consulate General, Buhl Bldg., 535 Griswold Ave., Suite 1840, Detroit, MI 48226
(313) 963-8560; Fax: (313) 963-8180

Italian Consulate General, 421 Chestnut St., Philadelphia, PA 19106
(215) 592-7329; Fax: (215) 592-9808

Italian Consulate General, 1300 Post Oak Blvd., Suite 660, Houston, TX 77056
(713) 850-7520; Fax: (713) 850-9113

Italian Consulate General, 12400 Wilshire Blvd., Suite 300, Los Angeles, CA 90025
(213) 826-6207; Fax: (213) 820-0727

Italian Vice Consulate, 744 Broad St., 28th Fl., Newark, NJ 07102
(201) 643-1448; Fax: (201) 643-3043

Italian Consulate General, 630 Camp St., New Orleans, LA 70130
(504) 524-2271; Fax: (504) 581-4590

Italian Consulate General, 690 Park Ave., New York, NY 10021
(212) 737-9100; Fax: (212) 249-4945

Italian Consulate General, 2590 Webster St., San Francisco, CA 94115
(415) 931-4925; Fax: (415) 931-7205

Italian Trade Commission, 2001 Peachtree St., NE, P.O. Box 56689, Atlanta, GA 30343
(404) 525-6600

Italian Trade Commission, 401 North Michigan Ave., Suite 3030, Chicago, IL 60611
(312) 670-4360

Italian Trade Commission, 1090 Natural Gas Pipeline Tower, 3050 South Post Oak Rd., Houston, TX 77056
(713) 626-5531

Italian Trade Commission, 1801 Avenue of the Stars, Suite 700, Los Angeles, CA 90067
(213) 879-0950

Italian Trade Commission, 499 Park Ave., New York, NY 10022
(212) 980-1500

Italian Trade Commission, 595 Market St., Suite 2150, San Francisco, CA 94105
(415) 398-1574

## U.S. AGENCIES IN ITALY

U.S. Embassy, Via Veneto 119A, Rome 00187
(06) 46 741; Fax: (06) 46 74 21 11

U.S. Consulate General, Lungarno Amerigo Vespucci 38, Florence 50100
(055) 23 98 276; Fax: (055) 28 40 88

U.S. Consulate General, Banca d'America e Italia, Piazza Portello, Genoa 6-16124
(010) 28 27 41; Fax: (010) 29 00 27

U.S. Consulate General, Centro Cooperazione Giulio Cesare, Milan 20145
(02) 46 96 451; Fax: (02) 48 14 161

U.S. Consulate General, Piazza della Repubblica, Naples 80122
(081) 76 14 303; Fax: (081) 76 11 869

U.S. Consulate General, Via Vaccarini 1, Palermo 90143
(091) 34 35 32; Fax: (091) 34 35 46

American Chamber of Commerce, Via Cantu 1, Milan 20123
(02) 86 90 661; Fax: (02) 80 57 737

## BANKS AND FINANCIAL INSTITUTIONS

Banca C. Steinhauslin & C., SpA, Via dei Sassetti 4, Florence 50123
(055) 27 621; Fax: (055) 23 02 391
Services: corporate, commercial banking

Banca di Credito di Trieste, SpA, Via Fabio Filzi 10, Trieste 34132
(040) 67 001
Services: corporate, commercial banking

Banca Toscana, SpA, Corso 6, Florence 50122
(055) 43 911; Fax: (055) 43 91 634
Services: corporate, commercial banking

Banco di Roma, SpA, Viale Umberto Tupini 180, Rome 00144
(06) 54 451
Services: international banking

Banco di Sicilia, Via Generale Magliocco 1, Palermo 90141
(091) 58 79 33
Services: international banking

Barclays International Finanziaria, Via della Moscova 18, Milan 20122
(02) 63 721; Fax: (02) 63 72 20 45
Services: corporate, commercial banking

Citibank NA Fillale Italiana, Foro Buonaparte 16, Milan 20121
(02) 85 421; Fax: (02) 85 42 407
Services: corporate, commercial banking

ICLE IST Nazionale Credito Lavoro It Estero, Via Sallustina 58, Rome 00187
(06) 48 28 404; Fax: 48 17 958
Services: corporate, commercial banking

Isveimer, Via Tufati 29, Naples 80133
(02) 65 71 95 12; Fax: (02) 65 71 952
Services: international banking

Republic National Bank of New York, Via dell'Orso 2, Milan 20121
(02) 72 10 21; Fax: (02) 86 46 17 68

## LAW FIRMS

Avvocati Bruno e Associati, Via P. Verri 10, Milan 20121
(02) 76 00 69 96; Fax: (02) 76 00 14 73
Services: corporate, foreign investment, local taxation and international law

Alberto Cajola, Via G. Rossini 5, Milan 20122
(02) 79 67 20; Fax: (02) 78 01 77
Services: international law

Enrico Ciantelli, Via dei Servi 9, Florence 50122
(055) 21 53 52; Fax: (055) 29 51 67
Services: international law

Studio Avvocati Colonna, Corso Siccardi 11, Turin 10122
(011) 51 14 23; Fax: (011) 53 75 21
Services: international law

Comito Viola & Partners, Viale Gramsci 17/B, Naples 80122
(81) 68 06 34; Fax: (81) 68 06 34
Services: admiralty, commercial, tax and financial law

Avvocati Ferruccio Mengaroni, Via della Camilluccia 35, Rome 00135
(06) 34 41 17
Services: trusts, estates, international and corporate law

Robert Horn & Co., Via di Porta Pinciana 4, Rome 00187
(06) 48 14 143; Fax: (06) 48 14 593

International Law Office G. Egidio, Via Archimede 59, Rome 00197
(06) 32 03 746; Fax: (06) 32 03 746
Services: admiralty, aviation, finance, tax and international law

International Law Studio, Piazza Independenza, Florence 30129
(055) 48 00 55; Fax: (055) 47 12 42

Studio Avvocati Morelli, Castello-Campo SS, Filippo e Giacomo 4512, Venice 30122
(041) 52 36 558; Fax: (041) 52 23 286
Services: international law

## ACCOUNTING FIRMS

Arthur Andersen & Co., SaS, Via della Moscova 3, Milan 20121
(02) 62 34 12; Fax: (02) 65 72 876
Services: auditing, tax and financial consulting

Carre, Orban, & Partners, Srl, Via Cerva 18, Milan 20122
(02) 76 00 44 41; Fax: (02) 78 45 03
Services: auditing, tax consultants

Coopers & Lybrand, SaS, Via Vittor Pisani 20, Milan 20124
(02) 67 831; Fax: (02) 66 98 14 33
Services: auditing, accounting, tax and financial consultants

Deloitte, Haskins & Sells, SnC, Via Monte di Pieta 24, Milan 20121
(02) 88 01; Fax: (02) 87 08 68
Services: auditing, accounting, tax and financial consultants

Interaudit, SpA, Viale Regina Margherita 279, Rome 00198
(06) 44 03 756; Fax: (06) 84 40 549
Services: auditing, accounting

Italaudit, SpA, Via Durini 18, Milan 20122
(02) 78 30 41; Fax: (02) 78 13 96
Services: auditing, tax consultants

Price Waterhouse, SaS, Via del Rione Sirignano 7, Naples 80121
(081) 76 14 100; Fax: (081) 66 78 02
Services: auditing, accounting, tax & financial consultants

Revisarda, SpA, Via Matta 1, Sassari 07100
(079) 23 45 48; Fax: (079) 23 93 16
Services: auditing, accounting
Contact: (079) 23 93 16

Servizio Italia, Salita San Nicola da Tolentino 1/B, Rome 00187
(06) 47 44 052; Fax: (06) 44 81 74 32
Services: auditing, tax consultants

Studio Jona Societa Fiduciaria e Revisione, C. Vinzaglio 16, Turin 10121
(011) 53 59 73; Fax: (011) 54 41 43
Services: auditing, accounting, financial analysis

## INSURANCE AGENCIES

Assicurazioni Generali, SpA, Piazza Duca degli Abruzzi 2, Trieste 34132
(040) 67 11; Fax: (040) 67 16 00
Services: insurance brokers, industrial and commercial risk management

Brokerban Insurance Brokers, SpA, Via Toledo 402, Naples 80132
(081) 55 23 143; Fax: (081) 55 24 481
Services: insurance brokers

Euroassicurazioni, SpA, Via Claudio Monteverdi 18, Rome 00198
(06) 88 40 910; Fax: (06) 85 41 149
Services: insurance brokers

GPA Gestione di Assicurazione, SpA, C.P.TA Romana 68, Milan 20122
(02) 55 10 917; Fax: (02) 54 51 593
Services: insurance brokers

Inalto, SpA, Corso G. Ferraris 86, Turin 10129
(011) 59 25 81; Fax: (011) 59 69 42
Services: insurance brokers

Marsh & McLennan Italia & Co., Via del Giardini 7, Milan 20121
(02) 63 451; Fax: (011) 63 45 300
Services: insurance brokers

Nikols Alpeadria Insurance Brokers, Srl, Via Donata 3, Trieste 34121
(040) 36 51 01; Fax: (040) 36 54 89
Services: insurance brokers

Sedgwick James, SpA, Via Fatebenefratelli 14, Milan 20121
(02) 65 96 041; Fax: (02) 65 72 587
Services: insurance brokers, industrial and commercial risk management

Studio Cantagallo, SaS, Via Fissiraga 10, Lodi 20075
(0371) 55 244; Fax: (02) 76 00 945
Services: accident management and settlement, industrial and commercial risk management

Unipol Assicurazioni, SpA, Via Stalingrado 45, Bologna 40128
(051) 50 71 11; Fax: (051) 37 53 49
Services: accident management and settlement, industrial and commercial risk management

## ADVERTISING AND MARKETING AGENCIES

Age Pubblicita Marketing Promozione, Srl, Via Leopard 14, Milan 20123
(02) 48 18 900; Fax: (02) 49 80 641
Services: corporate, commercial advertising and marketing

Brain Storming, Srl, Via Sacchi 38, Turin 10128
(011) 50 55 48; Fax: (011) 50 34 68
Services: corporate, commercial advertising and marketing

Commark Communicazione e Marketing, Srl, Via Isonzo 25, Rome 00198
(06) 85 49 394; Fax: (06) 84 16 677
Services: corporate, commercial advertising and marketing

Creative Consultant, SaS, Via Lattanzio 77, Milan 20137
(02) 54 50 751; Fax: (02) 54 56 470
Services: corporate, commercial advertising and marketing

Euro Advertising, SpA, Via Calzolari 47, Bologna 40128
(051) 37 41 98; Fax: (051) 37 44 85
Services: corporate, commercial advertising and marketing

Formula Advertising, SnC, Via Befiore 61, Turin 10126
(011) 65 09 509; Fax: (011) 65 08 804
Services: corporate, commercial advertising and marketing

Leodari Pubblicita, SnC, Via B. Marcello 6, Vecenza 36100
(0444) 56 31 14; Fax: (0444) 56 31 81
Services: corporate, commercial advertising and marketing

McCann-Erickson Italiana, SpA, Via Meravigli 2, Milan 20123
(02) 85 291; Fax: (02) 34 29 94
Services: corporate, commercial advertising and marketing

Publicitas, SpA, Via Eman Filiberto 4, Milan 20149
(02) 38 871; Fax: (02) 34 29 94
Services: corporate, commercial advertising and marketing

Zest, SrL, Via Mario Pagano 39, Milan 20145
(02) 48 12 746; Fax: (02) 48 17 755
Services: corporate, commercial advertising and marketing

## TRANSLATING AND INTERPRETING SERVICES

ABC Traduzioni, Via R. Lanciani 74, Rome 00162
(06) 83 23 512; Fax: (06) 83 22 261
Services: translating

Business Center, V. Savonaralo 217, Padova 35137
(049) 87 20 222; Fax: (049) 87 22 703
Services: interpreting, translating

Inlingua Genova, Via Brig. Partigiane 4, Genova 16129
(010) 58 67 88; Fax: (010) 58 67 88
Services: interpreting, translating

International Business Center, Corso Europa 12, Milan 20122
(02) 76 01 38 21; Fax: (02) 76 02 10 56
Services: interpreting, translating

International Service, Via della Palancola 20, Florence 50133
(055) 57 53 71; Fax: (055) 58 73 21
Services: interpreting, translating, convention organizing

Nexus Consulenze, Via Pompeo Magno 94, Rome 00192
(06) 32 22 062; Fax: (06) 32 21 057
Services: translating

Regency School, Via Arcivescovado 7, Torino 10121
(011) 51 74 56; Fax: (011) 54 18 45
Services: interpreting, translating

SIME Servizio Interpretie Marketing Estero, Via Stalingrado 24, 40128 Bologna
(051) 37 48 98; Fax: (051) 37 48 98
Services: interpreting, translating

Studio Nippon, Corso Lodi 24, Milan 20135
(02) 54 63 980; Fax: (02) 55 19 00 36
Services: translating

## TRANSPORTATION AND DISTRIBUTION COMPANIES

Aertrans, Srl, Salita San Nicola da Tolentino 1/B, Rome 00187
(06) 48 17 550; Fax: (06) 47 45 153
Services: international freight forwarders, terminal services, distribution

Albini & Piticliani International Forwarders, Via Zara 1, Seggiano-Pioltello, Milan 20096
(02) 92 16 08 28; Fax: (02) 92 16 08 55
Services: international freight forwarders, terminal services, distribution

Alisped, SpA, Viale Montegrappa 212/B, Prato 50047
(0574) 57 90; Fax: (0574) 57 01 75
Services: international freight forwarders, terminal services, distribution

Bergaglio Trasporti, Srl, Via Fantoli 28/3, Milan 20158
(0331) 26 15 70; Fax: (0331) 26 10 56
Services: international freight forwarders, terminal services, distribution

Eurotrans Spedizioni, Srl, Via Colombo 16, Santa Croce Sull'Arno 56029
(0571) 36 64 00; Fax: (0571) 36 64 05
Services: international freight forwarders, terminal services, distribution

Interglobo Morra, Srl, Via Carducci 5/3, Genova 16121
(010) 59 36 25; Fax: (010) 59 14 06
Services: international freight forwarders, terminal services

Perioli Dario, SpA, Viale Italia 33, La Spezia 19100
(0187) 31 334; Fax: (0187) 29 564
Services: loading, unloading, storage, transporting and treatment of solid fuels, ship brokers, buying and selling boats for tourism, international freight forwarders, terminal services, distribution

SADA-Spediz Autotrasporti Depositi, Via Fantoli 6/11, Milan 20138
(02) 50 60 241; Fax: (02) 50 22 64
Services: leasing of tank and special rail cars, pick up and delivery, international freight forwarders

Timat Spedizioni Internazionali, Srl, Via Pasubio 16, Creazzo 36051
(0444) 52 04 44; Fax: (0444) 52 04 25
Services: international freight forwarders, terminal services, distribution

Vicenzasped International Agency, Srl, Via Panizza 42, Vicenza 36100
(0444) 50 76 73; Fax: (0444) 51 38 29
Services: international freight forwarders, terminal services, distribution and security transport

## TRADE CONSULTANTS

Arpes, Srl, Via Mazzini 55, Rome 00195
(061) 32 17 786; Fax: (061) 32 17 783
Services: export consultants, management, production and general organization consultants

Bedaux Metodi, Srl, Via del Rondonel, Bologna 40122
(051) 55 37 54; Fax: (051) 55 30 95
Services: export consultants, industrial classification and coding services, management, production and general organization consultants, fashion and clothing business organization

Consulfidi, Srl, Via Padova 113, Milan 20127
(02) 28 40 929
Services: export consultants, management, production and general consultants, sales consultants

Egon Zehnder International, Srl, Piazza Meda 3, Milan 20121
(02) 77 081; Fax: (02) 78 00 29
Services: export consultants, general organization consultants

Euro Assembly, SnC, Via Lapidari 8, Bologna 40129
(051) 32 68 85; Fax: (051) 32 68 14
Services: export consultants, production organization consultants

Fienco, SpA, Via Chiossetto 18, Milan 20122
(02) 76 02 06 41; Fax: (02) 76 00 94 84
Services: export consultants, management consultants

Kover, Srl, Via Sebastiano Valfre' 3, Torino 10121
(011) 54 42 34; Fax: (011) 53 91 52
Services: export consultants, management consultants

Primeservice, Srl, Via Carducci 16, Florence 50121
(055) 23 41 141; Fax: (055) 23 41 143
Services: export consultants, general organization consultants

Somea Consult, SnC, Via del Giordano 34, Rome 00144
(06) 59 14 720; Fax: (06) 59 20 36 23
Services: export consultants, interventions at European level for industrial reorganization and opportunity studies

TMC Amrop International, Srl, Via Emanuele 15, Milan 20122
(02) 79 85 57
Services: export consultants, interventions at European level for industrial reorganization and opportunity studies

## TRADE SHOWS AND EXHIBITIONS

Milan International Tourism Exchange (BIT), Via Serbelloni 2, Milan
(02) 77 181; Fax: (02) 78 18 28
Description: annual (February) exhibit for tour operators, travel agents, hoteliers

Milan International Printing Machinery Exhibition Paper Converting, Delia Associates, Route 22 West, Whitehouse, NJ 08888
Fax: (908) 53 46 856
Description: triennial (March) exhibit of machinery and materials for converting industries, products, and printing of paper, plastics, rigid and flexible packaging

Turin International Motor Show, Corso Galileo Ferraris 61, Turin
(011) 57 611; Fax: (011) 535 366
Description: biennial (April) exhibit of current models, sports and special model cars

Milan International Furniture Exhibition (Salone del Mobile), Corso Magenta 96, Milan
(02) 48 00 87 16
Description: semi-annual (April, September) exhibit of furniture, indoor and outdoor

Milan International Trade Fair—Gifts, Perfumery, Fancy Goods, Costume Jewelry (Chibidue), Delia Associates, Route 22 West, Whitehouse, NJ 08888
Fax: (908) 53 46 856
Description: annual (May) exhibit of fashion jewelry, fashion accessories, novelties, promotional items, toys, and souvenirs

Verona International Foresting Fair (Euroforesta), Fiere di Verona, C.P. 525, Ente Autonomo, Verona
Description: annual (May) exhibit of forestry products, equipment, and restoration methods

Milan Exhibition Raw and Reworked Materials Transport and Recycling (Salvage and Recycle), Via Serbelloni 2, Milan
(02) 77 181; Fax: (02) 78 18 28
Description: annual (November) exhibit of vehicles, facilities and equipment for collection, transport, sorting, and control of waste

Milan International Exhibition Commerce Equipment, Via Serbelloni 2, Milan
(02) 77 181; Fax: (02) 78 18 28
Description: annual (November) exhibit of commerce equipment for shops, supermarkets, and warehouses

Milan International Ice Cream Confectionery Exhibition, Via Serbelloni 2, Milan
(02) 77 181; Fax: (02) 78 18 28
Description: annual (November) exhibit of machines, equipment and facilities for industrial and handicraft production of confectionery and ice cream

Turin International New Technologies Innovations Fair, Corso Massimo D'Azeglio 15, Turin
(011) 6569; Fax: (011) 650 9801
Description: annual (November) exhibit of factory and office technologies, automation, telematics, aeronautics and space, energy saving, home electronics, computers and optical electronics

# 21

# LUXEMBOURG

## GENERAL INFORMATION

Area: 1,000 square miles
Capital: Luxembourg
Languages: Luxemburgish, French, German
Population: 380,000
Currency: Franc (LuF)
Exchange Rate (June 1993): $1/LuF 34.9
International Trade*: $12 billion
Telephone Country Code: 352

The Grand Duchy of Luxembourg is a miniscule country, smaller in area than Rhode Island, with a population not much larger than the Baton Rouge metropolitan area. Being so small, Luxembourg has borrowed many of the things that countries need from its larger European neighbors. For example, it shares its franc with Belgium, the official language is French, but German is the most common language of business and the media, and the French-German patois known as Luxembourgish is what most people speak at home and on the street. Virtually every native speaks all three languages fluently, and many in business are comfortable in English, too.

As a result, the people of Luxembourg have always had a more European identity than the populations of larger countries with their own currencies, languages, and cultures. That was one reason—along with the fact that the new group needed any and all members it could get—that Luxembourg was one of The Six, the original members of the EC when it was formed in 1956.

Banking and other financial services have long been Luxembourg's bread and butter, and its "offshore" aspects have been attractive to many corporations, trusts, and wealthy individuals over the years. Some of the appeal may diminish, however, as Luxembourg comes under pressure to reform many of the practices of its financial services industry, such as its strict Swiss-style banking secrecy laws, and bring them in line with the more above-board regulations of other EC countries.

* This number represents total exports and imports.

Luxembourg is one of the wealthiest countries per capita in Europe, and perhaps one of the most formal, too. Suits are expected for businesspeople, even in informal meetings and semi-business gatherings, such as dinner at someone's home.

## LUXEMBOURG AGENCIES IN THE UNITED STATES

Embassy of Luxembourg, 2200 Massachusetts Ave., NW, Washington, DC 20008
(202) 265-4171; Fax: (202) 328-8270

Luxembourg Consulate, 1900 The Exchange, Suite 440, Atlanta, GA 30339
(404) 952-1157; Fax: (404) 984-2738

Luxembourg Consulate, 180 Grove St., Lexington (Boston), MA 02173
(617) 861-1104

Luxembourg Consulate, 180 North La Salle St., Suite 1400, Chicago, IL 60601
(312) 726-0355; Fax: (312) 726-6383

Luxembourg Consulate, 2001 Bryan Tower, 36th Fl., Dallas, TX 75201
(214) 746-7200; Fax: (214) 746-7123

Luxembourg Consulate, 43043 West Nine Mile Rd., Northville (Detroit), MI 48167
(313) 347-0100; Fax: (313) 349-5551

Luxembourg Consulate, 516 Avondale Ave., Los Angeles, CA 90094
(213) 394-2532

Luxembourg Consulate, 200 South Biscayne Blvd., Suite 3240, Miami, FL 33131
(305) 373-1300; Fax: (305) 373-1303

Luxembourg Consulate General, 801 Second Ave., 13th Fl., New York, NY 10017
(212) 265-4171; Fax: (212) 697-5529

Luxembourg-American Chamber of Commerce, Empire State Bldg., 350 Fifth Ave., Suite 703, New York, NY 10118
(212) 967-9885; Fax: (212) 692-0349

## U.S. AGENCIES IN LUXEMBOURG

Chamber of Commerce, 7 Rue Alcide de Gasperi, BP 1503, Luxembourg 2981
43 58 53; Fax: 43 83 26

U.S. Embassy, 22 Boulevard Emmanuel-Servais, Luxembourg 2535
46 01 23; Fax: 46 14 01

## BANKS AND FINANCIAL INSTITUTIONS

Banco di Napoli International, 1e-12 Avenue Pasteur, Luxembourg 2310
475 95 91

Bank of America International, SA, 35 Boulevard Royal Luxembourg, Luxembourg 2014
208 41

Credit Suisse Luxembourg, SA, 56 Grand Rue, Luxembourg 1660
460 01 11

Kredietbank, SA, Luxembourgeoise, 43 Boulevard Royal, Luxembourg 2955
479 71

Luxembourgeoise de Banque, 11 Avenue Emile Reuter, Luxembourg 2420
47 10 37

Societe Europenenne de Banque Luxembourg, SA, Avenue de la Porte Neuve, BP 21, Luxembourg 2010
46 14 11

The Pricoa International Bank, SA, 6 Avenue Pescatore, Luxembourg 2324
47 38 51

## LAW FIRMS

Bar rules preclude publication of adequate information.

Names of lawyers, addresses and contact numbers will be supplied on request from:

Professional Association
Ordre des Avocats
Palais de Justice
Postbox 15
Luxembourg 2010

## ACCOUNTING FIRMS

BDO Binder, Wirtschaftspruefungsgesellschaf, 17 Rue des Pommiers, Luxembourg 2343
42 30 42

Deloitte & Touche, 3 Route D'Arlon, Strassen Luxembourg 8009
40 28 03

Ernst & Young International, 6 Avenue Emile Reuter, Luxembourg 2420
468 11

Safilux, 2 Rue Tony Neuman, Luxembourg 2241
46 18 13

## INSURANCE AGENCIES

AG Luxembourg, SA, 1 Rue des Glacis, Luxembourg 1628
416 58

Assurance Liegoise, SA, 15-17 Avenue Guillaume, Luxembourg 1628
44 23 44

Assurlux, SA, 6 Rue Adolphe, Luxembourg 1116
44 24 24

Bureau International D'Assurances, SA, 89a Avenue Gaston Diderich, Luxembourg 1420
45 41 96

Interassurances, SARL, 40 Rue de Bragance, Luxembourg 1255
44 69 30

Sedgwick, SA, 257 Route d'Esch, Luxembourg 1471
49 52 41

Winterthur Assurance, 31bd G.D. Charlotte, Luxembourg 1331
45 22 80

Zurich, SA, 117 Avenue Gaston Diderich, Luxembourg 1420
44 50 50

## TRANSLATING AND INTERPRETING SERVICES

ECAT, SARL, 9-11 Rue Jean-Pierre, Luxembourg 2514
43 83 88

Eurotraduc, 10 bd Royal, Luxembourg 2449
46 03 55

Jones Pamela, 143 Rue du Cents, Luxembourg 1319
43 77 26

Systran Institut, 13-15 Rue Jean-Pierre, Luxembourg-Kirchberg 2514
43 30 65

Traducta, SV, Monterey Palace, 11c Boulevard Josef II, Luxembourg 1840
45 31 53

## ADVERTISING AND MARKETING AGENCIES

International Terry Consultants, 6 Place de Nancy,
Luxembourg 2212
44 03 53
Services: advertising, public relations

## TRANSPORTATION AND DISTRIBUTION COMPANIES

Eurotrack, International Transportation & Tracking Systems, 59
Rue Ernest Beres, Howald Luxembourg 1232
48 92 97; Fax: 48 03 31

TNT Express, Zone Industrielle, Rollach, Sandweiler
Luxembourg 5280
35 74 31; Fax: 35 74 30

Tranelux, SA, Zone Industrielle, Howald Luxembourg 2529
499 61; Fax: 49 09 27

## TRADE CONSULTANTS

Anthony & Partners, SC, 5 Rue Glesener, Luxembourg 1631
40 39 53
Services: industrial location consultants

Arthur Andersen & Co., 672 Rue de Neudorf, Luxembourg 2220
43 70 39
Services: export consultants

Infeurope, 17 Rue Glesener, Luxembourg 1461
40 20 20

SEDO, SA, 5 Rue de l'Eglise, Luxembourg 1458
49 94 37

World Systems, Rue Theodore Gillen, Howald Luxembourg 1625
40 40 51; Fax: 40 40 18
Services: trade consultants, business development

## TRADE SHOWS AND EXHIBITIONS

Luxembourg International Trade Fair, Societe des Foires
International de Luxembourg, Luxembourg 2088
439 91; Fax: 439 93 15
Description: semi-annual (May/October) exhibit

International Trade Fair for Police Equipment, Societe des Foires International de Luxembourg, Luxembourg 2088
439 91; Fax: 439 93 15
Description: annual (October) exhibit of police and security equipment

International Trade Fair for Office & Communications Technology, Societe des Foires International de Luxembourg, Luxembourg 2088
439 91; Fax: 439 93 15
Description: biennial (October) exhibit of office and communications technology

International Trade Fair for Gastronomy, Societe des Foires International de Luxembourg, Luxembourg 2088
439 91; Fax: 439 93 15
Description: every four years (November) exhibit of food, cooking methods, and equipment

# 22

# THE NETHERLANDS

## GENERAL INFORMATION

Area: 16,164 square miles
Capital: Amsterdam
Languages: Dutch, English, German
Population: 15 million
Currency: Guilder (Dfl)
Exchange Rate (June 1993): $1/Dfl 1.90
International Trade*: $275 billion
Telephone Country Code: 31

The Netherlands is an extraordinary little nation, much of it physically reclaimed from the sea and economically built on a history as one of the world's most aggressive traders. Its people are gruff, but friendly; kind, but stubborn; proud, but pragmatic.

The Dutch are Europe's most accomplished linguists. Most businesspeople speak English flawlessly, along with German and perhaps Spanish, French or Italian, too. Small talk is normal but does not dominate as in some southern European countries.

In the office, the Dutch are all business, and negotiations are typically straightforward, if not blunt. However, the Dutch often make time away from work, generally over beer or coffee, for personal chats in the many cafes. Some Dutch routinely invite foreign business visitors to their homes for supper, which is often served early in the evening by American standards.

Punctuality is extremely important. Being late equals being untrustworthy. Clothes may be a little more casual than in some other countries, though suits are still standard for formal business meetings. Everyone entering a meeting may shake hands with everyone else, and may do it again afterward.

In most respects, the Dutch are quite sophisticated about doing business internationally, and their style of doing business is comfortable for

* This number represents total exports and imports.

most Americans. The one thing the Dutch find personally irritating is pomposity; they are not known for their sense of humor, but the needles come out, however politely, whenever someone starts self-inflating.

## DUTCH AGENCIES IN THE UNITED STATES

The Netherlands Embassy, 4200 Linnean Ave., NW, Washington, DC 20008-3896
(202) 244-5300; Fax: (202) 362-3430

The Netherlands Consulate, Georgia Pacific Center, 113 Peachtree St., Suite 2500, Atlanta, GA 30303
(404) 525-4513; Fax: (404) 223-7155

The Netherlands Consulate, 6 James Ave., Suite 1001, Boston, MA 02116-3800
(617) 542-8452; Fax: (617) 542-3304

The Netherlands Consulate General, 303 East Wacker Dr., Suite 410, Chicago, IL 60601
(312) 856-0110; Fax: (312) 856-9218

The Netherlands Consulate, 7350 Young Dr., Walton Hills, Cleveland, OH 44146
(216) 232-5100; Fax: (216) 439-2760

The Netherlands Consulate, 2000 Town Center, Suite 1200, Southfield, MI 48075-1135
(313) 352-0620

The Netherlands Consulate General, 2200 Post Oak Blvd., Suite 610, Houston, TX 77056-4783
(713) 622-8000; Fax: (713) 622-3581

The Netherlands Consulate General, Central Plaza, 3460 Wilshire Blvd., Suite 509, Los Angeles, CA 90010-2270
(213) 380-3440; Fax: (213) 386-6380

The Netherlands Consulate, 2041 Coral Way, Suite 103, Miami, FL 33129-1449
(305) 858-7617; Fax: (305) 858-8474

The Netherlands Consulate, 643 Magazine St., New Orleans, LA 70130
(504) 596-2838; Fax: (504) 596-2800

The Netherlands Consulate General, 1 Rockefeller Plaza, 11th Fl., New York, NY 10020-2094
(212) 246-1429; Fax: (212) 333-3603

The Netherlands Consulate, 1 Maritime Plaza, Suite 750, San Francisco, CA 94111
(415) 981-6454; Fax: (415) 391-2493

## U.S. AGENCIES IN THE NETHERLANDS

American Chamber of Commerce, Carnegieplein 5,
The Hague 2571
(070) 365 98 08; Fax: (070) 364 69 92

U.S. Embassy, Lange-Voorhout 102, The Hague
(070) 462 49 11; Fax: (070) 361 46 88

U.S. Consulate General, Museumplein 19, Amsterdam 1071
(020) 664 81 11; Fax: (020) 675 28 56

## BANKS AND FINANCIAL INSTITUTIONS

ABN Bank, Postbox 669, Amsterdam 1000
(020) 629 91 11; Fax: (020) 629 80 62

AMRO BANK, NV, 22 Foppingadreef, Amsterdam BS 1102
(020) 628 93 93; Fax: (020) 691 16 68

Bank Mees & Hope, NV, 548 Herengracht, Amsterdam GC 1017
(020) 527 91 11; Fax: (020) 527 45 92

Credit Lyonnais Bank, NED, NV, Postbox 1045, Rotterdam BA 3000
(010) 469 59 11; Fax: (010) 414 83 91

Gelders-Utrechtse Spaarbank, 3 Stationsstraat, Wageningen
AM 6701
(08370) 971 11; Fax: (08370) 972 03

Hollandsche Bank Unie, NV, Postbox 554, Amsterdam AN 1000
(020) 629 92 22; Fax: (020) 629 20 23

NMB Postbankgroep, Postbox 1800, Amsterdam BV 1000
(020) 563 91 11; Fax: (020) 563 57 00

Rabobank Nederland, 18 Croeselaan, Utrecht CB 3521
(030) 90 91 11; Fax: (030) 90 26 72

## LAW FIRMS

Adriaanse & van der Weel, Postbox 240, Middelburg AE 4330
(01180) 353 65; Fax: (01180) 361 78

Hoegen Dijkhof & Van Brakel, 24 Wilhelminapark, Postbox
14215, NE Utrecht 3581
(030) 52 02 20; Fax: (030) 51 68 85
Services: banking, financial services, corporate, competition, EC,
international commercial contracts, mergers and acquisitions,
labor and industrial property law

Maaldrink Notarissen en Advocaten, 30 Wassenaarseweg, The Hague CJ 2596
(070) 346 96 46; Fax: (070) 356 04 90

Nauta Dutilh, Locatellikade 1, Postbox 7061, Amsterdam JB 1007
(020) 662 12 14; Fax: (020) 662 01 94
Services: EC and international law

Prinsen van der Putt, 15 Boschdijk, Postbox 666, Eindhoven AR 5600
(040) 43 34 33; Fax: (040) 43 30 33

Russell cs Advocaten, 202 Beethovenstraat, Amsterdam JZ 1077
(020) 664 91 11; Fax: (020) 662 35 94
Services: EC and international law

W. Martin Nijs, CS, BV, 146 Grotestraat, Postbox 105, Waalwijk AC 5140
(04160) 355 16; Fax: (04160) 306 73
Services: EC, Dutch and Swiss law

Zeeuwen & Van der Meeren Advocaten, 16 Merellaan, Postbox 144, Eindhoven AC 5600
(040) 45 25 45; Fax: (040) 44 58 97

## ACCOUNTING FIRMS

Ancona International Trading, 120 The Van Diemenstraat, Amsterdam CN 1013
(020) 625 25 83; Fax: (020) 625 25 83
Services: industrial and institutional investor accounting, stock control, international financial and taxation analysis, patent control, company constitution and relocation consultants

Bruijn en Ariaans Accountants, 138 de Hatertseweg, Nijmegen AS 6533
(080) 56 46 33; Fax: (080) 56 68 23
Services: industrial and institutional investor accounting, stock control, international financial and taxation analysts, patent control, company constitution and relocation consultants

Chaudron & Co., 3 Halverwege, Alphen ad Rijn NK 2402
(01720) 307 74; Fax: (01720) 343 42
Services: investor accounting, international financial and taxation analysts

Holland Trust Management, BV, 12E Hogehilweg, Amsterdam CD 1101
(020) 691 17 80; Fax: (020) 17 28
Services: industrial and institutional investor accounting, stock control, international financial and taxation analysts, patent control, company constitution and relocation consultants

Lodder Register Accountants, 7 C. van Heekstraat, Schiedam BN 3125
(010) 462 21 03; Fax: (010) 415 68 87
Services: corporate accounting

MEPI, BV, 30-10 Eekholt, Diemen XH 1112
(020) 699 81 11; Fax: (020) 600 11 76
Services: industrial and institutional investor accounting, stock control, international financial and taxation analysts, patent control, company constitution and relocation consultants

Paardekooper & Hoffman, 37a Stadionweg, Rotterdam AR 3077
(010) 436 49 44; Fax: (010) 436 04 66
Services: accounting

Schmidt & Orriens, BV, 39 Beukenhorstweg, Winterswijk DJ 7101
(05430) 181 25; Fax: (05430) 219 75
Services: accounting

## INSURANCE AGENCIES

Aegon Nederland, NV, Postbox 202, The Hague CE 2501
(070) 44 32 10; Fax: (070) 347 52 38

AMEV, NV, 10 Archimedeslaan, Utrecht BA 3584
(303) 57 91 11; Fax: (030) 52 23 94

BV Handelsmij.Rinjstroom, 1 Carnegialaan, The Hague KH 2517
(070) 352 64 75; Fax: (070) 350 67 98

Delta Lloyd Verz. Groep, NV, 4 Spaklerweg, Amsterdam BA 1096
(020) 659 49 11; Fax: (020) 693 79 68

Hudig-Langeveldt, 16 Marconistraat, Rotterdam AK 3029
(010) 448 89 11; Fax: (010) 425 34 31

Nat Ned Schadeverz Mij, NV, 15 PR Beatrixaan, The Hague AK 2595
(070) 341 80 80; Fax: (070) 347 59 62

NV Schadeverz.Mij UAP Nederland, 369 Keizersgracht, Amsterdam EJ 1016
(020) 523 71 11; Fax: (020) 627 76 32

Vezeno, NV, 83 Stationstraat, Zaandam DE 1506
(075) 51 51 51; Fax: (075) 51 54 44

## ADVERTISING AND MARKETING AGENCIES

Allick Bates, BV, Postbox 3586, Amsterdam AJ 1001
(020) 644 89 33; Fax: (020) 642 25 45

Burnett, BV, 5 Drentestraat, Amsterdam HK 1083
(020) 644 24 25; Fax: (020) 644 86 80

Delta Communications Groep, BV, 7 Takkebijster, Breda BL 4817
(076) 71 27 40; Fax: (076) 71 28 62

Douwes & Douwes, 11 Paradysweg, Zandvoort GC 2042
(02507) 190 46

Lintas Amsterdam, BV, 1641 Strawinskylaan, Amsterdam XX 1077
(020) 573 11 11; Fax: (020) 662 85 22

Publi-Air, 51a Eemnesserweg, Laren NB 1251
(02153) 824 30; Fax: (02153) 828 81

Saatchi & Saatchi Advertising, BV, 1-3 Welzijn, Amsterdam
VW 1181
(020) 647 61 11; Fax: (020) 647 56 50

Werkhoven Promotions, BV, VAN, Postbox 1141, Maarssen BC 3600
(03465) 744 00; Fax: (03465) 609 52

## TRANSLATING AND INTERPRETING SERVICES

Berlitz Language Centers, 87-89 Rokin, Amsterdam KL 1012
(020) 622 13 75; Fax: (020) 620 39 59

Goethe Institut, 470 Herengracht, Amsterdam CA 1017
(020) 623 0 21; Fax: (020) 638 46 31

Universala Esperanto Asocio, 176 Nieuwe Binnerweg, Rotterdam
BJ 3015
(010) 436 10 44; Fax: (010) 436 17 51

## TRANSPORTATION AND DISTRIBUTION COMPANIES

ACE Indep. Freight Service, 34 Olstgracht, Almere EC 1324
(03240) 307 00; Fax: (03240) 312 14

Emery Worldwide, 1 Leisteen, Hoofddorp ME 2132
(020) 654 03 21; Fax: (020) 654 03 33

Helvetica, BV, Postbox 1168, Barendrecht CA 2990
(01806) 167 77; Fax: (01806) 173 14

International Kuhlgutspedition, 20 Parmentierplein, Rotterdam
GN 3088
(010) 429 87 30; Fax: (010) 428 428 11 57

Kuhne & Nagel, NV, 35 Lloydstraat, Rotterdam EA 3024
(010) 478 99 11; Fax: (010) 476 05 15

Tromp, BV, Postbox 30032, Rotterdam EA 3024
(010) 411 11 15; Fax: (010) 433 25 07

Unipro, BV, 26 Paulus Potterstraat, Amsterdam DA 1071
(020) 675 01 76; Fax: (020) 675 34 03

## TRADE CONSULTANTS

ABB Advies en Bemiddeling, BV, 246 Rijnstraat, Amsterdam HW 1079
(020) 642 00 12; Fax: (020) 642 00 12

Coopers & Lybrand, NED, Postbox 2755, Rotterdam CT 3000
(010) 400 04 00; Fax: (010) 433 14 01

European Franchise Consultants, 11b Amersfoortsestraat, Soesterberg AD 3769
(03463) 539 74; Fax: (03463) 525 74

Imeconsult, BV, Postbox 525, Nijmegen AM 6500
(080) 22 81 00; Fax: (080) 23 30 46

Klockner Ina Nederland, BV, 4 De Horst, The Hague HA 2592
(070) 85 19 08; Fax: (070) 385 21 02

Marketresponse Amersfoort, BV, Postbox 1112, Amersfoort BC 3800
(033) 63 76 50; Fax: (033) 61 42 80

Research International Nederl, BV, 493 Karel Doormanstraat, Rotterdam GH 3012
(010) 427 67 89; Fax: (010) 433 24 82

The Research Center, 13 Noordse Bosje, Hilversum BD 1211
(035) 25 84 11; Fax: (035) 465 32

## TRADE SHOWS AND EXHIBITIONS

International Agricultural Exhibition, Rai Gebouw, BV, Europaplein, Amsterdam 1078 G2
(020) 549 12 12; Fax: (020) 46 44 69
Description: biennial (January) exhibit of agricultural machinery and farming methods

International Exhibition of Bicycles & Motorcycles, Royal Netherlands Fair, Postbox 8500, Utrecht
(030) 95 59 11; Fax: (030) 95 55 17
Description: annual (February)

Amsterdam International Boat Show, Rai Gebouw, BV, Europaplein, Amsterdam 1078 G2
(020) 549 12 12; Fax: (020) 46 44 69
Description: annual (March) exhibit of boats and equipment

International Consumer Goods Fair, Royal Netherlands Fair, Postbox 8500, Utrecht
(030) 95 59 11; Fax: (030) 95 55 17
Description: semi-annual (March/September) exhibit of consumer goods

International Furniture Fair, Royal Netherlands Fair, Postbox 8500, Utrecht
(030) 95 59 11; Fax: (030) 95 55 17
Description: annual (September) exhibit of furniture

Eurocomm, Rai Gebouw, BV, Europaplein, Amsterdam 1078 G2
(020) 549 12 12; Fax: (020) 46 44 69
Description: annual (December) exhibit of communications technology

# 23

# PORTUGAL

## GENERAL INFORMATION

Area: 35,550 square miles
Capital: Lisbon
Language: Portuguese
Population: 11 million
Currency: Escudo (Esc)
Exchange Rate (June 1993): $1/Esc 161
International Trade*: $35 billion
Telephone Country Code: 351

Portugal is a traditionally agrarian country that is turning to trade and industry to make up for declining farm production. Once self-sufficient, Portugal now imports a significant amount of its food. Textiles and clothing historically have been the major manufacturing sector, but now a number of multinationals are being drawn to Portugal because of its relatively low wages and many attractive incentives from both the EC and the Portuguese government.

Several major U.S. companies, particularly in automobiles and auto components, have established big factories in Portugal with the help of government and EC grants, loans, and tax breaks. When one U.S. company expressed concern about finding local managers to help with future expansion, the government set up a no-strings-attached management training program.

While Portugal shares some similarities with other southern EC countries, such as Spain and Greece, it has its own distinctive national character and flavor. The pace of life can be slow, sometimes too slow for Americans who want to do a deal and go on to the next place. The social niceties are often necessary, however, and are always conducted with the utmost courtesy. Casual attire is common. English is spoken widely in the business community, especially in larger corporations.

* This number represents total exports and imports.

Politically, Portugal is often seen on the wrong side of a two-tiered EC because of the inability of its economy in general and its currency in particular to keep up with its more prosperous northern neighbors. However, EC financial and technical assistance have already helped Portugal make great strides, and the prospects are bright for good long-term growth and expanded trade both in and out of the country. Large-scale modernization of the infrastructure, particularly in fields such as telecommunications, are sure to increase the demand for foreign products, while the lower production costs in Portugal will continue to help exporters find international markets.

## PORTUGUESE AGENCIES IN UNITED STATES

Embassy of Portugal, 2125 Kalorama Rd., NW, Washington, DC 20008
(202) 328-8610; Fax: (202) 462-3726

Portuguese Consulate General, 899 Boylston St., Boston, MA 02115
(617) 536-8740

Portuguese Consulate General, 1955 N. New England Ave., Chicago, IL 60365
(312) 889-7405; Fax: (312) 493-2433

Portuguese Consulate General, 3300 South Gessner St., Houston, TX 77063
(713) 953-1255

Portuguese Consulate General, 1801 Avenue of the Stars, Suite 400, Los Angeles, CA 90067
(213) 227-1491

Portuguese Consulate General, 100 N. Biscayne Blvd., Suite 1602, Miami, FL 33132
(305) 371-6333; Fax: (305) 381-6347

Portuguese Consulate General, 630 Fifth Ave., Suite 655, New York, NY 0111
(212) 246-4580; Fax: (212) 459-0190

Portuguese Consulate General, 3298 Washington St., San Francisco, CA 94115
(415) 346-3400

Portuguese Trade Commission, 590 Fifth Ave., Third Fl., New York, NY 10036
(212) 354-4610; Fax: (212) 575-4737

Portugal-U.S. Chamber of Commerce, 590 Fifth Ave., Third Fl., New York, NY 10036
(212) 354-4627; Fax: (212) 575-4737

## U.S. AGENCIES IN PORTUGAL

American Chamber of Commerce, Rua d. Estefania 155, Lisbon 1000
(01) 572 561

U.S. Embassy, Venida das Forcas Armadas, Lisbon 1600
(01) 726 6600; Fax: (01) 726 9109

## BANKS AND FINANCIAL INSTITUTIONS

Banco Portugues do Atlantico, Rua Aurea 110-116, Lisbon 1100
(01) 361 321; Telex: 42944
Services: corporate, commercial banking

Banco Totta & Acores, Avenida dos Aliados 48, Porto 4000
(02) 323 012; Telex: 25212
Services: corporate, commercial banking

Barclays Bank PLC, Avenida da Republica 50-2, Lisbon 1000
(01) 735 020; Telex: 42838
Services: corporate, commercial banking

BPI (Banco Portugues de Investimentos), Rua Tenente Valadim 284, Porto 4100
(02) 696 697; Telex: 26887 P
Services: corporate, commercial banking

Caixa Geral de Depositos, Rua 1 de Dezembro 118, Lisbon 1118
(01) 371 181; Telex: 42547
Services: corporate, commercial banking

Credito Predial Portugues, Rua do Ouro 139-2, Lisbon 1100
(01) 370 341; Telex: 12264
Services: corporate, commercial banking

Lloyds Bank, PLC, Rua Aurea 40-48, Lisbon 1100
(01) 361 211; Telex: 24370
Services: corporate, commercial banking

Manufacturers Hanover Trust, Rua Castilho 165-2, Lisbon 1000
(01) 692 200; Telex: 14740
Services: corporate, commercial banking

## LAW FIRMS

Carlos de Sousa e Brito & Associados, Rua Castilho 71, Lisbon 1200
(01) 540 407; Fax: (01) 561 705
Services: corporate, financial, tax, real estate, trademark and maritime law

Luis Brito Correia, Avenida Pedro Alvares Cabral 84-2,
Lisbon 1200
(01) 659 856; Fax: (01) 682 554

Dr. Luis Alberto Sequeira Lopes Gallego, Avenida Antonio Augusto Aguiar 165, Lisbon 1000
(01) 562 967; Fax: (01) 572 319
Services: commercial, civil, and mercantile law

Dr. Jose Osvaldo Gomes, Avenida Eng. Duarte Pacheco 28, 9th Fl., Lisbon 1000
(01) 689 146; Fax: (01) 685 338

Dr. Francisco Moncao Leao, Avenida Sidonio Pais 2-1, Lisbon 1000
(01) 540 522; Fax: (01) 555 231

Law Offices of Joao Maximiano, Rua Conselheiro Bivar 10, Faro (Algarve) 8000
(089) 803 219; Fax: (089) 21 972
Services: commercial and foreign investment law

Dr. Armando Felix Pereira, Avenida da Republica 14-8, Lisbon 1000
(01) 539 189; Fax: (01) 524 002
Services: EC, international, foreign investment, technology transfer, trademarks and copyright, insurance, tax and real estate law

Reynolds, Rankine, Lloyd & Robertson, Largo da Academia Nacional de Belas Artes 16, Lisbon 1200
(01) 346 2277; Fax: (01) 346 5079
Services: international, foreign investment and conveyancing law

## ACCOUNTING FIRMS

Arthur Andersen & Company, Avenida Ant. Augusto Aguiar 122-5, Lisbon 1000
(01) 571 200; Telex: 16904

Arthur Young & Company, Rua Marques de Subterra 10, Lisbon 1000
(01) 655 451; Telex: 16694

Coopers & Lybrand, Avenida Ant. Jose de Almeida 7-3, Lisbon 1000
(01) 730 023; Telex: 13664

Deloitte Haskins & Sells, Rua Silva Carvalho 234-4, Lisbon 1200
(01) 685 626; Telex: 16519

Ernst & Whinney, Avenida Ant. Augusto Aguiar 19-4, Lisbon 1000
(01) 524 849; Telex: 18887

KMG Thomson McLintock & Company, Rua Luciano Cordeiro 113-6, Lisbon 1100
(01) 543 585; Telex: 14237

Peat Marwick Mitchell & Company, Avenida Brasil 1-8, Lisbon 1700
(01) 733 498; Telex: 12435

Price Waterhouse, Rua Goncalo Cristovao 217/13, Porto 4000
(02) 312 614; Telex: 26687

## INSURANCE AGENCIES

Associacao Portuguesa de Seguradores, Avenida Jose Malhoa 1674-5, Lisbon 1000
(01) 726 8123; Telex: 43196

Commercial Union Assurance Co., Avenida Liberdade 38-4, Lisbon 1200
(01) 324 351; Telex: 18325

Eagle Star Insurance Co., Ltd., Avenida 5 de Outubro 70-8, Lisbon 1000
(01) 779 131; Telex: 42678

Fidelidade-Grupo Segurador, Largo do Corpo Santo 13, Lisbon 1200
(01) 360 321; Telex: 16483

Pearl de Portugal Companhia de Seguros, Rua Braancamp 88-3, Lisbon 1200
(01) 575 951; Telex: 63101

Rawes (Peritagens), Rua Julio Dinis 891-2, Porto 4000
(02) 667 116; Telex: 22120

Sedgwick Forbes (Portugal) Resseguros e Consultores de Seguros, Trav. do Corpo Santo 10-2, Lisbon 1200
(01) 363 191; Telex: 12216

Tranquilidade Seguros, Avenida da Liberdade 242, Lisbon 1200
(01) 538 866; Telex: 12164

## ADVERTISING AND MARKETING AGENCIES

Abrinicio, Publicidade e Marketing, LDA, Rua Castilho 201-1, Lisbon Codex 1093
(01) 688 002, Telex: 15389

Doyle Dane Bernbach & Guerreiro Publicidada, SARL, Rua D. Carlos Mascarenhas 75, Lisbon 1000
(01) 693 949

J. Walter Thompson Publicidade, Avenida Eng. Duarte Pacheco, Edificio Amoreiras, Torre 2, 15, Lisbon 1000
(01) 693 136; Telex: 42765 JWTLIS P

Phillip Ricardo, Casa S. Francisco, Rua das Mimosas, Cascais Birre 2750
(01) 285 1395; Telex: 12787

Sistema Tecnica de Gestao Publicit, SARL, Rua Marques da Fronteira 133-6, Lisbon 1000
(01) 652 538; Telex: 18885

Team—T. Protasio, LDA, Avenida Duque d'Avila 26-1-3, Lisbon Codex 1097
(01) 557 161; Telex: 13404

## TRANSLATING AND INTERPRETING SERVICES

Brithis Council, Rua Luis Fernandes 3, Lisbon Codex 1294
(01) 369 208; Telex: 42544

Cambridge School, Avenida Guerra Junqueri 8-1, Lisbon 1000
Telex: 12787

Escola Americana de Portugal, Camilo Blanco, Lisbon
(01) 418 7474

Eurocenter-Instituto de Linguas Cruz & Stuttaford, LDA, Avenida dos Bons Amigos 4-1, Cacem 2735
(01) 924 5549

## TRANSPORTATION AND DISTRIBUTION COMPANIES

Amorim—Servico Internacional de Contentores, LDA, Rua de Santa Catarina 882/886-1, Porto 4000
(02) 319 311; Telex: 23197

Broemme Portugal Transportes Internacionais, LDA, Rua Diogo Couto 1-6 e 9, Lisbon 1100
(01) 825 081; Telex: 12337

Cargoplan, LDA, Avenida dos EUA 8, Lisbon 1700
(01) 736 066; Telex: 64144

Eurofrete—Transportes Internacionais, LDA, Rua Diogo do Cuoto 1-7, Lisbon 1100
(01) 675 203; Telex: 13741

James Rawes & Co., Ltd., Rua Bernardino Costa 47, Lisbon 1200
(01) 370 231; Telex: 12341

Loisk Pires—Transportes Internacional, LDA, Rua Mousinho de Albuquerque 690, Matosinhos 4450
(01) 938 001; Telex: 26613

Transmaso—Transportes Internacional, LDA, Rua Infante D. Henrique 42-2, Porto 4000
(02) 312 667; Telex: 26253

Unimar—Soc. Maritima Commercial, SARL, Avenida 24 de Julho 3-1, Lisbon 1200
(02) 669 122; Telex: 22464

## TRADE CONSULTANTS

CGI Wolfram, Avenida Cumb. B. Pinheiro 103-2, Lisbon 1000
(01) 726 2566; Telex: 13341

CPI—Comercio e Projectos Industriais, Avenida da Boavista 970-2, Porto 4100
(02) 690 987; Telex: 26953

Ernst & Whinney & CIA, LDA, Rua Julio Dinis 891-3, Porto 4000
(02) 62 015; Telex: 23405

Eugenio Branco, LDA, Pc. Francisco Sa Carneiro 293-1, Porto 4200
(02) 490 276; Telex: 23458

Grant Thonton Kennard, Avenida Miquel Bombarda 21-3, Lisbon 1000
(01) 544 202; Telex: 12787

Meireles & Carneiro, LDA, Rua Nova de S. Crispim 356, Porto 4000
(02) 566 351; Telex: 23585

PA Consultores de Gestao e Organizacao, LDA, Rua Castilho 211-5, Lisbon 1000
(01) 658 420; Telex: 13137

Roderick Anthony Reynolds, Avenida Ant. Augusto de Aguiar 90-1, Lisbon 1000
(01) 549 205; Telex: 14199 EXINV P

## TRADE SHOWS AND EXHIBITIONS

International Trade Fair, Feira International de Lisboa, Praca das Industrias, Lisbon Codex 1399
(01) 362 0132; Fax: (01) 363 9048
Description: annual (May) exhibit of goods, services and innovations

International Furniture & Lighting Exhibit, Feira International de Lisboa, Praca das Industrias, Lisbon Codex 1399
Fax: (01) 363 9048
Description: annual (October) exhibit of furniture and lighting industries

# 24

# SPAIN

## GENERAL INFORMATION

Area: 194,897 square miles
Capital: Madrid
Languages: Spanish, Catalan
Population: 40 million
Currency: Peseta (Pta)
Exchange Rate (June 1993): $1/Pta 131
International Trade*: $150 billion
Telephone Country Code: 34

Economically, Spain has been one of the EC's most dramatic success stories. Under the Franco regime, Spain was politically and economically isolated. After Franco died in 1975, however, his Fascist dictatorship was replaced by democracy under a constitutional monarchy much like Britain's.

Since then, economic growth has been rapid and in some years spectacular, especially in the four years after Spain joined the EC in 1986. The worldwide recession slowed things, but Spain still rode the crest of 1992—the Year of the Fiesta, with the Columbus festivities, the Olympics, and the World Expo at Seville—on a flurry of infrastructure and other capital improvements.

As a result of the long years of the Franco oppression, Spain's business community has a sharp generational divide. On one hand are the parents and grandparents who built up safe, conservative family businesses. Courtesy to the point of old-fashioned chivalry was and is perhaps the most prominent feature of that part of Spain's business culture.

The new generation, the sons and daughters, have been educated in the United States or Britain, and are more attuned to doing business with an eye on profits than on the personal relationships so important to the older generation. Even the younger Spaniards, however, are still among the most gracious and polite Europeans, and many of them

* This number represents total exports and imports.

share the older generation's belief that being seen as a nice person with good character is more important than besting someone in a business deal. The Spanish are sometimes accused of being formally standoffish to the point of arrogance, but they must often like someone and feel that they are liked in return before they are comfortable doing business. Many Spaniards take any criticism personally, and some see words of personal praise as demeaning since it should be assumed they are doing a good job and making proper decisions.

Casual clothing is more acceptable in Spain than most other European countries, though formal suits are still expected for meetings, particularly in the booming financial services industry. Younger Spaniards take great pains to insist that the old days of the "*manana*" attitude are gone, but there is still ample evidence of long coffee breaks, lunch breaks, and, yes, the afternoon siesta.

## SPANISH AGENCIES IN THE UNITED STATES

Embassy of Spain, 2700 15th St. NW, Washington, DC 20009
(202) 265-0190; Fax: (202) 328-3212

Spanish Consulate General, 545 Boylston St., Suite 803, Boston, MA 02116
(617) 536-2506

Spanish Consulate General, 180 North Michigan Ave., Rm. 1500, Chicago, IL 60601
(312) 782-4588

Spanish Consulate General, 2411 Fountain View, Suite 130, Houston, TX 77057
(713) 783-6200

Spanish Consulate General, 6300 Wilshire Blvd., Suite 1530, Los Angeles, CA 90084
(213) 658-6050; Fax: (213) 628-1503

Spanish Consulate General, 151 Sevilla Ave., Coral Cables, Miami, FL 33134
(305) 446-5511; Fax: (305) 446-2602

Spanish Consulate General, 2101 World Trade Center, 2 Canal St., New Orleans, LA 70130
(504) 525-4951

Spanish Consulate General, 150 East 58th St., Fl. 16, New York, NY 10155
(212) 355-4080; Fax: (212) 644-3751

Spanish Consulate General, 2080 Jefferson St., San Francisco, CA 94123
(415) 922-2995; Fax: (415) 931-9706

Spanish Investment Office, 405 Lexington Ave., 44th Fl., New York, NY 10174
(212) 661-4959

Spain-USA Chamber of Commerce, 350 Fifth Ave., Suite 3514, New York, NY 10118
(212) 967-2170; Fax: (212) 564-1415

## U.S. AGENCIES IN SPAIN

American Chamber of Commerce, Avenida Diagonal 477, Barcelona 08036
(3) 321 8195; Fax: (3) 321 8197

U.S. Embassy, Serrano 75, Madrid 28006
(1) 577 4400; Fax: (1) 577 5735

U.S. Consulate General, Via Layentana 33, Barcelona 08003
(3) 319 3550; Fax: (3) 319 5621

U.S. Consulate General, Avenida Lehenda Kari Agirre 11-3, Bilbao 48014
(4) 475 8300; Fax: (4) 476 1240

## BANKS AND FINANCIAL INSTITUTIONS

Banco Bilbao Vizcaya, Plaza San Nicolas 4, Bilbao 48005
(4) 487 6000; Fax: (4) 423 2132
Services: commercial, corporate banking

Banco Commercial Español, Gran Via 5, Madrid 28013
(1) 521 1100
Services: industrial banking

Banco de Europa, Rosellon, Barcelona 08008
(3) 215 2312; Fax: (3) 215 9727
Services: industrial banking

Banco de Madrid, Carrera de San Jeronimo 13-15, Madrid 28006
(1) 429 2443
Services: commercial, corporate banking

Banco de Victoria, Dato, Victoria-Gasteiz 01001
(5) 233 900
Services: commercial, industrial and international banking

Banco Exterior de España, Carrera de San Jeronimo 36, Madrid 28014
(1) 429 4477; Fax: (1) 429 8342
Services: commercial, corporate banking

Banco Internacional de Comercio, Jose Ortega y Gasset 56, Madrid 28006
(1) 429 2693
Services: industrial banking

Citibank, NA, Jose Ortega y Gasset 29, Madrid 28006
(1) 404 3015
Services: commercial, corporate banking

## LAW FIRMS

Bufete Antonio de Fortuny, Francisco Gervas 15, Madrid 28020
(1) 270 7472; Fax: (1) 207 7331
Services: international investment, commercial, corporate, tax, banking and finance law

Bufete Cuatrecasas, Balmes 76, Barcelona 08007
(3) 215 4478; Fax: (3) 216 0347
Services: tax, corporate, commercial, banking, financial, bankruptcy, EC and international law

Bufete F. Gimenez Torres, Jose Abascal 47, Madrid 28003
(1) 441 5144; Fax: (1) 442 1051
Services: civil, corporate, and commercial law

J. & B. Cremades & Associados, Goya 18, Madrid 28001
(1) 431 8354; Fax: (1) 576 9794
Services: commercial, corporate, international investment, licensing, insurance, banking, finance, oil and gas, real estate, patent, arbitration and EC law

Despacho Melchor de las Heras, Jose Abascal 58, Madrid 28003
(1) 442 1077; Fax: (1) 442 6045
Services: international investment, banking, financial, corporate, international transactions, EC, tax, licensing and labor law

J.N. Estudio Juridico & Financiero, Rosellon 257, Barcelona 08008
(3) 237 8401; Fax: (3) 237 2407
Services: corporate, international investment, banking, financial, commercial, licensing, tax and real estate law

Fabregat & Bermejo, Paseo de la Castellana 8, Madrid 28046
(1) 521 7986; Fax: (1) 276 2332
Services: banking, financial, international investment, contracting, tax, mergers and acquisitions, licensing, real estate, patent, trademark and copyright law

Gabinete Juridico Julian Gil, Plaza Independencia 5, Madrid 28001
(1) 575 2503; Fax: (1) 576 4888
Services: international investment, civil, commercial, fiscal, labor and foreign trade law

Santiago Hernandez Izal, Calle del Rossello 79, Barcelona 08029
(3) 430 8529; Fax: (3) 419 5135
Services: maritime, transport, commercial and trade law

Ventura Garces, Freixa 26, Barcelona 08021
(3) 201 9444; Fax: (3) 209 8391
Services: commercial, corporate, fiscal, international investment, real estate, licensing, banking, finance and EC law

## ACCOUNTING FIRMS

Asesoria Mercantil, Plaza de España 5, Aviles 33400
(85) 549 929
Services: industrial and institutional accounting, international financial and tax system consultants, research and Trade Register work

Coopers & Lybrand, SA, Rasario Pino 14-16, Madrid 28020
(1) 572 0233; Fax: (1) 570 0042
Services: industrial and institutional accounting, international financial and tax system consultants, research and Trade Register work, social security legislation and wage and salary calculations, actuarial services

Deloitte & Touche, Torre Picasso Planta 38, Plaza de Pablo Ruiz Picasso, Madrid 28020
(1) 555 0252; Fax: (1) 556 7430
Services: industrial and institutional accounting, international financial and tax system consultants, company constitution analysts

Ernst & Young, Alberto Alcocer 24, Madrid 28036
(1) 250 2800; Fax: (1) 457 8917
Services: industrial and institutional accounting, international financial and tax system consultants, research and Trade Register work

Fernandez Martinez, Mayor 182, Molina de Segura 30500
(68) 610 186; Fax: (68) 615 951
Services: industrial and institutional accounting, international financial and tax system consultants, stock control, patents, social security, wages and salaries calculations

International Venture Consultants (IVC), Felix Boix 18-1, Madrid 28036
(1) 250 6905; Fax: (1) 457 5372
Services: industrial and institutional accounting, international social security, wages and salaries calculations

KPMG Peat Marwick, Po. de la Castellana 95, Torre Europa, Madrid 28046
(1) 555 5363; Fax: (1) 555 0132
Services: accountancy management

Soprecs, SA, Alda Mazarredo 25, Bilbao 48009
(4) 423 9636; Fax: (4) 423 8438
Services: industrial and institutional accounting, stock control tax and company constitution consultants, patents, social security, wages and salaries calculations

## INSURANCE AGENCIES

AGF Seguros, SA, Albacete 5, Madrid 28027
(1) 403 8800; Fax: (1) 403 0645
Services: general insolvency, export credits, agricultural, surety, employments risks, financial losses insurance

Alianza-Mutua Seguros & Reaseguros, SA, Barquillo 23, Madrid 28004
(1) 531 5200; Fax: (1) 531 5944
Services: general insolvency, export credits, agricultural, surety, employment risks, financial losses insurance

CAP Internacional, SA, Roger der Flor 16, Barcelona 08018
(3) 309 2412; Fax: (3) 309 3286
Services: general insolvency, export credits, agricultural, surety, employment risks, financial losses insurance

El Hercules Hispano, SA, de Seguros, Alcata 17, Madrid 28014
(1) 522 9030; Fax: (1) 521 8559
Services: general insolvency, export credits, agricultural, surety, employment risks, financial losses insurance

La Union & El Fenix, SA, Po. de la Castellana 33, Madrid 28046
(1) 319 8550; Fax: (1) 319 5260
Services: general insolvency, export credits, agricultural, surety, employment risks, financial losses insurance

Metropolis, SA, Alcala 39, Madrid 28014
(1) 532 4896; Fax: (1) 521 1491
Services: financial losses and general insurance

Plus Ultra, Plaza de las Cortes 8, Madrid 28014
(1) 589 9292; Fax: (1) 429 8921
Services: general insolvency, export credits, agricultural, surety, employment risks, financial losses insurance

Winterthru, Plaza Francesca Macia 10, Barcelona 08036
(3) 321 7800; Fax: (3) 239 1813
Services: general insolvency, export credits, agricultural, surety, employment risks, financial losses insurance

## TRANSPORTATION AND DISTRIBUTION COMPANIES

Danzas, SA, Berlin 11-17, Barcelona 08014
(3) 490 0000; Fax: (3) 490 5254
Services: international shipping and forwarding agents, customs clearance, distribution

DHM Express, Oviedo 1, 4C, San Fernando de Henaves 28830
(1) 673 2768; Fax: (1) 673 2768
Services: international shipping and forwarding agents, customs clearance, freight brokers, express transport

Fast Shipping, SA, Profesor Waksmann 4, Madrid 28046
(1) 458 2062; Fax: (1) 457 9971
Services: international shipping and forwarding agents, customs clearance, freight brokers, express transport

Lep International, Avda Francesc Cambo 21, Barcelona 08003
(3) 315 2363; Fax: (3) 315 4550
Services: international shipping and forwarding agents, customs clearance, freight brokers, express transport

Space Cargo Courier, Plaza Ciudad de Salta 2, Madrid 28043
(1) 416 9761; Fax: (1) 416 7498
Services: international shipping and forwarding agents, customs clearance, freight brokers, express transport

TACISA (Tecnicos Asesores Comercio Internacional, SA), Avda Senda Galiana S/N, Coslada 28042
(1) 673 8212; Fax: (1) 673 2914
Services: international shipping and forwarding agents, customs clearance, freight brokers, express transport

Tisamart Norte, SA, Aldapeta 2, 1B, Irun 20300
(43) 627 876; Fax: (43) 627 939
Services: international shipping and forwarding agents, customs clearance, freight brokers, express transport

Tradalco, SA, Edificio Belasco, 66-70, Irun 20300
(43) 629 766; Fax: (43) 629 355
Services: international shipping and forwarding agents, customs clearance, freight brokers, express transport

## TRANSLATING AND INTERPRETING SERVICES

Alpha, SA (Editorial), Via Layetana 30, Barcelona 08003
(3) 310 0244
Services: translating

CEUROSCOI (Cia Europeade Servicios al Comercio Internacional), Menendez Pelayo 2, Valladolid 47001
(83) 357 735; Fax: (83) 357 735
Services: translating and interpreting

Ercisa, Rodriquez Arias 23, Bilbao 48011
(4) 443 6282; Fax: (4) 416 9910
Services: translating and interpreting

Ink España, San Bernardo 97-99, Madrid 28015
(1) 593 0207; Fax: (1) 445 5612
Services: translating and interpreting

OEC (Organizacion de Exposiciones & Congresos, SA), Plaza Encarnacion 2, Madrid 28013
(1) 247 7042; Fax: (1) 542 7549
Services: translating and interpreting

Radar, Calvo Sotelo 3, Orense 32005
(88) 222 299
Services: translating

Sonido Electro & Comunicacione, Africa 1-3, Zaragoza 50080
(76) 374 566; Fax: (76) 373 775
Services: interpreting

Trades Servicios, SA, Plaza San Juan de la Cruz 7, Madrid 28003
(1) 535 6922; Fax: (1) 553 6922
Services: translating

## TRADE CONSULTANTS

ABZ, SA, Gran de Gracia, Barcelona 08012
(3) 415 1211; Fax: (3) 238 1602
Services: trade consultants, management consultants

Andersen Consulting, Plaza Pablo Ruiz Picasso, Torre Picasso, Madrid 28020
(1) 571 8187; Fax: (1) 571 9147
Services: trade and tariff advisors

Coopers & Lybrand, SA, Rosario Pino 14-16, Madrid 28020
(1) 572 0233; Fax: (1) 556 7430
Services: trade consultants and export advisory service, operational research and analysis

Deloitte & Touche, SA, Plaza Pablo Ruiz Picasso, Torre Picasso, plta 38, Madrid 28020
(1) 555 0252; Fax: (1) 556 7430
Services: trade consultants, management organization

Ernst & Young, Alberto Alcocer 24, Madrid 28036
(1) 250 2800; Fax: (1) 457 8917
Services: trade consultants, financing services, management organization

ICR Consultores, SA, Gran Via 17, Bilbao 48001
(4) 416 7055; Fax: (4) 416 5415
Services: trade consultants, financing services, management organization

Roland Berger, SA, Po. de la Castellana 140, Madrid 28046
(1) 564 7361; Fax: (1) 564 7275
Services: trade consultants, financing services, management organization

Tecplanhosa, Andres Mellado 29, Madrid 28015
(1) 544 6318
Services: trade consultants, financing services, management organization

Tesei, Alfonso Gomez 42, Madrid 28037
(1) 327 2532; Fax: (1) 327 2061
Services: trade consultants, financing services, management organization

Valores Integrad 2000, Avenida J. Tarradellas 130, Barcelona 08029
(3) 410 9798; Fax: (3) 310 5463
Services: trade consultants, financing services, management organization

## TRADE SHOWS AND EXHIBITIONS

Valencia International Textiles Home Decoration Exhibition, Avda de las Ferias BX476, Valencia
(6) 386 1100; Fax: (6) 363 6111
Description: annual (January) exhibit of home textiles, decorations, and accessories

Valencia International Toy Fair, Avda de las Ferias BX476, Valencia
(6) 386 1100; Fax: (6) 363 6111
Description: annual (February) exhibit of toys

Madrid International Security Safety & Fire Exhibit, Ifema-Ferial de Madrid, Avda de Portugal S/N, Madrid
(1) 479 4468; Fax: (1) 470 2703
Description: biennial (March) exhibit of security and safety equipment

International Exhibition of Automobile Components and Maintenance Equipment (Expomovil), Feria de Barcelona, Avenida Reinaa Ma. Cristina S/N, Barcelona
(3) 423 3101; Fax: (3) 423 8651
Description: biennial (April) exhibit of automotive spare parts, components, workshop tooling, garage equipment

Madrid International Municipal Services & Equipment Exhibition, Ifema-Ferial de Madrid, Avda de Portugal S/N, Madrid
(1) 722 5000; Fax: (1) 722 5791
Description: biennial (June) exhibit of drinking water supply, sheet lighting, urban engineering and construction

Spain International Machine Tool Exhibition, Apartado 468, Plaza de Basterrechea, Bilbao
Description: biennial (October) exhibit of machine tools

Bilbao International Environmental Protection Fair (PROMA), Apartado 468, Plaza de Basterrechea, Bilbao
Description: biennial (November) exhibit of environmental protection technology

Valencia International Woodworking Industry Hardware Carpentry Products, Avda de las Ferias BX476, Valencia
(6) 386 1100; Fax: (6) 363 6111
Description: biennial (November) exhibit of woodworking and carpentry industry

# 25

# UNITED KINGDOM

## GENERAL INFORMATION

Area: 94,247 square miles
Capital: London
Language: English
Population: 57 million
Currency: Pound Sterling (£)
Exchange Rate (June 1993): £1/US$ $1.50
International Trade*: $425 billion
Telephone Country Code: 44

In any given year, about half of the investment from the United States into the EC goes into the United Kingdom. In terms of geography, language, history, and business culture, Britain is closer to America than any of its friendly rivals in the EC.

Too many Americans, however, make the mistake of assuming overfamiliarity with Britain and Britons. It is still a foreign country, where things are often done differently. And it is a country where, for some reason—perhaps because of American ideals about British refinement and civility—many U.S. businesspeople find themselves making bad deals that they would never dream of making back home.

In the strictest sense, Great Britain refers only to England, Scotland, and Wales. The UK also includes the province of Northern Ireland, which is ruled by Britain. Don't make the mistake of confusing the separate countries and offending Scottish or Welsh national pride, especially by referring to them as English.

From blue or gray suits to fairly quick use of first names, the British style of doing business is outwardly quite comfortable for Americans. But the British are still relatively reserved and may be taken aback by American friendliness. Many Britons—calling them "Brits" is the same as them calling us "Yanks"—seem ill at ease about introducing themselves to strangers. They also often deflect questions that may seem

* This number represents total exports and imports.

innocent, but they regard as too personal; asking people about the schools they attended, for example, may be seen as prying into their social class.

Most business entertaining is done in restaurants, though the long liquid lunches traditional in parts of the City, as London's financial district is known, have become somewhat less popular in recent years. Some Britons have even adopted, begrudgingly, the American habit of the business breakfast, though so-called "power" teas are often afternoon meetings among Americans in London that include genuine English tea, English finger sandwiches, and English sweets but no actual Englishmen.

Many Britons in business regard Americans as cultural cousins, and show less resentment at U.S. commercial colonization than, say, the French. Americans are widely admired for their can-do business enthusiasm, and their positive attitude. Britons admit that in many situations where they might say something cannot be done because it has never been done that way before, Americans are more likely to go ahead with the changes and vow to make them work.

## BRITISH AGENCIES IN THE UNITED STATES

British Embassy, 3100 Massachusetts Ave., NW, Washington, DC 20008
(202) 462-1340; Fax: (202) 898-4255

British Consulate General, Marquis I Tower, Suite 2700, 245 Peachtree Center Ave., Atlanta, GA 30303
(404) 524-5856; Fax: (404) 524-3153

British Consulate General, Federal Reserve Plaza, 25th Fl., 600 Atlantic Ave., Boston, MA 02210
(617) 248-9555; Fax: (617) 248-9578

British Consulate General, 33 North Dearborn St., Chicago, IL 60602
(312) 346-1810; Fax: (312) 346-7021

British Consulate, 55 Public Square, Suite 1650, Cleveland, OH 44113-1963
(216) 621-7674; Fax: (216) 621-2615

British Consulate, 813 Stemmons Tower, 2730 Stemmons Freeway, Dallas, TX 75207
(214) 637-3600; Fax: (214) 634-9408

British Consulate General, Milam Bldg., Suite 2260, 1100 Milam, Houston, TX 77002-5506
(713) 659-6275; Fax: (713) 659-7094

British Consulate General, 3701 Wilshire Blvd., Suite 312, Los Angeles, CA 90010
(213) 385-7381; Fax: (213) 381-5450

British Consulate, Brickell Bay Office Tower, Suite 2110, 1001 South Bayshore Dr., Miami, FL 33131
(305) 374-1522; Fax: (305) 374-8196

British Consulate General, 845 Third Ave., New York, NY 10022
(212) 745-0200; Fax: (212) 735-3062

British Consulate General, 1 Sansome St., Suite 850, San Francisco, CA 94104
(415) 981-3030; Fax: (415) 434-2018

British Consulate, 820 First Interstate Center, 999 Third Ave., Seattle, WA 98104
(206) 622-9255; Fax: (206) 622-4728

British Trade & Investment Office, 845 Third Ave., New York, NY 10022
(212) 745-0495; Fax: (212) 745-0456

## U.S. AGENCIES IN THE UNITED KINGDOM

American Chamber of Commerce, 75 Brook St., London W1Y 2EB
(071) 493-0381; Fax: (071) 493-2394

U.S. Embassy, Grosvenor Square, London W1AE
(071) 499-9000; Fax: (071) 409-1637

U.S. Consulate General, Queens House, 14 Queens St., Belfast NI BT1 6EQ
(0232) 328-239

U.S. Consulate General, 3 Regent Terrace, Edinburgh, Scotland EH7 5BW
(031) 556-8315

## BANKS AND FINANCIAL INSTITUTIONS

Bank of Scotland, The Mound, Edinburgh EH1 1YZ
(031) 442-7777; Fax: (031) 243 5437
Services: domestic, merchant, corporate finance

Bank of Tokyo International, Ltd., 20/24 Moorgate, London EC2R 6DH
(071) 628-3000; Fax: (071) 628-8464
Services: merchant

Barclays Banks, 54 Lombard St., London EC3P 3AH
(071) 626-1567; Fax: (071) 929-0394
Services: financial

Guinness Mahon & Co., Ltd., 32 St. Mary at Hill, London EC3P 3AJ
(071) 623-9333; Fax: (071) 283-4811
Services: investment, corporate finance

IBJ International, Ltd., Bucklersbury House, 3 Queen Victoria St., London EC4N 8HR
(071) 236-1090; Fax: (071) 236-0484
Services: investment advisory services, syndicated loan management, securities

Lloyds Bank, PLC, 71 Lombard St., London EC3P 3BS
(071) 626-1500; Fax: (071) 626-6041
Services: merchant, investment, domestic and international banking

Merrill Lynch Europe, Ltd., Ropemaker Place, 25 Ropemaker St., London EC2Y 9LY
(071) 628-1000
Services: merchant, investment, industrial, finance

Midland Montagu, 10 Lower Thames St., London EC3R 6AE
(071) 260-9933; Fax: (071) 488-1630
Services: merchant, investment, finance

N.M. Rothschild & Sons, Ltd., 3 York Street, Manchester M2 2AW
(061) 833-0888; Fax: (061) 833-0293
Services: finance

Sumitomo Trust & Banking Co., Ltd., 155 Bishopgate, London EC2M 3XU
(071) 945-7000; Fax: (071) 945-7177
Services: merchant, investment, industrial, finance

## LAW FIRMS

Allen & Overy, 9 Cheapside, London EC2V 6AD
(071) 248-9898; Fax: (071) 236-2192
Services: international, commercial and corporate law

Alexanders, 203 Temple Chambers, Temple Ave., London EC4Y 0EN
(071) 353-6221; Fax: (071) 583-0662
Services: taxation, trust, conveyancing, corporate and commercial law

Barlow Lyde & Gilbert, Beaufort House, 15 St. Botolph St., London EC3A 7NJ
(071) 247-2277; Fax: (071) 782-8500
Services: corporate, commercial, international finance, banking, tax, property, aviation, aerospace, marine and industrial relations law

Bermans, Pioneer Bldgs., 65/67 Dale St., Liverpool L2 2NS
(051) 227-3351; Fax: (051) 236-2107
Services: banking, real estate, bankruptcy, liquidations and international transactions, commercial law

Clyde & Co., 51 Eastcheap, London EC3M 1JP
(071) 623-1244; Fax: (071) 623-5427
Services: international trade, commercial, corporate, shipping and marine law

Gamlens, 3/4 Stone Bldgs., Lincoln's Inn, London WC2A 3XS
(071) 831-7345; Fax: (071) 430-2566
Services: English, Italian and private international law

Reynolds Porter Chamberlain, Chichester House, 278/282 High Holborn, London WC1V 7HA
(071) 242-2877; Fax: (071) 242-1431
Services: corporate, commercial, property, indemnity litigation, construction, employment and intellectual property law

Russell Jones & Walker, Swinton House, 324 Gray's Inn Rd., London WC1X 8DH
(071) 837-2808; Fax: (071) 837-2941
Services: conveyancing, criminal, commercial litigation, corporate, industrial and regulatory law

Saunders Sobell Leigh & Dobin, 20 Red Lion St., London WC1R 4AE
(071) 242-2525; Fax: (071) 405-4202
Services: corporate, commercial, international trading distribution, licensing, franchising, new and joint ventures, tax, corporate restructuring, banking, financial services, UK and EC competition law

Silverman Sherliker, New City House, 71 Rivington St., London EC2A 3AY
(071) 739-3495; Fax: (071) 739-4309
Services: commercial, corporate, international, taxation, franchising, copyright, trademarks, EC, litigation, debt collection and property law

Bigger & Strahan, 89 Royal Ave., Belfast BT1 1 EX, Northern Ireland
(0232) 325-229; Fax: (0232) 244-086
Services: commercial, debt recovery, conveyancing law

## ACCOUNTING FIRMS

BDO Binder Hamlyn, Scottish Provident House, 52 Brown St., Manchester M2 2AU
(061) 831-7121; Fax: (061) 833-0669
Services: accounting services, management consultants

Cooper-Parry, Watson, Sowter, & Co. (CPWS), 26 The Ropewalk, Nottingham, NG1 5DW
(0602) 419-046; Fax: (0602) 483-813

Services: auditing, accounting, personal and corporate tax, corporate finance, management buyouts, business development, planning, computer consultancy, insolvency

Coopers & Lybrand Deloitte, Plumtree Court, London EC4A 4HT
(071) 583-5000; Fax: (071) 822-4652
Services: auditing, accounting, personal and corporate tax, corporate finance, insolvency, executive recruitment

Frane & Co., 29 Waterloo St., Glasgow G2 4BZ
(041) 226-3838; Fax: (041) 221-1397
Services: auditing, accounting, personal and corporate tax, corporate finance, insolvency, executive recruitment

Arthur D. Little, Ltd., Berkeley Square House, Berkeley Square, London W1X 6EY
(071) 409-2277; Fax: (071) 491-8983
Services: international management consultants, accounting services

Peat Marwick McLintock, Stokes House, 17 College Square East, Belfast BT1 6HD
(0232) 243-377; Fax: (0232) 326-970
Services: auditing, accounting, corporate finance, tax

Spicer & Oppenheim, Friary Court, 65 Crutched Friars, London EC3N 2NP
(071) 480-7766; Fax: (071) 480-6958
Services: auditing, accounting, corporate finance, tax

Stoy Hayward, 8 Baker St., London W1M 1DA
(071) 486-5888; Fax: (071) 487-3686
Services: auditing, accounting, business advisers, management consultants

Touche Ross & Co., Hill House, 1 Little New St., London EC4A 3TR
(071) 936-3000; Fax: (071) 538-8517
Services: auditing, accounting, corporate finance, tax

Harold Whitehead & Partners, Ltd., 27 Harcourt House, 19 Cavendish Square, London W1M 9AB
(071) 499-5342; Fax: (071) 629-1726
Services: auditing, accounting, management consultants

## INSURANCE AGENCIES

Alexander Stenhouse, Ltd., P.O. Box 214, 10 Devonshire Square, London EC2M 4LE
(071) 621-9990; Fax: (071) 621-9950
Services: international insurance brokers

C.T. Bowring & Co. (Insurance), Ltd., The Bowring Bldg., Tower Place, London EC3P 3BE
(071) 357-1000; Fax: (071) 929-2705
Services: international insurance, reinsurance brokers

Crusader Insurance, PLC (CIGNA), Cockshot Hill, Reigate RH2 8BL
(0737) 242-424; Fax: (0737) 223-111
Services: business insurance

Hogg Group, PLC, Lloyds Chambers, 1 Portsoken St., London E1 8DF
(071) 480-4000; Fax: (071) 480-4007
Services: international insurance, reinsurance brokers, corporate and personal financial planning services

London & Edinburgh Insurance Group, Ltd., The Warren, Worthing BN14 9QD
(0903) 820-8820
Services: international insurance, reinsurance brokers

Lloyd's of London, One Lime St., London EC3M 7HA
(071) 327-6950; Fax: (071) 327-6975
Services: international insurance

Sedgwick Group, PLC, Sedgwick House, The Sedgwick Center, London E1 8DX
(071) 377-3456; Fax: (071) 377-3199
Services: international insurance, reinsurance brokers

The Wilson Organisation, Ltd., Wilson House, 1–3 Waverly St., Nottingham, NG7 4HG
(0602) 420-111; Fax: (0602) 420-459
Services: international insurance, cargo, capital redemption, commercial and contractors, employers protection

Trade Indemnity, PLC, Trade Indemnity House, 12-34 Gt Eastern St., London EC2A 3AX
(071) 739-4311; Fax: (071) 729-7682
Services: private credit insurer

Willis Faber & Dumas, Ltd., Ten Trinity Square, London EC3P 3AX
(071) 488-8111; Fax: (071) 488-8228
Services: international insurance, cargo, capital redemption, commercial and contractors, employers protection

## ADVERTISING AND MARKETING AGENCIES

Baillie Marshall, Ltd., 8 Randolff Place, Edinburgh EH3 7TE
(031) 226-3794; Fax: (031) 225-2332
Services: advertising, marketing, public relations, market research

Hill & Knowlton (UK), Ltd., 5/11 Theobalds Rd., London WC1X 8SH
(071) 413-3000; Fax: (071) 413-4111
Services: public relations, marketing, corporate communications, financial and investor relations, parliamentary affairs

Lintas International, Ltd., 84 Eccleston Square, London SW1 V1PX
(071) 932-8840; Fax: (071) 932-8421
Services: corporate advertising, marketing, public relations, market research

The Marketing Workshop (Communications), Ltd., Glebe Farm, Draycote, Rugby CV23 9RB
(0926) 633-317; Fax: (0926) 632-801
Services: marketing consultancy service, new product and brand development, advertising and sales

Quadrangle Communications, Ltd., 81 Dean St., London W1V 3AR
(071) 287-2262; Fax: (071) 439-1537
Services: corporate advertising, marketing, public relations

Research International UK, Ltd., 6/7 Grosvenor Place, London SW1X 7SH
(071) 235-1277; Fax: (071) 235-2010
Services: market research organization, consultants

Saatchi & Saatchi Advertising, Ltd., 80 Charlotte St., London W1A 1AQ
(071) 636-5060; Fax: (071) 637-8489
Services: domestic and international advertising

J. Walter Thompson Co., Ltd., 40 Berkeley Square, London W1X 6AD
(071) 499-4040; Fax: (071) 493-8432
Services: advertising agency

Trimedia Communications, Ltd., 13–15 John Adams St., London WC2N 6LU
(071) 930-7642; Fax: (071) 839-3579
Services: advertising, public relations

Yellowhammer Advertising Co., Ltd., 76 Oxford St., London W1A 1DT
(071) 436-5000; Fax: (071) 436-4630
Services: advertising, public relations

## TRANSPORTATION AND DISTRIBUTION COMPANIES

Allport Freight, Ltd., 26 Chase Rd., London NW10 6QA
(081) 965-0678; Fax: (081) 965-1340
Services: international freight forwarding

Escombe Lambert, Ltd., Valentines House, 51–69 Ilford Hill, Ilford 1GL 2DR
(081) 478-6969; Fax: (081) 514-5851
Services: shipping and port agency

Geest North Sea Line, BV, Geest House, Hadleigh Rd., Ipswich IP2 0DH
(0473) 230-100; Fax: (0473) 230-130
Services: international distribution, warehousing services

Head International, Ltd., Flint St., West Thurrock RM16 1HA
(0708) 869-161; Fax: (0708) 860-198
Services: freight forwarding, procurement operations, export packing

Hayford & Beazley Group Transport, Ltd., Horseshoe House, London Rd., Harlow CM17 9LH
(0279) 439-637; Fax: (0279) 439-297
Services: transport, storage, contract hire

MAT Transport Management, Ltd., Arnold House 36/41, Holywell Lane, London EC2P 2EQ
(071) 247-6500; Fax: (071) 247-1991
Services: international transport, ancillary services

Spurling, Ltd., North Woolwich Rd., London E16 2BP
(071) 476-1466; Fax: (071) 474-9795
Services: national distribution, shipping, forwarding, export consignments

Stewart & Harvey, Ltd., Eldonwall Estate, 129/169 Whalebone Lane South, Dagenham RM8 1AU
(081) 517-0011; Fax: (081) 592-0827
Services: international packing, shipping

United Transport International, PLC, Stratton House, Piccadilly, London W1X 6DD
(071) 491-2633; Fax: (071) 629-4766
Services: international distribution

John C. Wheeler International, Ltd., Fishers Way, Belvedere DA17 6BS
(081) 310-2032; Fax: (081) 312-1913
Services: international distribution

## TRADE CONSULTANTS

CTA Economic & Export Analysis, Ltd., 96 London Rd., Reading RG1 5AU
(0734) 668-381; Fax: (0734) 351-440
Services: strategic consultants on single European market

Clydesdale Bank, PLC, P.O. Box 43, 30 St. Vincent Place, Glasgow G1 2HL
(041) 248-7070; Fax: (041) 204-0828
Services: business advisory

Dun & Bradstreet, Ltd., 11th Floor, Tower Block, Center City, 7 Hill St., Birmingham B5 4UN
(021) 631-2323; Fax: (021) 631-3268
Services: business advisory

Ernst & Young, Silkhouse Court, Titheham St., Liverpool L2 2LE
(051) 236-8214; Fax: (051) 236-0258
Services: business advisory

Euro Marketors Partnership, Wordpower House, Lower Rd., Cookham, Maidenhead SL6 9EH
(0628) 819-232; Fax: (0628) 819-141
Services: international strategic marketing, acquisitions, distribution search, development consultants, particularly in food, drink, agriculture, paper, packaging, leisure industries

KPMG Peat Marwick Management Consultants, 1 Puddle Dock, Blackfriars, London EC4V 3PD
(071) 236-8000; Fax: (071) 248-6552
Services: export consultants, purchasing consultants, business advisory

Modulus Management Consultancy, Ltd., Modulus House, 188 Washway Rd., Sale M33 1RN
(061) 905-1089; Fax: (061) 905-1578
Services: contract negotiation consultants, export consultants, business advisory

Performance Improvement, Ltd., Fitzjohns Country House, Rugby CV22 5QB
(0788) 75-156
Services: export consultants

REMIT Consultants, Ltd., 422 St. John St., London EC1V 4NJ
(071) 837-5498; Fax: (071) 833-5716
Services: export consultants, business advice, particularly in pharmaceuticals, health care, trade development, defense, food, beverages, information technology, consumer durables, competition

Strathclyde Business Development Unit, 20 India St., Glasgow G2 4PF
(041) 227-3866; Fax: (041) 227-3919
Services: business consultants, trade development, industrial promotion

## TRADE SHOWS AND EXHIBITIONS

International Hotel Catering Exhibit (HOTELYMPIA), Reed Exhibition Companies, Oriel House, 26 Quadrant, Surrey, England
(081) 948-9900; Fax: (081) 940-2171
Description: biennial (January) exhibit for international hotel products and services industries

Birmingham International Spring Fair (ISF), Exhibition House, Warren Lane, Trade Promotion Services, Ltd., London
(081) 855-9201; Fax: (081) 316-5719
Description: annual (February) spring fair

Electro-Optics Laser International Conference Exhibition, Cahners Expo Group, 999 Summer St., Stamford, CT 60905
(203) 694-000
Description: biennial (March, Birmingham National Exhibition Center) showcase for international electro-optic, fibre optic and laser industries

London International Book Fair (LIBF), Reed Exhibition Companies, Oriel House, 26 Quadrant, Surrey, England
(081) 948-9900; Fax: (081) 940-2171
Description: annual (March) exhibit for international magazines and book publishers

European Computer Communications Conference & Exhibition, Blenheim Online, PLC, Ash Hill Dr., Middlesex, England
Fax: (081) 868-9933
Description: annual (June) exhibit for international computer and communications industries

International Chemical Process Engineering Show & Conference, Cahners Expo Group, 999 Summer St., Stamford, CT 06905
(203) 964-0000
Description: triennial (June) exhibit for international chemical and process engineering industries

London Motor Show (Motorfair), Warwick Road, Earls Court CTEXH, Philbeach Events, Ltd., London
(071) 385-1200; Fax: (071) 244-7617
Description: biennial (October) exhibit of latest car models, accessories

International Plastics Rubber Fair (INTERPLAS), Reed Exhibition Companies, Radcliffe House, Blenheim, West Midlands, England
(021) 705-6707; Fax: (021) 705-4380
Description: triennial (November) exhibit for international plastics and rubber industries

World Travel Market, Reed Exhibition Companies, Oriel House, 26 Quadrant, Surrey, England
(081) 948-9900; Fax: (081) 940-2171
Description: annual (November) exhibit for international travel industry

London International Agricultural Machinery Exhibition, Royal Smithfield, Forbes House, Halkin St., London
(071) 235-0315; Fax: (071) 235-7112
Description: annual (December) exhibit of agricultural machinery

# INDEX